Selfless Intervention

Exercising Jurisdiction in the Common Interest

CEDRIC RYNGAERT

OXFORD
UNIVERSITY PRESS

OXFORD
UNIVERSITY PRESS

Great Clarendon Street, Oxford, OX2 6DP,
United Kingdom

Oxford University Press is a department of the University of Oxford.
It furthers the University's objective of excellence in research, scholarship,
and education by publishing worldwide. Oxford is a registered trade mark of
Oxford University Press in the UK and in certain other countries

First Edition published in 2020

Impression: 1

Published in the United States of America by Oxford University Press
198 Madison Avenue, New York, NY 10016, United States of America

British Library Cataloguing in Publication Data
Data available

Library of Congress Control Number: 2020932792

ISBN 978–0–19–885178–3

Printed and bound by
CPI Group (UK) Ltd, Croydon, CR0 4YY

This book is dedicated to Dominika, Sophie, and Alice.

Preface

This monograph is the outcome of two five-year research projects on unilateral jurisdiction and global values ('UNIJURIS'), funded by the European Research Council (ERC Starting Grant 336230—UNIJURIS) and the Dutch Organization for Scientific Research (VIDI Scheme, Project number 452-12-002). The research was conducted at Utrecht University School of Law, and more specifically in the context of the Utrecht Centre for Accountability and Liability Law (Ucall) and the research programme Regulation and Enforcement in Europe (Renforce). The author of this monograph was the Principal Investigator of these projects, which also involved seven junior (PhD) researchers: Nelson Coelho, Natalie Dobson, Friederycke Haijer, Arron Honniball, Lucas Roorda, Mistale Taylor, and Mark Zoetekouw. At the time of writing, most PhD researchers had defended their PhD manuscript at Utrecht University. The author is particularly grateful for their insights. References to their work can be found in the specific part (Chapter 5) of this monograph.

This monograph develops ideas contained in the author's inaugural lecture given at Utrecht University, upon accepting the chair of public international law, on 30 March 2015. A written version of this lecture was locally published by Eleven (Boom) as *Unilateral Jurisdiction and Global Values* (2015). Some parts of this booklet have been reproduced, in an amended and updated form, in this monograph. Parts of Chapter 3 have earlier been published in the *Handbook on Jurisdiction* (OUP 2019, chapter on cosmopolitanism and the national interest), and parts of section 5.5 have been published in an *American Journal of International Law*, vol 114, unbound issue on data protection extraterritoriality (2020).

For the final editing and production of this book, I wish to extend my thanks to student assistants Anouk van Midden and Matthieu van den Broeke, and to Jack McNichol at Oxford University Press. I am also most grateful for the support given by Merel Alstein (OUP) and the anonymous reviewers of the manuscript.

Utrecht,
6 December 2019

Table of Contents

Table of Cases

NATIONAL COURTS

Belgium

Canada

France

Netherlands

Spain

South Africa

Switzerland

United Kingdom

United States

INTERNATIONAL COURTS

Court of Justice of the European Union

European Court of Human Rights

International Court of Justice / Permanent Court of International Justice

International Tribunal for the Law of the Sea

World Trade Organization Dispute Settlement Mechanism

Table of Legislation

EU LEGISLATION

Decision

Directive

Regulation

INTERNATIONAL INSTRUMENTS

List of Abbreviations

AB	Appellate Body
AFDI	Annuaire Français de Droit International
AJIL	American Journal of International Law
AJILU	American Journal of International Law Unbound
ALF	Amsterdam Law Forum
ALI	American Law Institute
Am J Comp L	American Journal of Comparative Law
Am J Int'l L	Amsterdam Journal of International Law
Ariz J Int'l & Comp L	Arizona Journal of International and Comparative Law
ASIL Proceedings	Proceedings of the American Society of International Law
ASJIL	Asian Journal of International Law
ASL	Air and Space Law
ASR	African Security Review
ATS	Alien Tort Statute
AYIL	Australian Yearbook of International Law
Berkeley J Int'l L	Berkeley Journal of International Law
BHRJ	Business and Human Rights Journal
Brook J Int'l L	Brooklyn Journal of International Law
Buff L Rev	Buffalo Law Review
BULR	Boston University Law Review
BYBIL	British Yearbook of International Law
Camb Rev Int Aff	Cambridge Review of International Affairs
Case W Res J Int'l L	Case Western Reserve Journal of International Law
CBDR	common but differentiated responsibilities
CDEM	construction, design, equipment, or manning
CESCR	Committee on Economic, Social and Cultural Rights
CI	Critical Inquiry
CILJ	Cornell International Law Journal
CJEU	Court of Justice of the European Union
CJIL	Chicago Journal of International Law
CJTL	Columbia Journal of Transnational Law
CLF	Criminal Law Forum
CLR	Cornell Law Review
CMLR	Common Market Law Review
Col LR	Columbia Law Review
CORSIA	Carbon Offsetting and Reduction Scheme for International Aviation
COSRA	Council of Securities Regulators of America
CUP	Cambridge University Press

CYELS	Cambridge Yearbook of European Legal Studies
DPD	Data Protection Directive
DRC	Democratic Republic of the Congo
DSM	dispute-settlement mechanism
Duke J Comp & Int'l L	Duke Journal of Comparative and International Law
ECHR	European Convention Human Rights
ECtHR	European Court of Human Rights
EFAR	European Foreign Affairs Review
EILR	Emory International Law Review
EITI	Extractive Industries Transparency Initiative
EIW: a L Rev	Europe in the World: a Law Review
EJIL	European Journal of International Law
EJIR	European Journal of International Relations
EJPR	European Journal of Political Research
EFAR	European Foreign Affairs Review
EP	European Papers
Ethics	Ethics: An International Journal of Social, Political and Legal Philosophy
EU	European Union
EUP	European Union Politics
FAO	Food and Agriculture Organization
FATF	Financial Action Task Force
FCPA	Foreign Corrupt Practices Act
FIFA	Fédération Internationale de Football Association
Ford LJ	Fordham Law Journal
FSB	Financial Stability Board
GAIRAS	generally accepted international rules and/or standards
GAL	global administrative law
GAR	Global Antitrust Review
GATT	General Agreement on Tariffs and Trade
GC	Global Constitutionalism
GDPR	General Data Protection Regulation
GELJ	Georgetown Law Journal
GEP	Global Environmental Politics
Ger LR	German Law Review
GLJ	German Law Journal
GLR	Georgia Law Review
GLW	Griffith Law Review
GJIL	Goettingen Journal of International Law
GPG	global public goods
GTCJ	Global Trade and Customs Journal
GWILR	George Washington International Law Review
HICLR	Hastings International and Comparative Law Review
HILJ	Harvard International Law Journal

HLR	Harvard Law Review
Hous L Rev	Houston Law Review
HRILD	Human Rights and International Legal Discourse
HUP	Harvard University Press
ICAO	International Civil Aviation Organization
ICC	International Criminal Court
ICCPR	International Covenant on Civil and Political Rights
ICJ	International Court of Justice
ICJ Rep	International Court of Justice Reports
ICLQ	International and Comparative Law Quarterly
ICLR	International Criminal Law Review
IDPL	International Data Privacy Law
IICLR	Indiana International and Comparative Law Review
IJCL	International Journal of Constitutional Law
IJGLS	Indiana Journal of Global Legal Studies
IJHR	International Journal of Human Rights
IJIL	Indian Journal of International Law
IJMCL	International Journal of Marine and Coastal Law
IJS	Irish Journal of Sociology
ILM	International Legal Materials
ILR	International Law Reports
IMO	International Maritime Organization
Int'l Org	International Organization
IOSCO	International Organization of Securities Commissions
IPOA IUU	International Plan of Action to Prevent, Deter and Eliminate, Illegal, Unreported, and Unregulated Fishing
IRPL	International Review of Penal Law
Is LR	Israel Law Review
ITLOS	International Tribunal for the Law of the Sea
IUU	illegal, unreported, and unregulated
JCAEP	Journal of the Canadian Association of Emergency Physicians
JCMS	Journal of Common Market Studies
JECLP	Journal of European Competition Law and Practice
JEPP	Journal of European Public Politics
JGR	Journal of Genocide Research
JICJ	Journal of International Criminal Justice
JILIR	Journal of International Law and International Relations
JIEL	Journal of International Economic Law
J Int'l L & Int'l Rel	Journal of International Law and International Relations
JITAL	Journal of International Trade and Arbitration Law
JLEO	Journal of Law, Economics and Organization
JMAS	Journal of Modern African Studies
JPSP	Journal of Personality and Social Psychology
JWT	Journal of World Trade
Law and Humanities	Law Humanit

LCP	Law and Contemporary Problems
LJIL	Leiden Journal of International Law
Mich L Rev	Michigan Law Review
Mich JIL	Michigan Journal of International Law
Min JIL	Minnesota Journal of International Law
MICLW	University of Miami International and Comparative Law Review
MJIL	Melbourne Journal of International Law
MJILT	Maryland Journal of International Law and Trade
MLR	Minnesota Law Review
MOU	Memorandum of Understanding
MPEPIL	Max Planck Encyclopedia of Public International Law
MRV	monitoring, reporting, and verification
NASAL	NYU Annual Survey of American Law
NDLR	Notre Dame Law Review
NILR	Netherlands International Law Review
NoFo	No Foundations
NQHR	Netherlands Quarterly of Human Rights
NSACLR	National Security and Armed Conflict Law Review
NSJ	National Security Journal
NULR	Northwestern University Law Review
Nw J Int'l L & Bus	Northwestern Journal of International Law and Business
NYLR	New York Law Review
NYLSLR	New York Law School Law Review
ODIL	Ocean Development and International Law
OECD	Organisation for Economic Co-operation and Development
Osgoode Hall LJ	Osgoode Hall Law Journal
OUP	Oxford University Press
Pac McGeorge Global Bus & Dev LJ	Pacific McGeorge Global Business & Development Law Journal
Philosopical Topics	Phil Topics
PNR	passenger names records
PPMs	process and production methods
PSJ	port state jurisdiction
PT	Political Theory
PUP	Princeton University Press
RECIEL	Review of European, Comparative and International Environmental Law
REDD	Reducing Emissions from Deforestation and Forest Degradation
Renforce	Regulation and Enforcement in Europe
RIPS	Royal Institute of Philosophy Supplements
RJ	Ratio Juris
RPSP	Review of Personality and Social Psychology
SC	Social Cognition
SCLR	Southern California Law Review
SEC	Securities and Exchange Commission

STLV	Suffolk Transnational Law Review
SWIFT	Society for Worldwide Interbank Financial Telecommunication
TBT	Technical Barriers to Trade
TEJ	The Economic Journal
TEU	Treaty on the European Union
TFEU	Treaty on the Functioning of the European Union
Theoretical Inq L	Theoretical Inquiries in Law
TICLJ	Temple International and Comparative Law Journal
TILJ	Texas International Law Journal
TJIL	Texas Journal of International Law
TLD	Trade, Law and Development
TLT	Transnational Legal Theory
TMLR	The Modern Law Review
TLR	Tulane Law Review
TRIPS	Agreement on Trade-Related Aspects of Intellectual Property Rights
TWAIL	Third World Approaches to International Law
Ucall	Utrecht Centre for Accountability and Liability Law
U Ill L Rev	University of Illinois Law Review
UJIEL	Utrecht Journal of International and European Law
ULR	Utrecht Law Review
UN	United Nations
UNCLOS	UN Convention on the Law of the Sea
UNGP	United Nations Guiding Principles
UPLR	University of Pennsylvania Law Review
UTLJ	University of Toronto Law Journal
Vanderbilt J Transnat'l L	Vanderbilt Journal of Transnational Law
Vanderbilt L Rev	Vanderbilt Law Review
VJIL	Virginia Journal of International Law
VLR	Virginia Law Review
VPA	voluntary partnership agreement
Wayne L Rev	Wayne Law Review
WEP	West European Politics
WIPO	World International Property Organization
Wis Int'l LJ	Wisconsin International Law Journal
WLR	Willamette Law Review
WTO	World Trade Organization
WTR	World Trade Review
YHRDJ	Yale Human Rights and Development Journal
YILC	Yearbook of the International Law Commission
YILR	Yale International Law Review
YJIL	Yale Journal of International Law
YLJ	Yale Law Journal
YUP	Yale University Press
ZIS	Zeitschrift für Internationale Strafrechtsdogmatik

1
International Law and Cosmopolitanism

About 100 years ago, John Chipman Gray, a professor of property law at Harvard University, once said that with the exception perhaps of theology, there is nothing about which so much nonsense has been written as international law.[1] Still, property lawyers, for all their vices, have not been the most vehement critics of international law. In particular international relations scholars steeped in the realist tradition have cast doubt on the existence of something called 'international law', by attacking the normative power and ordering potential of international law. Almost inevitably, the characterization of international law as 'non-existent' impacts on the *raison d'être* of international legal scholarship: what kind of discipline studies something that does not exist?

In spite of the manifold criticisms that have been levelled at international law, there is no denying that international law has proved resilient. International law is frequently used as a discourse in international relations, not just by academics, but also by states. This tends to prove that international law is a reality, at least a terminological one. A legal scholar can, however, not satisfy himself with the observation that states use the language of international law in their reciprocal dealings. He should endeavour to understand whether international law has an impact on the conduct of international relations, and what parameters influence engagement and compliance with international law. In addition, he may inquire whether international law spawns, or is based on, a value-based international community that shapes the policy preferences of states or other members.

If such a value-based international community is proven to exist, one may venture to pose a next question: can states, as individual members of this community, also unilaterally further community values when other members fail to act jointly or separately? An aspect of this question is whether states could unilaterally exercise (prescriptive) *jurisdiction*, possibly with extraterritorial effects or overtones, to compensate for regulatory failures of the multilateral system, or of other states. It is this question which this study addresses. Its aim is to identify the conditions enabling and constraining the exercise of unilateral jurisdiction in the common interest by states that have not necessarily the strongest connection to a situation (sometimes denoted as 'bystander states'). In doing so, it seeks to find entry points in the international law of jurisdiction for 'selfless intervention', for the realization of *cosmopolitanism*, a political-philosophical notion that the international

[1] Hans J Morgenthau, *Human Rights and Foreign Policy* (Carnegie Council 1979).

Selfless Intervention. Cedric Ryngaert, Oxford University Press (2020). © Cedric Ryngaert.
DOI: 10.1093/oso/9780198851783.001.0001

community has a shared morality and that members of this community—whether states or individuals—have rights and duties towards each other.[2]

1.1 On Cosmopolitanism and Realism

Moral cosmopolitanism, or 'global justice' as it sometimes denoted,[3] has gained particular prominence in political theory since the 1990s. More recently, international lawyers have taken notice too,[4] while not specifically focusing on the law of jurisdiction. The debate as to the relationship between international law and cosmopolitanism is hardly new, however. In fact, many international legal scholars are intuitive cosmopolitans who wish to reform the international legal system to make it more just and reflective of the interests of the international community. Over the years, this reformist zeal has given rise to acrimonious exchanges between idealist and positivist international lawyers, or between idealist international lawyers and international relations realists. Positivists may accept that, to a certain extent, international law has incorporated cosmopolitan ideals, but they may assail idealists for mistaking international law for international morality and for denying the operation of the principle of state consent in the making and interpretation of international law. Realists may go one step further and deny the existence of any role for international law or morality in the conduct of international relations, even if moral norms have *on paper* integrated the international legal order.[5]

A fine example of the early debate between optimistic international lawyers and international relations scholars is the thought exchange, on the threshold of the Second World War, between EH Carr, one of the founding fathers of modern

[2] See for a fine account of cosmopolitanism: Kwame A Appiah, *Cosmopolitanism: Ethics in a World of Strangers* (Allen Lane 2006). See on the distinction between legal and moral cosmopolitanism: Thomas Pogge, 'Cosmopolitanism and Sovereignty' (1992) 103 Ethics 48, 49 (characterizing 'legal cosmopolitanism' as being 'committed to an ideal of a global order under which all persons have equivalent legal rights and duties, that is, are fellow citizens of a universal republic', whereas pursuant to 'moral cosmopolitanism', 'all persons stand in certain moral relations to one another: we are required to respect one another's status as ultimate units of moral concern'.

[3] *Eg* Thom Brooks (ed), *New Waves in Global Justice* (Palgrave Macmillan 2014).

[4] See notably Roland Pierik and Wouter Werner (eds), *Cosmopolitanism in Context* (CUP 2010) (discussing the strained relationship between moral cosmopolitanism and institutional reality with respect to the protection of the global environment, the World Trade Organization, the UN system of collective security, the International Criminal Court, and transboundary migration); Malcolm Langford, Wouter Vandenhole, Martin Scheinin, and Willem van Genugten (eds), *Global Justice, State Duties: The Extraterritorial Scope of Economic, Social, and Cultural Rights in International Law* (CUP 2014) (asking if states possess extraterritorial obligations under existing international human rights law to respect and ensure economic, social, and cultural rights and how far those duties extend).

[5] Such views have been particularly popular in the United States. See for an early characterization, at the beginning of the twentieth century: Harvard University professor of property law, John Chipman Gray, statement that 'with the exception perhaps of theology, there is nothing about which so much nonsense has been written as international law', cited in Hans J Morgenthau, 'Human Rights and Foreign Policy' in Kenneth W Thompson (ed), *Moral Dimensions of Foreign Policy* (Transaction Books 1994) 341.

realism as an academic discipline, and Hersch Lauterpacht, one of the towering figures in twentieth-century international law, who later became a judge at the International Court of Justice. EH Carr published *The Twenty Years Crisis (1919–1939)*[6] in 1939, in fact just days after Nazi Germany's invasion of Poland. In this book, he demolished legal-utopian ideas of world peace and stability, and showed—at first sight rather persuasively—that states' desire to strengthen the national interest disables the ordering and civilizing ambitions of international law and morality. According to Carr, states and their citizens have no sympathy for the fate or plight of foreigners, and thus do not consider themselves hamstrung by international rules, whether of a legal or moral nature, that limit their international scope of action.[7] Lauterpacht, the international lawyer, in contrast, admitted that the 'capacity for interest and sympathy is naturally determined by the geographical factor',[8] but was of the view that 'enlightened self-interest . . . admits the advisability in given circumstances, of the sacrifice of an immediate sectional interest for the sake of the general interest'.[9] Moreover, in his view, society and law perform the function of 'the creation of conditions and institutions for changing by proper political processes the existing law in accordance with equity and distributive justice'.[10]

This optimistic, Lauterpachtian notion of international law as a force for good has cast a long shadow. To this day, many contemporary international lawyers believe in the civilizing and ordering potential of international legal norms and a perceived 'international community' that goes beyond the accumulated interests of states.[11] On the other hand, many international relations scholars, and a number of US-based realist international law scholars, have further developed Carr's ideas on the impossibility of effective international law, let alone of 'idealist' cosmopolitanism that negates the importance of power in world politics.[12] Stephen Krasner, one of the leading contemporary international relations scholars, assumes 'that rulers want to stay in power and, being in power, they want to promote the security, prosperity, and values of their constituents', and that logics of consequences,

[6] Edward H Carr, *The Twenty Years' Crisis 1919–1939: An Introduction to the Study of International Relations* (first published 1939, Macmillan 1995).

[7] ibid, 209 ('our normal attitude to foreigners is a complete negation of the absence of discrimination on irrelevant grounds which we have recognized as the principle of equality').

[8] Hersch Lauterpacht and Elihu Lauterpacht (eds), *International Law: Being the Collected Papers of Hersch Lauterpacht. The Law of Peace. International Law in General* (Vol 2, CUP 1975) 85.

[9] ibid, 88.

[10] ibid, 89–90.

[11] Jack L Goldsmith and Eric A Posner, *The Limits of International Law* (OUP 2005) 205 (arguing that according to mainstream international law scholarship, states should 'act internationally on the basis of global welfare rather than state welfare').

[12] Jack L Goldsmith and Stephen D Krasner, 'The Limits of Idealism' (2003) 132 Daedalus 47 (criticizing the exercise of universal jurisdiction on these grounds). See also Hans Morgenthau and Kenneth W Thompson, *Politics Among Nations* (6th edn, New York: McGraw-Hill 1985) (original edition 1948). For a more nuanced position: Robert Jackson, *The Global Covenant: Human Conduct in a World of States* (OUP 2000) at 291 (arguing that pursuing international justice should not jeopardize international order).

reflecting power asymmetries, will normally prevail over logics of appropriateness, that is compliance with international norms.[13] Accordingly, also in his view there is no such thing as an international legal system with constitutive rules.[14] Somewhat ironically, similar views are held by some international lawyers themselves, inspired by international relations and the law and economics approach, especially in the United States. In their acclaimed book, *The Limits of International Law* (2005), Jack Goldsmith and Eric Posner strongly take issue with the so-called institutional turn in cosmopolitan theory, reasoning that voters have no widespread and intense cosmopolitan sentiments and will punish leaders who do harbour such sentiments.[15] This is an empirical assumption that may or not be true, but in any event grounds a nationalistic foreign policy paradigm that leaves committing to and complying with international law a function of the maximization of the welfare of the state. This is also the basic assumption of the law and economics approach to international law, which has become rather dominant in US international legal scholarship. Thus, Andrew Guzman observes in *How International Law Works* (2008): 'States do not concern themselves with the welfare of other states ... [They] will only cooperate when doing so increases their own payoffs.'[16] This approach does not exclude the formation of and compliance with international law, but these are not based on an endogenous attractiveness of international legal norms but rather on the basis of a rational calculus, factoring in exogenous factors known as the 'three Rs': reciprocity,[17] retaliation,[18] and, in particular, reputation[19]. This view is still rooted in a black-box approach to the state as a maximizer of some ill-defined national interest but, unlike hard-core realists such as Carr and Krasner, it admits that states may in fact be rather far-sighted and decide to enter into and comply with international law, at least insofar as in a not-too-distant future, it will enjoy payoffs that are higher than those it would enjoy as a result of a failure to sign up to international law, or of non-compliance with existing obligations.[20] There is only

[13] Stephen D Krasner, *Sovereignty: Organized Hypocrisy* (PUP 1999) 7–8.

[14] ibid 229 ('[The international system] does not have constitutive rules, if such rules are conceived of as making some kinds of action possible and precluding others.').

[15] Jack L Goldsmith and Eric A Posner, *The Limits of International Law* (OUP 2005) 212–9.

[16] Andrew T Guzman, *How International Law Works: A Rational Choice Theory* (OUP 2008) 17.

[17] Reciprocity is a pull for compliance in that a state, by threatening to withdraw its own compliance with international law, encourages compliance by other states. Reciprocity does not always work well; however, as an incentive for compliance with international human rights and environmental obligations, it may lack credibility as there are no consequences for the violating state in case a bystander states withdraws its own compliance. cf Guzman (n 16) 45.

[18] Retaliation is a pull for compliance if states are deterred from violating the law where they know that other states will punish them. However, as Pauwelyn has observed (Joost Pauwelyn, *Optimal Protection of International Law* (CUP 2008) 158), since states 'are hesitant to enter a regime with strict remedies and tough punishments', the overall cost of breach is minimized, and a compliance pull may not be generated.

[19] Guzman (n 16) 33 ('A good reputation is valuable because it makes promises more credible and, therefore, makes future cooperate both easier and less costly.').

[20] Guzman (n 16) 41; Sergio Dellavalle, 'Opening the Forum to the Others: Is There an Obligation to Take Non-National Interests Into Account Within National Political and Juridical Decision-Making-Processes?' (2014) 6 Göttingen Journal of International Law 217, 240 ('the attitude of international

limited room for cosmopolitanism in this view, as solidarity with non-nationals will not normally increase the payoffs for states.

All these international relations and law and economics-inspired scholars are essentially rehashing old philosophical views on the role of the state as a utility maximizer in international relations. Such a state has no qualms about violating legal commitments and does not normally have an interest in developing a morally just international legal framework. Spinoza, for instance, in his somewhat lesser known work, *Tractatus Politicus*, published posthumously in 1677, already wrote that the relations between states are characterized by anarchy and lawlessness, that the state has no moral obligations towards other states, but only towards the individuals who compose it, and that the prosperity of the state trumps treaty compliance (*'Imperii salus summa lex'*).[21] Somewhat similarly, Hegel averred in his *Grundlinien der Philosophie des Rechts* ('Elements of the Philosophy of Right', 1820) that '[the state's] government is ... a matter of particular wisdom, not of universal providence' and that it is animated not by 'a universal (philanthropic) thought, but [by] its actually offended or threatened welfare in its specific particularity'.[22] Bosanquet, for his part, echoed Spinoza and Hegel's opinions in his 1899 publication, *The Philosophical Theory of the State*, where he held that '[m]oral relations presuppose an organized life; but such a life is only within the State, not in relations between States and other communities'.[23] These views, with perhaps the exception of Hegel,[24] essentially doubt the existence of an international community as a substrate for the development of international law, as states are only motivated to maximize their own welfare.

However, as the law and economics school has not failed to highlight, the maximization of a state's welfare does not preclude the development of international law, as international law could, under the right conditions, indeed maximize the state's welfare. Moreover, a state's aspiration to maximize its own welfare does not exclude the maximization of *other states'* welfare through international law. In fact,

actors [in multilateral contexts including iteration] will be significantly more prone to complying with international law and, generally, less hostile to cooperation since they would take into account possible remuneration or retaliation in the next rounds of interaction'—thereby taking issue with the narrow approach espoused by Goldsmith and Posner).

21 Tractatus Politicus, ch iii, 14, also discussed in Lauterpacht and Lauterpacht (eds) (n 8) 371–72.

22 Georg Wilhelm Friedrich Hegel, *Elements of the Philosophy of Right* (CUP 1991) para 337 (adding that '[the state's] concrete existence, rather than any of those many universal thoughts which are held to be moral commandments, can be the principle of its action and behaviour'). See on the maximization of internal state welfare ibid, para 332: 'independent states are primarily wholes which can satisfy their needs internally'.

23 Bernard Bosanquet, *The Philosophical Theory of the State* (4th edn, Macmillan 1930) 302.

24 Hegel appeared to believe that there was a role for international *law* in international relations through this belief in a 'universal spirit'. Hegel (n 22) para 340 (writing that universal spirit produces itself through a 'dialectic of the finitude of these spirits', even if '[t]he principles of the *spirits of nations* are in general of a limited nature because of that particularity in which they have their objective actuality and self-consciousness').

as early as 1770, Emmer de Vattel, in his highly influential *Le droit des gens* ('The Law of Nations'), while writing in Book I of this work that the state is under an obligation to preserve itself and its members, and has a right to 'every thing necessary for its preservation',[25] emphasized the duties of a nation for the preservation of *others*, and the duty to contribute to the perfection of *other states* in Book II.[26] Vattel may not have considered these duties to be contradictory. Arguably, he may have believed that the state may have a duty to act in the best interests of other states and their citizens insofar as so doing does not (substantially) decrease the former's welfare.[27] In this respect, contemporary political theorist Simon Caney refutes the notion that the state has a contractual duty towards its own people as an argument against duties towards other nations; he reasons that states are free to pursue their own ends and to discharge their duties towards their own citizens, but they should do so 'within the context of a fair overall framework'; that is 'a set of parameters defined by a theory of justice'.[28] In this strand, international law could be conceived of as a set of norms that not only maximizes the welfare of the individual states subscribing to them but also the welfare of all participating states. This is essentially an institutional cosmopolitan view, pursuant to which domestic as well as international institutions purportedly have duties toward non-citizens.

Sure enough, in pure cosmopolitanism, states or institutions disappear, and individuals have ethical duties towards other individuals who are worse off, wherever in the world they may be. This strand has been advocated in a seminal 1972 article, spurred by a famine in Bangladesh caused by its bloody secession from Pakistan, in which moral philosopher Peter Singer posited that 'if it is in our power to prevent something bad from happening, without thereby sacrificing anything of comparable moral importance, we ought, morally, to do it', even when the person in need is geographically distant.[29] For Singer, it did not matter morally whether this person is a neighbour's child drowning in a pond 10 yards from me or an unknown Bengali 10,000 miles away. But obviously, individual agency is not particularly practical. Therefore, subsequent global justice proponents have advocated mediating ethical duties via institutions, such as states or international organizations.[30] According to these advocates, who are steeped in a consequentialist ethical tradition, political

[25] Emer de Vattel, *Le droit des gens* (Guillaumin 1863) Book I, Ch II, paras 16–18.

[26] ibid Book I, Ch I, paras 1–6. Justifying the latter duties toward others, he approvingly cites the Roman orator Cicero, who said in *De Officiis* that 'nothing is more agreeable to nature, more capable of affording true satisfaction, than, in imitation of Hercules, to undertake even the most arduous and painful labours for the benefit and preservation of all nations'. (Marcus Tulllius Cicero, *De Officiis* (CUP 1899), lib. iii. cap. 5, para 1).

[27] See also Paul Mertenskoetter, 'National Courts as "Trustees of Humanity"?', GlobalTrust Working Paper Series 04/2013, pp 9–10 (discussing Eyal Benvenisti's work and characterizing it as based on a weak Pareto principle).

[28] Simon Caney, *Justice Beyond Borders: A Global Political Theory* (OUP 2005) 139–40.

[29] Peter Singer, 'Famine, Affluence and Morality' (1972) Philos Public Aff 229, 235.

[30] *Eg* Michael J Green, 'Institutional Responsibility for Global Problems' (2002) 30 Phil Topics 79, 85–86.

institutions need to be oriented towards furthering cosmopolitan ideals and tackling collective action problems, such as protecting human rights and the environment, and ensuring distributive justice (in particular, alleviating world poverty).[31]

The cosmopolitan views set out above stand in stark contrast with the realist assumption or observation that states are not interested in maximizing the interests of other states and their citizens. However, at the same time, they accord with the reality of a vast legal-institutional machinery which states have developed over the years, a machinery that is indeed aimed at constraining state action in the field of human rights and the environment, and at ensuring North–South financial transfers. A multitude of human rights and environmental treaties have been concluded, often coming with their own supervisory mechanisms, and a host of UN specialized agencies funnel Northern donor funds to the global South for development purposes.

1.2 From Multilateral to Unilateral Cosmopolitanism

Through multilateral agreements and institutions, states indeed appear to be willing to support some form of cosmopolitan action. Surely, cosmopolitans would claim that not nearly enough is being done in this respect. Realists, for their part, would claim that such legal arrangements are in fact toothless, and in reality do not (empirically), or even should not (normatively) constrain selfish state behaviour. For the international lawyer, these external views, which are both correct from their own perspective, are sobering. They require him to question the morality and effectiveness of the current international legal system. However, we cannot deny that the deficiencies ascribed to international law precisely reinforce its existence. When international law is considered worth criticizing it must be so because it exists, whatever ills may afflict it. The reform-minded international lawyer, adhering to the optimistic Lauterpachtian tradition of international legal scholarship, will subsequently ponder how international law could be improved, notably become more cosmopolitan and more attuned to human dignity and human rights,[32] while remaining grounded in actual state practice so as not to become utopian.[33]

This is the challenge that this study takes up, at least with respect to the 'selfless' exercise of state jurisdiction in the common interest. This is not a wide-ranging treatise on cosmopolitan international law, or on how cosmopolitan ideals have

[31] Caney (n 28) 159. See on poverty in particular Thomas Pogge, *World Poverty and Human Rights: Cosmopolitan Responsibilities and Reforms* (2nd edn, Polity Press 2008).

[32] Hersch Lauterpacht, *International Law and Human Rights* (Archon Books 1968) 68.

[33] The most notable contribution to the theoretical debate as to the nature of international law has obviously been made by Martti Koskenniemi, *From Apology to Utopia: The Structure of International Legal Argument* (CUP 2006).

been translated, or should be translated in international law.[34] Instead, it answers a number of more circumscribed, although no less relevant questions, from both a normative and doctrinal point of view: (a) whether the international legal system can accommodate the exercise of unilateral jurisdiction in a cosmopolitan fashion by states, or geographically limited regional organizations such as the European Union (EU) on which Member States have conferred powers; and (b) whether there are indications in practice that such jurisdiction is indeed exercised.

The limitation of the research object to the exercise of *(prescriptive) jurisdiction* means that only the legal opportunities for, and limits to states' (and the EU's) *application of their laws to situations with a foreign component* will be studied. Such application is sometimes denoted as 'extraterritorial' jurisdiction, although this term is not entirely apt. As will be seen throughout this book, when states act unilaterally in a cosmopolitan manner, they often do so on the basis of a *territorial* nexus, however weak it may be.[35] For instance, states may exercise universal criminal jurisdiction over gross human rights violations insofar as the presumed perpetrator is *present on their territory*, or states may impose environmental requirements on foreign production processes insofar as the finished goods *enter their territory*, at which point market access conditions are applied. Nevertheless, for reasons of convenience, 'extraterritoriality' will be used as shorthand for situations that have an extraterritorial *dimension*. This is typically the case with cosmopolitan jurisdictional unilateralism: while the relevant measures have an internal/territorial character or link, their *effects* are extraterritorial in that foreign countries and foreign country nationals (and economic operators) may be—more or less—forced to adjust their behaviour in order to satisfy the requirements set by the unilaterally acting regulator. Sometimes the terms 'internal measures with extraterritorial impact' or 'indirect extraterritorial laws' are used in this context, especially when denoting unilateral trade restrictions pursuing public values, for example related to the environment.[36]

This study does not as such focus on the lawfulness of extraterritorial *enforcement* jurisdiction, the enforcement of a state's laws or policies abroad. This implies, for instance, that the legality of unilateral humanitarian intervention or the legality of special operations on foreign soil against terrorist targets will not be addressed. Enforcement jurisdiction falls within the scope of the study, however, to the extent

[34] Reference is made again to this fine collection: Pierik and Werner (eds) *Cosmopolitanism in Context* (n 4).

[35] See also Anthony J Colangelo, 'What is Extraterritorial Jurisdiction?' (2013) 99 CLR 1303, 1306 (observing that 'the concept of territoriality can be, and has been, finessed to embrace foreign activity').

[36] See Ioanna Hadjiyianni, 'The Extraterritorial Reach of EU Environmental Law and Access to Justice by Third Country Actors' in Special Section 'The New Frontiers of EU Administrative Law, Is There an Accountability Gap in EU External Relations?' (2017) 2(2) European Papers 519; Charlotte Blattner, 'Can Extraterritorial Jurisdiction Help Overcome Regulatory Gaps of Animal Law? Insights from Trophy Hunting' in Symposium on Global Animal Law, Part II: The Case for Global Legal Animal Studies (2017) 111 AJILU 420 ('Indirect extraterritorial laws also regulate domestic affairs, but have an ancillary effect on foreign territory.').

that it is exercised territorially to enforce extraterritorial legislation, such as where port state authorities impose sanctions on foreign-flagged vessels in respect of the latter's activities on the high seas, or where states take enforcement problems into account when contemplating the exercise of prescriptive jurisdiction.[37]

1.3 Techniques of Extraterritoriality: Private Regulation Versus State Unilateralism

A limitation of this study is that it concentrates on regulation (and adjudication) taking place at the level of the *state*,[38] that is the traditional actor exercising prescriptive, adjudicatory, and enforcement jurisdiction. Modesty and perspective are in order, however: these days, the state is no longer the only norm-setter. Notably, transnational law scholars have made much of the potential of private actors to govern social relations on their own, such as by establishing multi-stakeholder initiatives setting norms for corporate activity with little intervention by the state. From an epistemic perspective, private regulation speaks to the 'de-territorialization' of regulation, meaning loss of relevance for legal norms, conceived as territorial state-sanctioned regulation, in social interactions.[39] Such norms would gradually be replaced by social norms developed by private actors partaking in the same, self-regulating transnational communities.[40] Where these functionally differentiated communities are structurally coupled, these social norm systems can acquire systemic autonomy, and supplant the state as the central *locus* of governance.[41] In this approach, jurisdiction is no longer dependent on a

[37] Alex Mills, 'Rethinking Jurisdiction in International Law' (2014) 84 BYBIL 187, 195 (noting that while prescriptive and enforcement jurisdiction are theoretically distinct, 'they are not necessarily unrelated in practice', citing the taking into consideration of 'restrictions on the possibility of effectively enforcing national laws or judgments' in determining whether to exercise prescriptive jurisdiction).

[38] Or regional organizations, such as the European Union, to which states have transferred sizable powers, also in the international realm.

[39] Peer Zumbansen 'Defining the Space of Transnational Law: Legal Theory, Global Governance and Legal Pluralism' in Gunther Handl, Joachim Zekoll, and Peer Zumbansen (eds), *Beyond Territoriality: Transnational Legal Authority in an Age of Globalization* (Martinus Nijhoff Publishers 2012) 59–60.

[40] Gralf-Peter Calliess and Peer Zumbansen, *Rough Consensus and Running Code: A Theory of Transnational Private Law* (Hart Publishing 2010). Such norms could be subsumed under a broad, pluralist conception of law as a set of norms guiding social behaviour, but it remains no less true that a full understanding of such norms, and their genesis, is beyond the toolkit of the lawyer, and rather belongs to the social science realm of research. See Zumbansen (n 39) 59–60, noting the importance of sociology and anthropology in this respect, as these disciplinary perspectives 'question the association of legal-rule creation with a territorially-fixed place'.

[41] Larry Catá Backer, 'Governance Without Government: An Overview' in Gunther Handl, Joachim Zekoll, and Peer Zumbansen (eds), *Beyond Territoriality: Transnational Legal Authority in an Age of Globalization* (Martinus Nijhoff Publishers 2012) 118–20 (referring in particular to social norms governing the behaviour of economic non-state actors); John Haskell, 'Ways of Doing Extraterritoriality in Scholarship' in Daniel S Margolies and others (eds), *The Extraterritoriality of Law* (Routledge 2019) 21–22 (referring to this literature as 'theoretical contextualization' of extraterritoriality, in which 'the state is only one of many actors vying for authority').

territorial or nationality-based nexus to a state, but is a matter of individual/community choice and even right.[42] From a cosmopolitanism perspective, this means that states, as long as they are in existence, should facilitate such a choice, and offer fora that realize the jurisdictional autonomy of individuals and communities. Or put differently, state sovereignty should be at the service of individual sovereignty rather than just realize the narrow self-interest of the state.[43]

This study recognizes that a post-territorial, community-based spatiality could lead to the disappearance of 'the state' as a governance system, and to the emergence of non-state transnational governance, especially for economic transactions. It remains to be seen, however, whether fully autonomous non-state governance could adequately address current global governance challenges. These require that economic non-state actors adequately deal with the negative externalities caused by their profit-maximizing activities. Concerns could be raised that their self-regulatory activities merely amount to green- and blue-washing.[44] While acknowledging the important role to be assumed by transnational private authority in the twenty-first century,[45] this study is of the view that such authority is in need of flanking policies by public institutions, such as states.[46] In the contemporary world, power not only resides in non-state actors but continues to reside in states and other public organizations, even if, with the disaggregation of the state, organized non-state actors may have a major impact on the formulation of state policy, or even the very identity of the state.[47]

To address global governance challenges, states could use unilateral vertical authority in the international sphere, that is normative power emanating from one rule-making agency and addressed to transnationally active non-state actors, especially to fill a void left by multilateral failures. Such unilateral action, characterized

[42] Mills (n 37) at 233 (citing 'outmoded conceptions of public international law, which conceive of jurisdiction as purely a matter of (territorial or nationality-based) state rights and powers', and suggesting instead the incorporation of 'the idea of jurisdiction as individual right').

[43] cf Mills (n 37) at 237 (pointing to the 'emergence of a more "cosmopolitan" conception of sovereignty, which attempts to accommodate the normative value of both state and individual actors').

[44] Also Mills (n 37) at 239 ('The deeper challenge for international lawyers is whether the door can be opened to recognition of the normative authority of individuals without losing sight of the other interests and values, national and international, which have traditionally been protected by the law, and whose protection we may need to preserve.').

[45] Compare Martti Koskenniemi 'International Law and Hegemony: A Reconfiguration' (2004) 17 Camb Rev Int Aff 197, 213–14 ('By focusing on war and great crises—the great power perspective—international law will continue to be implicated in the marginalisation of problems that touch by far the greatest and the weakest part of the world's population. It is therefore necessary that its agenda will be enlarged so as to cover questions that have been presently relegated to the unregulated, private network of transnational relations.').

[46] Also Sara L Seck, 'Beyond the E-word in the Anthropocene' in Margolies and others (eds), *The Extraterritoriality of Law* (n 41) 53 ('[I]t is critical to embrace a polycentric mode of governance that preserves a key role for the state in accordance with international law', while noting the responsibility of corporations and the contributions of non-state civil society).

[47] Carly Nyst, 'Solidarity in a Disaggregated World: Universal Jurisdiction and the Evolution of Sovereignty' (2012) 8 J Int'l L & Int'l Rel 36, 50. See on the disaggregation of the state on the basis of (governmental) networks: Anne-Marie Slaughter, *A New World Order* (PUP 2004).

by competition between different power centres, is actually on the rise. It is in need of proper scholarly treatment, also by public international lawyers who may so far mainly have been concerned with studying horizontal, often cooperative relationships between states, or between states and organizations.[48]

When acting unilaterally, states question the territorial jurisdictional structure of the international system in ways similar to how theorists of non-state governance cast doubt on the continued relevance of territoriality.[49] In fact, advocates of (cosmopolitan) state unilateralism and advocates of transnational private regulation may invoke the same extraterritorial jurisdictional model as an alternative to territoriality: the community-based one.[50] However, where private regulation theorists advance functionally differentiated communities as jurisdictional centres, theorists of unilateral state jurisdiction may refer to the international community as the relevant jurisdictional linchpin, the interests of which are mediated via the state in the absence of a global government. Pursuant to cosmopolitan unilateralism, the state could be said not to exercise its own jurisdiction but rather the jurisdiction of the international community, which the state merely *represents*.[51] Or put differently, the state exercises its sovereignty in the service of the international community.[52]

Focusing on the role of the *state* in realizing international community values obviously comes down to assuming that state power is still meaningful in the

[48] Michael L Buenger, 'Regulatory Legality: Extraterritorial Rule across Domestic and International Arenas' in Nikolas M Rajkovic, Tanja E Aalberts, and Thomas Gammeltoft-Hansen (eds), *The Power of Legality* (CUP 2016) (arguing that 'a narrative that often frames international law as an ever-expanding, self-reinforcing, systematized movement of cooperation between various actors ... fails to recognize the growing role of domestic regulatory actors in the international arena'). Buenger refers in particular to EU unilateral action with extraterritorial effects in the environmental sphere, examining the EU Renewable Energy Directive and the Aviation Directive.

[49] In fact, Gunther Handl, Joachim Zekoll, and Peer Zumbansen (eds), *Beyond Territoriality: Transnational Legal Authority in an Age of Globalization* (Martinus Nijhoff Publishers 2012), addresses both non-state transnational regulation *and* extraterritorial jurisdiction exercised by states. See also Buenger (n 48) 272 ('Unilateral regulatory projection then is the power to "determine one's fate" by using domestic law to circumvent territory as inviolable geopolitical space and redefine it as more malleable and untethered normative space.').

[50] Note, nevertheless, that, *formally speaking*, state unilateral assertions will typically be justified under the territoriality principle, in particular on the grounds that a (foreign-based) activity produces effects within the territory.

[51] The concept of 'representational' or 'vicarious' jurisdiction is not unknown in legal systems. See Jürgen Meyer, 'The Vicarious Administration of Justice: An Overlooked Basis of Jurisdiction' (1990) 31 HILJ 108. See notably the *stellvertretende Rechtsprinzip* codified in § 7 (2), 2° of the German *Strafgesetzbuch*, which provides that all offences by foreigners committed abroad may be subject to German penal law, if the conduct is punishable under the legislation of the territorial state (or if no state has authority over the place where the conduct has taken place), if the offender is found in Germany, and—although the Extradition Law permits the extradition on the basis of the nature of the offense—he or she is not extradited because an extradition request has not timely been filed, because it has been refused, or because the extradition could not be executed.

[52] Compare David S Koller 'The End of Geography: The Changing Nature of the International System and the Challenge to International Law: A Reply to Daniel Bethlehem' (2014) 25 EJIL 25, 28–29 (adding that territoriality delays the emergence of a global human community with universal jurisdiction 'holding all individuals accountable independently of any linkages to the state').

current political constellation characterized by an onslaught of non-state actors encroaching on state sovereignty. The assumption here is that state power is indeed still meaningful but could be repurposed to pursue a cosmopolitan, extraterritorial agenda.[53] This study acknowledges the reality of powerful non-state actors—in particular transnational corporations—at times impacting on individual lives in equal measure as states. However, based on empirical observations, it does not subscribe to the idea that state power necessarily has receded. Rather, it is posited that state sovereignty has undergone an ontological transformation, while not entirely forfeiting its classic 'command and control' legal nature. In various domains the role of the state has shifted from issuing commands to steering, facilitating, and orchestrating more private forms of governance and regulation, for example where states or intergovernmental organizations set minimum standards with respect to the institutional design of private or multi-stakeholder initiatives dealing with public values (human rights, security, the environment).[54] In other fields, the state employs its sovereign power to further global values, such as where a state initiates an international corruption investigation.[55] In yet other fields, classic state regulation persists, notably in the criminal law, which protects public values par excellence. Because the addressees of unilateral regulation, and at times even its architects, if one does not consider the state as a black box, tend to be non-state actors rather than states,[56] such regulation may seem to belong to *transnational law*, at least its formal rule-based incarnation,[57] rather than classic, state-to-state

[53] See also Matthew Craven and Rose Parfitt, 'Statehood Self-Determination, and Recognition' in Malcolm Evans (ed) *International Law* (5th edn, OUP 2018) 2015, noting the two broad contemporary themes regarding the discussion on sovereignty, namely the 'sociological reflection on the changing character of international society and the declining power and authority of the nation State' (addressed above), and the 'ethical variant which regards the tradition of State "sovereignty" to be an archaic impediment to the pursuit of humanitarian or other cosmopolitan agendas (human rights, environmental protection, etc) and which has recommended various interventionist policies of a unilateral or multilateral character'. I admit that by thus reconceiving the role of the state, even in relation to 'that which exceeds or transgresses a given set of "territorial" frontiers', I '[reinforce] the very state system that so many have struggled to destabilise'. See Daniel S Margolies and others, 'Introduction' in Margolies and others (eds), *The Extraterritoriality of Law* (n 41) 1.

[54] Kenneth W Abbott and others (eds), *International Organizations as Orchestrators* (CUP 2015).

[55] *Eg* when the US Department of Justice (DoJ) relied on its racketeering laws to indict FIFA officials for worldwide bribery in 2015. DoJ, indictment Webb and others, 15 CR 0252(RJD)(RML), 20 May 2015.

[56] Notably when private plaintiffs act as private attorneys-general and ask courts to give extraterritorial application to statutes in court litigation. This is especially the case in the United States. cf Paul B Stephan, 'The Political Economy of Extraterritoriality' [2011] SSRN 8 ('[T]he lower courts are more greatly influenced by litigant choices and thus prone, *ceteris paribus*, to produce outcomes that litigating lawyers favor.'). Stephan regrets this state of affairs as it may lead to welfare losses. ibid 19 (characterizing this as a 'classic public choice story, in which a homogenous and concentrated interest group (litigators) obtains rents that produce a net loss in social welfare'). In an extreme situation, the state may even be entirely 'captured' by private interests. See on state capture, although not in the context of extraterritorial regulation: *eg* Joel S Hellmann and others, 'Measuring governance, corruption, and State capture—how firms and bureaucrats shape the business environment in transition economies', Policy Research Working Paper Series, No 2312, The World Bank.

[57] cf Philip Jessup, *Transnational Law* (YUP 1956) 1–2 (stating that 'the term "international" is misleading since it suggests that one is concerned only with the relations of one nation (or state) to other nations (or states)', and that '[t]ransnational situations, then, may involve individuals, corporations,

public international law. At the same time, because unilateral regulation is formally enacted by *states*, and may impact on the regulatory sphere of other states, it *is* a concern of public international law, in particular the law of jurisdiction.

1.4 Methodology

In attempting to answer the research questions identified above, an eclectic methodology is applied: reliance is placed on a combination of multiple methods and theories. This 'toolkit' methodology is in accordance with recent insights from interdisciplinary work straddling international law and international relations.[58] To answer the empirically tinged question whether states exercise jurisdiction in the global interest the classic doctrinal methodologies drawn from legal positivism will be applied: identifying relevant state practice and *opinio juris*, and analysing the discourse states officially use to justify their action. The argument is, however, not just doctrinal but also *theoretical*. A *normative*[59] although *empirically grounded* perspective is espoused to examine how the ambitions of cosmopolitan theory have informed, and could further inform actual legal practices. In so doing, it takes up the challenge posed by theorists of global justice, who have highlighted that a reflexive theory of global justice requires empirical analysis to overcome 'the impotence of the ought'. This implies that global justice concepts need to be viable in the world of actual political and legal decision-making.[60] As Koskenniemi has also observed, principles of justice are in need of decision processes 'through which they can be translated into social action'; such decision processes are even 'prior to the principles and delimit how they can be applied'.[61]

states, organizations of states, or other groups') (emphasis added). Many contemporary scholars of transnational law have been particularly interested in non-formal law without, however, necessarily excluding formal rules that govern cross-border transactions. cf Carrie Menkel-Meadow, 'Why and How to Study "Transnational" Law' [2011] SSRN 103 (defining transnational law as 'law that transcends or crosses borders but may not be formally enacted by states', and as including 'customary practices, norms, and patterns of behavioral regulation that are broader than, and perhaps, even more complex than formal law').

[58] See Jeffrey L Dunoff and Mark A Pollack, 'Reviewing Two Decades of IL/IR Scholarship: What We've Learned, What's Next' in Jeffrey L Dunoff and Mark A Pollack (eds), *Interdisciplinary Perspectives on International Law and International Relations: The State of the Art* (CUP 2013) 627 (writing that international law/international relations scholarship should 'adopt an eclectic or "toolkit" approach, drawing insights from multiple bodies of theory as a function of their specific research questions').

[59] Normative legal research has been defined as a method of 'articulating the normative foundations for the reconstruction, interpretation, and progressive development of the existing global order'. Rafael Domingo, 'The New Global Human Community' (2012) 12 CJIL 568.

[60] Erik Oddvar Eriksen, 'Three Conceptions of Global Political Justice' (2017) 1 ARENA Working Paper 2. See also ibid, 22–23 ('The context of justice is mixed and cannot be settled solely with reference to moral responsibility—to duties of right. Many questions related to global political justice must instead be resolved through a blend of empirical social science and political philosophy, as they stem from the increasing level of interdependence and affectedness ... Consequently, there is a need for an approach and a method that can integrate empirical analyses with normative, conceptual analyses.').

[61] Martti Koskenniemi, 'The Wonderful Artificiality of States' (1994) ASIL Proceedings 22, 28.

This study is cognisant of a reality of a decreasing relevance of state borders in an age of globalization (at least in certain fields), and the nagging enforcement deficit of substantive international law. Thus, it inquires in particular how unilateral jurisdiction is, and can be tapped to protect 'global values' and other community interests. Embracing a reconstructionist and empirically grounded perspective, it is explored to what extent the law of jurisdiction, in light of its historical pedigree and its path dependency, is conceptually amenable to such cosmopolitan understandings, and to what extent actual practice has so far shown such amenability. If the law of jurisdiction is or should be evolving in view of contemporary challenges, the next question is *how* it should precisely evolve, and more particular, how political theories of legitimacy, democracy, and public participation could inform, and have already informed, the imposition of jurisdictional restraints on cosmopolitan unilateralism.

Such theoretical work does not just describe or interpret the existing law and legal practices but has a normative, prescriptive, and reformist ambition too. This ambition is part and parcel of an international law tradition that aims at advancing the international legal order.[62] It shifts existing system paradigms that no longer reflect reality or justice,[63] and is interested in realizing just outcomes in accordance with human dignity and common values through broadly defined processes rather than strict formal rules.[64] At the same time, such an endeavour starts from and interprets actual practices that testify to jurisdictional shifts.

The methodology used—using moral theories to analyse, interpret, and critique actual legal practices—somewhat resembles the one used by Ewan Criddle and Ewan Fox-Decent in *Fiduciaries of Humanity* (OUP 2016),[65] and by Steven Ratner

[62] Jeffery L Dunoff and Mark A Pollack, 'International Law and International Relations: Introducing an Interdisciplinary Dialogue' in Jeffery L Dunoff and Mark A Pollack (eds), *Interdisciplinary Perspectives on International Law and International Relations: The State of the Art* (CUP 2013) 13.

[63] Mills (n 37) 237 ('Law and the social sciences are fundamentally different from the natural sciences in that the adoption of a theoretical perspective does not merely describe, but may also change its subject... The choice of a theoretical paradigm in law is not only a question of its descriptive accuracy, but also a question of its normative implications.').

[64] See notably the New Haven policy-oriented school of jurisprudence: W Michael Reisman and others, 'The New Haven School: A Brief Introduction' (2007) 32 YILR 575, 576 ('[L]aw is policy, but [the New Haven School] is an approach that is policy-oriented in a much broader sense... It also undertakes to improve the performance of decision processes themselves and enhance their capacity to achieve outcomes more consonant with human dignity.'). Such an approach assumes that states are not just interested in maximizing their own narrowly defined welfare, as international relations realists would claim. See for the seminal work of the New Haven School: Myres S McDougal and Harold D Lasswell, 'The Identification and Appraisal of Diverse Systems of Public Order' in Myres S McDougal and others (eds), *Studies in World Public Order* 3 (Martinus Nijhoff 1960). See for a critical reflection Molly Land, 'Reflections on the New Haven School' (2013–14) 58 NYLSLR 919.

[65] Ewan Criddle and Ewan Fox-Decent, *Fiduciaries of Humanity* (OUP 2016) 4 ('The fiduciary model of sovereignty developed in this book is both a conceptual and normative theory of the philosophical foundations of state authority and a positive or interpretive theory of the juridical structure that already exists under international law of the relationship between the state and each person subject to its jurisdiction.'). The authors use the process of 'reflective equilibrium under which the specific particulars of international law are tested against the general requirements of the fiduciary theory, which at this stage of analysis is a theory enriched and strengthened by inclusion of the core elements of international law well-suited to a fiduciary explanation.' (pp 4–5). The 'reflective equilibrium' approach draws on John

in *The Thin Justice of International Law* (OUP 2015).[66] The work draws on political theory and philosophy as well as on some empirically oriented international relations scholarship.[67] To use the words of Howse and Teitel, the book attempts to 'imagin[e] the way in which the social and political world would look if the law's aim was fully attained',[68] an attempt that finds its roots in Kant's ideas about the perfectibility of law, laid down most famously in his essay *Perpetual Peace* (1795).[69] While this perfectibility of positive law is an aspiration that may never be fully realized,[70] it should not keep us from trying. Like all scholarship on extraterritoriality, this book also aims 'to advance legal arguments in order to obtain specific outcomes', to use John Haskell's assessment of extraterritoriality literature.[71]

While drawing on other disciplines from the humanities and the social sciences, this study remains a primarily a legal one, however. The last, 'specific' part of the book even contains a close doctrinal-technical analysis of how the law of jurisdiction has furthered and can still further common interests in discrete fields of the law. Ultimately, how the law of jurisdiction works in practice depends on the particular issue-area in which it is applied.[72] This should come with a proper,

Rawls, *A Theory of Justice* (1971 HUP) 20. Rawls explains that a state of reflective equilibrium is reached after 'a person has weighed various proposed conceptions and he has either revised his judgments to accord with one of them or held fast to his initial convictions'. In this work, I start from the conception that jurisdictional practice is, and should reflect, cosmopolitan understandings. This general conception is tested against actual (particular) practice and rival theoretical (general) conceptions, especially those that are realist and national interest-based. The expectation is that the cosmopolitan theory initially set out will undergo some adjustments after confrontation with practice and rival theory.

66 Steven Ratner, *The Thin Justice of International Law* (OUP 2015) 64 (testing international law rules for their compatibility with precepts of global justice—an ethical theory—positing that '[i]nternational law rules will be deemed just if and only if they (a) advance international and interstate peace, and (b) respect, in the sense of not interfering with, basic human rights').

67 See, however, the recent discovery of normative international political theory by international relations, making a debate with legal theory's normativity possible, as cited in Dunoff and Pollack, 'Reviewing Two Decades of IL/IR Scholarship' (n 58) 653. See for a forerunner: Stanley Hoffmann, *Duties beyond Borders: On the Limits and Possibilities of Ethical International Politics* (Syracuse University Press 1981).

68 Robert Howse and Ruti Teitel, 'Does Humanity-Law Require (or Imply) a Progressive Theory of History? (and Other Questions for Martti Koskenniemi)' (2013) 27 TICLJ 377, 379.

69 Immanuel Kant, *Perpetual Peace: A Philosophical Sketch* (1795) (T Humphrey trans, Hackett Publishing 2003).

70 Also Roland Pierik and Wouter Werner, 'Can Cosmopolitanism Survive Institutionalization?' in Roland Pierik and Wouter Werner (eds) *Cosmopolitanism in Context: Perspectives from International Law and Political Theory* (CUP 2010) 288–89 (calling it impossible and even undesirable to close the gap between moral cosmopolitanism and actual institutions, as the 'actual effects of cosmopolitanism should be constantly revealed, discussed and re-examined').

71 Indeed, at the most fundamental level, my approach to extraterritoriality, although it focuses specifically on common interests, may not differ that much from other approaches, as all of them somehow aim at 'moving history' and changing legal practices. See notably John Haskell, 'Ways of Doing Extraterritoriality in Scholarship' in Margolies and others (eds), *The Extraterritoriality of Law* (n 41) 26 (arguing that in all scholarship on extraterritoriality 'enacting a conceptual revolution among a given set of legal professionals is thought to lead to more effective, identifiable outcomes').

72 Cedric Ryngaert, 'The Limits of Substantive International Economic Law: In Support of Reasonable Extraterritorial Jurisdiction' in Bert Keirsbilck, Wouter Devroe, and Erik Claes (eds), *Facing the Limits of the Law* (Springer-Verlag 2009) 237–52, 247.

grounded understanding of how knowledge is created in these areas, and how valid arguments are constructed. This part ensures that the principles set out in the more theoretical first part of the book can be adequately translated into legal practice.

1.5 Structure

In terms of structure, this study starts, in Chapter 2, by presenting a theoretical argument in favour of 'selfless' cosmopolitan extraterritoriality by means of the exercise of jurisdiction. This study is fully aware, however, of the realist critique of pie-in-the-sky selflessness. Therefore, Chapter 3 explores how the exercise of prescriptive jurisdiction in the common interests oscillates between cosmopolitanism and national interest-based parochialism. The study is also aware of the risk of imperialism and abuse that may accompany the exercise of prescriptive jurisdiction in the common interest. Thus, Chapter 4 discusses various limiting principles that should condition or already condition the exercise and design of jurisdictional assertions. Chapter 5 road-tests the arguments set out in Chapters 2 and 3 by examining how jurisdictional doctrine and practice in specific fields of the law have effectuated or could effectuate cosmopolitan extraterritoriality. Four manifestations of unilateral jurisdiction have been selected: (i) port state jurisdiction over illegal, unreported, and unsustainable fishing and marine pollution; (ii) trade measures regarding global environmental challenges; (iii) transnational tort litigation with respect to human rights abuses committed by corporations; and (iv) the extraterritoriality of data protection law. Chapter 6 concludes.

2
Selfless Intervention
The Promise of Unilateral Jurisdiction

Advocates of 'global justice' or 'cosmopolitanism' propound that ethical duties are universal, and apply regardless of nationality, citizenship, race, etc. In pure cosmopolitanism, individuals owe ethical duties towards other individuals who are worse off, wherever in the world they may be. Individual agency is not particularly practical, however.[1] Therefore, global justice advocates have proposed mediating individuals' ethical duties via institutions, in particular international (governmental) organizations.[2] In this institutional view, international organizations ought to be oriented towards furthering cosmopolitan ideals and tackling collective action problems, such as protecting human rights and the environment, guaranteeing collective security, and ensuring distributive justice.[3] Some such institutions, such as the United Nations, have been duly created. However, because of design faults, political unwillingness, or resource limits, they have not been able to deliver fully on the promises they initially held. Human rights are still trampled on, corruption remains rampant, and global warming continues unabated.

In the face of international institutions' failure to adequately tackle collective action problems, the question may arise whether well-positioned *bystander (third) states* could, or even should tackle these problems. These states would assume a cosmopolitan responsibility, that is, act 'selflessly', apart from catering to the needs of their own citizens. Contemporary political theorist Simon Caney, in any event, is of the view that individual states *do* have such global responsibilities. While they are free to pursue their own ends and to discharge their 'contractual' duties towards their own citizens, they should do so 'within the context of a fair overall framework', 'a set of parameters defined by a theory of justice'.[4] In this book, an aspect of this state cosmopolitanism is addressed, namely the question whether states can *unilaterally extend their (prescriptive) jurisdiction* to address global ills.

Unilateral action is defined here as conduct 'to opt out of a multilateral framework (whether existing or proposed) or to act alone in addressing a particular

[1] Judith Lichtenberg, 'Negative Duties, Positive Duties and the "New Harms"' (2010) 120 Ethics 557.
[2] Michael J Green, 'Institutional Responsibility for Global Problems' (2002) 30 Phil Topics 79, 85–86.
[3] Simon Caney, *Justice Beyond Borders: A Global Political Theory* (Oxford 2005) 159. See on poverty in particular Thomas Pogge, *World Poverty and Human Rights: Cosmopolitan Responsibilities and Reforms* (2nd edn, Polity 2008).
[4] ibid, 139–40.

Selfless Intervention. Cedric Ryngaert, Oxford University Press (2020). © Cedric Ryngaert.
DOI: 10.1093/oso/9780198851783.001.0001

global or regional challenge rather than choosing to participate in collective action'.[5] From a (prescriptive) jurisdictional perspective, the inquiry regards how a state can apply its own laws to address globally undesirable situations that arise or occur (largely) extraterritorially, that is, beyond its borders. Well-known instances of such exercises of jurisdiction are the US Department of Justice's indictment of corrupt FIFA (Fédération Internationale de Football Association) officials,[6] Spanish investigating judge Garzon's attempts to have former Chilean dictator Augusto Pinochet extradited to Spain to stand trial for international crimes,[7] and the EU's move to subject foreign air carriers to the EU's own stringent climate change legislation to the extent that they frequent EU airports.[8]

This chapter fleshes out, from a theoretical perspective, how such unilateral, 'extraterritorial' action could be justifiable. The starting point of the analysis is that, in light of institutional failures to adequately protect global values and common interests, unilateral action may at times be necessary to dispense global corrective justice (section 2.1). This begs the question, however, as to whether such values and interests actually exist, or more fundamentally, is there such a thing as an 'international community' on whose behalf individual states purport to act (section 2.2)? And even if some interests or values are more or less universally shared, should individual states rather than international institutions be entrusted with cosmopolitan jurisdictional powers? Can benevolent hegemons be trusted, or does their 'cosmopolitan' action risk degenerating into imperialist imposition of idiosyncratic hegemonic values (section 2.3)? While acknowledging the risk of self-serving behaviour, this monograph is inclined to support benevolent unilateralism, as the alternative—no action—may be worse. It argues that the justification of such unilateralism should be sought in a reinterpretation of the notion of sovereignty (section 2.4), as well as in the substantive values supposedly furthered by unilateral action (section 2.5). Finally, section 2.6 draws a rough sketch of *existing* treaty- and customary law-based authorizations and obligations to exercise

[5] Armin Steinbach, 'The Trend towards Non Consensualism in Public International Law: A (Behavioural) Law and Economics Perspective' (2016) 27 EJIL 643, 650, citing David M Malone and Yuen Foong Khong (eds), *Unilateralism and US Foreign Policy: International Perspectives* (Rienner 2003) 3. See for a definition of unilateralism also Maggie Gardner, 'Channeling Unilateralism' (2015) 56 HILJ 297, 299 ('the independent actions of a state taken without any expectation that other states will reciprocate'). Jurisdictional unilateralism denotes the exercise of prescriptive jurisdiction by states or regional organizations (such as the European Union), acting individually to address governance challenges that other states will reciprocate.

[6] The US Department of Justice's FIFA indictments can be found here: https://www.nytimes.com/interactive/2015/05/27/sports/soccer/document-fifa-indictments.html. See also Conor Slattery, 'A New World Order: FIFA Fiscal Scandal Opens the Door for the United States Department of Justice to Prosecute Crimes Committed across the Globe through the Use of Extraterritorial Jurisdiction' (2018) 41 Suffolk Transnat'l L Rev 201.

[7] See on the proceedings in *Pinochet:* Andrea Gattini, 'Pinochet Cases' (2007) MPEPIL, https://opil.ouplaw.com/view/10.1093/law:epil/9780199231690/law-9780199231690-e859?print=pdf

[8] Directive 2008/101/EC of the European Parliament and of the Council of 19 November 2008 amending Directive 2003/87/EC so as to include aviation activities in the scheme for greenhouse gas emission allowance trading within the Community, [2009] OJ L 8/3.

prescriptive jurisdiction in the common interest, a sketch which will be further elaborated on in Chapter 5.

2.1 Unilateral Action Compensating for Multilateral Failures

Advocates of unilateral cosmopolitanism in essence posit that states *can*, and perhaps *should* assume responsibility for, and on behalf of all members of a perceived international community, irrespective of artificially created national borders. This laudable position is in apparent tension with a principle on which the entire edifice of contemporary international law has been built: the principle of territorial sovereignty. The pedigree of this principle can be traced from the Peace of Westphalia of 1648, a series of treaties which ended the Thirty Years' War and introduced the concept of coexisting states with full internal and external sovereignty, until the present day.[9] Territorial sovereignty implies that final political authority and jurisdiction is exclusively vested in a territorially delimited political community, and that no other authority has jurisdiction, that is a legal say ('*juris dicere*'), over this community. The role of international law is simply to ensure that this sovereignty is not trampled on and that the territorial state-based system survives. In practice, state sovereignty has at times been violated when one state reasoned that respect for another state's sovereignty was not in its interest—which may lead one to question indeed whether sovereignty is not just organized hypocrisy.[10] But it remains an enduring 'cognitive script' that guides the actions of participants in international relations.[11] It requires that they at least pay lip service to the principles of non-intervention and territoriality.

The law of jurisdiction, with which we are concerned here, is closely related to the principle of territorial sovereignty, and may even be coextensive with it. It contains rules that limit the reach of a state's prescriptive, adjudicatory, and enforcement jurisdiction to the state's territorial boundaries, with some limited exceptions to protect and punish its own nationals (personality principle), its political independence (protective principle), and certain enemies of mankind (universality principle). The basic rule of territoriality, and the limited extraterritorial exceptions to it, are geared towards protecting the sovereignty and self-interest of states.[12] Jurisdictional rules may also be inspired by a utilitarian rationale based

[9] See for a historical account: Derek Croxton, *Westphalia: The Last Christian Peace* (Palgrave Macmillan 2013); and for a discussion of the influence of the peace until the twentieth century: Leo Gross, 'The Peace of Westphalia, 1648–1948' (1948) 42 AJIL 20.

[10] See also Stephen D Krasner, *Sovereignty: Organized Hypocrisy* (PUP 1999) 11.

[11] ibid, 69 (arguing that sovereignty—while being organized hypocrisy in his opinion—has proved remarkably 'durable in the sense that it has affected the talk and conception of rulers since at least the end of the 18th century, despite substantial changes in the international environment').

[12] This applies both in a positive and a negative sense: states are allowed to project their power unilaterally, but when so doing, they should not unduly interfere in other states' affairs. Theoretically, reciprocity ensures that States will by and large respect the requirement of non-interference, although in

on efficiency and procedural economy.[13] As such, they ensure that courts and prosecutors do not waste scarce state resources to address problems that are another state's concern, apart from preventing international discord.

Understandings of jurisdiction that consider states, with territorial boundaries, as the primary units of analysis, are not particularly amenable to cosmopolitan action. For cosmopolitans indeed, individuals, making up an international community with common values, are the focus of attention.[14] Nevertheless, in recent international law scholarship and practice, sovereignty has lost some of its discursive power, and considerations of humanity and solidarity have instead risen to prominence.[15] This humanity-centredness has also found its way to the law of jurisdiction, part of which has become based on the rationale of corrective justice; that is, on the cosmopolitan notion that states owe duties based on ethics towards citizens of other nations.[16] In the law of jurisdiction, the idea that a state has certain

reality, as a result of disparities of power, strong states have an incentive to extend their jurisdiction to the detriment of other states' sovereignty, without being hampered by a concern over adverse foreign reactions (notably the United States, European states, and the European Union have been at the vanguard of exercising 'extraterritorial' jurisdiction).

[13] Adeno Addis, 'Community and Jurisdictional Authority' in Gunther Handl, Joachim Zekoll, and Peter Zumbansen (eds), *Beyond territoriality: Transnational Legal Authority in an Age of Globalization* (Brill | Nijhoff 2012) 16–17, 'appears to consider this efficiency-based rationale to be the main informant of the norms of jurisdiction, stating that 'jurisdictional norms emerge for the purpose of maximizing aggregate social welfare'.

[14] Rafael Domingo, 'The New Global Human Community' (2012) 12 CJIL 563, 570 (referring to individuals' 'human dignity'). Cosmopolitans do not necessarily deny the existence or use of states, but for them, states only have instrumental value, insofar as they contribute to the primary cosmopolitan ideal of realizing the worth of every human being. See Roland Pierik and Wouter Werner, 'Cosmopolitanism in Context: An Introduction' in Roland Pierik and Wouter Werner (eds), *Cosmopolitanism in Context: Perspectives from International Law and Political Theory* (CUP 2010) 4–5. Note that non-cosmopolitan moral philosophers, however, may well ascribe moral value to (territorially delimited) states. See eg Mervyn Frost, *Ethics in International Relations* (CUP 1996) 155 ('sovereign states and the system of sovereign states are necessary to the flourishing of individuals'). A similarly 'Hegelian' view is even embraced by John Rawls, whose theory on—national—justice cosmopolitans have applied to international relations. In one of his last works, John Rawls, *The Law of Peoples* (HUP 1999), Rawls adheres to a society of states approach to international morality, considering peoples organized in states as the primary units of analysis. This is reminiscent of the work of Frost and Hedley Bull, the main representative of the so-called English school in international relations, who similarly regarded the state-based system as the best system to realize justice. See Hedley Bull, *The Anarchical Society: A Study of Order in World Politics* (Palgrave 1977) 287–88. Pierik and Werner have incisively observed that Rawls's approach is very much in keeping with the Westphalian structure of current international law: it gives pride of place to state sovereignty, self-determination, and the principle of non-intervention (Pierik and Werner, this n, 8).

[15] Theodor Meron, *The Humanization of International Law* (Brill 2006); Ruti G Teitel, *Humanity's Law* (OUP 2011). See on solidarity: Sergio Dellavalle, 'Opening the Forum to the Others: Is There an Obligation to Take Non-National Interests Into Account Within National Political and Juridical Decision-Making-Processes?' (2014) 6 GJIL 2, 217, at 220 (defining solidarity as the 'legal obligation to take non-national interests into account'); Rüdiger Wolfrum, 'Solidarity amongst States: An Emerging Structural Principle of International Law' in Pierre-Marie Dupuy and others (eds), *Völkerrecht als Wertordnung—Common Values in International Law: Festschrift für Christian Tomuschat* (Engel 2006), 1087–88 ('States in shaping their positions in international relations should not only take into consideration their own individual interests but also those of other States or the interests of the community of States or both.').

[16] Addis (n 13) 17.

moral duties towards outsiders has already grounded legal principles that allow, and, under certain circumstances, even require states to exercise so-called universal jurisdiction over a number of treaty- and customary law-based international crimes, such as war crimes and torture,[17] in the absence of any territorial or personal link of the crime or the presumed offender with the asserting state.[18] The incorporation of the obligatory dimension of this imperative—jurisdiction as a duty of states rather than just a discretionary choice that is restricted by international law—has in fact been hailed as a momentous shift in jurisdictional thinking. For Alex Mills, it points to a reconceptualization of the regulation of jurisdiction 'as not merely a "ceiling", defining the maximum limits of state power, but also ... as a "floor", reflecting minimum requirements for the exercise of regulatory power by states in order to satisfy their international obligations'.[19] This chimes with arguments from legal philosophy pursuant to which addressing the global problems afflicting humanity 'is not just a moral *option,* but a moral and political *duty* with important legal implications'.[20]

One could envisage that this notion of jurisdiction as corrective, cosmopolitan justice may also inform and justify jurisdictional assertions beyond the sphere of international criminal law. To address acute global governance problems, individual states may wish to regulate corporations' overseas business practices that adversely affect human rights or the environment, or violate global anti-corruption standards. They may fine foreign-flagged vessels docking in their ports, even in relation to activities on the high seas such as illegal or unsustainable fisheries, or pollution of the marine environment. They may restrict or prohibit the importation of goods produced abroad in substandard conditions, or which contribute to global warming. When states, or regional organizations such as the European Union, thus flex their muscles, they might exercise unilateral jurisdiction to protect some notion of 'global values' or 'the common interest'.

Standard accounts of institutional cosmopolitanism have not directly addressed this kind of unilateral jurisdictional action. Instead, such accounts typically emphasize the role of international agreements and institutions as media to

[17] *Eg* Convention Against Torture and Other Cruel, Inhuman or Degrading Treatment or Punishment (opened for signature 10 December 1984, entered into force 26 June 1987) 1465 UNTS 85, art 7(1).

[18] States may, however, require the presumed offender's posterior territorial presence for jurisdiction to be triggered. Also the operation *aut dedere aut judicare* clause that features in a number of international conventions is based on the presence of the offender within the territorial jurisdiction of the state, as States Parties to such conventions only have the choice to extradite or prosecute the presumed offender when the latter is present in their territory in the first place. See *eg* art 5(2) of the UN Torture Convention (n 17), 'Each State Party shall ... take such measures as may be necessary to establish its jurisdiction over such offences in cases where the alleged offender is present in any territory under its jurisdiction and it does not extradite him.').

[19] Alex Mills, 'Rethinking Jurisdiction in International Law' (2014) 84 BYBIL187, 209–12 (also stating at 212 that 'the fact that (particularly positive) jurisdictional obligations have been recognized with growing frequency and scope supports the thesis of a broader shift in international law').

[20] Domingo (n 14) 565.

effectuate cosmopolitan duties. Standard-setting, administrative, and enforcement competences may transferred to multilateral institutions, which—to the extent possible—objectively decide on the allocation of resources to alleviate the plight of disenfranchised people or to solve global environmental problems. However, while such institutions have been established, in the non-ideal world in which we live, they may lack power, resources, and ambition as they are hamstrung by the principle of consent. Consent, which remains a central characteristic of the international legal system, implies that progress on global governance issues requires the participation of all, or at least a substantial number of members of the international community.[21] Precisely this requirement of consent may immobilize international agreements and institutions, and fail to deliver the expected global benefits.[22] For instance, international agreement has so far not been reached in a way that would measure up to the challenge of adequately combatting climate change.[23] Nor have international legal instruments substantially limited multinational corporations' scope of action, with the attendant externalities going partly unaddressed (*eg* in terms of human rights violations).[24] If such collective action problems were to arise in a purely domestic setting, states could just address them by adopting laws as the domestic law-making process does not require that the consent of every single citizen be secured; it suffices that a majority agrees. But this is obviously not how international law works, or at least not how states have wanted it to work. In international law, there are hardly any constraints on liberalism's 'free exchange of entitlements',[25] with the attendant negative externalities.

The limitations of multilateralism should give us pause and invite us to ponder the benefits of states *unilaterally* taking action to compensate for the lack of

[21] Nico Krisch, 'The Decay of Consent: International Law in an Age of Global Public Goods' (2014) 108 AJIL 1. This may not apply to single-best effort global public goods, for the realization of which no aggregate effort is required, for example geo-engineering techniques in which only one state, or a small group of states invests, but that may deliver benefits for the entire international community.

[22] See: Eyal Benvenisti, 'Sovereigns as Trustees of Humanity: On the Accountability of States to Foreign Stakeholders' (2013) 107 AJIL 295, 312 (writing that sovereignty is 'potentially immobilizing', and referring to an 'anti-commons' regime that requires everybody's consent to achieve socially beneficial outcomes').

[23] Joeri Rogelj et al, 'Paris Agreement climate proposals need a boost to keep warming well below 2 °C' (2016) 534 Nature 631–39.

[24] But see zero draft on a Legally Binding Instrument on Business and Human Rights, submitted by the Embassy of Ecuador, July 2018.

[25] Liberal international theory traditionally sees the principle of consent and the freedom of states undergirding it, as global welfare *maximizers*, much in the same way as liberals, within a nation state context, assume that individual freedom and choice, without (or with limited) collective intervention, furthers the public good. See Joost Pauwelyn, *Optimal Protection of International Law* (CUP 2008) 31, reflecting on the consent-based structure of international law, Pauwelyn has observed that international law is in fact 'the prototype of a market-based property rule regime', which can be said to mirror our capitalist economy. See Pauwelyn at 31. Limited exceptions to the principle of consent in international law are peremptory norms of international law (*jus cogens*), which invalidate treaties that violate such norms (see arts 53 and 64 Vienna Convention on the Law of Treaties (opened for signature 23 May 1969, entered into force 27 January 1980) 1155 UNTS 331), and UN Security Council resolutions adopted under Chapter VII of the UN Charter, which, in accordance with art 103 of the UN Charter, prevail over other legal commitments entered into by States Parties to the UN Charter.

international progress on governance challenges regarding global public goods, values, and interests. Should individual states perhaps be allowed to exercise unilateral action to further common interests, at least temporarily, until adequate multilateral action is taken? In light of the democratic deficit of international organizations,[26] one may even wonder whether international institutions are ontologically desirable to further common interests, given their democratic deficits.[27] Instead, perhaps space should be created for pluralistic experimentation by the *loci* of democratic governance: states.[28] Should these states, acting as agents of the international community, not be allowed to prescribe their laws to further global values and common interests? Possibly out of a disciplinary bias against sovereign statehood, international ethics largely shuns the state as a cosmopolitan duty-bearer, possibly seeing the state as the problem of, rather than the solution to the world's ills. This bias is understandable: leaving the realization of global justice to individual states may well be a recipe for doing nothing, as electoral politics may render cosmopolitanism a non-starter. But on closer inspection, empowering individual states to further the global interest in fact sits well with our current pluralistic and pluri-centric world, where different centres of power take experimental, bottom-up global action, thereby providing best practices and inspiration for others to follow.[29] The sociologist Saskia Sassen's work on global cities comes to mind here.[30] Moreover, some cosmopolitans themselves, wary of a Leviathan-like supreme world government responsible for dispensing global justice,[31] have

[26] Discussing the democratic deficit of the European Union see *eg* Andreas Follesdal and Simon Hix, 'Why There is a Democratic Deficit in the EU: A Response to Majone and Moravcsik' (2006) 44 JCMS 533. Discussing the democratic deficit at the international level in general see *eg* Hans Born and Heiner Hänggi (eds), *The 'Double Democratic Deficit': Parliamentary Accountability and the Use of Force under International Auspices* (Ashgate 2004).

[27] See *eg* Eyal Benvenisti, 'Sovereigns as Trustees of Humanity: On the Accountability of States to Foreign Stakeholders' (2013) 107 AJIL 295, 332 (inveighing against a strong supervisory role of international bodies on grounds of reliability and democratic legitimacy, arguing that intrusion into national policy-making raises serious legitimacy concerns, 'especially regarding the impartiality of global decision-makers and judges, their competence to make better judgment calls than the reviewed sovereigns, and the potentially stifling impact of their interventions on domestic democratic processes').

[28] Jed Rubenfeld, 'Unilateralism and Constitutionalism' (2004) 79 NYLR 2012 ('International constitutionalism, which Habermas favors, does damage to the prospects for variation, experimentation, and pluralism that national democracy opens up', and, in opposition to 'European' international constitutionalism, which arguably has its roots in the excesses of 'democratic' Nazism, at 1999, favouring US democratic constitutionalism that is 'answerable to the nation's project of political self-determination over time').

[29] See also Pamela Bookman, 'The Unsung Virtues of Global Forum Shopping' (2016) 92 NDLR 579. *Contra* Austen L Parrish, 'Fading Extraterritoriality and Isolationism? Developments in the United States' (2017) 24 IJGLS 207, 210 (worrying 'that the unilateral use of domestic law to regulate foreigners for activity occurring abroad ... will further fragment the international legal system in a particularly pernicious way'.).

[30] Saskia Sassen, *The Global City: New York, London, Tokyo* (PUP 2013). This work chronicles how New York, London, and Tokyo became command centres for the global economy and in the process underwent a series of massive and parallel changes. What distinguishes Sassen's theoretical framework is the emphasis on the formation of cross-border dynamics through which these cities and the growing number of other global cities begin to form strategic transnational networks.

[31] See already Immanuel Kant, *Perpetual Peace: A Philosophical Sketch* (1795), reprinted in Hans Reiss (ed), *Kant Political Writings* (CUP 1991) (submitting that 'laws progressively lose their impact as

admitted that 'there is a case for different institutions operating at different levels', which has the advantage of preventing the centralization of coercive power.[32] They may have in mind, in the first place, different international organizations addressing different policy issues, and keeping each other in check. But there is no reason to exclude individual states from this pantheon. In fact, Kant saw separate states rather than international organizations as the cosmopolitan duty-bearers in his *Perpetual Peace*.[33] Rawls defended the society of states in his approach to justice in *The Law of Peoples*, although then he famously went on to doubt the possibility of global justice and solidarity within a society of states that do not all share a liberal justice outlook.[34] And Bartelson, one of the leading contemporary sovereignty theorists, foregrounded the role of states as media and instruments of global justice in *Sovereignty as Symbolic Form*: 'the universalistic visions invoked to justify the projection of ... governmental strategies into the global realm today operate under the assumption that the international system of states is the only available medium for realizing such visions in the near future'.[35] Ultimately, the state remains a—or even *the*—central actor in international law-making and implementation. States could well be cosmopolitan actors,[36] which means that they recast global problems in local terms in order to take advantage of local political or social resources.[37] In legal practice, this could take the form of prosecuting corporations engaging in foreign corrupt practices or foreign human rights abuses, or prosecuting individuals who committed atrocities abroad. Such jurisdictional action may be inevitable if multilateral avenue are (temporarily) foreclosed, or if more closely connected states fail to assume their regulatory and enforcement responsibilities. As Ankersmit and others have argued, 'unilateralism is sometimes the only available path toward regulation to protect important values',[38] or as Seck

the government increases its range, and a soulless despotism, after crushing the germs of goodness, will finally lapse into anarchy').

32 Caney (n 3) 163.

33 Robert Howse and Ruti Teitel, 'Does Humanity-Law Require (or Imply) a Progressive Theory of History? (and Other Questions for Martti Koskenniemi)' (2013) 27 TICLJ 377, 383 writing that 'according to Kant, we need the state as well as an order of cosmopolitan right where individuals can claim, as humans, to be treated in a certain way regardless of territorial boundaries', citing Kant's emphasis on the republican federation in *Perpetual Peace*); Thomas Pogge, 'Cosmopolitanism and Sovereignty' (1992) 103 Ethics 48.

34 Rawls, *The Law of Peoples* (n 14) 13.

35 Jens Bartelson, *Sovereignty as Symbolic Form* (Routledge 2014) 78.

36 Roland Pierik and Wouter Werner, 'Can Cosmopolitanism Survive Institutionalization?' in Roland Pierik and Wouter Werner (eds), *Cosmopolitanism in Context: Perspectives from International Law and Political Theory* (CUP 2010) 283 (noting also that 'international treaties that embrace cosmopolitanism endow States with the primary task of guarding the interests of individuals and global society as a whole'); Joel P Trachtman, *The Future of International Law* (CUP 2013) 11.

37 Hannah L Buxbaum, 'National Jurisdiction and Global Business Networks' (2010) 17 IJGLS 165, 167.

38 Laurens Ankersmit and others, 'Diverging EU and WTO Perspectives on Extraterritorial Process Regulation' (2012) 21 MJIL 12, 33, citing Daniel Bodansky, 'What's So Bad about Unilateral Action to Protect the Environment?' (200) 11 EJIL 339, 339 ('the choice is not between unilateral-ism and

has submitted, '[e]ffective legal governance in the Anthropocene ... requires state laws to reach further, extending beyond territorial borders to capture transnational corporate conduct'.[39] From a global welfare perspective, inaction may be a worse option than action.

2.2 The 'International Community' Served by Unilateral Action

When a state wants to tackle global problems through the exercise of unilateral jurisdiction, from a justice perspective it may obviously want to ensure that others view these problems as global too, lest such jurisdiction be seen as illegitimate, self-serving, and intruding on other states' policy choices. In this respect, it can be posited that the justification of a unilateral/extraterritorial measure hinges on the international community's recognition of the object of regulation (*eg* a stable climate, human rights, sustainable fisheries, a corruption-free world), and thus on internationally shared values. When the international community has recognized an object as in need of protection, the assumption is that states may be (more) justified to protect this good unilaterally,[40] as they are, *arguendo*, just vicariously enforcing community values. The international dimension encourages[41] and 'multilateralizes' unilateral action, and adds nuance to its interventionist character. Therefore, unilateralism and multilateralism should not be seen as opposites.

multilateralism, but between unilateralism and inaction'). Ankersmit and colleagues are however fully aware of the potential for abuse. ibid, 20–33.

[39] Also Sara L Seck, 'Beyond the E-word in the Anthropocene' in Daniel S Margolies and others (eds), *The Extraterritoriality of Law* (Routledge 2019) 57.

[40] cf Appellate Body Report, *United States—Import Prohibition of Certain Shrimp and Shrimp Products*, WT/DS58/AB/R (12 October 1998), para 31 (observing that extraterritorial trade measures could in principle be justified when the measure concerns a shared resource, of which the value of its protection is as such recognized by the international community: '[g]iven the recent acknowledgement by the international community of the importance of concerted bilateral or multilateral action to protect living natural resources, and recalling the explicit recognition by WTO Members of the objective of sustainable development in the preamble of the WTO Agreement, we believe it is too late in the day to suppose that Article XX(g) of the GATT 1994 may be read as referring only to the conservation of exhaustible mineral or other non-living natural resources. Moreover, two adopted GATT 1947 panel reports previously found fish to be an "exhaustible natural resource" within the meaning of Article XX(g). We hold that, in line with the principle of effectiveness in treaty interpretation, measures to conserve exhaustible natural resources, whether living or non-living, may fall within Article XX(g).' (footnotes omitted). See also Friedl Weiss, 'Extra-Territoriality in the Context of WTO Law' in Gunther Handl, Joachim Zekoll, and Peter Zumbansen (eds), *Beyond Territoriality: Transnational Legal Authority in an Age of Globalization* (Brill | Nijhoff 2012), (observing in respect of art XX(g) GATT that trade-restrictive environmental measures adopted pursuant to multilateral environmental agreements easier to justify than fully unilateral measures).

[41] cf Daniel Bodansky, 'What's in a Concept? Global Public Goods, International Law, and Legitimacy' (2012) 23 EJIL 651, 660 (citing the transformative effect of a characterizing an obligation as an international one: 'The existence of an international obligation ... gives domestic actors both within and outside government a "hook" for their arguments.').

Contextualized unilateralism may in fact resemble multilateralism, where the unilaterally acting actor enforces multilaterally shared norms and values.[42]

The persuasiveness of this thesis is obviously a function of the actual existence of such shared norms, and of an international community of which the state purportedly is a guardian. It is an understatement in this respect that the notion of 'international community'—an 'imagined community' of principle that transcends borders and in which the members do not know each other—[43] is a particularly elusive and contested one.[44] Still, the notion is widely used in international legal scholarship, where it denotes a community premised on common international interests that prevail over individual state interests.[45] This 'international community' in fact echoes Stoic, medieval, and early modern cosmopolitan views which referred to a community of humankind under the law of God (over which the Holy See would exercise 'universal jurisdiction'),[46] and later, after the religious wars of the early seventeenth century, under a rational, natural law-based *jus gentium*,[47] or cosmopolitan law.[48] Pursuant to the latter, individuals have specific entitlements against states of which they are not citizens simply because individuals, regardless of state borders, socially interact and communicate (a Kantian perspective, later also theorized by Jürgen Habermas).[49]

[42] Pierik and Werner, 'Can Cosmopolitanism Survive Institutionalization?' (n 36) 286, relying on Jack M Balkin, 'Nested Oppositions' (1990) 99 YLJ 1169 (drawing attention to the specific context in which conceptual opposites receive their meaning, and arguing that 'in certain contexts concepts may appear to be radically opposed, while in others they may look quite similar').

[43] Benedict Anderson, *Imagined Communities: Reflections on the Origin and Spread of Nationalism* (Verso Books 2006); Addis (n 13) 20. It is pointed out that the very fact that its members do not know each other has been used to discredit the notion of international community. See Pierik and Werner, 'Cosmopolitanism in Context: An Introduction' (n 14) 9–10 (citing the critique of cosmopolitanism that 'humanity as a whole too large and abstract to evoke genuine passions of unity, loyalty and obligation').

[44] *Eg* Herbert R McMaster and Gary D Cohn, 'America First Doesn't Mean America Alone' Wall Street Journal (Europe Edition) 1 June 2017, A11 (presenting the US Trump Administration's view on international relations, and endorsing 'a clear-eyed outlook that the world is not a "global community" but an arena where nations, nongovernmental actors and businesses engage and compete for advantage'.

[45] *Eg* Eyal Benvenisti and Georg Nolte (eds), *Community Interests Across International Law* (OUP 2018).

[46] Domingo (n 14) 564 (listing the Stoic cosmopolitan vision, the Roman aspiration 'toward an empire without end', the 'Christian ideal of a world united by charity', and 'the Dantian longing for a universal monarchy'). Note that the principle of *territorial* jurisdiction has *also* been grounded on divine mandates. See Gregor Noll, 'Theorizing Jurisdiction' in Anne Orford and Florian Hoffman (eds), *The Oxford Handbook of the Theory of International Law* (OUP 2016) 6.

[47] See, *eg*, Grotius's natural law views, pursuant to which the obligatory force of natural laws derive from the dictates of (human) reason. Note, however, that for Grotius 'the ultimate source of law in De iure belli is [still] the will of God, in a genealogical sense, because God had willed the existence of human beings in the first place'. See Benjamin Straumann, 'Early Modern Sovereignty and Its Limits' (2015) 16 Theoretical Inq L 423, 429.

[48] Sergio Dellavalle, 'On Sovereignty, Legitimacy and Solidarity—Or: Solidaristic Idea of Legitimate Sovereignty Be Justified' (2015) 16 Theoretical Inq L 367, 367–77.

[49] ibid, 393. See on communicative rationality also Jürgen Habermas, *Theory of Communicative Action, Volume One: Reason and the Rationalization of Society* (Beacon Press 1984); Jürgen Habermas, *Theory of Communicative Action, Volume Two: Lifeworld and System: A Critique of Functionalist Reason* (Beacon Press 1987). In practice, of course, this global community withered, and nation states ascended, a process which was also fuelled by scholarly views. Domingo (n 14) 573 (citing Gentili in particular).

In international law, the best-known contemporary proponent of the international community and its interests is arguably former judge of the International Court of Justice (ICJ) Bruno Simma, who defined international community interests as a 'consensus according to which respect for certain fundamental values is not to be left to the free disposition of States, individually or *inter se*, but is recognized and sanctioned by international law as a matter of concern to all States'.[50] This definition—which harks back to such ethically inspired international lawyers as Suarez, Grotius, Vattel, and Lauterpacht, who assumed the existence of an 'international society' with a 'general interest'—brackets the principle of state consent and signals that the notion of international community has natural law roots.[51]

In Alberico Gentili, *De jure belli libri tres* (1598), Gentili had indeed advocated studying the actual practices of states, and had dismissed the universal authority of the Church in matters of international law.

[50] Bruno Simma, *From Bilateralism to Community Interest in International Law* (Brill| Nijhoff 1994) 217, 233 (also expressly including environmental protection as a community interest). See also, against consensualism, Accordance with international law of the unilateral declaration of independence in respect of Kosovo (Advisory Opinion) [2010] ICJ Rep 403 (speaking out against 'anachronistic, extremely consensualist vision of international law, expressed in the *Lotus* judgment'). Also other ICJ judges have not shied away from referring to the 'international community', including in their judicial opinions. Former ICJ Judge Mohammed Bedjaoui famously declared in the *Nuclear Weapons* advisory opinion that '[t]he resolutely positivist, voluntarist approach of international law ... has been replaced by an objective conception of international law, a law more readily seen as the reflection of a collective juridical conscience and a response to the social necessities of States organised as a community'. Legality of Threat or Use of Nuclear Weapons (Separate Opinion of Judge Bedjaoui) 1996 ICJ 1345 (para 13). Current ICJ Judge Cançado Trindade even has the habit of appending lengthy individual, and often dissenting opinions to ICJ judgments, in which he criticizes the majority for taking the interests of the international community, humanity, or justice insufficiently into account (*eg* Application of genocide convention (*Croatia v* Serbia) (Dissenting Opinion Cancado Trindade) [2015] ICJ Rep 3, para 2) 'I thus present with the utmost care the foundations of my own entirely dissenting position ... guided above all by the ultimate goal of precisely the *realization of justice*.'). In fact, many international lawyers have embarked on a reformist project to give the interests of the international community a more prominent place in the current legal system. Martti Koskenniemi, 'International Law in a Post-Realist Era' (1995) 16 AYIL 1–19 ('our discipline has implied a program for reforming the present international structures, perhaps to reflect better the "interests of the world community"'). Note that a journal is also named after it: International Community Law Review (Brill).

[51] See, for probably the earliest legal articulation, Francisco Suarez, *Tractatus de Legibus ac Deo Legislatore Book II* (1612) ch 19 § 5 ('Mankind, though divided into numerous nations and states, constitutes a political and moral unity bound up by charity and compassion; wherefore, though every republic or monarchy seems to be autonomous and self-sufficing, yet none of them is, but each of them needs the support and brotherhood of others, both in a material and a moral sense. Therefore they also need some common law organizing their conduct in this kind of society.'). See for Vattel: One state owes to another state whatever it owes to itself, so far as that other stands in real need of its assistance, and the former can grant it without neglecting the duties it owes to itself. Such is the eternal and immutable law of nature. Emer de Vattel, *The Law of Nations, Or, Principles of the Law of Nature, Applied to the Conduct and Affairs of Nations and Sovereigns, with Three Early Essays on the Origin and Nature of Natural Law and on Luxury* (Liberty Fund 2008) (1797) 262 bk 2, ch 1, sec 3. See also Hersch Lauterpacht, 'The Law of Peace' in Elihu Lauterpacht (ed), *International Law: Being the Collected Papers of Hersch Lauterpacht Volume 2 The Law Of Peace* (Vol 2 CUP 1975) 88 (opining that the relation of the state to the international community was not based on 'self-sacrifice nor blind acceptance of the overriding superiority of the general interest of the international society, but enlightened self-interest which admits the advisability in given circumstances, of the sacrifice of an immediate sectional interest for the sake of the general interest'). Note that Lauterpacht did not explicitly state that there is an international community that could be dissociated from the consent of states; rather he urged states to consensually abandon narrow state interests for the sake of the general interest.

The problems with natural law are well-known. Universal morality is arguably subjective and enables powerful states to articulate a particularist view of it, while downplaying the potential conflict between conceptions of natural law held by different actors.[52] Modern international law's father Grotius, for instance, opened his *Mare Liberum* (1609) with a vehement critique of the great maritime nations of the era, Spain and Portugal—whose hold on the oceans had to be broken to advance the maritime interests of the Dutch United Province—on the ground that they mistook their particularist justice conceptions for universal justice.[53] Invoking humanity or objective justice may in fact just be a front for furthering one's own subjective preferences and interests.[54] Or as Proudhon and Schmitt have famously pointed out: 'whoever invokes humanity, wants to cheat'.[55] Thus, the question is whether global values can really exist in a non-egalitarian world, dominated by Western powers in particular,[56] and characterized by very divergent value conceptions.

Cosmopolitan theorists would counter this critique by positing that certain values are truly internationally shared. Since there is a common human nature, there is often no principled disagreement regarding basic moral norms, which can be said to converge globally,[57] even if a 'community of sentiment' may be lacking.[58] Communities may sometimes cherish other ideals, but this may be so because they face different scenarios and challenges[59] or because they may be misled by self-interested rulers.[60] Even where some divergence is noticeable, cosmopolitan philosophers would argue that this can be accommodated within a culturally sensitive universalist framework that affirms a pluralism of values.[61]

[52] Zygmunt Bauman, *Postmodern Ethics* (Blackwell 1993) 42 (arguing that 'there is more than one conception of universal morality, and that which of them prevails is relative to the strength of the powers that claim and hold the right to articulate it'); Immanuel Wallerstein, *European Universalism: The Rhetoric of Power* (The New Press 2006) 45 ('there are multiple versions of natural law that are quite regularly at direct odds with each other').

[53] Hugo Grotius, *Mare Liberum*, trans Ralph van Deman Magoffin, *The Freedom of the Seas, A Dissertation by Hoge Grotius* (OUP 1916) 1.

[54] *Eg* Bartelson (n 35) 33, 71 (pointing to the danger of universal thinking that 'whatever is subsumed under the category of the global and its cognates will always necessarily reflect particularistic interests and identities, and will thus also represent imperial or hegemonic aspirations in disguise'); Ulrich Beck, 'War is Peace: On Post-National War' (2005) 36 Security Dialogue 5, 36 (arguing that in so-called humanitarian military interventions, state interests may play a larger role than humanitarian concerns).

[55] Carl Schmitt, *The Concept of the Political* (University of Chicago Press 2007) 54.

[56] Wallerstein (n 52) 28. (noting that 'we are far from yet knowing what [global universal] values are', which requires 'a structure that is far more egalitarian than any we have constructed up to now'), observing at 51 that Europeans have considered their universalist claim as a scientific 'assertion of objective rules governing all phenomena at all moments of time'.

[57] Caney (n 3) 45–46.

[58] Andrew Clapham, 'The Role of the Individual in International Law' (2010) 21 EJIL 25, 31 (noting that 'states are abstract entities and I wonder if the solution does not rather partly lie in ensuring that individuals feel more sentimental about each other'), seconding Antonio Cassese, *The Human Dimension of International Law. Selected Papers* (OUP 2008), 78.

[59] Caney (n 3) 45–46.

[60] ibid, 49 (pointing out that some disagreement arises from error, selfishness, and indoctrination, and that 'values can be justified to all persons when those persons' reasoning is not distorted by self-interest, factual mistakes, complacency, and so on').

[61] ibid, 47 (citing Isaiah Berlin).

International lawyers steeped in the modern 'positivist' tradition, however, have intuitive reservations about an instinctive reliance on a common human nature. In order to escape the risk of subjective determinations, they would demand evidence of officially sanctioned commonalities ('state practice') before they dare speak of 'global values' or an 'international community'. Still, when espousing this positivist mindset, an analysis of relevant state practice yields the conclusion that, indeed, some version of an international community, although a relatively thin one at that, could be witnessed, as states have entered into particular treaties affirming community interests that go beyond states' (joint) immediate interests. This reality had already been observed as early as 1936 by Brierly.[62] Currently, a substantial number of treaties and customary norms protect interests that are considered as common to humanity, such as human rights and the environment. These treaties and norms do not maximize states' interests, but they limit states' scope of action to the benefit of their true addressees: a global community consisting of individuals, the environment, and the global commons.[63]

2.2.1 *Erga omnes* obligations

The international community character of at least some of these treaties is reinforced by the fact that States Parties to the relevant treaty may have been given the power to invoke the responsibility of the violating state on behalf of the international community, or at least of the collective state parties to that treaty.[64] This non-injured state's 'cosmopolitan' right to unilaterally invoke another state's responsibility in respect of violations of obligations owed to the international community is laid down in the International Law Commission's Articles on the Responsibility of States for Internationally Wrongful Acts (2001).[65] These articles

[62] 'The Rule of Law in International Society', reprinted in James L Brierly, *The Basis of Obligations in International Law and Other Papers* (OUP 1958), 250–52 ('[C]ommon standards, too, do sometimes issue in common action, and though the action may be half hearted and its results meagre, it is evidence of the general acceptance of at least some degree of common responsibility for the common welfare.'), citing the Mandates system, the Minorities treaties, the Nansen office for refugees, the International Red Cross organization, the manifold social and humanitarian work of the League of Nations, which he considered as 'not enough', but also as 'not negligible'. But see Domingo (n 14) 565 ('Since the international community lacks both the ability to take common action and universal awareness of common interests, it could be said to be more like a partnership than a community in the strict sense.').

[63] See also James Crawford, 'The Current Political Discourse Regarding International Law' (2018) 81(1) TMLR 1–22, 4 (arguing that 'whether or not there is a "global community"—a matter that rather depends on one's definition of community—there are incontestably global, communal or collective interests, such as "environmental stewardship" and "the prevention as far as possible of wars of destruction and weapons of mass destruction"').

[64] Individuals and the environment do not often have the power or capacity to call directly to account state violators of obligations laid down in the treaty, although some human rights treaties, such as the European Convention on Human Rights [1950] ETS 5, provide for standing of individuals before a supranational court.

[65] Draft Articles on Responsibility of States for Internationally Wrongful Acts [2001] YILC vol II Part Two, art 48(1)(b), November 2001, Supplement No 10 (A/56/10). This article provides that any

codify the *erga omnes* obligations pioneered by the ICJ in the *Barcelona Traction* case, in which the Court held that 'the obligations of a State towards the international community as a whole' are 'by their nature' 'the concern of all States', and that, '[i]n view of the importance of the rights involved, all States can be held to have a legal interest in their protection; they are obligations *erga omnes*'.[66] In so doing, the Court developed an idea enunciated by Kant in *Perpetual Peace*.[67]

This recognition of norms in which the 'international community' and its constituent parts—states—have an interest, is surely a watershed in international law. It is an acknowledgment that international law is not just concerned with the interests of states but also those of individuals and the international community at large.[68] The doctrine of *erga omnes* enables states not injured by violations of international law (*eg* international human rights law) to act in a cosmopolitan fashion, and represent the international community through the mechanism of invocation of state responsibility. Regardless, the international community established by such obligations is necessarily a partial one. Given the abiding relevance of the principle of state consent to be bound by international legal norms, states are under no obligation to enter into treaties or to accept the validity of a customary norm of general international law in the common interest. Thus, legally speaking, the positivistic international community is a limited, consent-based one. It is composed of states rather than individuals and therefore does not necessarily serve a global cosmopolitan purpose.[69] As long as states do not formally sign up to legal commitments, they are not bound, and fellow states, posing as guardians of the international community, cannot invoke their responsibility, since legally such an international community does simply not exist beyond the treaty or customary law regime.

This state of affairs may lead to serious collective action problems, where (major) states fail to join the protective legal regime, and global values accordingly do not enter the legal realm. Moreover, even the partial international community—or

state other than an injured state is entitled to invoke the responsibility of another state, among other scenarios, 'if the obligation breached is owed to the international community as a whole'. The articles also make reference to the 'international community' in art 25(1) regarding necessity as a circumstance precluding wrongfulness: 'Necessity may not be invoked by a State as a ground for precluding the wrongfulness of an act not in conformity with an international obligation of that State unless the act: (a) is the only way for the State to safeguard an essential interest against a grave and imminent peril; and (b) does not seriously impair an essential interest of the State or States towards which the obligation exists, or of *the international community as a whole*.' (emphasis added)

66 Barcelona Traction, Light and Power Company, Limited (*Belgium v Spain)* [1970] ICJ Rep 3 para 33.

67 Kant, *Perpetual Peace* (n 31) 107–08 ('The peoples of the earth have ... entered in varying degrees into a universal community, and it has developed to the point where a violation of rights in one part of the world is felt everywhere.').

68 Mills, 'Rethinking Jurisdiction in International Law' (n 19) 213 (although not using the term *erga omnes* in this respect).

69 Compare Domingo (n 14) 565 (noting that the current international community is a community of nation states, whereas the new global community is a community of individual persons).

rather communit*ies*—established by law are hardly beyond reproach when it comes to addressing collective action problems for a variety of reasons. First, states joining treaty regimes protecting community interests often only pay lip service to these interests; they may join out of reputational concerns rather than out of conviction.[70] Second, the *erga omnes* character of the community obligations in practice rarely has the consequence that bystander states invoke the responsibility of the violating state, for obvious political reasons.[71] Third, invocation of responsibility, when it occurs, rarely has far-reaching consequences, as it is just a speech act naming and shaming an alleged violator.[72] It does not come with any enforcement powers, except retorsions, unfriendly but lawful measures that states can take anyway, even in the absence of a prior breach.[73] And fourth, while the characterization of an obligation as *erga omnes* may foster the legitimacy of the exercise of unilateral jurisdiction over a violation of an obligation, it does not automatically confer a legal right on states parties to exercise extraterritorial jurisdiction over the violation. After all, as Seck has argued, the relevant treaties 'are premised on the idea of a bounded regulatory state that is able and willing to control . . . conduct effectively within its borders'.[74] In the words of Scott, such treaties are based on territorial 'system boundaries': they apportion responsibility for regulating conduct to the state where the relevant activity takes place or originates.[75] Only some treaties, typically in the sphere of international and transnational criminal law, contain a clause conferring extraterritorial jurisdiction on states parties.[76]

[70] Andrew Guzman, 'Reputation' in Andrew Guzman, *How International Law Works: A Rational Choice Theory* (OUP 2008) 71–118.

[71] Pauwelyn (n 25) 190–91 arguing that no-one is willing to invoke the responsibility of others if they are not directly harmed, and that the ensuing collective action problem—no-one protects the good—is the 'result of the nature of the subject-matter'). See for a rare example of a state invoking another state's responsibility for violating *erga omnes* obligations, even before the International Court of Justice: Questions Concerning the Obligation to Prosecute or Extradite (*Belgium v* Senegal), (Merits) [2012] ICJ Rep 422 (Belgium invoking the international responsibility of Senegal for failing to comply with the duty to either prosecute or extradite a presumed torturer present on Senegal's territory).

[72] Where a bystander state invokes another state's responsibility before an international court, however, the chances that change is brought about, are much higher, as non-compliance within binding decision has reputational repercussions for the state proved wrong by the decision. See on the role of reputation in inducing compliance with international law: Guzman, 'Reputation' (n 70) 67. For example, after the ICJ rendered its judgment in *Belgium v Senegal* (n 71), and found that Senegal had violated its obligations under the UN Torture Convention (n 17), Senegal established Extraordinary Chambers within its criminal justice system, so as to bring the presumed torturer to justice. See Statute of the Extraordinary African Chambers within the courts of Senegal created to prosecute international crimes committed in Chad between 7 June 1982 and 1 December 1990 (Unofficial translation by Human Rights Watch), available at http://www.hrw.org/news/2013/09/02/statute-extraordinary-african-chambers (accessed 17 March 2015).

[73] Non-affected states cannot take countermeasures, only 'lawful' measures. See Draft Articles (n 65) 54. *Contra* Christian Tams, *Enforcing Obligations Erga Omnes in International Law* (CUP 2005) 250.

[74] Also Seck, 'Beyond the E-word in the Anthropocene' (n 39) 49 (discussing global environmental treaties).

[75] Joanne Scott, 'The Global Reach of EU Law' in Marise Cremona and Joanne Scott, *EU Law Beyond EU Borders: The Extraterritorial Reach of EU Law* (OUP 2019) 40.

[76] *Eg* art 5 UN Torture Convention (n 17).

A contradiction may thus be discerned: although *erga omnes* treaties appear to offer a high level of protection to community values, and give more states the right to address a breach, in practice fewer take the initiative. Pauwelyn has observed in this respect that 'the actual protection of international entitlements is ... inversely related to how strongly international law aims or pretends to be protecting the entitlement'.[77] This is not to say that the norms enshrined in these treaties are not enforced. Sometimes international courts have been established to bring states or individuals to account, such as the European Court of Human Rights (ECtHR), which offers direct standing to individual plaintiffs, or the International Criminal Court (ICC), which has an independent prosecutor who can start investigations. And obviously, reputational concerns and fear of sanctions may exert a pull towards compliance. But it remains that the international community obligations confirmed in such treaties are under-enforced.

Accordingly, the formal international community conception based on *erga omnes* obligations fails in its mission to protect international community interests and to address collective action problems—even those which the *erga omnes* regime was precisely supposed to address. It overestimates the potential of the invocation of state responsibility as a remedial mechanism and does not *as such*—as a matter of positive international law—give states a mandate to exercise unilateral jurisdiction to protect the said obligations.[78] Furthermore, it is held hostage by the 'anti-commons' principle of consent, which allows states *not* to subscribe to a globally desirable collective regime. In other words, we are confronted with the inherent limits of a purely positivist approach to international community interests: such an approach may fail to ground the exercise of states' unilateral jurisdiction in the common interest.

2.2.2 Global public goods and global problems

Faced with the collective action problems relating to international community interests that have not (yet) risen to the level of international obligations, recent scholarship, borrowing from institutional economics, has cast the international community in non-legal global public goods (GPG) terms. GPGs could be defined as goods that are 'non-rival' and 'non-excludable', meaning that no-one can be excluded from their benefits and that consumption by one person does not diminish consumption by another.[79] The provision of such goods in not self-evident, as

[77] Pauwelyn (n 25) 194–95.

[78] But see Charlotte Beaucillon, 'Practice Makes Perfect, Eventually?' in Natalino Ronzitti (ed), *Coercive Diplomacy, Sanctions and International Law* (Brill | Nijhoff 2016), 105 (arguing that the legitimacy of unilateral measures is increased if justified on the basis that the target has violated *erga omnes* obligations).

[79] Inge Kaul and others (eds), *Providing Global Public Goods: Managing Globalization* (OUP 2003).

prisoners' dilemmas may prevent necessary multilateral action from being taken. Where individual states take action, other states may tend to free-ride, that is, fail to take action but hope to profit from other states' investment in providing GPGs. The potential for free-riding behaviour may ultimately discourage individual state action. However, if such action could bring free-riders within the state's jurisdictional ambit through extraterritorial jurisdiction, GPGs could yet be provided, even without multilateral intervention. Accordingly, the GPG approach holds particular promise for legitimizing unilateral action in the common interest, as the relevant question is not whether states have enshrined this interest in international law but rather whether it is *expedient* for such action to be taken so as to avert a perceived threat posed to the GPG. In GPG-inspired unilateralism discourse, the end, GPG protection, may justify the means, nonconsensual action. State consent becomes less material and unilateral action is hailed as a mechanism to compensate for multilateral regulatory failures,[80] and the lack of third-party enforcement in international law.[81]

GPGs have been defined rather broadly. Not only do they include common resources or goods that belong to 'the common concern of mankind', such as the global climate, the ozone layer, the prevention of pollution, the preservation of fish stocks, and biodiversity,[82] they may also cover such 'values' as human rights, peace, and accountability for international crimes.[83] This may render them indistinguishable from 'global problems', problems that concern the world at large, and they 'cannot be separated into different sub-problems that can be solved individually'.[84] In this respect, Ralph Michaels has usefully categorized global problems as 'global by nature' (*eg* climate change and other collective action problems that need to be solved by aggregate efforts of the international community), 'global by design'

[80] Krisch (n 21), 2 (stating that unilateral action appears 'more useful for problem solving and the effective exercise of power than formal institutions and the increasingly firm and demanding processes of multilateral treaty making'). ibid, 4 ('consent-based structure presents a structural bias against effective action on global public goods, especially given the large number of foreign states today'); see also, but critically Jack L Goldsmith and Eric A Posner, *The Limits of International Law* (OUP 2006) 87.

[81] It is conspicuous that Pauwelyn, after concluding that third-party enforcement does not work, suggests as alternatives robust community enforcement, direct standing for private parties, international procedure against individual criminals, and domestic courts, but not unilateral action (Pauwelyn (n 25), 196–97).

[82] UN General Assembly, Protection of global climate for present and future generations of mankind, UN Doc A/RES/43/53 (1988), para 1 ('Recognizes that climate change is a common concern of mankind, since climate is an essential condition which sustains life on earth'); Frank Biermann, 'Common Concern of Humankind: The Emergence of a New Concept of International Environmental Law' (1996) 34 Archiv des Völkerrechts 426, 449; Thomas Cottier, *The Emerging Principle of Common Concern: A Brief Outline*, Working Paper No 2012/20, NCCR Trade Regulation (2012). Compare with the 'common heritage of mankind', a term used to denote in particular areas beyond national jurisdiction, such the deep seabed and the celestial bodies. See *eg* Treaty on Principles Governing the Activities of States in the Exploration and Use of Outer Space, Including the Moon and Other Celestial Bodies, 27 January 1967, 18 UST 2410, 610 UNTS 205.

[83] See with respect to peace Goldsmith and Posner (n 80) 87.

[84] Ralf Michaels, 'Global Problems in Domestic Courts' in Sam Muller and others (eds) *The Law of The Future of Law* (Torkel Opsahl Academic EPublisher 2011) 167.

(*eg* the globally accessible Internet), and 'global by definition', even if these problems occur within one territory (*eg* crimes against humanity, which are directed at humanity at large, and thus at what it means to be an international community).[85] All these problems may arguably be amenable to the exercise of extraterritorial jurisdiction in the common interest.

However collective action failures are precisely characterized, what unites these characterizations is that they consider state consent and inaction, and ultimately sovereignty, as threats to the realization and protection of GPGs, global interests, or global values.[86] It is believed that unilateral action may remedy these failures where one state (or group of states such as the European Union) extends its jurisdiction to include within its ambit foreign-based persons subject to an unduly permissive regulatory or enforcement regime in their home or territorial state. Such unilateral action could be based on a—territorial or personal—nexus with the asserting state (*eg* a foreign corrupt person wired the proceeds of his activities to a bank account located in the state), or simply on the underlying global value or interest to be protected (*eg* a suspected *génocidaire* is brought to trial in a state without the latter having any territorial or personal connection with the crime or the suspect).

Approaches based on GPGs or on global problems attempt to bypass the subjectivity of natural law approaches to the common interest by casting global remedial action in terms of efficiency, welfare enhancement, urgency, scientific determinism, or even plain human or planetary survival. However, also these approaches cannot entirely escape the legitimacy problems coming with 'subjective' unilateral action. Even where an objective, quasi-scientific consensus exists on the good to be protected, unilateral action can cause distributional effects that lack international legitimacy in the absence of multilateral consent. States exercising unilateral jurisdiction could thus single-handedly decide on a global distribution of resources, with major resource allocation shifts being brought about as a result of the choice for a specific jurisdictional trigger. For instance, a broadly defined territoriality principle which brings foreign economic operators within the ambit of the asserting state may shift important resources from these operators and their home states to the asserting state.[87] The danger is real here that individual states will in reality be self-serving by bringing about inward shifts of international resources under cover of defending the global interest. Having calculated the efforts

[85] ibid, 171 (stating that a crime against humanity 'is by definition de-territorialized, simply because humanity transcends all territoriality', and terming it a 'world event').

[86] Also Martti Koskenniemi, 'What Use for Sovereignty Today?' (2011) 1 ASJIL 61 (writing that international lawyers have criticized sovereignty from a *functional* perspective on the ground that it fails to deal with global threats).

[87] See *eg* Joanne Scott, 'The New EU "Extraterritoriality"' (2014) 51 CMLR 1343, with respect to the territorial extension of EU law (arguing that 'the EU's choice of trigger bears deeply upon the distribution of the burden of complying with EU law and upon how easy this burden is to evade', and 'also impacts significantly upon how great a contribution a measure may make to the attainment of its stated objectives as well as upon the distribution of the benefits that flow from EU law').

required to address a global public good challenge, for example reducing greenhouse gas emissions, individual states may well impose disproportionate burdens on foreign operators and states such as via market access requirements or criminal prosecution. Moreover, different global public goods and values may be in tension with each other.[88] For example, justice considerations, which are arguably served by prosecuting human rights offenders, even in the courts of bystander states, may be in tension with the imperative to create peace and reconciliation, which is arguably served by deferring or foregoing prosecution of high-ranking perpetrators with a vocal constituency. Climate change mitigation for its part, which militates in favour of important emissions reductions, even if unilaterally imposed via market access requirements, may be in tension with the right to social and economic development of people living in less advanced nations, a right which may precisely militate against such reductions. Balancing conflicting public goods and values, as well as deciding on issues of burden-sharing, are inherent to global public goods or unilateralism inspired by global problems. They are essentially *moral choices* which states make in—what they believe is—the global interest.

2.3 The Cosmopolitan State as a Benevolent Hegemon

Where global problems have not been addressed by treaties or multilateral institutions, or where treaties or customary law have not conferred remedial jurisdiction on states to act in the global interest, pure positivism will equal defeatism. Those who believe in humanity's progress, however, may not consider such defeatism as a viable option in light of contemporary global justice and governance challenges. As an alternative, the relaxation of the principle of state consent to the exercise of cosmopolitan jurisdiction could be explored. In so doing, however, as argued in section 2.2, in essence, one replaces positivism with naturalism as a legitimating doctrine.

When advocating natural law, however rationally its contents may have been constructed, one should be keenly aware of the charges of subjectivism that have been levelled at it. These charges pertain particularly to the danger of unilateral hegemonic imposition of the values and norms of the powerful on the weak, with the former's life choices supplanting the latter's. Cosmopolitan unilateralism's goal of 'serving humanity' could thus be conceived as a thinly disguised attempt at realizing imperialist or hegemonic ambitions,[89] that is at dominating a weaker

[88] Bodanksy, 'What's So Bad about Unilateral Action to Protect the Environment?' (n 38) 651 and 656 (submitting that 'different actors will have different preferences about which norm to choose', and that every choice will accordingly have distributive consequences).

[89] Austen Parrish, 'The Interplay Between Extraterritoriality, Sovereignty, and the Foundations of International Law' [2017] SSRN 10 ('extraterritorial regulation is not the friend of international law, but rather evidence of a hegemonic state seeking to exempt itself from the world system'). This critique may also be directed at non-state-based, multi-stakeholder initiatives protecting global values, *eg* regarding

group,[90] and at promoting an internal agenda.[91] This concern was in fact already voiced by Grotius,[92] Vattel,[93] and Kant.[94] Ultimately, is the exercise of prescriptive jurisdiction with extraterritorial overtones not merely a projection of a state's power abroad?[95] Is such jurisdiction not just normative foreign policy repackaged in the form of legal rules that are supposedly more legitimate and carrying more ready obedience than simple policies and interests?[96] Would it not be more cosmopolitan, and respectful of human dignity, to stick to the principle of territorial sovereignty, which has, historically speaking, after the Peace of Westphalia, protected individuals from (religious) violence?[97]

There is no denying that ideas such as 'human fellowship' and 'the protection of others' interests' have been abused to justify colonial empire-building and subjection of foreign peoples.[98] As we write, they may continue to be used in pursuit

the environment and human rights, especially if they originate in the West. See *eg* regarding aquaculture certification: Peter Vandergeest and Anusorn Unno, 'A New Extraterritoriality? Aquaculture Certification, Sovereignty, and Empire' (2012) 31 Political Geography 335.

[90] Unilateralism indeed generally remains a suspect word, conjuring up images of subjectivism at best and colonialism at worst. See *eg* Jürgen Habermas, 'Interpreting the Fall of a Monument' (2003) 4 GLJ 701, 706 ('justification through international law can, and should be replaced by the unilateral, world-ordering politics of a self-appointed hegemon'); Pierik and Werner, 'Cosmopolitanism in Context: An Introduction' (n 14) 9–10, citing the concern that cosmopolitanism may risk 'becoming part and parcel of imperialistic policies', and referring in this respect to Costas Douzinas, *Human Rights and Empire: The Political Philosophy of Cosmopolitanism* (Routledge-Cavendish 2007). See also Jean L Cohen, 'Whose Sovereignty? Empire versus International Law' (2004) 18 Ethics & Int'l Affairs 1. Note that the terms 'imperialism' and 'hegemony' have also been used in the context of extraterritorial jurisdiction, especially as exercised by the United States. See Jeffrey Lena and Ugo Mattei, 'U.S. Jurisdiction over Conflict Arising Outside of the United States: Some Hegemonic Implications' (2001) 24 HICLR 381, 382 ('[T]he expansionist thrust of the jurisdiction of U.S. courts . . . may be viewed as a sort of legal imperialism.').

[91] In the context of unilateral regulation by transnational corporations' home states: Sara L Seck, 'Transnational Business and Environmental Harm: A TWAIL Analysis of Home State Obligations' (2011) 3 TLD 164, 196.

[92] 'Antient and modem History indeed informs us, that Avarice and Ambition do frequently lay hold on such Excuses; but the Use that wicked Men make of a Thing, does not always hinder it from being just in itself', Grotius, RWP, at 1162; Grotius, IBP, at 1.1.10.3.

[93] Vattel (n 51), bk 2, ch 1, sec 7 ('[Grotius's] opinion opens a door to all the ravages of enthusiasm and fanaticism, and furnishes ambition with numberless pretexts').

[94] Kant, *Perpetual Peace* (n 31) (noting European colonizers' abuse of the cosmopolitan right to communicate with other peoples).

[95] Michael Farbiarz, 'Extraterritorial Criminal Jurisdiction' (2016) 114 MLR 507, 512.

[96] Michael L Buenger, 'Regulatory Legality: Extraterritorial Rule across Domestic and International Arenas' in Nikolas M Rajkovic and others (eds), *The Power of Legality: Practices of International Law and their Politics* (CUP 2016) 275 (submitting, in the context of a reflection of regulatory unilateralism as a foreign policy tool that 'we must be cognizant of the degree to which the linguistics of "law" and "rule" are being requisitioned to transform idiosyncratic policy interests into global normative practices using domestic law as a vehicle').

[97] Evan Fox-Decent and Evan J Criddle, *Fiduciaries of Humanity: How International Law Constitutes Authority* (OUP 2016) 10 (who, however, ultimately go on to reject the absolute conception of sovereignty, and instead embracing the concept of 'relational sovereignty', pursuant to which states are fiduciaries of humanity).

[98] See for a fine historical discussion of how *prima facie* progressive ideas were used, and possibly even devised to justify territorial expansion and subjugation: Andrew Fitzmaurice, 'Sovereign Trusteeship and Empire' (2015) 16 Theoretical Inq L 447.

of political and economic hegemony. Sometimes, the parochialism of pursuing narrow foreign policy goals by means of the meting out of extraterritorial 'justice' is quite apparent.[99] At other times, the pursuit of political and economic hegemony may be more implicit, but no less real nevertheless. For instance, the rule of law, human rights, and governmental accountability may be promoted in developing countries precisely so that they become ripe for capitalist exploitation by economically dominated powers. Even well-intentioned extraterritorial human rights litigation, initiated by Western non-governmental organizations (NGOs), may thus, intentionally or not, pave the way for opening up protected economies to the Western capitalism. It has been argued that this charitable practice 'can take the character of both assistance and intervention',[100] and that 'the West practiced colonialism around the time it was advancing its classical theories of rights'.[101]

However that may be, as Andrew Fitzmaurice has observed, an awareness of particular concepts' historical susceptibility to rhetorical manipulation, may precisely alert us to their potential for contemporary abuse.[102] Alertness may have a cathartic effect, dispel cynicism and distrust, and allow concepts that are intrinsically just to blossom fully. Thus, awareness of the potential for abuse of unilateral action furthering the common interest should not yield an outright ban on such action, but rather in imposing restrictive conditions on its exercise,[103] for example,

[99] For instance, the 2016 US *Justice for Sponsors of Terrorism Act*, which authorizes US federal courts to exercise personal jurisdiction over any foreign state's support for acts of international terrorism against a US national or property, may be considered as a naked US foreign policy tool enabling courts to play an additional role against US enemies, even if formally speaking it empowers victims of terrorism to obtain compensation. cf Stephen J Schnably, 'The Transformation of Human Rights Litigation: The Alien Tort Statute, the Anti-Terrorism Act, and JASTA' (2017) 24(2) MICLW 285, 294 ('The weaponization of judicial redress for severe human rights violations disrespects the victims whose interests it claims to vindicate and undercuts the integrity of the judicial process.').

[100] Dorothea Anthony, 'Resolving UN Torts in US Courts: Georges v United Nations; (2018) 19(2) MJIL 462.

[101] ibid, citing Jeffrey N Wasserstrom, 'The Chinese Revolution and Contemporary Paradoxes' in Jeffrey N Wasserstrom and others (eds), *Human Rights and Revolutions* (2nd edn, Rowman & Littlefield Publishers 2007) 21, 23.

[102] Fitzmaurice (n 98) 471 ('If we abandon contextualism, we open ourselves to the danger that sovereigns may, for example, hide expansionist politics behind claims to protect the rights of others without being subject to critical scrutiny.').

[103] These mitigating principles play an important role in WTO litigation pertaining to trade restrictions based on 'extraterritorial' non-product-based process and production methods, *eg* conditions that require a product to be produced in an environmentally sustainable manner abroad. As Ankersmit and colleagues have observed, the WTO dispute settlement body has so far seemingly recognized the legitimacy of state pursuing the realization of particular values through trade restrictions (or at least it has ignored this), but it has strictly assessed the domestic processes that led to the adoption of the restriction. Ankersmit and others (n 38). See also Philippe Sands, '"Unilateralism", Values and International Law' (2000) 11 EJIL 291, 300. In *EC—Seals*, for instance, the WTO Appellate Body acknowledged EU consumers' interest in the animal welfare of seals outside the European Union, and thus the principled legitimacy of the EU's ban of seal products, but it nevertheless went on to find the actual design of the measure to lack even-handedness. WTO, *European Communities—Measures Prohibiting the Importation and Marketing of Seal Products—Report of the Appellate Body* (22 May 2014) WT/DS400/AB/R and WT/DS401/AB/R.

requirements of connection,[104] legitimate interest, non-discrimination, obligations to pursue multilateral negotiations before resorting to unilateralism,[105] and allowing outsiders the participate (principle of other-regardingness).[106] These restrictive conditions will be discussed in-depth in Chapter 4.

The fundamental argument posited here is that hegemonic states, that is, internationally leading states, may, under certain circumstances, harness their power and capacities to extend their sovereignty with a view to protecting global values and common interests. Hegemony may have acquired an imperialist connotation of one society exercising power over a subordinate society, with the former forcing the latter to adapt to its own wishes and its own benefit.[107] Etymologically speaking, however, the Greek word 'hegemon' simply means 'leadership' or 'rule'.[108] In order to address global collective action problems, some leadership of 'first movers' may be needed. Such first movers may want to push the envelope at the multilateral level by convincing other participants of the need for international action.[109] Yet when these efforts fail to bear fruit as a result of myopic anti-cosmopolitan sentiment harboured by those participants, unilateral action may be appropriate and even desirable.[110] Such action need not be hegemonic in the domination sense of the word; that is, interfering on an arbitrary basis with the range of options available to another agent.[111] Cosmopolitan action is not aimed at subordinating foreign peoples. Instead, it has emancipatory and empowering potential in that it may

[104] *Eg* United States—Import Prohibition of Certain Shrimp and Shrimp Products [1998] WT/DS58/AB/R , para 133 ('We do not pass upon the question of whether there is an implied jurisdictional limitation in Article XX(g), and if so, the nature or extent of that limitation. We note only that in the specific circumstances of the case before us, there is a sufficient nexus between the migratory and endangered marine populations involved in the United States for the purposes of Article XX(g) [GATT].').

[105] ibid, para 150

[106] Eyal Benvenisti, 'The Paradoxes of Sovereigns as Trustees of Humanity: Concluding Remarks' (2015) 16 Theoretical Inq L 535, 543 ('[CS Lewis's] admonition [that a tyranny sincerely exercised for the good of its victims may be the most oppressive] is apt when contemplating how to promote global justice. It reminds us that the key is effective voice in and meaningful accountability of both national and transnational decision-making processes.').

[107] *Eg* Ernesto Laclau and Chantal Mouffe, *Hegemony and Socialist Strategy: Towards a Radical Democratic Politics* (Verso Books 1985).

[108] In ancient Greek times 'hegemony' was notably used to denote one city-state's exercise of leadership over a league of city-states. Sparta, for instance, was the hegemon of the Peloponnesian League (sixth to the fourth century BC), Athens was the hegemon of the Delian League (fifth century BC), and Macedonia was the hegemon of the League of Corinth (fourth century BC). See *eg Encyclopaedia Britannica*, available at http://www.britannica.com/ (accessed 6 December 2019).

[109] See *eg* the adoption of the OECD Guidelines for Multinational Enterprises, first adopted in 1976, which set out a number of corporate social responsibility principles, available at http://mneguidelines.oecd.org/about.htm (accessed 6 December 2019). Elisa Morgera, 'Corporate Accountability' in Elisa Morgera and Kati Kulovesi (eds), *Research Handbook on International Law and Natural Resources* (Elgar 2016) 113 ('The success of this initiative has been ascribed to the smaller number of like-minded states involved in the negotiations, notably major capital-exporting States.').

[110] Aravind Ganesh, 'The EU's Human Rights Obligations Towards Distant Strangers' [2015] 7 GlobalTrust Working Paper Series 45 ('unilateral assertions of authority might be the only way to solve the coordination problems plaguing the provision of global public goods such as environmental protection').

[111] Bartelson (n 35) 101.

be protective of the human rights of the world's downtrodden or of a neglected natural environment.[112]

To the extent that unilateral action serves this purpose, even scholars and activists hailing from the Third World Approaches to International Law (TWAIL) tradition, which has been so critical of hegemonic attempts by the Global North, may support it. As Sara Seck has written, such action may give voice to 'resistance by the South within the North' in that it may enable host state (South) individuals and local communities to prevent and seek redress from harm in the North in ways that are impossible in the South.[113] Obviously, this requires that we do not conceive of states as black boxes but instead that we sometimes understand them as entities in which venal elites may have grabbed power to the detriment of the masses, or of particular disenfranchised communities. This has been described well by Leif Wenar in *Blood Oil*, a book in which the author denounces governmental elites living lavishly off the proceeds of resource exploitation without much concern for the development of the country or the fate of their citizens.[114] Wenar suggests that powerful Western states can break this deadlock by taking unilateral trade measures, such as by conditioning the import of oil from a country to that country's compliance with minimum human rights and democratic standards. He shows how states in a position of power can make good use of this power by forming alliances with, or at least assist foreign citizens oppressed or denied life-opportunities by their own regime. By acting unilaterally, such states may, under certain conditions, serve humanity. Or in the words of Eyal Benvenisti: '[T]he unilateral law-making for humanity should not be deprecated as imperialist and hegemonic. Rather, international law should be positively open to initiatives of relatively strong actors to promote global public goods unilaterally, if they have the capacity, willingness and skills to do so, and if the procedures they follow while designing and enforcing the policies they adopt take all affected interests into account.'[115]

It is obviously true that powerful, 'hegemonic' states taking the lead in the exercise of 'selfless' prescriptive jurisdiction[116] may able to effectively influence

[112] Howse and Teitel (n 33) 384–85 (admitting that one may perhaps discern kinds of hegemonic power structures underlying or supporting 'law among liberal nations', but arguing that this need to be fatal to hopefulness concerning the direction of the cosmopolitan project, citing the *empowering* potential of cosmopolitanism is the most important point). ibid, 385 (submitting that worrying on behalf of the non-West may in itself be 'a form of neo-colonial condescension').

[113] Seck, 'Transnational Business and Environmental Harm' (n 91) 199–200.

[114] Leif Wenar, *Blood Oil* (OUP 2016).

[115] Eyal Benvenisti, 'Legislating for Humanity: May States Compel Foreigners to Promote Global Welfare?' [2013] 2 GlobalTrust Working Paper Series, 16. See also, although more critical: Sara L Seck, 'Transnational Corporations and Extractive Industries' in Sawkat Alam and others (eds), *International Environmental Law and the Global South* (CUP 2015) 398 ('The presumption under the traditional story of international environmental law is that the developed states of the First World have both strong laws and sufficient governance capacity and political will to enforce them. But in the resource extraction context, colonialism runs deep.').

[116] Beaucillon (n 78) 126 (considering unilateralism to be a function of a non-institutionalized international society and citing the balance of power between the leading economies of the world).

extraterritorial conduct according to their value preferences and interests.[117] This need not disqualify them, however, as they may not necessarily be intent on just furthering their own interests. Powerful states could well be enlightened and, as benevolent hegemons, use their stronger enforcement capacities to protect international community interests.[118] In fact, precisely because they have more power and capacity, in accordance with the principle of common but differentiated responsibilities, it may be *incumbent* on them to do more than others to further the global interest, and thus to behave in—what may just in appearance be—a hegemonic fashion.[119] Such 'global responsibilities' could also be normatively grounded in a powerful state's contribution to, or complicity in assaults on community interests. Thus, Scott has argued that the concept of complicity may justify the EU's 'territorial extension' of its own legislation—the effectiveness of which is a function of its global market power—insofar as such extension aims to mitigate the negative global environmental impacts of the EU's own consumption pattern (ecological footprint).[120] All this means that the notion of 'power' should not be reified or negatively stereotyped as militating against cosmopolitan action. Rather, as Howse and Teitel have observed, it may be a shifting reality, becoming intertwined with 'humanity-law'.[121]

The view that state power should be used to further the international, rather than just the national interest is not new. It was a wildly popular idea in progressive internationalist circles in the United States in the early twentieth century, circles which came to be championed by US President Woodrow Wilson (in office from 1913 through 1921). Triggered by the cataclysm of the First World War, Wilson held in his 1914 4th of July address that a great nation such as the United States should use its influence and power not for aggrandizement and material benefit only but to improve the world ('it is patriotic to concert measures for one

[117] Buenger (n 96) 269 ('The effective use of domestic law in international space, therefore, depends upon a regulatory actor's relative capacities and ability to produce rules that have "sticking power"; that is, rules that align extraterritorial behavior with a particular interest, value, or need.')

[118] See also Farbiarz (n 95) 557 (regretting that 'the [US] Constitution, as currently interpreted in the extraterritorial due process doctrine, does not allow the United States to act as the world's police force', clarifying that 'under the extraterritorial due process doctrine as it is currently formulated, distant horrors cannot justify returning an indictment precisely because of their distance, their lack of connection and "nexus" to America'); Eyal Benvenisti, 'Legislating for Humanity: May States Compel Foreigners to Promote Global Welfare?' [2013] 2 GlobalTrust Working Paper Series 11.

[119] Karinne Coombes, 'Universal Jurisdiction: A Means to End Impunity or a Threat to Friendly International Relations' (2011) 43 GWILR 419, 457 ('there is the danger that universal jurisdiction may be *perceived* as hegemonistic jurisdiction exercised mainly by some Western powers against persons from developing nations') (emphasis added).

[120] Scott, 'The Global Reach of EU Law' (n 75) 51–57. Intriguingly, Scott notes a 'bias in environmental measures giving rise to territorial extension in favor of regulating the qualitative/efficiency aspects of third country production rather than the quantitative aspects of EU consumption', which in her view 'would be difficult to justify from a complicity point of view'. ibid, 62. Indeed, EU territorial extension does as such not tackle quantitative consumption patterns in the European Union itself, which give rise to a high EU demand for foreign products and materials.

[121] Howse and Teitel (n 33) 396 (citing 'the endlessly dynamic relation of law to social reality').

another').[122] For Wilson, confronted with similar global governance challenges more than 100 years ago, this task was not just a matter of political morality but of plain historical necessity:[123] the very survival of mankind arguably depended on the United States taking the lead. This Wilsonian view informed the multilateral establishment of the League of Nations, and later the United Nations, but also the taking of US unilateral action to spread global values such as democracy and human rights.[124] It may strike the reader that this position is a far cry from the Trump administration's America First policy.[125] But from a prescriptive jurisdiction perspective, the United States may have done a service to humanity by extending its laws to address such global ills as corruption (Foreign Corrupt Practices Act), racketeering (Racketeer Influenced and Corrupt Organized Act),[126] antitrust conspiracies (Sherman Act), human rights violations (Alien Tort Statute), illegal arms trade, and drug trafficking.[127] This holds even if the presumption against extraterritoriality has sometimes militated against a wide reach of US legislation.[128] Also 'Europe', another hegemonic actor, may be serving humanity by projecting EU environmental legislation abroad via trade measures, for example to counter global warming,[129] to prevent illegal logging of rainforests,[130] to protect biodiversity at risk because of palm oil plantations abroad,[131] and by prosecuting

[122] Woodrow Wilson, 4th of July address, 4 July 1914, PWW 30:251.

[123] Frank Ninkovich, *The Wilsonian Century* (University of Chicago Press 1999) 68–69.

[124] Before Wilson took office, the United States also acted unilaterally, notably in its Latin American backyard under the Monroe doctrine. As Ninkovich has pointed out, however, such interventions were justified by anxiety about European intervention, or by economic rhetoric, whereas the interventions authorized by the Wilson were justified on the ground that they spread law, order, and democracy (Ninkovich, n 123, 51–52).

[125] See on the Trump administration's relationship with international law: Harold H Koh, *The Trump Administration and International Law* (OUP 2018).

[126] Foreign governmental actors have even served as plaintiffs under RICO in respect of extraterritorial harm done to them, thereby testifying to their support of the statute. See notably *RJR Nabisco, Inc. v European Community*, 136 S Ct 2090 (2016), in which the Court, however, found against extraterritorial application of the statute. See on that case also Julie Rose O'Sullivan, 'The Extraterritorial Application of Federal Criminal Statutes: Analytical Roadmap, Normative Conclusions, and a Plea to Congress for Direction' (2018) 106 GELJ 1021, 1082 (noting that 'the European Community aggressively fought to have U.S. law apply overseas').

[127] Farbiarz (n 95) 513 (citing the use of US extraterritorial criminal jurisdiction to shore up stable and legitimate governments elsewhere, *eg* in Africa and Colombia). See as regards drug-trafficking: Aaron J Casavant, 'In Defense of the U.S. Maritime Drug Law Enforcement Act: A Justification for the Law's Extraterritorial Reach' (2017) 8 NSJ 191, 234 (defending US law enforcement regarding extraterritorial maritime drug trafficking, on the grounds that it 'threatens the security of the United States and its regional partners and is condemned by virtually all nations'); O'Sullivan (n 126) 1082 (noting the lack of protest against US extraterritorial enforcement of its drug-trafficking legislation).

[128] *Eg* William S Dodge, 'The New Presumption against Extraterritoriality' (2019) 133 HLR.

[129] Directive 2008/101/EC of the European Parliament and of the Council of 19 November 2008 amending Directive 2003/87/EC so as to include aviation activities in the scheme for greenhouse gas emission allowance trading within the Community (Aviation Directive) [2008] OJ L8/3.

[130] Regulation (EU) No 995/2010 of the European Parliament and of the Council of 20 October 2010 laying down the obligations of operators who place timber and timber products on the market (Timber Regulation) [2010] OJ L295/23.

[131] European Parliament, Report on palm oil and deforestation of rainforests (2016/2222(INI)).

the vilest international criminals under the universality principle.[132] Sometimes, the targets of such extraterritorial jurisdiction may even be treated more humanely than under national or territorial jurisdiction, in case due process protections in the former are higher than in the latter.[133]

Admittedly, unilateral jurisdictional action may at times be heavy-handed, but it should be recalled that asserting prescriptive 'extraterritorial' jurisdiction is in itself already a form of restraint as compared to the military enforcement actions of the past.[134] Bearing this in mind, to prevent states from resorting to military solutions relatively unconstrained by the law, doctrines of jurisdiction may arguably have to be construed relatively broadly so as to enable states to conduct foreign policy within the bounds of the law. Thus, Farbiarz, a former US federal prosecutor for national security matters, suggested that the US practice of carrying out lethal drone strikes abroad may have been the consequence of the unviability of US criminal justice options, given that federal prosecutors may not have been able to prosecute the presumed terrorists because of the extraterritorial due process doctrine.[135]

Critics may go on to object that often the powerful are not very likely to exercise extraterritorial jurisdiction in the global interest without some national interest being present, and that this national interest rationale is bound to engender justified international suspicion.[136] In the field of business regulation, for instance, states will typically exercise unilateral jurisdiction when (also) the integrity of domestic regulation is undermined, and domestic actors' rights and interests are affected by foreign activity, such as where foreign cartels are preying on domestic

[132] Julia Krebs, Cedric Ryngaert, and Florian Jeβberger, 'Universal Jurisdiction and International Crimes: Constraints and Best Practices' Study European Parliament (2018), http://www.europarl.europa.eu/RegData/etudes/STUD/2018/603878/EXPO_STU(2018)603878_EN.pdf (last accessed 6 December 2019).

[133] Farbiarz (n 95) 555, criticizing a US line of court cases that requires a nexus between the United States and the defendant to satisfy due process requirements of extraterritorial criminal jurisdiction ('one wonders how many alleged terrorists have been consigned to local prosecutions, off-loaded to terribly rough criminal justice in Afghanistan or Somalia—not prosecuted in the incomparably freer and fairer U.S. courts out of fealty to, of all things, the terrorists' own rights').

[134] Kal Raustiala, *Does the Constitution Follow the Flag? The Evolution of Territoriality in American Law* (OUP 2009) 20. See also Noah Bialostozky, 'Extraterritoriality and National Security: Protective Jurisdiction as a Circumstance Precluding Wrongfulness' (2014) 52 CJTL 617, 656 ('The very reason why protective jurisdiction is a useful method of national self-defense is because it presents a more nuanced tool than the blunt instrument of force.').

[135] Farbiarz (n 95) 554. This is a doctrine of US constitutional criminal law which requires a sufficient *nexus* between the defendant and the United States, so that the application of US criminal law would not be 'arbitrary or fundamentally unfair'). *US v Davis,* 905 F.2d 245 (9th Cir. 1990); *US v Al Kassar,* 660 F.3d at 118. To prevent recourse to such forcible measures—which are not restrained by any form of due process—Farbiarz proposed focusing the due process doctrine only on actual conflicts between federal criminal law and the foreign criminal law of the *locus delicti, ie* when one law prohibits what the other allows. These conflicts are in fact very rare, as most crimes are crimes everywhere, as a result of which extraterritorial jurisdiction would be substantially widened. Farbiarz (n 95) 548–52.

[136] See on extraterritorial regulation and the national interest also Paul B Stephan, 'Global Governance, Antitrust, and the Limits of International Cooperation' (2005) 38 CILJ 173; and Chapter 3 of this monograph.

markets, or foreign companies import substandard products.[137] This focus on safeguarding the business opportunities of domestic operators tends to create an impression of self-centredness, arbitrariness,[138] exclusivity to the detriment of less powerful actors,[139] protectionism,[140] domination,[141] or outright legal imperialism.[142] One should realize, however, that such action is not simply meant to advance, in some sort of zero-sum game, one state's national interest to the detriment of another state's.[143] Rather, as further argued in Chapter 3, it levels a playing field that has become unbalanced as a result of globally undesirable lax foreign regulation that puts domestic operators, who had *already* become subject to stricter regulation, at a competitive disadvantage. For instance, in the environmental field, the European Union, in response to market distortions and citizen pressure, provided for such a high level of environmental protection,[144] also with respect to global environmental goods such as a stable climate, that EU-based businesses have lost economic opportunities. Such a loss could only be repaired by either scaling backing regulation, or by 'extraterritorializing' regulation, subjecting foreign operators to EU law in the global interest. Surely the latter option is preferable from an international community vantage point?

'Hegemonic' actors such as the United States or the European Union may thus be, and have been first movers as far as globally desirable regulation is concerned, subjecting their domestic operators to strict rules regarding, for example, accountability for human rights violations, corruption, antitrust conspiracies, securities fraud, or climate change. They subsequently wish to cast the regulatory net wider, so as to allow their domestic operators to remain in business, and at the same time to tackle global problems more efficiently which may be exacerbated by

[137] Tonya L Putnam, 'Courts Without Borders: Domestic Sources of US Extraterritoriality in the Regulatory Sphere' (2009) 63 Int'l Org 459, 468 (2009); Jonathan Turley, 'When in Rome: Multinational Misconduct and the Presumption Against Extraterritoriality' (1990) 84 NULR 598.

[138] Anthony J Colangelo, 'A Unified Approach to Extraterritoriality' (2011) 97 VLR 1019, 1107 ('Unlike international law, other nations may not have consented to, say, unilateral projections of U.S. securities or antitrust laws within their territories, and absent a U.S. nexus, the choice of U.S. law appears arbitrary.').

[139] Krisch (n 21) 31 ('nonconsensualism ... creates more exclusive decision-making structures that reduce the number of decision-makers'); ibid, 39 (nonconsensualism 'does away only with the consent of the less powerful, and it can easily become a tool of hierarchy and control').

[140] Paul B Stephan, 'The Political Economy of Extraterritoriality' [2011] SSRN 1, voicing the concern that states can use extraterritorial regulation 'as a form of trade protection by imposing stricter standards on foreign firms than on domestic producers'.

[141] Jeffrey A Meyer, 'Dual Illegality and Geoambiguous Law: A New Rule for Extraterritorial Application of U.S. Law' (2010) 95 MLR 110–11 ('A superpower [the US] no longer bent on conquering more territory stands to benefit when it instead can unilaterally project its law and corresponding enforcement resources to regulate what people do in other countries.').

[142] Raustiala (n 134) 224 (submitting that extraterritorial jurisdiction 'enabl[es] the United States to unilaterally manipulate legal difference so as to better serve its interests' while 'enhancing American power and interests on the world stage').

[143] Gardner (n 5) 346 ('[C]hanneled unilateralism is not a zero-sum game: even if the motivated state comes out furthest ahead, other states will also have made progress down the field.').

[144] Natalie L Dobson, *Extraterritorial Climate Protection Under International Law: A Jurisdictional Analysis of EU Unilateralism*, PhD manuscript Utrecht University (2018), Chapter 2.1 and 2.2.

businesses moving offshore to evade strict regulation. In this second stage, states 'extraterritorialize' their laws, but in a manner that is less unilateral than may meet the eye.[145] Ultimately, they may just be enforcing shared values of, or challenges facing the international community. These may, for that matter, have already been recognized by various binding or non-binding international instruments,[146] and may have been tackled by various national initiatives.

Accordingly, unilateral action by powerful states may represents just an additional enforcement tool. At the same time, jurisdictional assertions may allow existing instruments and initiatives to develop further, also at the multilateral level,[147] and thus constitute incentives for international regulatory cooperation.[148] They allow for the authoritative enunciation of a state's value preferences and require other states to take a position. Such a position could obviously be one of

[145] Hannah L Buxbaum, 'Transnational Regulatory Litigation' (2006) 46 VJIL 251, 255, 268, 298 (arguing that in 'transnational regulatory litigation' cases, the US domestic regulatory law that is applied extraterritorially, *eg* regarding antitrust, securities, and corruption, 'reflects an internationally shared norm'). But see *F Hoffmann-LaRoche Ltd v Empagran SA*, 542 US 155, 169 (Breyer, J) ('where foreign injury is independent of domestic effects, Congress might have hoped that America's antitrust laws ... would commend themselves to other nations as well ... if America's antitrust policies could not win their own way in the international marketplace for such ideas, Congress, we must assume, would not have tried to impose them, in an act of legal imperialism, through legislative fiat').

[146] See *eg* UN Convention against Corruption (New York 2004), UN General Assembly resolution 58/4 of 31 October 2003; OECD Convention on Combating Bribery of Foreign Public Officials in International Business Transactions' (Paris 1997); Kyoto Protocol to the UN Framework Convention on Climate Change (1997); Convention on the Prevention and Punishment of the Crime of Genocide, UN General Assembly Resolution 260 (III) A (1948); Rome Statute of the ICC (1998). See as regards cooperation in the field of antitrust law: the International Competition Network, which counts 104 competition agencies from 92 jurisdictions (http://www.internationalcompetitionnetwork.org). For cooperative networks in the field of securities/capital markets regulation: International Organization of Securities Commissions (IOSCO), the Financial Stability Board (FSB), the Council of Securities Regulators of the Americas (COSRA), and the Financial Action Task Force (FATF).

[147] Commission Staff Working Document Impact Assessment Accompanying the document Proposal for a Directive of the European Parliament and of the Council amending Council Directives 78/660/EEC and 83/349/EEC as regards disclosure of nonfinancial and diversity information by certain large companies and groups (COM(2013) 207 final) (SWD(2013) 128 final), p 42, pp 68–69. See also Chapter 10 in the EU Directive 2013/34/EU of the European Parliament and of the Council of 26 June 2013 on the annual financial statements, consolidated financial statements and related reports of certain types of undertakings, amending Directive 2006/43/EC of the European Parliament and of the Council and repealing Council Directives 78/660/EEC and 83/349/EEC (OJ 2013, L182/19), or EU Financial Report on Payments to Governments Directive, which builds on the Extractive Industries Transparency Initiative (EITI), a voluntary scheme regarding transparency on payments from corporations to governments, developed by a multi-stakeholder group, including governments, oil, gas, and mining companies, industry bodies, international institutions, investors, and NGOs. Many resource-rich countries have not signed up to this initiative, however (see for a critique: Leif Wenar, *Blood Oil* (OUP 2016) 317–18). Accordingly, the EU Directive broadens the scope of the EITI, and adds teeth to it.

[148] An Hertogen, 'Letting *Lotus* Bloom' (2015) 26 EJIL 901, 924 ('By creating an incentive for cooperation to avoid concurrent jurisdiction, the principle of locality [pursuant to which jurisdiction is based on an act's effects on states] can thus also help achieve the second goal for international law—that of promoting cooperation between states.'). Hertogen observes in this respect that 'the PCIJ's decision in *Lotus* prompted negotiations on an alternative allocation of jurisdiction over collisions on the high seas, and this may have been exactly what the Court intended'). The principle that the flag state does not have exclusive jurisdiction over collisions on the high seas was indeed rather swiftly set aside by multilateral treaty. See art 11 of the 1958 Convention on the High Seas; currently art 97 UNCLOS.

rejection and denunciation[149] but also one of cooperation or tagging along on second thought. Especially where powerful 'first moving' states have taken the lead, game theory predicts that others will tend to follow regulatory innovation, even if initially reluctantly.[150] A fine example is the EU's catalysing of a 2016 multilateral agreement, reached at the level of the International Civil Aviation Organization (ICAO), on a global market-based measure to regulate carbon emissions from civil aviation.[151] That said, hegemonic norm-setting and norm-developing unilateralism does not automatically give rise to the development of global standards that apply to all operators in a particular field. Only if a state can exercise authority over a relatively large group of foreign operators is it likely that standards migrate to other states and to the international level, thereby eventually making the initially local standard a global one.

When a multilateral solution is eventually reached, the hegemonic promoter may decide to suspend its unilateral action, at least when certain minimum conditions are met. In the specific case mentioned, the European Union, taking note of the ICAO agreement, announced its cautious willingness to stop applying its own unilateral measures provided that the multilateral agreement meets certain conditions.[152] However, even if a multilateral agreement materializes, states may

[149] See regarding private international law-based unilateralism: Alex Mills, 'Private International Law and EU External Relations: Think Local Act Global, or Think Global Act Local?' (2016) 65 ICLQ 541, 577–78 ('stating that [i]f private international law rules could effectively be used to leverage other States to comply with EU policies, this technique is unlikely to be viewed favourably by States who become subject to such pressure' and submitting that 'cooperative means of addressing the relevant policy goals may be just as effective without the accompanying risk of perceived regulatory overreach').

[150] Steinbach (n 5) 668 ('Non-multilateral initiatives become frames that subsequently become the points of orientation of lawful conduct among party states.'); Gardner (n 5) 322 ('[M]otivated states' investigations of extraterritorial misconduct will increase available information about the transnational criminal problem and generate possible solutions that other states can mimic. They also shed light on other states'—particularly lagging states'—lack of enforcement effort.') (footnote omitted). The EU's standard-setting effect has been well-documented in this respect. See A Bradford, *The Brussels Effect* (OUP 2020). Doubts have, however, been cast over whether international agreement is likely to result from private international law unilateralism in respect of substantive policy values (*eg* the use of particular choice of law or jurisdictional rules in the field of human rights or the environment). Alex Mills, 'Private International Law and EU External Relations: Think Local Act Global, or Think Global Act Local?' (2016) 65 ICLQ 541, 570.

[151] Carbon Offsetting and Reduction Scheme for International Aviation (CORSIA), https://www.icao.int/environmental-protection/CORSIA/Pages/default.aspx (last accessed 6 December 2019). See for an analysis of this agreement: Uwe M Erling, 'International Aviation Emissions Under International Civil Aviation Organization's Global Market Based Measure: Ready for Offsetting?' (2017) 42(1) ASL 1.

[152] See on the pressure brought to bear by the European Union on the ICAO to reach an agreement: EU Regulation 421/2014. The EU Commission has not proved willing to simply forgo its unilateral measures in light of the multilateral agreement, however. In a 2017 communication, it proposed 'a further assessment and review the EU [Emissions Trading Scheme] for the post-2020 period', '[o]nce there is more clarity about the nature and content of the legal instruments adopted by ICAO for the implementation of the [global market-based mechanism] as well as about the intentions of our international partners regarding the implementation of the GMBM'. Commission Proposal 2017: https://ec.europa.eu/transparency/regdoc/rep/1/2017/EN/COM-2017-54-F1-EN-MAIN-PART-1.PDF. See for a critical note: Natalie L Dobson, 'Maintaining the pressure: The EU leaves ICAO hanging despite "historic" emissions agreement for civil aviation' RENFORCE Blog, 19 March 2017, http://blog.renforce.eu/index.php/en/2017/03/19/maintaining-the-pressure-the-eu-leaves-icao-hanging-despite-historic-emissions-agreement-for-civil-aviation/ (last accessed 6 December 2019).

eventually not prove willing to relinquish their unilateral instincts entirely. This is not only because the content of a multilateral agreement may have been watered down so as to accommodate all participating states, but also because it is uncertain whether states will comply with the agreement, especially if strong supervisory and enforcement mechanisms are absent,[153] as well as because the bureaucracy involved in multilateral regulation may be (prohibitively) expensive. In light of potential substantive shortcomings of multilateralism, the likelihood of free-riders benefiting from others' efforts and issues of cost, unilateral regulation and enforcement aimed at such free-riders may remain attractive options. Where unilateral action has been in place for a relatively long time, this attraction may endure even if multilateral solutions might enhance global welfare: having become used to unilateral action, individual states may worry that they stand to lose from concessions reached multilaterally, whereas others stand to win. For instance, a global antitrust framework, while desirable in view of its global welfare-enhancing consequences, has arguably not materialized because the cooperation gains for some parties—notably the main unilateral actors, the United States and the European Union—are not considered as sufficiently high: these actors perceive their own concessions in multilateral bargains as losses, and the actual effects of 'unknown' multilateral action may be hard to predict.[154] Such 'parochial' unilateralism is obviously not to be applauded, given its global welfare-decreasing effects, but political-economic dynamics may make it difficult to avoid.[155]

2.4 Reinterpreting Sovereignty

One of the major doctrinal obstacles to allowing leading states to exercise prescriptive jurisdiction in the common interest is the principle of territorial sovereignty. This principle may be said to have an exclusionary character: it bars one state from extending its jurisdiction to events occurring on the territory of another state, save in exceptional circumstances. Sure enough, one can argue that the principle is simply unsuited for an era of globalization.[156] A more sophisticated argument,

[153] See also Andrew T Guzman, 'Against Consent' (2012) 52 VJIL 747, 749, 752 ('Giving consent does not eliminate a state's incentives to violate the law or necessarily increase the compliance-pull of the rule.').

[154] Steinbach (n 5) 651–53. The first perspective is a rational choice one, the second a behavioural economics one, based on the concepts of loss aversion and 'sunk costs' in case of well-established legal regimes and practices in which states have in the past been invested. Steinbach adds that 'actors are ambiguity averse when probabilities cannot be easily predicted' and that 'actors prefer known outcomes over unknown ones'.

[155] Steinbach (n 5) 653 ('These insights collectively prevent states from neutrally perceiving and assessing the benefits of the international level playing field by following the same set of rules.').

[156] *Eg* Alan Hudson, 'Beyond the Borders: Globalisation, Sovereignty and Extra-territoriality' in *Geopolitics* (vol 3, Routledge 1998) 89–105, 102. Sovereignty as a particular spatiality of power and authority seems unsuitable for an increasingly globalized world.

which is made here, is that sovereignty, jurisdiction, and territory[157] are enduring cognitive scripts that may require reconceptualization in light of current governance challenges.[158] These capacious scripts have in fact historically been 'sites or spaces of enunciation' that allow powers and authorities to concretize multiple political discourses,[159] to include or exclude persons or events,[160] and to realize material justice.[161] They are 'legal constructs whose meanings and uses vary depending on the context in which they are employed',[162] that are subject to conceptual manipulation,[163] have little essentialist meaning,[164] and are not socially neutral.[165] Reinterpretations and innovations of these notions, which favour action to tackle novel problems, may well be possible within the current structure of international law. This depends on the evolution of international relations such as the increasing interdependence between states[166] and international justice conceptions.[167]

[157] See on the 'mutually constitutive relations between sovereignty, jurisdiction, and territoriality': Daniel S Margolies and others, 'Introduction' in Daniel Margolies and others (eds), *The Extraterritoriality of Law: History, Theory, Politics* (Routledge 2019) 2.

[158] Sovereignty as originally defined by Grotius as '[t]hat power [potestas] is called sovereign [*summa potestas*] whose actions are not subject to the legal control of another, so that they cannot be rendered void by the operation of another human will.' Grotius, *De Jure Belli ac Pacis* 1.3.7.1. An alternative is to erase 'sovereignty' from the vocabulary of international law altogether, but given its historical trajectory and the spell it has cast on our imagination of the world, this appears next to impossible. cf Michel Troper, 'Sovereignty and Natural Law in the Legal Discourse of the Ancien Regime' (2015) 16 Theoretical Inq L 315, 316 (noting that it may be 'difficult to eliminate the concept of sovereignty altogether, because it is an essential part of the language of the law'). See also John D Haskell, 'Ways of Doing Extraterritoriality in Scholarship' in Daniel Margolies and others (eds), *The Extraterritoriality of Law: History, Theory, Politics* (Routledge 2019) 19 (categorizing this approach as a 'technical' approach to territoriality, as it is characterized by a 'core belief that international law is a coherent system', in which 'state sovereignty remains intact').

[159] Peter Rush, 'An Altered Jurisdiction: Corporeal Traces of Law' (1997) 6 GLW 144, 150 (reflecting on the concept of jurisdiction).

[160] Peter Goodrich, 'Visive Powers: Colours, Trees and Genres of Jurisdiction' (2008) 2(2) Law Humanit 213, 215–16 ('jurisdiction is first and foremost a power to allow entry, a threshold condition of access wherein the subject holding the keys can determine who enters and who is excluded from the country, community or court that the gate protects'), also noting at p 223 that 'jurisdiction, understood as the technical species of discourse of foundation, opens a door to a plurality of discourses about the imagined community, the faith or bond that ties the group together').

[161] Noll (n 46) 2 ('The practice of international law confirms that jurisdictional questions are prior to questions of material justice.').

[162] Anthony J Colangelo, 'What is Extraterritorial Jurisdiction?' (2014) 99 CLR 1303, 1304 (also mentioning the concept of 'extraterritoriality' in this respect).

[163] *Eg* regarding the United States, Colangelo, 'What is Extraterritorial Jurisdiction?' (n 162) 1323 ('How lawmakers, litigants, and judges manipulate those constructs directly influences the geographic scope of U.S. regulatory power under the Constitution.').

[164] The lack of meaning of the concept of jurisdiction has been decried, *eg*, by Rain Liivoja, 'The Criminal Jurisdiction of States: A Theoretical Primer' (2010) 7 NoFo 25, 54 ('Discussion of State jurisdiction under international law is hampered by a danger of terminological and conceptual misunderstandings, not least because of the myriad meanings of the term "jurisdiction".').

[165] Compare the discussion of extraterritorial disputes in Hudson (n 156) 102 ('The allocation of jurisdiction, spatially and otherwise, is never socially neutral... Processes of re-scaling are simultaneously processes of re-valuing.').

[166] cf Abram Chayes and Antonia Handler Chayes, *The New Sovereignty: Compliance with International Regulating Agreements* (HUP 1995) 27 (defining sovereignty as a 'connection to the rest of the world and the political ability to be an actor within it').

[167] cf Hertogen (n 148) 915, 919.

The same malleability can, for that matter, be found in systems where the reach of domestic law is a matter of statutory construction rather than international law, such as in the United States, where federal courts, applying the established presumption against extraterritorially, have struggled to classify statutes as either territorial or extraterritorial.[168]

Conceptual malleability may be manipulated to narrow still further political and economic interests of states and corporations and to prevent meaningful accountability. However, the concepts of sovereignty and jurisdiction could also be productively reinterpreted, based on a sense of growing solidarity manifested by the adoption of a number of substantive international law rules,[169] to serve inclusive, cosmopolitan purposes, and to tame power.[170] Sovereignty then becomes relational and more adept at responding to contemporary problems 'which do not respect the mythical boundedness of the sovereign state'.[171] As Gareth Davies observed, it is perhaps the 'mood of this age' to add nuance to the historical dogma of sovereignty to accommodate concerns over global well-being.[172] In the contemporary era, epistemic forces have embedded the social construct of sovereignty in a larger international governance project that requires state authority to be exercised 'responsibly'.[173] While the international community may leave a margin of appreciation to states as to the implementation of responsible authority, the core contours of the concept are arguably defined at the international rather than national level. Such a strategy may necessarily embrace a truncated view of sovereignty that isolates desirable, individual autonomy-enhancing aspects of sovereignty (democracy, human rights, accountability, the ability to deliver public goods) from undesirable aspects

[168] Colangelo, 'What is Extraterritorial Jurisdiction?' (n 162) 1347. Colangelo sees only a limited role of international law in determining the reach of US law under the US Constitution, namely to the extent 'it acts as a proxy for whether the exercise of jurisdiction is "arbitrary or fundamentally unfair" by imputing to defendants knowledge of its substantive and jurisdictional rules'. ibid, at 1306. Note that the presumption does not apply to the reach of state law in the United States. This has created even more flexibility in determining the reach of the law. See Katherine Florey, 'State Law, U.S. Power, Foreign Disputes: Understanding the Extraterritorial Effects of State Law in the Wake of Morrison v. National Australia Bank' (2012) 92 BULR 535.

[169] Carly Nyst, 'Solidarity in a Disaggregated World: Universal Jurisdiction and the Evolution of Sovereignty' (2012) 8 JILIR 36, 48.

[170] *Eg* regarding the underlying political concerns regarding the extraterritorial human rights obligations of states: Daniel Augenstein, 'Paradise Lost: Sovereign State Interest, Global Resource Exploitation and the Politics of Human Rights' (2016) 27 EJIL 669, 690 ('Doctrinal arguments about the conditions under which a state can be held legally accountable for extraterritorial human rights violations reflect normative judgments about the appropriate role of human rights in construing an agency relationship between that state and an individual located outside its borders.')

[171] Seck, 'Beyond the E-word in the Anthropocene' (n 39) 50.

[172] Gareth Davies, 'International Trade, Extraterritorial Power, and Global Constitutionalism: A Perspective from Constitutional Pluralism' (2012) 13 Ger LJ 1212.

[173] Bartelson (n 35) 10 (drawing on the linguistic turn in philosophy and social sciences and stating that 'sovereignty is what we make of it through our linguistic practices, given the contextual constraints at hand').

(militarization, quest for great power status, beggar-thy-neighbour economic policies).[174]

Accordingly, in an era of interdependence, sovereignty no longer equals non-interference and it should not be raised as a defence against well-meaning international, possibly unilateral, efforts to promote GPGs and human rights through more expansive assertions of jurisdiction.[175] This reinterpretation of sovereignty and its twin jurisdiction draws on the urgency of the challenges and the method of the veil of ignorance and allows international law to progressively develop beyond its rudimentary state towards justice.[176] Inclusive jurisdictional cosmopolitanism may well be the answer to Gregor Noll's question whether after the death of God, when jurisdiction in international law lost its stable metaphysical base, we are capable of 'discerning a calling beyond that cacophony, a calling that evokes faith in its justness?'[177] Inclusive, more just cosmopolitan jurisdiction[178] could replace the time-worn notion of territoriality as the jurisdictional linchpin, as territoriality, while originally meant to temper the imperial ambitions of the great powers, may in fact entrench injustice.

In this respect, Jenny Martinez observed that reliance on territoriality in two of the most important jurisdictional judgments of the US Supreme Court, in the human rights case of *Kiobel* (2013) and in the older antitrust case of *American Banana* (1909), has yielded particularly unjust outcomes, namely a lack of 'oversight and accountability for the conduct of powerful, but nominally private, transnational actors that operate outside the territorial bounds of any one government'.[179] Indeed, private corporations having worldwide activities could game an international system based on sovereign equality and territorial jurisdiction to escape the reach of

[174] Bartelson (n 35) 80 (submitting that 'recent strategies for interfering in the domestic affairs of states are justified on grounds that such interference is necessary to *strengthen* their sovereignty' and that the concept of sovereignty is disaggregated and unbundled 'so that its unnecessary or destructive aspects can be eliminated, before the health and useful aspects can be glued back together and imposed on the target state').

[175] Paul Mertenskoetter, 'National Courts as "Trustees of Humanity"?' [2013] 4 GlobalTrust Working Paper Series 4 ('In today's world, so the argument goes, states are not sovereign equals and the principle's non-interference doctrine is not a practical reality of an interdependent world . . . no good justifications for state sovereignty in its strict form exists, both a utilitarian argument for efficient administration of the world and its resources as well as a deontological argument for the respect of human rights require a reconceptualization of state sovereignty.').

[176] See also Goodrich (n 160) 225 ('Jurisdiction . . . is a recuperation, a telling and retelling of the story of a just law, of law's ligeance [sic] with faith, its common, shared, amicable properties within the realm.').

[177] Noll (n 46) 11 (also, relatedly, observing at p 14 that general international law offers a terminology of jurisdiction, yet lacks a coherent conception underpinning it).

[178] See on sovereignty (jurisdiction) as inclusive and fiduciary: Alon Jasper, 'Participation of Foreigners in Environmental Decision-Making & the Aarhus Convention' [2017] 6 GlobalTrust Working Paper Series, 2 ('[T]he interlocking, interdependent nature of our globalized world, with its diverse phenomena, has been accompanied by a normative and legal shift in—or struggle over—the dominant conception of sovereignty: from a property concept, according to which the right to exclude is considered a basic attribute of sovereignty, to an inclusionary-fiduciary concept').

[179] Jenny S Martinez, 'New Territorialism and Old Territorialism' (2014) 99 CLR 1387, 1390.

any jurisdiction. In *American Banana*, United Fruit, a major multinational corporation, convinced the Supreme Court to rule that '[a]ll legislation is *prima facie* territorial',[180] and on the basis to dismiss US jurisdiction over the corporation's activities abroad. Liberal anti-imperialism informed this high-water mark of territoriality, and is rooted in a US self-image defined in opposition to the imperialism and colonialism of the European powers of the time.[181] However, as Martinez points out, this anti-imperial territoriality is naïve in that it enables multinational corporations 'to exercise and abuse strong de facto power in regions with underdeveloped public authority', without fear of being amenable to US jurisdiction;[182] in fact, *American Banana* helped create the Latin American 'banana republics'.[183] Application of the presumption against extraterritoriality in *Kiobel* was a replay of this anti-imperial attitude: holding that the United States is not the *custos morum* of the entire world, the Supreme Court rejected the exercise of US jurisdiction over alleged human rights violations committed abroad absent a strong (territorial) nexus with the United States. [184] Again, as Philip Liste has also highlighted, corporations manipulated the principle of territoriality—aiming at keeping states apart rather than at empowering non-state actors—to suit their own ends of making profit with as little regulatory oversight as possible.[185] The upshot was a sanctioning of multinational corporations' predatory ambitions abroad, corporations which, since *Kiobel*, can engage in extraterritorial abusive practices without fearing the long arm of US law, especially if they are incorporated abroad. Empirical research has demonstrated that following *Kiobel*, extractive industry firms with headquarters abroad (unlike US firms) experienced larger cumulative abnormal returns, and that 'mining firms based abroad with subsidiaries in countries with poor human rights records benefitted most'.[186] This shows that multinationals' cost of doing business in such countries, and possibly becoming involved in human rights violations, has significantly decreased as a result of the Supreme Court's reliance on territoriality in *Kiobel*. To address such injustices, which arise as a result of a disconnect between the abstract principle of state territoriality and the concrete reality of sometimes pernicious transnational activity, cosmopolitan jurisdiction, which de-emphasizes formal territory as the relevant jurisdictional link, may be required.[187]

[180] *American Banana Co. v United* Fruit Co., 213 US 347 (1909).

[181] Martinez (n 179) 1399, 1408.

[182] ibid, 1399, 1408.

[183] ibid, 1400.

[184] *Kiobel v Royal Dutch Petroleum*, 133 S Ct 1659, 1669 (2013).

[185] Philip Liste, 'Transnational Human Rights Litigation and Territorialised Knowledge: Kiobel and the 'Politics of Space' (2014) 5 TLT 1; Philip Liste, 'Geographical Knowledge at Work: Human Rights Litigation and Transnational Territoriality' (2016) 22 EJIL 217.

[186] Darin Christensen and David K Hausman, 'Measuring the Economic Effect of Alien Tort Statute Liability' (2016) 32 JLEO.

[187] Martinez (n 179) 1414 ('[F]ormal legal categories (like the focus on territories under the power of a particular sovereign) can obscure actual power and political dynamics underlying a given dispute. In a legal world governed by territorial formalism, entities (like corporations) that lack corporeal and

Existing law may offer opportunities for less territorial interpretations of the law of jurisdiction,[188] although obviously simply because a state of affairs is desirable does not mean that it can be accommodated by existing law.[189] Chapter 5 will analyse in detail the opportunities for the exercise of common interest-based jurisdiction in a number of thematic areas.

2.5 Reinterpreting State Consent: Beyond Formalism

It will have become clear by now that the cosmopolitan action addressed in this study cannot be captured by orthodox legal positivism that puts a high premium on explicit state consent. Where legal and political instruments do not confer extraterritorial jurisdictional authority on states to enforce the values enshrined in them, the exercise of such authority may transcend the explicit consent of states and thus undermine the main tenet of positivism. For 'selfless intervention' by means of unilateral, prescriptive jurisdiction to gain entry in international legal scholarship, the notion of consent—one of the hallmarks of modern international law, just like sovereignty—may have to be reconstructed.

Arguably, in the face of the assertions of jurisdiction which concern us here, consent can be safeguarded, if only just, insofar as such assertions find their normative basis in international instruments and broadly defined international norms and policies, which can be traced back to the consent of states. Assertions of extraterritorial jurisdiction may indeed enforce values which the community of states has deemed worthy of protection: international crimes and human rights violations are proscribed by treaties and customary international law, anti-corruption conventions have been widely ratified, and global environmental goods (*eg* a stable climate, biodiversity) have been recognized by a host of legal and political instruments. State consent may possibly not extend to all procedural issues of enforcement, but the relevant issue is that it pertains to certain substantive values and common interests. So as to strengthen the impact of such values, and eventually

territorial forms can too easily escape necessary regulation... At the dawn of a new century, these problems deserve new and better solutions.'). See also Daniel Augenstein and David Kinley, 'Beyond the 100 Acre Wood: In Which International Human Rights Law Finds New Ways to Tame Global Corporate Power' (2015) 19 IJHR 828–48; Augenstein (n 170) 689 (suggesting to oblige states to provide access to justice in litigation for extraterritorial corporate human rights violations, *ie* to exercise extraterritorial (or even universal) jurisdiction over corporate abuses).

[188] Regarding tort law: L Roorda and Cedric Ryngaert, 'Business and Human Rights Litigation in Europe and Canada: The Promises of Forum of Necessity Jurisdiction' (2016) 80 RabelsZ 783. Regarding criminal law: Cedric Ryngaert, 'Accountability for Corporate Human Rights Abuses: Lessons from the Possible Exercise of Dutch National Criminal Jurisdiction over Multinational Corporations' (2018) 29 CLF 1.

[189] cf South West Africa *(Liberia v South Africa)* [1966] ICJ Rep 48 ('Rights cannot be presumed to exist merely because it might seem desirable that they should.').

the rule of law, unilaterally acting states can be said to only place their legal enforcement machinery at the disposal of states which have given prior consent to the protection of values and interests.

This view ties in well with recent anti-formalistic legal scholarship that emphasizes extra-positivist sources of international law authority, namely those based on substantive authority and effectiveness. Nijman and Nollkaemper put it as follows:

> Part of the answer [as to who or what validates non-positive law sources of international law] is found in the fact that deformalization is a parallel development to the emergence of common values. International law does not (only) find its authority in binding rules and principles, ie in conformity with the positivist model, but is in a way more substantive since it is grounded on international norms as keepers of universal common *values* rather than as binding rules of positive international law. In this role (binding or non-binding) international norms have authority because of the values they represent.[190]

This reasoning allows us to justify unilateralism on the basis of a legalized form of Kantian, deontological ethics,[191] with an international norm providing the requisite substantive authority for unilateral action. From a constructivist international relations perspective, such unilateralism may, theoretically at least, be likely to gain acceptance by states, as the existence of the international norm or value which unilateral action intends to propagate may serve a socializing function and influence the perception of legitimate behaviour.[192]

That being said, it may happen that no international norm can (yet) be discerned, namely where prisoners' dilemmas have made any agreement on substantive norms impossible. Assume, for instance, that an international agreement on tackling climate change fails to materialize, even if all scientific evidence shows that collective action should be taken to avert a catastrophe. If states take unilateral remedial action, such action may not be justified on the basis of codified internationally shared values, let alone on the basis of classic international law, as there is simply no substantive norm to be enforced. The fiction of prior state consent may carry little justificatory force for such action. Still, such action could perhaps find its legitimation in states' constructive consent, inferred from Rawls' method of the 'veil of ignorance'. Rawls' moral theory puts agents in an 'original position' where

[190] Janne E Nijman and André Nollkaemper, 'Beyond the Divide' in Janne E Nijman and André Nollkaemper (eds), *New Perspectives on the Divide between International and National Law* (OUP 2007) 353.

[191] Immanuel Kant, *Groundwork of the Metaphysic of Morals* (1964).

[192] Jeffrey L Dunoff and Mark A Pollack, 'International Law and International Relations: Introducing an Interdisciplinary Dialogue' in Jeffrey L Dunoff and Mark A Pollack (eds) *Interdisciplinary Perspectives on International Law and International Relations: The State of the Art* (CUP 2012) 8–12. See for an exposition of the relationship between constructivism and international law in the same volume: Jutta Brunnée and Stephen J Toope, 'Constructivism in International Law', 119–45.

'no one knows his place in society, his class position or social status; nor does he know his fortune in the distribution of natural assets and abilities, his intelligence and strength, and the like'.[193] Personal tastes, self-interest, and power differentials disappear in this constellation, and genuine moral choices will be made. Just like individuals, ignorant of what position they will hold upon entering society, will not normally choose a slave-owning society (where they could well end up on the receiving end), ignorant states are unlikely to want to enter a society characterized by environmental disaster, international crimes, rampant corruption, and corporate abuses. One can instead presume that they would *a priori* give their consent to an international society that is based on some minimum rules of conduct. From this perspective, the empirical reality that states, for self-interested reasons, do not give their *actual* consent to the protection of a global value or to global welfare-enhancement, nor of states' right to extraterritorially protect the value, is not decisive. Key to this is that in the original position, states, for reasons of rational morality, would have given their consent if their vision had not been clouded by particularist considerations.

The question remains, however, whether salvaging consent is a worthwhile endeavour in the first place. It has notably been argued that, from the perspective of the structure of international law, explicit consent to be bound by a norm is not, and has not been a prerequisite for norm legitimacy. As Kumm put it:

> [S]tate consent cannot plausibly be the foundation of international law. The legitimacy of a sovereign state is not self-standing. Rather, a sovereign state's legitimacy and its legal order also depends on its integration into an international system whose purpose it is to first establish the conditions under which the exercise of state sovereignty is legitimate ... International law seeks to create the conditions and define the domain over which states can legitimately claim sovereignty... Only a cosmopolitan state—a state that incorporates and reflects in its constitutional structure and foreign policy the global legitimacy conditions for claims to sovereignty—is a legitimate state.[194]

This approach to state consent strongly relates to our earlier discussion of sovereignty. What is posited here is a concept of 'relative sovereignty',[195] pursuant to which state sovereignty is not a pre- or a-legal notion ('sovereignty as fact') but is created by and embedded in international law ('sovereignty as law').[196]

[193] John Rawls, *A Theory of Justice* (HUP 1999) 118.
[194] Mattias Kumm, 'Sovereignty and the Right to Be Left Alone: Subsidiarity, Justice-Sensitive Externalities, and the Proper Domain of the Consent Requirement in International Law' (2016) 79 Law & Contemp Probls 239, 24.
[195] See on relative sovereignty Hans Aufricht, 'On Relative Sovereignty' (1945) 30 CLR 318.
[196] Also Koskenniemi, 'What Use for Sovereignty Today?' (n 86). See also *SS* 'Wimbledon' (*United Kingdom and others v Germany*), Judgment (1923) PCIJ Series A no 1, 25 (PCIJ 1923) ('the right of entering into international engagements is an attribute of State sovereignty').

Sovereignty is conditional and has to be earned,[197] and, in keeping with the *Lotus* judgment—the World Court's pre-eminent enunciation of the principles of the law of jurisdiction—needs to be exercised to ensure coexistence cooperation between states.[198] The relative notion of sovereignty implies that where states withhold consent to global welfare-enhancing regulation without good reason, such consent may have to be disregarded. Deciding otherwise could have a chilling effect on globally desirable regulation, even if it is based on unilateral action. One should bear in mind in this respect that non-action or a failure to consent is itself a unilateral act,[199] which holds other states, the international community, or even local citizens hostage. Thus, requiring consent and permission from other states has been considered as hindering the progressive development of the law of jurisdiction,[200] and from a Kantian perspective, 'contrary to right'.[201]

Accordingly, clinging to a global welfare-decreasing principle of consent is normatively inferior to, and should arguably give way to regulatory unilateralism that enhances global welfare and subjects other states and their individuals and operators to 'extraterritorial' regulation, for example unilateral action that tackles

[197] This view has notably informed the global interventionist discourse regarding failed states, *ie* incapable or illegitimate states. See Kenneth Chan, *Intervention and State Failure in International Law* (PhD thesis KU Leuven 2016). See for a critique Matthew Craven and Rose Parfitt, 'Statehood Self-Determination, and Recognition' in Malcolm Evans (ed) *International Law* (5th edn OUP 2018) 225 (noting, in respect of the discourse of failed states, that the 're-emergence of this "liberal anti-pluralist" theme within international legal doctrine . . . recalls the intellectual structures of nineteenth century imperialism'). See on conditional sovereignty also Fox-Decent and Criddle (n 97) 3 (espousing a fiduciary conception of sovereignty and stating that 'a state's claim to exercise sovereign authority is derived from, and wholly dependent upon, the satisfaction of its relational duties to the people subject to its legal powers').

[198] Hertogen (n 148) 917, also citing Judge Shahabuddeen, opinion in Nuclear Weapons Advisory Opinion, 393 (referring to the 'objective structural framework within which sovereignty must necessarily exist'. This notion, somewhat surprisingly perhaps, harks back to early modern writings on what was thought of as 'absolute' sovereignty. Troper, 'Sovereignty' (n 158) 326–33 (arguing that in the early modern age, 'being absolute' was not defined as exercising a power with no limits, but 'exercising a power limited only by natural or divine laws', citing, *inter alia*, the phrase of Jean Bodin—the main theorist of absolute sovereignty in the early modern age—that 'whereas the King respects the laws of nature, the tyrant violates them', and the fact that natural law enabled the English Parliament to review the King's law). See also nineteenth-century and early twentieth-century ideas on freedom being organized by international law, and international law being based on the society of states rather than on state consent. cf Eyal Benvenisti, 'The Paradoxes of Sovereigns as Trustees of Humanity: Concluding Remarks' (2015) 16 Theoretical Inq L 535, 538–39, citing *inter alia* Hans Kelsen, Foundations of Democracy (1955) 66 Ethics 1, 34 ('absolute sovereignty is not and cannot be an essential quality of the state existing side by side with other states', and 'recognizing the possibility of an international legal order constituting an international community of which the state is a member').

[199] Ankersmit and others (n 38) 33 (discussing unilateral process and production-based measures).

[200] Hertogen (n 147) 915 ('[A] system that requires permission before states can act is undesirable. It fails to remove the "baneful spell" of consent that hinders the progressive development of international law . . . a requirement of permission is problematic not because the acting state will have a de facto veto right over a rule that prohibits its actions but, rather, because the state will have a de facto veto right over the creation of any rule that permits an affected state to respond.').

[201] Aravind Ganesh, 'Unilateral Jurisdiction to Provide Global Public Goods: A Republican Account' (2018) 42 Brook J Int'l L 571, 640 (2018) (submitting that 'requiring the State to pursue its purpose solely through multilateral channels would place it at the mercy of other persons, State and Non-state. This is contrary to right.').

criminal activity with cross-border effects, or unilateral action that addresses a global environmental good such as a stable climate.[202] After all, following Kant, one cannot tolerate a state of affairs that allows one actor to coerce another (*ie* subject him to one's will), and in so doing limit the latter's autonomy.[203] Instead, the latter can coerce the former by subjecting him to unilateral regulation with a view to entering 'into a rightful condition', in this case the autonomy-enhancing subjection to global welfare, and global values-promoting unilateral regulation. Indeed, as Ganesh reminds us, in Kantian contractual thinking, one can be coerced if one does not enter into a rightful condition, as in the original contract, coercive authority grounds freedom.[204] Consequently, unilateral coercion of states by other states, that is states' subjection to legal authority without their explicit consent, is legitimate, insofar as it enhances justice and (broadly defined) freedom of individuals, for example where it contributes to the fight against human rights abuses, nefarious forms of cross-border criminality or dodgy business practices, or climate change, all of which directly or indirectly have an adverse impact on individual freedom.[205]

States that are not in 'a rightful condition' arguably forfeit their right to protest alleged violations of their sovereignty because such states no longer qualify as proper states. This is an idea which in fact predates Kant, and could already be found in Spinoza's writings. Admittedly, Spinoza does not tie governmental authority to the furthering of individual autonomy. Instead, he is interested in state *interests* rather than moral obligations and constraints. Nevertheless, he grounds the legitimacy of sovereign authority in its capacity to generate compliance-inducing law effectively that promotes the interests of the community or commonwealth. This capacity is a function of the state's capabilities to have prescriptive human laws (positive law) adequately reflect descriptive human laws (the law of nature). To the extent that the state fails in this endeavour, it risks non-compliance of its laws by its subjects, thereby losing its effective authority, and risking its own demise as a state.[206]

[202] Kumm, 'Sovereignty and the Right to Be Left Alone' (n 194) 251 ('Justice concerns are not merely raised by negative externalities of state action, but also by omissions that result in the failure to realize positive externalities when the state has a responsibility to act.').

[203] Immanuel Kant, 'Theory and Practice' in Hans Reiss (ed) *Kant's Political Writings* (CUP 1970) 73–75.

[204] Ganesh, 'Unilateral Jurisdiction' (n 201) 608 ('First, authority is necessary for freedom. You become free by submitting to authority. If you do not submit, you are unfree, and therefore can be compelled. Second, if you do not enter into a rightful condition, you are reserving for yourself the opportunity to use arbitrary violence against others as and when you please, and this they need not, in fact *must* not abide. Conversely, you can coerce others into entering into a rightful condition with you because of your innate right—your only right—to be free.' Citing *inter alia* Ak §6:316 [DR].

[205] Kumm, 'Sovereignty and the Right to Be Left Alone' (n 194) 251 ('Given that these are areas in which states lack legitimate authority to effectively control what may or may not be done, no injustice is done to states when they are subjected to legal obligations without having consented to them. On the contrary, deep legitimacy questions arise when individual states have the capacity to effectively veto the emergence of universally binding obligations in contexts where the behavior of an individual state raises justice-sensitive externality concerns.').

[206] Lorenzo Zucca, 'A Genealogy of State Sovereignty' (2015) 16 Theoretical Inq L 399, 416–18, citing Johnathan Israel (ed), *Spinoza: Theological-Political Treatise* (CUP 2007) 426.

Zucca has extrapolated Spinoza's effectiveness-based view of state authority to the global realm and argued that the state which 'is no longer capable of providing the adequate responses to global problems of coordination' loses its existence.[207] This is not so much out of moral considerations but out of the state's very interest: in an increasingly interdependent world, 'the survival of states relies on their ability to provide answers to transnational problems'.[208] Accordingly, something counterintuitively such as extraterritorial cosmopolitan action, aimed at promoting global stability and global public goods, could serve the very interest and survival of the 'targeted state'.[209] Such a state can be considered as lacking legal power and authority and as having no voice in protesting other state's actions that do provide answers to pressing global problems, even if such answers superficially impinge on its interests. After all, by failing to collaborate, states not just worsen global problems but they also undermine the rational interests of their own subjects who benefit from international collaboration and regulation.[210] On these views, a state which commits or tolerates human rights violations, or does not address climate change, does not just fail 'the international community' but first and foremost its own citizens. Such a state does not have any international or domestic authority and may legitimately be subjected to multilateral or unilateral intervention which adequately responds to global problems, thereby also vindicating the rights and interests of the target states' citizens.

Ultimately, also the latter justification of 'selfless intervention' could be normatively grounded in constructive state consent as it presupposes or requires that foreign states consent to extraterritorial action. More convincingly, however, the legitimacy of such action can be considered as a function of the challenges facing humanity rather than some form of 'consent' given by states. In this view, legitimacy does not derive from a deontological, rule-based, consensual perspective (codified shared values), but rather from a *consequentialist* or *utilitarian* ethical angle which takes into account an action's potential to enhance global welfare,[211]

[207] ibid, 419.

[208] ibid, 420. See on sovereignty as independence also Chayes and Chayes, *The New Sovereignty* (n 166); Jochen von Bernstorff, 'Georg Jellinek and the Origins of Liberal Constitutionalism in International Law' (2012) 4 GJIL 659, 672–73.

[209] Zucca (n 206) 421 ('A sovereign state that does not understand its interest in collaborating with other states to provide answers to pressing global problems is first and foremost undermining its chances of future survival.').

[210] Ideas of enlightened self-interest characterized by obligations towards others, can, for that matter, also be found in Vattel (n 51), where he considers that allowing international commerce should trump reason of state, in the interests of justice. Straumann (n 47) 446 citing Isaac Nakhimovsky, 'Vattel's Theory of the International Order: Commerce and the Balance of Power in the Law Nations (2007) 33 History of European Ideas 157, 162.

[211] See notably the works of the nineteenth-century British philosophers Jeremy Bentham and John Stuart Mill: Jeremy Bentham, *Introduction to the Principles of Morals and Legislation* (printed for publication 1780, published 1789) and John Stuart Mill, *The Principles of Political Economy: with some of their Applications to Social Philosophy* (1848).

even if it may decrease one or more states' national welfare.[212] Such a position may find its conceptual roots in Weber's 'ethics of responsibility,[213] and possibly in the legal processes emphasized by the New Haven policy approach to international law.[214] It remains an anti-formalist view par excellence, as it values the supply of global public goods and the provision of global justice higher than compliance with the formal requirement of state consent.[215] If such a view, which disregards any form of state consent, informs actual jurisdictional practices, these practices will in any event have to be surrounded by stringent limiting conditions to prevent jurisdictional overreach. These limiting conditions will be discussed in Chapter 4.

2.6 Positive Law Authorizations and Obligations to Exercise Jurisdiction in the Common Interest

The lawyer's task of finding a normative basis for the exercise of unilateral jurisdiction in the common interest is considerably eased where positive international law explicitly authorizes or even obliges states to exercise jurisdiction in the global interest. In this case, the international or multilateral authorization of a jurisdictional assertion decreases, or even removes its unilateral character. Such an assertion may then no longer be perceived as violating another state's sovereignty insofar as that state has given its consent to the exercise of jurisdiction by bystander states, for example via signing and ratifying a relevant treaty.

Notably in the field of criminal law, a number of treaties authorize or even oblige states to exercise forms of extraterritorial jurisdiction in the common interest, forms which have sometimes been labelled—although perhaps wrongly so—as universal jurisdiction.[216] Thus, the UN Torture Convention provides that '[e]ach State Party shall ... take such measures as may be necessary to establish its

[212] Guzman, 'Against Consent' (n 153) 757 (arguing in favour Kaldor–Hicks rather Pareto efficiency improvements, as the former only require 'that the total pie get larger, not that every state receive a larger piece', while the latter requires 'that somebody be made better off and nobody be made worse off').

[213] Max Weber, '*Politik als Beruf*' in Max Weber *Gesammelte Politische Schriften* (3rd edn, 1971) ('You should resist evil with force, otherwise you are responsible for its getting out of hand.').

[214] See for the seminal work of the New Haven School, emphasizing processes over formal rules: Myres S McDougal and Harold D Laswell, *The Identification and Appraisal of Diverse Systems of Public Order* in Myres S McDougal and others (eds) *Studies in World Public Order* (Springer 1986). *Contra* Martti Koskenniemi, *The Gentle Civilizer of Nations* (CUP 2001) 485 (decrying this instrumentalism that replaces formal law by a wider standard policy guideline and the 'values of liberal democracy').

[215] Guzman, 'Against Consent' (n 153) 749 ('An excessive commitment to consent can cripple efforts to use international law as a tool to help solve the world's largest problems.'). *Contra* Koskenniemi, 'What Use for Sovereignty Today?' (n 86) 65 (denouncing the anti-formalist nature of contemporary global law, which in his view does no longer protect formal sovereignty, but replaces it by 'global systems of management' that renders everything 'negotiable, revisable in view of attaining the right outcome').

[216] On the non-existence of universal jurisdiction: Matthew Garrod, 'Unraveling the Confused Relationship Between Treaty Obligations to Extradite or Prosecute and "Universal Jurisdiction" in the Light of the *Habré Case*' (2018) 59 HILJ 125.

jurisdiction over such offences in cases where the alleged offender is present in any territory under its jurisdiction and it does not extradite him' to another state having jurisdiction.[217] A similar mandatory *aut dedere aut judicare* clause could be found in the Geneva Conventions regarding grave breaches of the laws of war, and in a number of anti-terrorism conventions.[218] The UN Convention against Corruption requires a state party to establish its jurisdiction when it does not extradite a person on the ground that he or she is one of its nationals,[219] and authorizes—although does not require—states to do the same in other cases.[220] The UN Convention on the Law of the Sea (UNCLOS) authorizes the exercise of 'universal' criminal jurisdiction over piracy.[221]

Jurisdictional authorizations and even obligations to exercise criminal jurisdiction could also follow from customary international law. For instance, crimes of genocide, crimes against humanity, and war crimes committed in non-international armed conflicts have been considered to be amenable to permissive universal criminal jurisdiction under customary international law, even if treaties do not confer such jurisdiction.[222] It is doubtful whether currently there are offences amenable to obligatory universal jurisdiction under customary international law.[223]

Outside the criminal law, only few treaties explicitly authorize or require the exercise of 'selfless' jurisdiction. The most notable examples can be found in the field of port state jurisdiction, jurisdiction exercised by port states over foreign-flagged visiting vessels, possibly in respect of acts done in an area beyond national jurisdiction. Thus, article 218 UNCLOS authorizes the exercise of apparently 'universal' port state jurisdiction over discharges on the high seas, and the Port State Measures Agreement even requires port states to exercise jurisdiction over foreign vessels engaged in illegal, unreported, or unsustainable (IUU) fishing.[224]

In the absence of a treaty, selfless jurisdiction will have to be based on customary international law. The customary principle of territorial jurisdiction,

[217] Art 5(2) UN Torture Convention (n 17).

[218] Art 49 of the 1949 Geneva Convention I, art 50 of the 1949 Geneva Convention II, art 129 of the 1949 Geneva Convention III and art 146 of the 1949 Geneva Convention IV; art 4(b) of the Convention on Offences Committed on Board Aircraft, Tokyo, 14 September 1963, 220 UNTS 10106; art 6(2)(b) of the Convention for the Suppression of Unlawful Acts Against the Safety of Maritime Navigation, Rome, 10 March 1988, 222 UNTS 29004.

[219] Art 42(3) UN Convention against Corruption.

[220] ibid, art 42(4).

[221] Art 105 UNCLOS.

[222] Cedric Ryngaert, *Jurisdiction in International Law* (2nd edn OUP 2015) 126–28.

[223] See also Constitutional Court of Spain, Sentencia 140/2018, 20 December 2018 (BOE núm. 22, de 25 de enero de 2019), ECLI:ES:TC:2018:140. The Court held that 'customary law permits states to grant universal jurisdiction to their municipal courts, without imposing any obligation to do so', and that 'Spanish courts and parties do not have an absolute right to bring claims before Spanish courts'. As discussed in Nicolás Zambrano-Tévar, 'Ruling of the Spanish Constitutional Court Legitimising Restrictions on Universal Criminal Jurisdiction' EJIL:Talk!, 6 February 2019.

[224] Agreement on Port State Measures to Prevent, Deter and Eliminate Illegal, Unreported and Unregulated Fishing (FAO 2016), arts 7–9.

which operates on the basis of a territorial nexus of a situation with the regulating state, appears to be most attractive in this respect.[225] The role of territoriality as a jurisdictional vehicle for cosmopolitan action will be discussed in more detail in Chapter 5, where it is demonstrated that states typically ground unilateral jurisdiction in the common interest on the principle of territoriality (broadly construed, however).

Absent a territorial nexus, justifying the exercise of non-criminal jurisdiction under customary international law becomes more challenging. Particularly instructive in this regard is the discussion regarding the authorization or even obligation of states to exercise universal civil jurisdiction over international crimes. Existing treaty clauses on the exercise of state jurisdiction typically do not address the 'extraterritorial' exercise of civil or tort jurisdiction over such crimes.[226] This has not stopped legal interpreters from reading extraterritoriality into such clauses.[227] Actual state practice, however, appears to go the other way, as also acknowledged by the ECtHR in *Nait-Liman* (2016, 2018), the only supranational court case addressing universal civil jurisdiction.[228] In these judgments, the Court held that there was no international obligation to exercise universal civil jurisdiction over torture, and even entertained doubts as to its permissibility under international law, given its potential for diplomatic tension.[229]

From a positive law perspective, in the absence of persuasive state practice evidencing the existence of a treaty-based or customary norm requiring states to exercise jurisdiction in the common interest, the exercise of such jurisdiction could alternatively be grounded on the structure of international obligations, in particular obligations under international human rights treaties. While such treaties do not normally contain a clause on the exercise of unilateral state jurisdiction,

225 *Eg* Court of Justice of the EU, Judgment of the Court (Grand Chamber) of 21 December 2011. *Air Transport Association of America and Others v Secretary of State for Energy and Climate Change*. Reference for a preliminary ruling: High Court of Justice (England & Wales), Queen's Bench Division (Administrative Court)—United Kingdom. Case C-366/10. ECLI:EU:C:2011:864 (EU 'climate change' jurisdiction over aviation justified on the basis of the territoriality principle, on the ground that the jurisdictional assertions only extend to aircraft landing at, or departing from an EU aerodrome).

226 Treaties may feature a clause on reparations, but such a clause typically remains silent about its jurisdictional scope. See art 14(1) UN Torture Convention (n 17) (' Each State Party shall ensure in its legal system that the victim of an act of torture obtains redress and has an enforceable right to fair and adequate compensation, including the means for as full rehabilitation as possible. In the event of the death of the victim as a result of an act of torture, his dependents shall be entitled to compensation.').

227 The Committee against Torture, for one, held that an obligation to exercise universal civil jurisdiction followed from art 14 of the UN Torture Convention. UN Committee Against Torture, Conclusions and recommendations, 34th Sess, 2—20 May 2005, UN Doc CAT/C/CR/34/ CAN, 7 July 2005, paras 4(g), 5(f).

228 *Nait-Liman v Switzerland* (GC), Application no 51357/07, Judgment of 15 March 2018, on appeal from *Naït-Liman v Switzerland*, Judgment of 21 June 2016.

229 See for a general discussion regarding the existence of public international law limits to adjudicatory jurisdiction in civil matters, as triggered by the ECtHR's judgment in *Nait-Liman*: Lucas Roorda and Cedric Ryngaert, 'Public International Law Constraints on the Exercise of Adjudicatory Jurisdiction in Civil Matters' in S Forlati and P Franzina (eds), *Universal Civil Jurisdiction* (forthcoming Brill 2020).

they may contain one requiring contracting parties to secure the human rights of individuals 'within their jurisdiction'. This applies especially to treaties on civil and political rights, such as the European Convention on Human Rights (ECHR) and the International Covenant on Civil and Political Rights (ICCPR).[230] Pursuant to current understandings of such a jurisdictional clause, contracting parties have 'extraterritorial' human rights obligations insofar as they exercise effective territorial control or public authority over individuals abroad.[231] From a remedial perspective, insofar as states incur such obligations abroad, they may have to extend their state jurisdiction by offering a procedural remedy in case such obligations are breached. This may include allowing their courts to hear 'extraterritorial' tort claims (*ie* to exercise adjudicatory jurisdiction) or instructing their prosecutors to initiate 'extraterritorial' criminal proceedings against the persons allegedly responsible for the violations.

The widening of the geographic scope of human rights treaties to include non-residents and the accompanying remedial exercise of jurisdiction to discharge such human rights obligations may be characterized as an exercise of cosmopolitan jurisdiction to the extent that it confers rights on distant others.[232] However, human rights jurisdictional clauses have so far mainly served the purpose of offering accountability for the contracting state's violations of its own, negative human rights obligations (*eg* the right to life),[233] typically in the context of the state's military operations abroad.[234] Still, such clauses could as well ground 'extraterritorial' positive obligations for the contracting state to protect foreign individuals from violations committed by third parties. This means that foreign individuals whose enjoyment of human rights is adversely affected by acts of foreign state or a non-state actor may fall within the contracting state's jurisdiction, at least if it can be shown that the latter state has a sufficiently strong connection with these acts and actors,[235]

[230] Art 2 European Convention Human Rights (ECHR); art 1 International Covenant Civil and Political Rights (ICCPR).

[231] See notably *Al-Skeini and Others v the United Kingdom* [2011] Appl No 55721/07.

[232] Fox-Decent and Criddle (n 97) 41 (stating that 'the fiduciary character of sovereignty has a cosmopolitan aspect, in that states must refrain from treating foreign nationals abroad as mere objects that they are at liberty to harm or destroy without justification', although limiting this to the exercise of the use of force abroad).

[233] *Al-Skeini and Others v the United Kingdom* (n 231) (concerning violations of art 2 of the ECHR—right to life). This may however also extend to positive obligations that are closely tied to these obligations, *eg* procedural obligations regarding violations of the right to life. See *Jaloud v The Netherlands* [2014] Appl No 47708/08.

[234] There is a large literature on extraterritorial human rights obligations, *eg* Marko Milanovic, *Extraterritorial Application of Human Rights Treaties* (OUP 2011).

[235] See notably Inter-American Court of Human Rights, The Environment and Human Rights (State obligations in relation to the environment in the context of the protection and guarantee of the rights to life and to personal integrity—interpretation and scope of arts 4(1) and 5(1) of the American Convention on Human Rights). Advisory Opinion OC-23/17 of 15 November 2017. Series A No 23 (holding that an individual falls within the jurisdiction of a contracting state 'when the State of origin exercises effective control over the activities carried out that caused the harm and consequent violation of human rights' (para 104(h)).

or if it can be said to have the capacity to influence them.[236] Whether and how human rights jurisdictional clauses also ground the establishment of mandatory state jurisdiction will be explored in Chapter 5,[237] in the particular contexts of the right to a tort remedy for extraterritorial human rights violations by corporations and of data protection legislation with extraterritorial effect.[238]

2.7 Concluding Observations

In the Grotian tradition, reason, ethics, and the law of nature may demand that international legal action be taken beyond the express will of states,[239] and that existing positive law should be reinterpreted or even modified to this effect.[240] In this

[236] The UN Committee on Economic, Social and Cultural Rights (CESCR), in any event, has taken a wide view concerning states' extraterritorial obligations. Regarding the right to health, for instance, it has held that 'States parties have to respect the enjoyment of the right to health in other countries, and prevent third parties from violating the right in other countries, if they are able to influence these third parties by way of legal or political means, in accordance with the Charter of the United Nations and applicable international law.' CESCR General Comment No. 14 (2000). The right to the highest attainable standard of health (art 12 of the International Covenant on Economic, Social and Cultural Rights), UN Doc E/C.12/2000/4 (2000), para 39.

[237] Note however, as also pointed out by Steven R Ratner, *The Thin Justice of International Law* (OUP 2015) 268, that the extraterritorial application of human rights and state jurisdiction are 'distinct doctrinal boxes and labels'. The extraterritoriality of human rights law does not normally raise the concerns over jurisdictional overreach, imperialist intervention, and violations of state sovereignty typically associated with the exercise of unilateral jurisdiction in the global interest. In fact, foreign states and foreign persons will ordinarily *welcome* the exercise of state jurisdiction based on the extraterritoriality of human rights, as such jurisdiction protects their rights. Extraterritorial human claims against the state and state officials are indeed—necessarily—initiated by victims of foreign harm, who thus purposely seek the exercise of state jurisdiction. That being said, some commentators have voiced concern over imperialist imposition of 'foreign' human rights standards undermining local, democratic choices as to the desired standard of protection. *Eg* Naz K Modirzadeh, 'The Dark Sides of Convergence: A Pro-Civilian Critique of the Extraterritorial Application of Human Rights Law in Armed Conflict' (2010) 86 US Naval War College ILS 349, 375

[238] International human rights treaties, while they provide for the right to privacy, do not as provide for a right to data protection. However, the EU Charter on Fundamental Rights, a *regional* human rights instrument, does consider data protection to rise to the level of a fundamental right (art 8). For data protection, the question then becomes whether the EU Charter has extraterritorial effect, in the case whether the European Union has human rights obligations towards EU data subjects in respect of these subjects being targeted by foreign operators, and in respect of the transfer of their data to third countries.

[239] Hersch Lauterpacht, 'The Grotian Tradition in International Law' (1946) 1 BYBIL 21–22, relying on Grotius's *De Jure Belli ac Pacis* ('The significance of the law of nature in the treatise is that it is the ever-present source for supplementing the voluntary law of nations, for judging its adequacy in the light of ethics and reason, and for making the reader aware of the fact that the will of states cannot be the exclusive or even, in the last resort, the decisive source of the law of nations.'). Zucca (n 206) 410 (discussing how for Grotius *ius* is superior to *lex* and that '[o]bjective right is not dependent on the exercise of will—it is antecedent to human will and independent of divine will'), contrasting this at 411 with Hobbes's view ('For Hobbes, it is not possible to ascertain an objective moral standard (ius) above and beyond the state.').

[240] Dellavalle, 'On Sovereignty, Legitimacy and Solidarity (n 45) 397; Dellavalle, 'Opening the Forum to the Others' (n 15) 230 (noting that, for Kant, morality serves as 'a conceptual basis for criticism of the existing law, as a precondition for further development of the legal system').

chapter, it has been argued that interests common to the international community may suffer if notions of sovereignty and state consent are given a strict interpretation, if this leads to multilateral blockage and lack of accountability for extraterritorial abuses.[241] Instead, the progressive development of international law may have to be geared towards relaxing the principles of non-intervention and territorial jurisdiction,[242] so that unilateral action by states in the common interest may more easily be taken.[243] Borrowing from Dyzenhaus,[244] it could be posited that such states advance the *ius* of the international rule of law project (*ie* the progressive development of international law so that it protects common concerns and individual freedom) against the *lex* of positive international law (*ie* the strict principles of non-intervention and state consent).

Cosmopolitan consequentialism requires us to take substance rather than formality seriously. Therefore, 'consent' and 'sovereignty' are in need of reinterpretation so that they can facilitate and not inhibit the realization of global values and common interests. On this view, while (state) unilateralism eventually remains rooted in (state) sovereignty, this is a reconstructed sovereignty that serves cosmopolitan and solidaristic purposes and is not bound to one state's territory.[245] Arguably, for a state to be legitimately subjected to regulation by a third state, the former state need not have voluntarily participated and consented to it, providing that such a third state acts 'selflessly', that is it contributes to the building of an international community.[246] Consent has less traction in this scheme because in the

241 Also Augenstein (n 170) 690 (arguing that this is 'part of a broader project to reconfigure the legal and political landscape of the "late" Westphalian world' and that one should prevent that 'the retreat behind the veil of state sovereignty degenerates into a realpolitical charade').

242 This also extends to some related, restrictive doctrines under domestic foreign relations law. *Eg* Farbiarz (n 95) 552–53 (regretting that in the United States, many extraterritorial prosecutions that would further global public safety are not even brought because of the extraterritorial due process doctrine which requires a *nexus* with the United States, and illustrating that the leader of Boko Haram, while formally subject to US law, *eg*, legislation proscribing child conscription, because Boko Haram has no nexus with the United States).

243 Guzman, 'Against Consent' (n 153) 788.

244 David Dyzenhaus, 'Kelsen, Heller and Schmitt: Paradigms of Sovereignty Thought' (2015) 16 Theoretical Inq L 337, 363. See also Zucca (n 206) 304 (arguing that, in the context of factional tensions in his home city of Florence, Dante is committed to the *ius commune*, considered 'as the product of natural reason, reflecting the real order', and opposes the jurisdictional autonomy of city-states producing particularistic and unjust law *(lex)*, being 'merely the product of factional majority interests'). ibid. 404 (contrasting this view with Machiavelli's position that politics needs to be separated from ethics, and that the state stands for 'an impersonal rule that has the monopoly of coercion over a boundary-defined territory').

245 See on the malleability of sovereignty: Dyzenhaus (n 244) 342 (submitting that 'sovereignty becomes an instrument for whatever ideological purposes those who occupy sovereign office choose', drawing on Schmitt and Kelsen). See on non-territorial sovereignty: Dellavalle, 'On Sovereignty, Legitimacy and Solidarity (n 48) 368 (arguing that 'sovereignty' consists of 'the legitimate exercise of public power … generally but not necessarily with reference to a specific territory'). ibid, 370 ('legitimate sovereignty has to be updated and integrated with a further aspect, namely a solidaristic attitude towards aliens' interests').

246 Domingo (n 14) 584 ('The most important consequence of universality is that the global human community is a non-voluntary community.').

face of globalization and planetary challenges, the existence of such a global community is arguably a legal necessity; that is, not arising by an explicit prior agreement among its members.[247] It remains, nevertheless, that consent to the exercise of unilateral jurisdiction by bystander states could sometimes be explicitly found in existing international legal instruments, some of which may even *require* states to exercise jurisdiction in given circumstances. It could also be derived from the structure of international obligations in human rights treaties which may ground (consent-based) duties to exercise state jurisdiction. Moreover, states could rely on traditional principles of jurisdiction, in particular territoriality, to regulate matters that are in essence extraterritorial in nature, and in so doing possibly further the common interest.

At the end of the day, allowing calibrated common interest-based prescriptive jurisdiction with extraterritorial effect may be preferable to prohibiting it altogether, with the attendant negative consequences for planetary survival and the enjoyment of rights.[248] Calibration means that, in order counter illegitimate domination and abuse of unilateralism, techniques that mitigate its impact and increase its legitimacy have to be explored. This will happen in Chapter 4. But before discussing these techniques, Chapter 3 will address the *likelihood* of states intervening selflessly by means of the exercise of prescriptive jurisdiction. If such interventions are unlikely anyway, there is little point in elaborating on limiting conditions for its exercise.

[247] ibid, 578 (decrying at 577 that today, a 'strong sense of contractualism has fueled disregard for the tripartition of sources of law into consent, custom, and necessity', a tripartition which he traces back to the Roman jurist Modestinus's first book of legal rules, in which stated that 'all law has been made either by consent, or established by necessity, or confirmed by custom'.) ibid, 577 (raising the 'need to recover the concept of necessity in order to develop the correct approach to the law in this era of globalization').

[248] Thus, states and regional organizations willing to act unilaterally in the common interest, as 'benevolent hegemons', may have to be applauded rather than criticized. Practice shows that such applause may be forthcoming indeed. For instance, when in 2015 US prosecutors indicted FIFA officials under US racketeering laws for accepting foreign bribes, international opinion was largely supportive of the US taking steps to clean up international football. 'The World's Lawyer: America's Legal Reach' (The Economist, 6 June 2015); John Gapper, 'America is the Best Referee to Discipline FIFA' (Financial Times, 27 May 2015).

3

Selfless Jurisdiction and the National Interest

Between Cosmopolitanism and Parochialism

The previous chapter set out how states may want to intervene 'selflessly' by exercising jurisdiction in case the common interest cannot be otherwise protected or furthered, notably because of multilateral failures, or failures of states more closely connected to the matter. However, it would be intellectually dishonest to dismiss the observation of realists that cosmopolitan action is in reality not or rarely taken, unless it is in the state's interest, or when the state has a jurisdictional nexus (link, a connection) to the situation subject to regulation, often a territorial one. In the absence of state ability and willingness to act as an agent of the international community, cosmopolitanism may well remain dead letter.[1]

This chapter examines the variables that may determine the exercise of jurisdiction in the common interest. It inquires what explanatory variables determine the dependent variable of the (non-)exercise of jurisdiction in the common interest, based on actual jurisdictional practice of states. However, the chapter's approach is also normative where it seeks to justify particular interest-based practices of jurisdiction or recommends reform.[2]

Drawing on realist theory and actual practice, it is posited that the exercise of jurisdiction in the common interest is unlikely unless the state has a nexus to the situation subject to regulation. The presence of a nexus may in fact serve to allocate jurisdictional authority and responsibility and encourage action in the common interest. In practice, however, because the exercise of jurisdiction under international law is in principle discretionary, there is no guarantee that the state to whom jurisdiction is allocated will also assume it. As such failure to exercise jurisdiction may have detrimental effects for global justice, a second-order jurisdictional authority for 'bystander' states (*ie* less closely connected states) may be called for (section 3.1). However, realistically, bystander states are only likely to exercise selfless jurisdiction if this also serves their national interests (section 3.2).

[1] Ronald Pierik and Wouter Werner, 'Can Cosmopolitanism Survive Institutionalization?' in Ronald Pierik and Wouter Werner (eds), *Cosmopolitanism in Context: Perspectives from International Law and Political Theory* (CUP 2010) 284.

[2] This chapter is partly based on Cedric Ryngaert, 'Cosmopolitan Jurisdiction and the National Interest' in Stephen Allen and others (eds), *Oxford Handbook on Jurisdiction* (OUP 2019) 218–27.

Selfless Intervention. Cedric Ryngaert, Oxford University Press (2020). © Cedric Ryngaert.
DOI: 10.1093/oso/9780198851783.001.0001

It is argued that this limitation of cosmopolitan action need not be regrettable. Instead, it could be justified from a normative perspective. In particular, the variables determining the (non-)exercise of universal criminal jurisdiction as well as the jurisdictional extension of domestic economic regulation will be discussed to support the argument (sections 3.3 and 3.4). The last section of the chapter examines whether domestic courts, which are supposed to operate independently from the political branches, are possibly more likely to exercise 'selfless' cosmopolitan jurisdiction (section 3.5).

3.1 Allocating the Exercise of Jurisdiction

Realists posit that the taking of state action is a function of the maximization of national welfare. Thereby, they all but close the door to jurisdiction in the common interest.[3] A more benign realist would however observe that the likelihood that action is effectively taken is higher when a state nexus is present.[4] The presence of a 'nexus', however constructed,[5] ordinarily points to the presence of an interest of the state. This logically renders the exercise of jurisdiction more likely.[6]

Using 'nexus' may increase the prevalence of jurisdictional action in the common interest as it goes some way to allocate responsibility: it circumscribes and thus defines the circle of actors competent to take action. If, in contrast, one were to promote a version of non-nexus-based, universal, cosmopolitan jurisdiction, no-one may take action at all. The irony is apparent. Such jurisdiction may have been designed to address multilateral free-rider behaviour, but comes with its

[3] *Eg* Jack Goldsmith and Stephen D Krasner, 'The Limits of Idealism' (2003) 132 Daedalus 47.

[4] *Eg* Rain Liivoja, 'The Criminal Jurisdiction of States a Theoretical Primer' (2010) 7 NoFo 25 ('A State generally has little interest in spending its scarce resources on investigating offences that it has little or no connection to.').

[5] When exactly a transnational activity has a nexus with a state is not self-evident, but depends on what law-appliers consider as a relevant nexus. This means that transnational acts could sometimes rather artificially be 'located' within a particular state's territory. Anthony J Colangelo, 'What is Extraterritorial Jurisdiction?' (2014) 99 CLR 1303, 1323 ('[E]ven seemingly straightforward jurisdictional questions of geography often hinge on some predicate legal determination about where, exactly, one locates the relevant aspect or aspects of a claim or suit.'). See *eg* the US Supreme Court's principle that application of the presumption against extraterritoriality requires an analysis of the 'statutory focus'. In *Morrison,* for instance, the Court held that the relevant (securities law) statute's focus was not on fraudulent conduct but rather on the sale and purchase of securities. As the latter occurred abroad, there was no relevant nexus to the United States, and hence no jurisdiction. *Morrison v National Australia Bank*, 561 US 247 (2010).

[6] However, the precise ambit of the legal norm applied may vary, depending on the strength of the nexus, or the nature of the norm. See Liivoja (n 4) 36 (submitting that 'every individual norm possesses some sort of ambit'). Compare *eg Morrison* (n 5) (considering fraudulent acts in the United States producing effects abroad as not sufficient to find jurisdiction under US securities regulations) with *Pasquantino v United States*, 544 US 349 (2005) 365 (finding jurisdiction over a wire fraud devised in the United States but producing effects in Canada). Not, however, that the ambit of categories of norms may be laid down by law, *eg* in the general part of the criminal law, which typically considers territory to be the relevant nexus.

own free-rider problems: making everyone responsible for tackling a problem may in practice be a recipe for doing nothing. Indeed, social psychologists have experimentally proved that group size has an impact on the likelihood that people help others in a state of emergency.[7]

The prosecution, or rather non-prosecution, of piracy is instructive in this respect. Under international law, every state has the right to arrest and prosecute pirates under the universality principle because such pirates are considered to be *hostes humani generis*; they threaten the community of states at large. In practice, however, universal jurisdiction over piracy is hardly exercised. Even when patrolling vessels, such as those off the coast of Somalia, come across pirates and arrest them, they are likely not to prosecute them, in particular if no merchant vessel flying the flag of the intervening state has been attacked or threatened with attack. Even when a national interest is involved, patrolling vessels are likely either to release pirates after catching them, or turn them over to another state—notably Kenya, which operates anti-piracy courts sponsored by the international community—rather than to their own prosecutorial authorities. This may be so for a variety of reasons. Bystander states may not have national laws allowing for piracy prosecution.[8] If they have them, prosecution in the arresting state's own courts may be far too costly, and unsuccessful prosecution may well cause the pirate to seek asylum in the bystander state which, by virtue of the principle of *non-refoulement*, may be prevented from sending him back to his home state.[9] Possibly most importantly, states may just reason that it does not increase national welfare—rather on the contrary—to prosecute a foreign pirate who has hijacked a foreign ship with foreign crew.[10] Kontorovich and Art have succinctly put this conundrum as follows: 'perhaps the most obvious reason for the lack of universal jurisdiction is the fact that it is universal'.[11] Or as Kontorovich argued

[7] See for early work in social psychology: John M Darley and Bibb Latané, 'Bystander Intervention in Emergencies: Diffusion of Responsibility' (1968) 8 JPSP 377; Mark R Leary and Donelson R Forsyth 'Attributions of Responsibility for Collective Endeavors' (1987) 8 RPSP 167. See for more recent work: Karin E Tobin and others, 'Calling Emergency Medical Services During Drug Overdose: An Examination of Individual, Social and Setting Correlates' (2005) 100 Addiction 397; Christian Vaillancourt and others, 'Understanding and Improving Low Bystander CPR Rates: A Systematic Review of the Literature' (2008) 10 JCAEP 51; Karl H Teigen and Wibecke Brun, 'Responsibility is Divisible by Two, but not by Three or Four: Judgments of Responsibility in Dyads and Groups' (2011) 29 SC 15. See, however, for recently voiced doubts over the bystander effect: R Philpot and others, 'Would I be helped? Cross-national CCTV footage shows that intervention is the norm in public conflict' (2008) AP DOI:10.1037/amp0000469 (accessed 5 December 2019).

[8] Yvonne Dutton, 'Maritime Piracy and the Impunity Gap: Insufficient National Laws or a Lack of Political Will?' (2011) 86 TLR 1111, 1120.

[9] Emmanuel Obuah, 'Outsourcing the Prosecution of Somali Pirates to Kenya: A Failure of International Law, or a Response to Domestic Politics of States?' (2012) 21 ASR 40, 50.

[10] Milena Sterio, 'Piracy off the Coast of Somalia: The Argument for Piracy Prosecutions in the National Courts of Kenya, The Seychelles, and Mauritius' (2012) 4 ALF 104, 111 (wondering why the United Kingdom should pay for the exercise of universal jurisdiction on behalf of a Liberian vessel owned by a Dutch corporation and employing a Philippine crew).

[11] Eugene Kontorovich and Steven E Art, 'An Empirical Examination of Universal Jurisdiction for Pirates' (2010) 104 AJIL 436, 453. From these authors' research it transpires that between 1998 and 2009,

in another publication: in economic terms, universal jurisdiction transforms claims 'into a global common resource, preventing several ownership', which in turn prevents them from being 'put to their social highest valued use', thus ultimately decreasing global welfare.[12] In other words, universal jurisdiction may lead states to shirk their cosmopolitan responsibilities: their reasoning that other states should also bear the enforcement burden may ultimately yield the outcome that no state takes action.[13]

Relying on 'nexus', instead, could precisely serve as an incentive for states to assume their responsibility to intervene selflessly. Indeed, the immediacy of the encounter produced by the nexus of an act, actor, or situation with the state may bring to its attention how this jeopardizes common as well as local interests and create opportunities for remedial action through the exercise of jurisdiction.[14] At the same time, from a positivist international law perspective, 'nexus' allows states to err on the safe side of jurisdictional caution: jurisdictional claims that are grounded on a nexus with the state, in particular a territorial nexus, are much more likely to pass the legality test. In addition, they provide some legal certainty to individuals and operators who can anticipate falling within the ambit of the law if their conduct has a nexus with the state.[15]

Accordingly, from an enforcement point of view, the law of jurisdiction may have to be geared towards facilitating nexus-based jurisdiction. Moreover, to ensure that the incentive remains for 'nexus states' to exercise their jurisdiction, bystander states—which have no or only a weak nexus to the case—may perhaps want to refrain from exercising jurisdiction. Indeed, the availability of remedies elsewhere may discourage nexus states from assuming their own jurisdiction. In the long run, this may have a detrimental impact on common interests, which nexus states are normally better placed to protect, and more. Hence, one could have some sympathy with the argument of the United Kingdom and the Netherlands, made in their *amicus curiae* brief in the *Kiobel* litigation arising under the US Alien Tort Statute (ATS) before the US Supreme Court, that the exercise of universal civil jurisdiction by a bystander state (in this case the United States) would give states with a nexus to the case 'reason to downplay and even ignore their own international

1,158 pirate attacks on the high seas were reported. Only seventeen prosecutions were brought under the principle of such universal jurisdiction, even though all those attacks were subject to universality.').

[12] Eugene Kontorovich, 'Inefficiency of Universal Jurisdiction' (2008) U Ill L Rev 389, 395, arguing in respect of universal jurisdiction over piracy.

[13] See also Frédéric Mégret, 'The "Elephant in the Room" in Debates about Universal Jurisdiction: Diasporas, Duties of Hospitality, and the Constitution of the Political' (2015) 6 TLT 89, 95.

[14] See on the ethics of encounter: Emmanuel Levinas, *Totalité et Infini: Essai sur l'Extériorité* (The Hague Martinus Nijhoff 1961).

[15] cf An Hertogen, 'Letting *Lotus* Bloom' (2015) 26 EJIL 901, 919 ('The territorial allocation of prescriptive jurisdiction provides certainty to individuals, who do not need to determine the nationality of those with whom they interact to determine which legal system governs their interaction.'). Hertogen argues against an overly strict interpretation of territoriality, however. ibid, at 920.

human rights law obligations' and that '[t]hey will also not come under pressure to provide a remedy, and indeed prevent abuses, if plaintiffs have recourse to redress elsewhere'.[16] Possibly swayed by these arguments, the Court eventually went on to reject a broad jurisdictional construction of the ATS.[17] Regardless of the technicalities, this decision may partly have been informed by the concern that US courts may become global human rights enforcers undercutting the responsibility of other states. Indeed, holding that it was not the duty of the United States to be the '*custos morum* of the entire world', the Court implied that the US legal system should not spend precious judicial resources that other, more closely connected, free-riding states may be unwilling to spend.[18] The same concern comes to the force in the earlier US Supreme Court decision in *Empagran* (2004), in which the Court dismissed a claim brought by foreign victims of a worldwide vitamins cartel in respect of foreign harm.[19] Arguably, the Court feared that opening up US courts to such a claim would come down to the United States bearing the international antitrust enforcement burden alone and becoming the 'global antitrust cop', thereby undermining the jurisdiction of nexus states.[20]

Thus, the argument is that in order to prevent free-riding by more closely connected states and to forestall an eventual overall decrease in state willingness to act, it may be advisable to allocate jurisdiction to states with a convincing nexus to a situation, and for more loosely connected states to refrain from exercising their 'cosmopolitan' jurisdiction. This nexus-based allocation principle prevents 'institutional displacement', that is the long-term substitution of local institutions by bystander state institutions.[21] It encourages regulatory

[16] Supplemental Brief of the Governments of the Kingdom of the Netherlands and the United Kingdom of Great Britain and Northern Ireland as *Amici Curiae* in Support of Neither Party, *Kiobel v Royal Dutch Petroleum Co* 133 S Ct 1659 (2013) (No 10-1491), available at <www.americanbar.org/content/dam/aba/publications/supreme_court_preview/briefs/10-1491_neutralamcunetherlands-uk-greatbritain-andirelandgovs. authcheckdam.pdf> (accessed 5 December 2019) 25.

[17] *Kiobel v Royal Dutch Petroleum Co 133 S Ct 1659* (2013) (applying the presumption against extraterritoriality).

[18] *Kiobel* (n 17) 1668. See also ibid 1669 (quoting *Morrison v Nat'l Austl Bank Ltd.*, 130 S Ct 2869, 2878 (2010) (citing the 'presumption that United States law governs domestically but does not rule the world').

[19] *F. Hoffmann-LaRoche Ltd. v Empagran S.A.*, 542 US 155 (2004) 159–65.

[20] Hannah L Buxbaum, 'National Jurisdiction and Global Business Networks' (2010) 17 IJGLS 165, 175 ('[T]he court retreated into its "natural" space of engagement. It did not really engage the substance of the plaintiffs' argument regarding global under-deterrence.'). Formally speaking, the Court declined to exercise jurisdiction over separate foreign antitrust harm, on the ground that the non-economic principle of non-intervention in the affairs of foreign states carried more weight. However, as there was little evidence of foreign nations taking issue with the US exercise of jurisdiction in the case, the Court in fact feared that foreign plaintiffs would flock to US courts if the Court would construe the geographical ambit of US antitrust law too widely.

[21] See regarding the exercise of bystander state jurisdiction over foreign corrupt practices: Kevin E Davis, 'Why Does the United States Regulate Foreign Bribery: Moralism, Self-Interest or Altruism?' (2012) 67 NASAL 497, 508 ('second concern about using the FCPA to combat corruption in foreign countries . . . is that reliance on U.S. institutions as substitutes for local anti-corruption institutions will, over time, inhibit the development of the local institutions').

and democratic learning-by-doing by nexus states,[22] boosts local ownership, and—as far as localized human rights abuses are concerned—facilitates transnational justice efforts steered by the directly affected society rather than by distant strangers.[23]

Allocating jurisdiction to states with a (strong) nexus, and disavowing the jurisdiction of *prima facie* less concerned third states, along the lines sketched above, sounds attractive. Unfortunately, however, it falls short in practice. This is because the law of jurisdiction is largely based on discretionary authority rather than obligation.[24] Consequently, jurisdictional deference by one state does not always result in the assumption of jurisdiction by another state, even if the facts call for regulatory intervention of some sort. Abstract concerns over free-riding behaviour flowing from all too ready selfless intervention by bystander states may in fact result in the absence of *any* state exercising jurisdiction, to the detriment of the common interest. *Kiobel* and *Empagran* demonstrate this well. The Court's declining of jurisdiction in *Empagran* left the victims of the vitamins cartel in the cold because they could not recover their damages anywhere as their local courts were inaccessible.[25] From a global justice perspective, this outcome may appear satisfactory. Instead, the Court could have heeded the argument advanced in an *amicus* brief drafted by two economists who called on the Court to take into account global deterrence in US antitrust litigation and thus to provide a remedy for antitrust harm suffered in foreign transactions.[26] Also, *Kiobel* shows that concerns over foreign nations free-riding on the efforts of one state risks leaving individual plaintiffs without any remedies.[27] The aforementioned *amicus* brief of the United Kingdom and the Netherlands in fact appears to be a classic example of states' own narrowly-conceived national economic interests masquerading as global welfare arguments. Both states obviously wished to shield Shell, an Anglo-Dutch

[22] ibid 510, regarding the prosecution of foreign corrupt practices by the United States as bystander state ('Another possibility is that the performance gap between local and U.S. institutions will be so great that neither the effects of "voice" nor learning-by-doing can close the gap.').

[23] cf Hilly Moodrick-Even Khen, 'Revisiting Universal Jurisdiction: The Application of the Complementarity Principle by National Courts and Implications for Ex-Post Justice in the Syrian Civil War' (2015) 30 EILR 261.

[24] See, however, on the shift from permission to duty: Alex Mills, 'Rethinking Jurisdiction in International Law' (2014) 84 BYBIL 187.

[25] Ralf Michaels, 'Global Problems in Domestic Courts' in Sam Muller and others (eds), *The Law of the Future and the Future of the Law* (Torkel Opsahl Academic EPublisher 2011).

[26] Brief of *Amici Curiae* Economists JE Stiglitz and PR Orszag in Support of Respondents, *F. Hoffmann-LaRoche v Empagran S.A.*, 542 US 155 (2004) (No 03-724).

[27] But see the civil case brought in early 2017 by Esther Kiobel against Shell in the Netherlands. See 'Nigeriaanse activiste daagt Shell voor rechter in Nederland' Het Financieele Dagblad (13 January 2017) https://fd.nl/ondernemen/1182792/nigeriaanse-activiste-daagt-shell-voor-rechter-in-nederland (accessed 5 December 2019). The Dutch case is, however, not exactly the same as the case brought in the United States. The latter concerned Shell's aiding and abetting of the Nigerian government's crushing of Ogoni resistance to oil development in the Niger River Delta, whereas the former only concerns Shell's complicity in the killing of Barinem Kiobel in 1995.

corporation, from liability in US courts rather than to allocate responsibility among states. US litigation under the universality principle did not diminish the opportunities or incentives for the United Kingdom or the Netherlands to assume their own legal responsibility with respect to Shell's activities in Nigeria, but both states arguably never had an interest in doing so in the first place.[28] On the contrary, litigation in bystander state courts could set in motion processes of broader social and legal reform in the more closely connected states by exposing patterns of misconduct. For instance, the 'Pinochet effect' in Latin America—the impact of the Spanish indictment, under the universality principle, of the former Chilean dictator on criminal proceedings against torturers in Chile and elsewhere in South America—has been well-documented.[29] Thus, the initial exercise of cosmopolitan jurisdiction, rather than encouraging free-riding, may *prevent* future free-riding in that strengthened local jurisdictional capacity reduces reliance on foreign jurisdiction. For this reason, when the exercise of 'local' jurisdiction is unlikely, bystander states showing only a weaker nexus may want to give 'temporary' protection with a view to spurring other states into action in the global interest. This could be defined as positive jurisdictional subsidiarity or complementarity,[30] or contingent unilateralism.[31]

[28] Uta Kohl, 'Corporate Human Rights Accountability: The Objections of Western Governments to the Alien Tort Statute' (2014) 63 ICLQ 665, 684, ('States that have a connection with the dispute based on the nationality of the parent company (in *Kiobel, the UK and the Netherlands*) also have no real interest in holding the parent accountable for its or its subsidiary's behaviour abroad which injures people to whom they are not politically accountable.').

[29] Naomi Roht-Arriaza, *The Pinochet Effect: Transnational Justice in the Age of Human Rights* (University of Pennsylvania Press 2006). See on the impact of Spanish universal jurisdiction on proceedings in Guatemala: Amy Ross, 'The Ríos Montt Case and Universal Jurisdiction' (2016) 18 JGR 361. See on the impact of universal jurisdiction on proceedings in Rwanda: Leila Sadat, 'Transjudicial Dialogue and the Rwandan Genocide: Aspects of Antagonism and Complementarity' (2009) 22 LJIL 543. Note that cases have also been filed in Latin America under the universality principle, notably in Argentina, to bring pressure to bear on Spain to open investigations into crimes committed by the Franco regime—a sort of reverse Pinochet effect. See Maximo Langer and Mackenzie Eason, 'The Quiet Expansion of Universal Jurisdiction' 24–25 (ResearchGate March 2019, forthcoming EJIL 2020). See ibid, 27, for the effects of this investigation in Spain (citing the uncovering of a series of mass graves in Spain).

[30] See on subsidiarity and universal jurisdiction: Cedric Ryngaert, 'Universal Jurisdiction over International Crimes and Gross Human Rights Violations: The Role of the Principle of Subsidiarity' in Guliana Ziccardi Capaldo (ed) *The Global Community. Yearbook of International Law and Jurisprudence* (OUP 2015) 275. Note that the bystander state does not necessarily have the weaker nexus or interest than the territorial or national state. In this case, reliance on subsidiarity may make little sense. For instance, Mégret has criticized the subsidiarity principle on the ground that there is no unproblematic metric to compare whether prosecution of an international criminal in the territorial state is more important than in the 'bystander' state, especially not when the alleged criminal has fled to the bystander state where survivors of his crimes are also present. Mégret (n 13) 105. Mégret's view should however not be viewed as an indictment of the subsidiarity principle, as the latter should arguably only counsel deference to the territorial or national state in case that state also has the stronger nexus to the situation, in the sense of suffering the most 'deviance from expressed norms of legal behaviour'. See on the latter Danielle Ireland-Piper, 'Extraterritorial Criminal Jurisdiction and the Cosmopolitan: A Double-Edged Sword' (2017), paper on file with the author, 13.

[31] Joanne Scott and Lavanya Rajamani, 'EU Climate Change Unilateralism' (2012) 23 EJIL 469.

3.2 Cosmopolitan Jurisdiction and the National Interest

In section 3.1, two arguments were made. It was submitted that states are, realistically speaking, more likely to exercise jurisdiction in the global interest when they have a nexus to the situation at hand. At the same time, a warning was sounded not to draw the normative inference that the presence of a strong nexus is a necessary condition for the legitimate exercise of jurisdiction. Where global and individual justice are jeopardized, bystander states with only a weak nexus should be allowed to exercise complementary or subsidiary jurisdiction. However, for the actual exercise of jurisdiction, whether or not a nexus is present, is ultimately of lesser relevance than the presence of a national interest or a national goal.[32] The realist paradigm indeed has it that states will follow a particular course of conduct if they perceive such a course to be in their—or their constituents'—*interest*, however defined.[33] Realist approaches normally limit the space for cosmopolitan action because such action by bystander states is not likely to further the latter's interests. The outcomes in the aforementioned *Kiobel* and *Empagran*, for instance, could be explained by a concern that a more cosmopolitan jurisdictional outlook may diminish, or at least not further 'the national interest'.[34] These cases are concrete instantiations of a more general and rather well-entrenched jurisdictional realism that is distrustful of cosmopolitanism on the ground that rulers of states are beholden to their voters, who may punish them in case they prioritize the interests of others over theirs. In theory, state rulers will thus be forced to abandon a cosmopolitan discourse, or when using it, do so strategically to advance their voters' interests. Even when harbouring cosmopolitan sentiments, states may be unwilling to shoulder the cosmopolitan burden alone. Exercising unilateral 'selfless' jurisdiction may, as argued earlier, cause other states to free-ride on the former's efforts, or invite protest against jurisdictional overreach as the case may be, thereby inducing states in turn to scale back their efforts. This is a classic collective action problem.

A perception that the national interest is not at stake,[35] fear of upsetting foreign nations and thus inviting retaliatory action,[36] or concerns over judicial

[32] *Eg* Michael Farbiarz, 'Extraterritorial Criminal Jurisdiction' (2016) 114 Mich L Rev 507, 508. ('Over and over during the past few decades, the federal government has launched ambitious international prosecutions in the service of *U.S. national security goals*.') (emphasis added).

[33] In the most general sense, a national interest could be defined as the advantage or benefit enjoyed by a state (nation), or, alternatively as a common concern of a territorially delimited polity (state). cf *Oxford English Dictionary* (online), definition of 'interest'.

[34] Kohl (n 28) (arguing that 'unconnected States have no obvious economic or political interest in monitoring these obligations towards foreign citizens to whom they are not legally or politically accountable').

[35] Note that, rather exceptionally, outside a cosmopolitan context, even when a national interest is at stake and a jurisdictional grant is apparent, courts may for technical jurisdictional reasons not exercise jurisdiction. See *eg* Lindsay Farmer, 'Territorial Jurisdiction and Criminalization' (2013) 63 UTLJ 225, 226–27.

[36] It is observed that not exercising (extraterritorial) jurisdiction might under certain circumstances also lead to foreign protest. See *eg* the case of *R v Bernard*, [1858] 1 F & F 240, in which an English court acquitted a man involved in a plot on the life of Napoleon III for reasons of uncertainty as to whether

complications,[37] costs and wasting scarce national resources, all militate against cosmopolitan action. Research into the actual exercise of universal criminal jurisdiction, for instance, has shown that such jurisdiction is normally only exercised when the stakes are not very high, for example over lower-ranking perpetrators, in which case the risk of upsetting foreign nations is limited.[38] In addition, resource and capacity problems have undoubtedly informed decisions not to prosecute[39] because domestic resources are more likely to be spent to address domestic problems. In the end, prosecutors are unlikely to take action in the global interest when there is not at least a national interest at stake. This is illustrated by a statement of the chief prosecutor of Hamburg in Germany regarding the prosecution of piracy: '[T]he German judicial system cannot, and should not, act as World Police. Active prosecution measures will only be initiated if the German State has a particular, well-defined interest.'[40] In civil cases, the courts have also often construed broad jurisdictional mandates restrictively, and ultimately emphasized the state's national interest. The vagaries of the ATS illustrate this well. On its face, this US statute is a cosmopolitan's dream in that it appears to confer universal tort jurisdiction over US federal courts in respect of violations of international law, and after its 'rediscovery' in 1980, some US courts were indeed willing to offer a remedy to foreign victims in respect of foreign harm committed by foreign perpetrators.[41] However, ultimately, in *Kiobel*, the Supreme Court limited the jurisdictional scope of the ATS to claims 'touching and concerning' the United States 'with sufficient force'.[42] Even the minority judges in *Kiobel* were of the view that the ATS should be interpreted as 'providing jurisdiction only where distinct American interests are at issue'.[43]

the man had committed a crime under English law. The acquittal led to French protests. Case cited in Farmer (n 35).

[37] *Eg* Helen L Trouille, 'France, Universal Jurisdiction and Rwandan *génocidaires*: The *Simbikangwa* Trial' (2016) 14 JICJ 195, 214. Note that in that very case, universal jurisdiction *was* exercised, and the accused was convicted.

[38] Maximo Langer, 'The Diplomacy of Universal Jurisdiction: The Political Branches and the Transnational Prosecution of International Crimes' (2011) 105 AJIL 1.

[39] *Eg* when the South African Police Service considered itself unable to initiate an investigation into torture committed in Zimbabwe, citing practical problems in particular. Republic of South Africa Constitutional Court, *National Commissioner of The South African Police Service v Southern African Human Rights Litigation Centre and Another* (CCT 02/14) [2014] ZACC 30; 2015 (1) SA 315 (CC); 2015 (1) SACR 255 (CC) (30 October 2014), paras 15, 64.

[40] Cited in Kontorovich and Art (n 11) 451. See also Nico Krisch, 'The Decay of Consent: International Law in an Age of Global Public Goods' (2014) 108 AJIL 1, 28 ('US courts do not see their role as solving problems of a global nature as such.').

[41] See *eg Filártiga v Peña-Irala* 630 F 2d 876 (2nd Cir 1980); *Kadic v Karadzic* 70 F 3d 232 (2nd Cir 1995).

[42] *Kiobel v Royal Dutch Petroleum Co* (n 17) 1669 ('[E]ven where the claims touch and concern the territory of the United States, they must do so with sufficient force to displace the presumption against extraterritorial application.').

[43] *Kiobel v Royal Dutch Petroleum Co* (n 17) 1674. See also Jonathan Hafetz, 'Human Rights Litigation and the National Interest: *Kiobel's* Application of the Presumption against Extraterritoriality to the Alien Tort Statute' (2013) 28 MJILT 107.

Nevertheless, to the extent that global values are seen as reflecting domestic values, institutions, and interests, the former may actually strengthen the latter and thus open up a space for cosmopolitan action. In international relations, this is termed 'second image reversed'.[44] When states have had a strong influence on the making of international law, the odds of domestic 'cosmopolitan' enforcement of international law in such states may be higher.[45] And even where states and their officials consider the 'national interest' to be their guiding light, they need not understand this as a parochial concept per se at loggerheads with cosmopolitan action. For instance, the aforementioned minority judges in *Kiobel* were in favour of the exercise of jurisdiction in case the defendant's conduct substantially and adversely affects an important US national interest, including a distinct interest in preventing the United States from becoming a safe harbour (free of civil as well as criminal liability) for a torturer or other common enemy of mankind.[46] As international criminals are unlikely to repeat their crimes on US soil in the absence of a context propitious to their commission, this scenario actually has cosmopolitan overtones. It is arguably in the interest of every state, including the United States, to see to it that justice is done regarding international crimes because such crimes affect the international community and all its constituent members.[47] A similar view can be found in the 2014 decision of the South African Constitutional Court in the *Zimbabwe* case, in which it ruled that '[g]iven the international and heinous nature of the crime of torture, South Africa has a substantial connection to it'.[48] This appears to be selfless jurisdictional intervention in its purest form: international crimes are considered as having a nexus with every state, and every community interest is considered as a national interest.[49] The South African decision is a fine example of how unconnected states, in spite

[44] Peter Gourevitch, 'The Second Image Reversed: The international Sources of Domestic Politics' (1978) 32 Int'l Org 881. This theory holds that domestic structures and institutions are the *consequences* of states' positions of relative power in international politics.

[45] See Lisa Conant, 'Whose Agents? The Interpretation of International Law in Domestic Courts', in Jeffrey L Dunoff and Mark A Pollack (eds), *Interdisciplinary Perspectives on International Law and International Relations: The State of the Art* (CUP 2012) 411–12.

[46] *Kiobel v Royal Dutch Petroleum Co* (n 17) 1674 (going on to find, however, that the impugned conduct and the parties did not have a sufficient nexus with the United States under this test).

[47] Compare ibid, 1675 (writing that in the *Filartiga* decision, '[j]urisdiction was deemed proper because the defendant's alleged conduct violated a well-established international law norm, and the suit vindicated our Nation's interest in not providing a safe harbor, free of damages claims, for those defendants who commit such conduct').

[48] *National Commissioner of The South African Police Service* (n 39) para 78 (adding that, hence, '[a]n investigation within the South African territory does not offend against the principle of non-intervention').

[49] See also Constitutional Court of Spain, Sentencia 140/2018, 20 December 2018 (BOE núm. 22, de 25 de enero de 2019), ECLI:ES:TC:2018:140, 29. However, the Court held that while all states have an interest in such prosecution each state determines the specific formula with which to apply such principle, in order to avoid concurrent jurisdiction and conflicts. See Nicolás Zambrano-Tevár, 'Ruling of the Spanish Constitutional Court Legitimising Restrictions on Universal Criminal Jurisdiction' (EJIL:Talk!, 6 February 2019) https://www.ejiltalk.org/ruling-of-the-spanish-constitutional-court-legitimising-restrictions-on-universal-criminal-jurisdiction/ (accessed 5 December 2019).

of realist considerations militating *against* jurisdictional cosmopolitanism, *have* assumed their responsibility, especially by exercising universal jurisdiction over gross human rights violations.[50] Or as Uta Kohl has observed, bystander states may want to act in such a cosmopolitan fashion 'perhaps simply because it is the right thing to do'.[51]

This idea that states should exercise universal jurisdiction because it is morally appropriate may be compelling. However, states exercising 'cosmopolitan' jurisdiction rarely do so only because it is the right thing to do, but rather because it is—also—in their national interest.[52] Below, this is illustrated by how universal criminal jurisdiction (section 3.3) and jurisdiction in regulatory matters (section 3.4) is normally exercised. The analysis does not limit itself to observing empirical patterns, however. It is also argued that sound reasoning based on national interest may be normatively preferable over abstract cosmopolitanism because it provides reasons for action that strengthen a polity's identity and values.

3.2.1 Universal criminal jurisdiction: public prosecutors and the national interest

A vast pool of cases potentially qualify for universal jurisdiction. However, a specific pattern may be discerned in the kind of cases that are *actually* brought. Such cases, while formally brought by an independent public prosecutor, typically result from migration patterns[53] and from pressure brought to bear on prosecutors by victim communities that have sought refuge in a bystander state. Thus, Frédéric Mégret has pointed out that universal jurisdiction 'is almost never exercised in a pure supranationalist void by states "sacrificing themselves" for the global public good', but instead 'almost always follows existing patterns of transnational interaction between states'; in particular 'victim diasporas' are 'the crucial variable in understanding the evolving practice of [universal jurisdiction] as it actually unfolds in reality'.[54] The cases brought in Spain under the universality principle against alleged human rights offenders from Latin America, or cases brought in

[50] In the South African case, the Constitutional Court, after confirming the cosmopolitan connection of the case with South Africa, eventually rejected the practical problems cited by the police, held that there *was* a reasonable possibility that the police would gather evidence that may satisfy the elements of the crime of torture, and subsequently ordered the police to investigate the complaint. In so doing, it confirmed that practical difficulties should not be used as an excuse for a failure to act in the global interest. *National Commissioner of The South African Police Service* (n 39).

[51] Kohl (n 28) 685.

[52] See also Pierik and Werner (n 1) 286–87 (notions of cosmopolitan justice may foster the pursuit of what states perceive to be in their interest, drawing particular attention to the mixture of national security with imperial agendas).

[53] Langer and Eason (n 29) 42–44, who go on to call on states not to limit universal jurisdiction proceedings to perpetrators who have sought refuge in the forum state).

[54] Mégret (n 13) 99.

Belgium or France against offenders from Rwanda, could thus be better comprehended contextually.[55]

This empirical reality of universal jurisdiction being exercised at the behest of victim diasporas can, according to Mégret, even be considered as normatively defensible to the extent that it becomes an 'integral part of the normal process of welcoming refugees' and contributes to the strengthening of a state's multicultural society, in which newcomers' citizenship is a function of the host state demonstrating empathy and solidarity.[56] Thus, by exercising universal jurisdiction, states may not (just) show international solidarity but also, and more so in fact, vindicate their own national interest in building a stable society in which immigrants feel welcome and integrated.

Integrating immigrants from diasporas is, however, only one national interest that can be served by the exercise of universal jurisdiction. Arguably, *any* national interest that is grounded in political community and identity could qualify as an empirical trigger for the exercise of jurisdiction based on the common interest as well as a normative reason for action. Thus, as Itamar Mann has noted, the Jerusalem District Court in *Eichmann*, when it established its universal jurisdiction, acted not only as a 'Court of Humanity', vindicating the interests of the international community pursuant to the universality principle, but also as a 'Court of Violence', exercising the state's (Israel's) right to punish Eichmann on the grounds of the 'special connection the State of Israel has with such crimes, seeing that the People of Israel—the Jewish People—constituted the target and the victim of most of the crimes in question'.[57]

The question then arises as to what national political interests *appropriately* trigger the exercise of universal jurisdiction?[58] Mann refrains from giving an all-encompassing definition of 'appropriateness'. Still, the examples which he gives

[55] In the French case of *Munyeshyaka*, for instance, the accused—who was charged for his involvement in the 1994 Rwandan genocide—had sought refuge in France, where some of his victims also lived. On that ground, Sadat considered the exercise of universal jurisdiction to be not 'exorbitant'. See Sadat (n 29) 558 (also noting that the presence requirement, used to trigger universal jurisdiction in France, 'served to insulate France from some of the political controversies surrounding the use of universal jurisdiction in cases with fewer connections to the forum'). Munyeshyaka was acquitted in 2014. For a description of the case, see 'Wenceslas Munyeshyaka' (Trial International, 7 May 2018) https://trialinternational.org/latest-post/wenceslas-munyeshyaka/ (accessed 5 December 2019). The presence of a victim diaspora (in the case of Rwandan victims of genocide present in France organized as the *Collectif des Parties Civiles pour le Rwanda*) is not the only explanatory variable for the exercise of universal jurisdiction in a particular case, however. It may happen that state authorities discover that a person may have committed international crimes in the context of investigations into another crime. The French case of *Simbikangwa* is instructive in this respect. This Rwandan genocide suspect had fled to the French Indian Ocean island of Mayotte, where his true identity was revealed in the context of an investigation into false identity documents. See Trouille (n 37) 196.

[56] Mégret (n 13) 108–14, *eg* stating at p 111 that 'the criminal law becomes a way of constituting the political'. From this perspective, the exercise of universal criminal jurisdiction can be regarded as *benefiting* the national interest. ibid, 114 ('the exercise of UJ should be seen not as a net liability for the state').

[57] Cited in Itamar Mann, 'The Dual Foundation of Universal Jurisdiction: Towards a Jurisprudence for the "Court of Critique"' (2010) 1 TLT 485, 503.

[58] ibid, 517.

of appropriate and inappropriate interests undergirding actual prosecutions give some guidance. Thus, Kenyan prosecutors may be justified in prosecuting Somali pirates under the universality principle insofar as piracy adversely affects Kenya's access to waterways. In contrast, insofar as these prosecutions may have been outsourced by Western states unwilling to shoulder the jurisdictional burden and instead paying other bystander states to prosecute the pirates on the basis of universal jurisdiction, questions as to the appropriateness of these prosecutions can be raised.[59] Mann voices similar concerns regarding the appropriateness of Belgium's issuance of a warrant for the arrest of then Minister of Foreign Affairs of the Democratic Republic of the Congo Yerodia (2000) on charges of incitement to genocide, a crime amenable to universal jurisdiction, even *in absentia* pursuant to Belgian law applicable at the time (a warrant which sparked the *Arrest Warrant* case before the International Court of Justice (ICJ)). Echoing the individual opinion of ICJ Judge Bula-Bula in the *Arrest Warrant* case,[60] as well as David Luban's writings on crimes against humanity,[61] Mann suggests that Belgium's prosecution should be precluded because of Belgium's 'bloody history' as the former colonial power in the Congo.[62] That former colonizers have no 'moral right' to exercise universal criminal jurisdiction over former colonies has also informed the African Union's position on universal jurisdiction[63] as well as on the International Criminal Court (ICC) for that matter.[64]

The latter position is understandable from the perspective of (a variation of) the clean hands doctrine.[65] Nonetheless, without wanting to press the argument too far, it is debatable whether Western states should perforce be precluded from sitting in judgment of heinous crimes committed in their former colonies, in light of transgressions committed at the time. Precluding Western states' reliance on universality may in fact foreclose valuable opportunities for the exercise of universal jurisdiction, as large diaspora communities—the actors precisely triggering universal jurisdiction—live on the territory of their former colonial masters. In fact, it could be argued that precisely *because* Western states have historically oppressed colonial peoples, with all the attendant consequences such as a legacy of

[59] ibid, 519.

[60] *Case Concerning the Arrest Warrant of 11 April 2000 (DRC v Belgium)* (judgement) [2002] ICJ Rep 3, individual opinion Judge Bula-Bula. Note that the Court itself did not address the legality or appropriateness of the exercise of universal jurisdiction, limiting itself to the question of the international immunity *ratione personae* of an incumbent Minister of Foreign Affairs.

[61] David Luban, 'A Theory of Crimes Against Humanity' (2004) 29 YJIL 85.

[62] Mann (n 57) 518.

[63] African Union Model Law on Universal Jurisdiction: An African Response to Western Prosecutions based on the Universality Principle (2012), available at http://www.ejiltalk.org/wp-content/uploads/2012/08/AU-draft-model-law-UJ-May-2012.pdf (accessed on 5 December 2019).

[64] See African Union Withdrawal Strategy Document (12 January 2017) available at https://www.hrw.org/sites/default/files/supporting_resources/icc_withdrawal_strategy_jan._2017.pdf (calling for mass withdrawal from the ICC).

[65] *Diversion of Water from the River Meuse (Netherlands v Belgium)* [1937] PCIJ (ser A/B) No 70, 4, 77.

weak governance and armed conflict, they have a moral interest in atoning for their past sins by assisting their former colonial possessions, including by exercising universal jurisdiction over crimes committed by individuals in the latter. Such prosecutions under the universality principle may not only contribute to the entrenchment of accountability and the rule of law in former colonies. They also serve the purpose of reconstituting the polity of the former colonial oppressor as a polity that no longer defines itself as a victimizer, but as an emancipator of those victimized by the governance gaps left when the colonial power departed.

The change in national identity resulting from former colonial powers' prosecutions under the universality principle could well be defined as an appropriate national interest, and may have informed actual jurisdictional practices. Bystander states' assumption of a role, on the basis of the universality principle, as emancipator of foreign peoples may even be seen as a means to atone for *purely domestic* historical injustices or pave the way for the prosecution (whether domestic or extraterritorial) of these injustices. Spain's universality-informed prosecutions of Latin American human rights violators are instructive in this regard. As Amy Ross has argued, Spain's engagement with the prosecution of the (alleged) genocide in Guatemala can chiefly be explained by 'Spain's own problematic regarding its failure to achieve justice for violations, the lack of accountability for crimes committed under Franco, and the persistence of silence and impunity'.[66] This political background—Spain's failure to come to terms with its own past—was brought into even starker relief after the adoption of a Historical Memory Law in 2007, which failed fully to break official silence on the crimes committed by the Franco regime.[67] In 2008, this emboldened Judge Baltasar Garzon of the Spanish National Court—who had earlier filed a warrant for the arrest of former Chilean head of state Augusto Pinochet—to order the exhumation of mass graves and to charge Franco-era figures, a step which, for that matter, led to his fall from grace.[68] Mass graves was also uncovered in 2018, following Argentina's initiation of investigations into Franco-era crimes under the universality principle, in what has been characterized as an '*extraterritorial backfire effect* against Spain's own attempts to hold universal jurisdiction proceedings for international crimes committed

[66] Ross (n 29) 367.

[67] Ley de Memoria Historica or Ley por la que se reconocen y amplian derechos y se establecen medidas en favor de quienes padecieron persecucion o violencia durante la Guerra Civil, Law 52/2007 of 16 December (Spain).

[68] Ross (n 29) 369–70. Note that Argentine courts, in a remarkable turning of the tables, later invoked the universality principle to investigate the Franco regime's crimes. Associated Press Madrid, 'Human rights abusers in Franco-era Spain could be tried in Argentina' The Guardian (London, 2 November 2014) https://www.theguardian.com/world/2014/nov/02/buenos-aires-spain-franco-argentina (accessed 5 December 2019). An Argentinian investigating judge issued arrest warrants against twenty former officials of the Franco era, but Spanish authorities refused to arrest the suspects, citing the statute of limitations and an amnesty law. Luciana Bertoia, 'Spain rejects Franco-era extradition' Buenos Aires Herald (Buenos Aires, 26 April 2014) http://www.buenosairesherald.com/article/157940/spain-rejects-francoera-extradition (accessed 5 December 2019).

outside its territory, including in Argentina, while not being willing to reckon with its own past of international crimes committed during its own civil war (or "coup") and the ensuing decades of authoritarian rule under Franco'.[69]

While 'appropriateness' could be construed broadly as including the wish to atone, there are obviously assertions of universal jurisdiction that should be considered 'inappropriate'. Inappropriate assertions of jurisdiction lack civic character, for example because a prosecution under the universality principle has been brought with ulterior motives, such as to force regime change or isolate politically inconvenient figures. In that case, while a national interest may be present, the exercise of universal jurisdiction on which it is based may not be considered as appropriate. For instance, French investigating judge Bruguière's issuance in 2006 of warrants for the arrest of nine senior Rwandan officials of the Kagame regime for their alleged role in the shooting down of the Rwandan President's aircraft which triggered the 1994 Rwandan genocide, may be suspect, not just because it was technically based on the *in absentia* exercise of passive personality-based jurisdiction but more importantly because of a lingering suspicion that France was somehow involved in the genocide, or at least did not do enough to prevent it. Because of France's possible complicity in the Rwandan genocide, France may not have come to the prosecution with clean hands, and thus the exercise of jurisdiction in the case might be considered inappropriate.[70]

3.2.2 Jurisdiction and transnational business regulation

Although universal jurisdiction has captured the imagination of activists and legal scholars, examples of it actually being exercised are few and far between.[71] Much more common is the exercise of 'extraterritorial' jurisdiction to level the international playing field and to protect the integrity of domestic business regulation tackling transnational challenges, such as foreign corrupt practices, pollution, or climate change. 'Extraterritorializing' such regulation remedies the disadvantages

[69] Langer and Eason (n 29) 27, 34.

[70] Sadat (n 29) 562. Sadat added, however, that '[o]ne can also make a strong counter-argument to the effect that if one disaggregates the notion of the "state", and a state has an independent judiciary, the unclean-hands doctrine should have no application'. It happened that the French investigating judges succeeding to Bruguière found that the missiles were found to be fired from positions controlled by the Rwandan Armed Forces, not by Kagame's RPF. See Tanguy Berthemet, 'Rwanda: les vérités gênantes des juges français' Le Figaro (12 January 2012) http://www.lefigaro.fr/international/2012/01/12/01003-20120112ARTFIG00456-rwanda-les-verites-genantes-des-juges-francais.php (accessed 5 December 2019). French proceedings regarding the attack were relaunched in 2016, however. See 'Rwanda: l'enquête sur l'attentat contre Habyarimana relancée en France' Le Parisien (Paris, 7 October 2016) http://www.leparisien.fr/international/rwanda-l-enquete-sur-l-attentat-contre-habyarimana-relancee-en-france-07-10-2016-6184261.php (accessed 5 December 2019).

[71] This applies even if the number of universal jurisdiction prosecutions appears to be rising, *eg* in the context of Syrian war criminals fleeing to Europe. Langer and Eason (n 29).

at which domestic operators are put as a result of lax foreign regulation or enforcement, and prevents harmful or criminal activities from being relocated abroad where they would go unpunished and adversely affect global welfare.[72] A state's interest in exercising 'extraterritorial' jurisdiction in such cases is to prevent domestic rule evasion. Such jurisdiction appears to be closely tied to parochial concerns. In Chapter 5, discrete fields of business regulation and litigation will be discussed in great detail. This section discusses, at a more general level, how 'extraterritorial' economic regulation oscillates between serving common interests and national interests.

For a proper understanding of the subject matter, let us start with giving a number of examples. The European Union has attempted to force foreign airlines to surrender emissions allowances under its Aviation Directive so as to treat foreign operators on the same footing as domestic ones for climate regulation purposes, and to prevent 'carbon leakage'.[73] To counter the threat which illegal, unreported, and unsustainable (IUU) fishing poses to legitimate fishing opportunities of their own fishing fleets, states have exercised port state jurisdiction to clamp down on foreign-flagged rogue fishing vessels.[74] And some states vigorously enforce their foreign corrupt practices legislation, arguably in order to safeguard the business opportunities of their own corporations in developing countries, which are at risk of being outcompeted by foreign corporations subject to laxer regulation.[75]

On its face, the exercise of such jurisdiction furthers the interests of national operators and the integrity of domestic regulation, and hence 'the national interest'.

[72] cf Ireland-Piper (n 30) 19–20 (discussing the displacement or substitution of child sex offences to destinations less willing or able to prosecute, and the exercise of extraterritorial criminal jurisdiction to prevent this from occurring); Juscelino F Colares, 'The Extraterritorial Impact of the EU and Australian Carbon-Restricting Reforms' in Larry Kreiser and others (eds), *Market-Based Instruments. National Experiences in Environmental Sustainability* (Edward Elgar, 2013) 106 (discussing the extraterritorial impact of national measures to prevent 'carbon leakage', which would result from a state's limiting emissions regulation to its own territory); Alex Mills, 'Private International Law and EU External Relations: Think Local Act Global, or Think Global Act Local?' (2016) 65 ICLQ 541, 565 (arguing that 'rules governing the conduct of EU Member State companies in developing States might, for example, aim to ensure that those companies are governed by the substantive legal standards which are applicable in their home States, as a means of giving extraterritorial effect to those standards, to protect or constrain the company concerned').

[73] More broadly, EU global leadership in the environmental field may be meant to spur innovation and economic growth as a result of boosting EU green energy industries. cf Michael L Buenger, 'Regulatory Legality: Extraterritorial Rule Across Domestic and International Arenas' in Nikolas M Rajkovic and others (eds), *The Power of Legality: Practices of International Law and their Politics* (CUP 2016) 279.

[74] See Chapter 5.2.

[75] Emily Willborn, 'Extraterritorial Enforcement and Prosecutorial Discretion in the FCPA: A Call for International Prosecutorial Factors' (2013) 22 Min JIL 422. It has even been alleged that a US Department of Justice's 'extraterritorial' FCPA investigation into corrupt acts involving the French company Alstom facilitated (or was perhaps meant to facilitate?) the latter's takeover at a lower price by the US company General Electric. 'How the American takeover of a French national champion became intertwined in a corruption investigation' The Economist (Paris, 17 January 2019) https://www.economist.com/business/2019/01/17/how-the-american-takeover-of-a-french-national-champion-became-intertwined-in-a-corruption-investigation (accessed on 5 December 2019).

However, a concurrent aim, or at the very least a consequence, may be cosmopolitan in nature.[76] In our examples, this is the stabilization of the climate, the protection of global fish stocks, and the safeguarding of the development prospects of communities harmed by foreign corrupt practices. To the extent that these cosmopolitan goals are universally shared, for example because they have been laid down in an international treaty,[77] or because a relatively strong international political consensus has coalesced around them,[78] foreign protest may be muted and, if it occurs, lack legitimacy.

However, even if the goals of domestic laws are *not* unambiguously shared globally, states may tend to extend the reach of their laws in case there are strong economic or moral rationales, backed up by sizable enforcement opportunities, that is, where administrative agencies have sufficient resources at their disposal to supervise compliance and take enforcement action,[79] and where foreign operators have substantial economic connections with, and assets in, the regulating state.[80] Such

[76] See also Laurens Ankersmit and others, 'Diverging EU and WTO Perspectives on Extraterritorial Process Regulation' (2012) 21 Min JIL 14, 31 ('Protecting domestic producers and protecting foreign actors in that case could be said to go hand in hand.'); Buenger (n 73) 285 (discussing regulatory unilateralism and submitting that 'rulemaking becomes a multifarious exercise containing elements of multilateralism and unilateralism, of cooperation and competition, of addressing common concerns and unilaterally leveraging law's force to protect parochial values and interests').

[77] Such as the Port State Measures Agreement, the UN Convention against Corruption, or the Paris Agreement regarding climate change.

[78] *Eg* the isolation of rogue regimes through economic sanctions. The United States has extended its economic sanctions regulations to foreign-based entities on the basis of the US currency denomination of an economic transaction between foreign-based entities, and the fact that, pursuant to banking practices, a US correspondent bank has to clear such a transaction. The US (territorial) nexus for such jurisdiction is very weak, which should cast doubt on its international legality. See Susan Emmenegger, 'Extraterritorial Economic Sanctions and their Foundation in International Law' (2016) 33 Ariz J Int'l & Comp L 631, 656 ('[T]he correspondent account nexus as sufficient basis for jurisdiction is tantamount to accepting a limitless US jurisdiction. There is no basis in international law for such a far-reaching assumption.') (footnote omitted). However, as these sanctions typically concern trade with internationally isolated rogue regimes, *eg* Syria, regarding which other states have also put in place (admittedly less draconic) economic sanctions, international governmental protest has remained relatively absent. See, however, the recent conflict between the European Union and the United States triggered by the reinstatement of US secondary sanctions following US President Trump's denunciation of the Iran Nuclear Accord. This conflict led to the reactivation of the EU Blocking Statute (Regulation 2271/96), aimed at countering the adverse effects of the US sanctions for EU businesses.

[79] See on the institutional dimension of market-based extraterritoriality: Nikhil Kalyanpur and Abraham L Newman, 'Mobilizing Market Power: Jurisdictional Expansion as Economic Statecraft' (2019) 73 Int'l Org 1, 28 (concluding, on the basis of empirical research into the extraterritoriality of financial law, that 'powers will not only need to generate large markets but will also need to create the political institutions that can oversee and, thus, mobilize them'). See on the institutional rationale of the EU's extraterritorial projection of its data legislation: Christopher Kuner, 'The Internet and the Global Reach of EU Law' in Marise Cremona and Joanne Scott, *EU Law Beyond EU Borders: The Extraterritorial Reach of EU Law* (OUP 2019) 145 ('Regulation of the Internet has proved a convenient vehicle through which the EU can assert itself on the world stage without having to take coordinated action geo-politically in a way that would exceed its current capabilities. By focusing on the Internet, the EU has been able to use its strengths in law and regulation, areas where it is a superpower, to make itself heard globally.').

[80] Tonya Putnam, *Courts Without Borders: Law, Politics and US Extraterritoriality* (CUP 2016), 265 ('[T]he conditions that enabled broad-ranging U.S. extraterritorial practices are disappearing. U.S. enforcement capacity is experiencing a long, slow decline tied to the decreasing centrality of the United

jurisdictional assertions appear to be more blatantly parochial. The extraterritorial application of US and EU competition, data protection, intellectual property, and animal welfare laws can serve as examples. US and EU antitrust and competition laws have been applied 'extraterritorially' as soon as (qualified) domestic effects were discernable.[81] Even if no global antitrust regime has been put in place,[82] states have a clear incentive to give extraterritorial effect to such laws because of the adverse territorial impact of the impugned anti-competitive conduct. Also data protection and intellectual property legislation appear to be triggered by states' desire to protect local interests, notably local residents whose rights may be compromised everywhere in the borderless online world. Thus, EU data protection law applies to (foreign) data controllers which offer goods to, or monitor the behaviour of EU residents.[83] In the field of animal welfare then,[84] the incentive for the European Union to externalize its norms has been less the adverse economic effects of particular practices or products on EU territory or for EU residents and rather the implications of such practices and products for EU citizens' deeply held local moral beliefs that only products produced with sufficient respect for animal welfare should be sold in the European Union.[85] 'Parochial' ethical concerns have exercised a strong pull towards the exercise of 'extraterritorial' jurisdiction in this field

As these examples of jurisdictional extension of domestic economic regulation are in the first place triggered by a desire to protect 'local interests' and do not enforce a pre-existing international normative consensus, one may perhaps want to discard them as relevant instances of cosmopolitan, selfless jurisdiction. Still, they come with strong cosmopolitan aspirations, even if coupled with subjective motivations. The trigger for the exercise of such jurisdiction is a state's strong belief in the suitability of its laws to address transnational and foreign-originating threats to values which it holds dear and would prefer other states to espouse in the common

States in the global economy. This has helped to underwrite a growing trend toward U.S. judicial minimalism in U.S. extraterritorial practice.').

[81] *United States v Alcoa*, 148 F 2d 416 (2d Cir 1945); Case C-89/85 DEP *A. Ahlström Osakeyhtiö and others v Commission of the European Communities* [1988] ECLI:EU:C:1988:447; Case C-413/14 P *Intel Corporation Inc. v Commission* [2017] ECLI:EU:C:2017:632.

[82] See for a discussion of jurisdiction in antitrust matters: Cedric Ryngaert, *Jurisdiction over Antitrust Violations in International Law* (Intersentia 2008).

[83] Art 3(2) General Data Protection Regulation.

[84] See on extraterritoriality and animal welfare at length: Charlotte E Blattner, *Extraterritorial Jurisdiction and the Challenges of Globalization* (OUP 2019).

[85] In Case C-424/13 *Zuchtvieh-Export GmbH v Stadt Kempten* [2015] OJ C 205, the Court of Justice of the European Union held that the application of an EU regulation concerning the welfare of animals during transport does not limit itself to road transports within the European Union but also applies to such transports between an EU place of departure and a non-EU place of destination, or *vice versa*, regardless of the rules on animal welfare applicable outside the European Union, and absent an international consensus on appropriate animal welfare standards. Another example in the same field is the ban on trade in seal products in the European Union, which applies to seal products produced in the European Union *and* to imported seal products, a ban which was imposed in the absence of an international consensus on the welfare of seals. See Regulation (EC) No 1007/2009, as amended.

interest.[86] Domestic law which is thus projected abroad may eventually become the global standard of conduct where operators have no other choice than to comply with strict regulation from important states (*eg* because non-elastic markets or the non-divisibility of production processes limit opportunities for reorienting business).[87] In turn, these operators' compliance may pave the way for the approximation of local and foreign law[88] and to a globally uniform legal standard that may initially not have been preferred by a large number of states. Insofar as such jurisdictional assertions have global goals, consequences or overtones, they are also included in the research, *provided that they further at least emerging global values.* Data protection could be considered as such an emerging value, even if it is a contested one.[89] It is examined at greater length in section 5.5.[90]

When the goals or consequences of domestic regulation are global and may perhaps enhance global welfare, at least in the regulating state's view, the *normative* question subsequently arises why such states' jurisdictional assertions should hinge on the presence of a state nexus or interest. This is a rather similar question to the one posed above with respect to universal criminal jurisdiction: if such jurisdiction promotes global justice, is there a logic of appropriateness that justifies conditioning the exercise of cosmopolitan jurisdiction on the presence of an interest or a connection, on some form of 'parochialism'? Assuming that conditioning the exercise of universal jurisdiction on the existence of an (appropriate) national interest may be defensible, is the interest-based exercise of unilateral jurisdiction to protect domestic rule integrity—although with extraterritorial, cosmopolitan aspirations—equally so?

A first observation is that, because such jurisdiction extends domestic law and, unlike universal jurisdiction, does not give effect to a jurisdictional grant based on international law, it is only logical that it should be based on a connection or

86 Farbiarz (n 32) 508–09 (first stating that US extraterritorial criminal jurisdiction is exercised in the US national security interest, but then noting that '[f]orcing the United States to forego major extraterritorial prosecutions harms *global public safety*') (emphasis added).

87 Anu Bradford, 'The Brussels Effect' (2012) 107 NULR 2012.

88 Putnam (n 80) 75 ('Extraterritorial assertiveness on the part of U.S. courts, for example, may make it more costly for foreign governments whose domestically influential nationals are targeted by U.S. litigation to maintain regulatory rules or policies that are strongly at odds with U.S. preferences.').

89 Kuner (n 79) 136–38 (discussing the EU's promotion of EU law as a set of universal values, but citing the 'the risk is that this may lead not to genuine, disinterested universalism, but to "false universalism"', and the risk that a data protection norm is based on a political interest rather than a fundamental legal value).

90 Also in other fields, 'global values' may be emerging even if, as such, positive international law may not yet have proscribed or addressed particular harmful conduct. See *eg* regarding animal welfare: Katie Sykes, 'Sealing Animal Welfare into the GATT Exceptions: The International Dimension of Animal Welfare in WTO Disputes' (2014) 13 WTR 471, 480 ('almost all the world's domestic legal systems—the traditional source of general principles of international law—include some kind of broad legal prohibition on unnecessary cruelty to animals'), relying *inter alia* on Michael Bowman and others, *Lyster's International Wildlife Law* (2nd edn, CUP 2010) 678–82, which posited that a general principle of international law concerning animal welfare exists). Sykes argues that this general principle concerning animal welfare should inform treaty interpretation in the WTO context, in particular in the context of art XX GATT.

interest of the state. After all, exercising jurisdiction without a connection or an interest would, from the point of view of international legal doctrine, violate the principle of non-intervention. International trade law, in any event, has recognized that such jurisdictional assertions could be justified, even if they constitute a barrier to trade, provided that they have a nexus with the state.[91] The World Trade Organization (WTO) Appellate Body has also recognized the principled legality of banning the importation of products of which the extraterritorial production processes go against the moral beliefs of a particular community, in keeping with the public morals exception of Article XX(a) GATT (General Agreement on Tariffs and Trade).[92] In that case, the particular geographic community which has those beliefs arguably serves as the relevant jurisdictional nexus. However, positive law can only give a truncated answer to the question of whether jurisdictional assertions are appropriate in the moral sense of the term. In some domestic legal contexts, such as in the United States, the strictures of international law do not necessarily pose obstacles to, and thus have no strong bearing on, the exercise of jurisdiction.[93] And where international law does in theory pose an obstacle, broad constructions of territoriality will ordinarily allow many, if not most, jurisdictional assertions to pass muster with international law.[94] The justification of states' auto-limitation may then have to be sought elsewhere.

At the most fundamental level, it appears that a society's conditioning of its global ambitions regarding a particular subject matter on the availability of a (territorial) connection is normatively justified on the grounds that this very connection marks the difference between what is inside and what is outside the society, thereby strengthening its particular identity,[95] cohesiveness, and perceptions of safety. More specifically, by exercising unilateral jurisdiction regarding products and services crossing a border—the point of connection between the inside and the outside—such a society reaffirms its beliefs and value systems and differentiates itself from foreign polities harbouring alternative views, while nevertheless

[91] The WTO Appellate Body, while refusing to 'pass upon the question of whether there is an implied jurisdictional limitation in Article XX(g) GATT', *ie* the provision which exceptionally allows the imposition of trade-restrictive measures relating to the conservation of exhaustible natural resources has recognized trade measures that aim to protect extraterritorial natural resources if there is a 'sufficient nexus' with territorial resources. See WTO Appellate Body, *Shrimp-Turtle*, WT/DS58/AB/R (decided 12 October 1998) (adopted 6 November 1998) para 133.

[92] WTO Appellate Body, European Communities—Measures Prohibiting the Importation and ... Importation and Marketing of Seal Products, WT/DS400/DS401/AB/R (22 May 2014).

[93] See *eg* section 204, comment b, Restatement (Fourth) of US Foreign Relations Law, Council Draft No 3 (2016) ('Interference with the sovereign authority of foreign states may be reasonable if such application would serve the legitimate interests of the United States.').

[94] See in the online context: Dan Svantesson, *Solving the Internet Jurisdiction Puzzle* (OUP 2017) chs 2 and 3.

[95] Gareth Davies, for instance, writes that measures making market access conditional upon social norms supplies a 'moral comfort which adds to the quality of life in a way quite comparable to good health or public order', regardless even of whether such measures make a global impact in practice. See Gareth Davies, 'International Trade, Extraterritorial Power, and Global Constitutionalism: A Perspective from Constitutional Pluralism' (2012) 13 Ger LR 1203, 1212 (2012).

also hoping to convince the latter to adopt its own. In short, in the act of exercising connection-based jurisdiction, the society (re-)constitutes itself. Without a tangible connection with a product or service that requires an actual position-taking and regulatory intervention, a society may not be able to define its own identity and expound its views as persuasively.

From a more practical perspective, of course, states' reliance on tangible connections is closely related to the territorial nature of enforcement jurisdiction: states can often only enforce their prescriptions provided that the relevant goods, services, and persons are on their territory, or are about to enter it. Territorial location and border control offer states practical opportunities to effectively bring their laws to bear, and give them extraterritorial effect.

3.3 Independent Courts and the National Interest

So far in this chapter, it has been argued that states are likely to pursue their own interests and thus to be wary of pursuing global interests, unless these can be translated into, or align with (broadly construed) national interests and connections. The emphasis was put on the role of states as (business) regulators and law-enforcers. In this role, states are indeed likely to espouse a relatively narrow interpretation of the national interest, especially when political representatives have been elected on a platform of 'making the country great again', and regulators and prosecutors are beholden to their political overlords. However, these imperatives may apply to a far lesser extent to the *judicial* branch of government. At least in states based on the rule of law, the judiciary is an independent branch of government and neutrally adjudicates cases. Accordingly, courts need not directly explain their actions to voters and thus need not fear punishment when not advancing the national interest. Hence, there is reason to expect that domestic courts harbour more cosmopolitan sentiments than the political branches. In the literature, indeed, the 'modern internationalist' role of domestic courts as enforcers of international law, dispensers of global justice, and independent arbitrators in transnational disputes,[96] has duly been acknowledged.[97] Notably in international business regulation and international crimes prosecutions, domestic courts have assumed a prominent role.[98] It may even be said that domestic courts are the *main* (state) actors when it comes to unilaterally addressing global

[96] Austen L Parrish, 'Reclaiming International Law from Extraterritoriality' (2009) 93 MLR 815, 829–31, also citing constructivist theory, pursuant to which judges have 'internalized' international norms, and apply them without regard to furthering the interests of 'the state'.

[97] Kohl (n 28) 682 (noting that 'the prevailing wind appears to be changing').

[98] Buxbaum (n 20) 166 (referring to the 'much more pervasive involvement of domestic courts in the regulation of international business' and the fact that 'litigants and judges are increasingly conscious of the impact that local litigation has on global regulatory process').

governance issues through the law; or as Michaels put it, unilateral adjudication is 'the predominant legal response to globalization'.[99]

At first sight, domestic courts may appear to be bit players when it comes to exercising jurisdiction in the common interest. After all, courts are tasked simply to apply the law created by state legislatures and regulators. However, all law application may come with law development. When applying the law to cases before them, courts may explore its outer bounds, and possibly construe and even *create* norms in a cosmopolitan manner,[100] without having to fear direct censure by political constituencies. They may ingeniously tap the resources of domestic law to give effect to, or even make cosmopolitan law, sometimes unwittingly perhaps.[101] Formally speaking, they may perhaps only adjudicate the case before them, but eventually they give authoritative interpretations to the law that are valid for all future similarly situated cases, thereby 'developing' the law.[102]

However, there is a whiff of wishful thinking in conceiving of domestic courts as 'selfless interveners'. First, domestic courts may be aware that even in rule of law-based societies, it is entirely legitimate for the political branches to adopt legislation that curbs courts' ambitions, or even to repeal broadly construed statutory authorizations altogether. For instance, domestic courts' progressive interpretations of international crimes legislation in Belgium and Spain—which included the establishment of universal criminal jurisdiction *in absentia*, as well as the rejection of international immunities—resulted in legislative intervention that severely curtailed the possibilities to exercise universal jurisdiction.[103] Second, and

[99] Ralf Michaels, 'Global Problems in Domestic Courts' in Sam Muller and others (eds), *The Law of the Future and the Future of the Law* (Torkel Opsahl Academic EPublisher 2011).

[100] cf Liivoja (n 4) 31 (stating, with respect to the exercise of jurisdiction, that 'all adjudication and public administration can be seen as norm creation').

[101] Obviously, courts do not act *proprio motu* as 'selfless interveners'. They are typically seized, or even instrumentalized, by non-state 'norm entrepreneurs' intent on refining and developing transnational and international law in line with their interests, sometimes also when legislative process is not readily available to address global challenges. Carly Nyst, 'Solidarity in a Disaggregated World: Universal Jurisdiction and the Evolution of Sovereignty' (2012) 8 JILIR 36, 39 ('universal jurisdiction is a clear example of the way in which non-state actors can fundamentally alter the principles and dynamics of international society and the norms by which it is constituted'). See for the seminal work on norm-entrepreneurs and transnational advocacy by NGOs obviously Margaret E Keck and Kathryn Sikkink, *Activists beyond Borders: Advocacy Networks in International Politics* (Cornell University Press 1998). This does not only apply to tort litigation, which plaintiffs can directly initiate, but also to criminal law. Even if the state (in the form of the public prosecutor) formally initiates investigations, in a transnational context, the state will often do so after receiving information from non-state entities, who may *de facto* trigger the investigation. Insofar as these entities represent victims, they may even legally challenge a decision not to prosecute. See *eg* art 12 of the Dutch Code of Criminal Procedure (art 12 Sv). Note that plaintiffs are not necessarily inspired by cosmopolitan motives. Ultimately they may have just wanted to see justice done for themselves. David Luban, 'Carl Schmitt and the Critique of Lawfare' (2010) 43 Case W Res J Int'l L 457, 462 ('Anyone who voluntarily has recourse to the institutions of the law has ulterior motives: nobody ever files a lawsuit out of disinterested curiosity in the answer to a legal question.').

[102] Putnam (n 80) 85.

[103] Rosa AA Fernández, 'The 2014 Reform of Universal Jurisdiction in Spain From All to Nothing' (2014) 13 ZIS 717; Luc Reydams, 'The Rise and Fall of Universal Jurisdiction' in William A Schabas and Nadia Bernaz (eds), *Handbook of International Criminal Law* (Routledge 2010) 337; Luc Reydams,

relatedly, domestic courts may fear a political backlash against the judiciary, or fear being branded 'enemies of the people' in the populist press.[104] This may give them some pause in their cosmopolitan ambitions and to apply auto-censorship when contemplating the exercise of cosmopolitan jurisdiction.[105] Natalie Davidson, for instance, has highlighted how, in the 1980 *Filartiga* torture case, the 'rediscovery' of the US ATS, which appears to provide for the exercise of universal civil jurisdiction over violations of international law,[106] was accompanied by a narrative that remained silent on US institutional involvement in repressive practices in Paraguay.[107] By weaving a narrative of a lone foreign official torturing just one boy, the courts arguably hoped to prevent a political backlash in the United States.[108] Third, in some cases, domestic courts may in fact fully internalize parochial political considerations and thus limit space for 'progressive' judicial outcomes that could adversely affect the political interests of the forum state. Thus, regarding a claim for compensation filed in US courts, in relation to extraterritorial death and injury caused by a cholera epidemic allegedly attributable to Nepalese UN peacekeepers deployed in Haiti, Anthony has explained US courts' confirmation of the UN's *immunity* in that case, by the United States having a 'vested interest in Haitian affairs and a history of imposing its will on Haiti'.[109] In the case, the US government arguably had an interest in the United Nations keeping the peace in Haiti, located in its own backyard, and had obviously no interest in eventually footing the bill of a judgment ordering the United Nations to pay compensation, regardless of the adverse human rights ramifications for the claimants in *Georges*. Fourth, domestic courts may simply take an agnostic position and argue that they have no expertise

'Belgium Reneges on Universality: The 5 August 2003 Act on Grave Breaches of International Humanitarian Law' (2003) 1 JICJ 679. See also the UK Police Reform and Social Responsibility Act, 2011 c 13, which requires that the direct of public prosecutions consent to the issuance of a universal jurisdiction-based arrest warrant in a private prosecution. This Act was adopted after an outcry over the issuance of a warrant for the arrest of the former Israeli Minister of Foreign Affairs in 2010.

[104] cf 'Enemies of the People' Daily Mail (4 November 2016) (populist newspaper denouncing three judges who had ruled that the UK Government would require the consent of Parliament to give notice of Brexit).

[105] Mark A Pollack, 'Is International Relations Corrosive of International Law? A Reply to Martti Koskenniemi' (2013) 27 TICLJ 339, 373 ('most political scientists would argue that international judicial decisions are likely to reflect . . . also *extra-legal* factors including . . . pressures from state institutions and public institutions') (emphasis in original).

[106] *Filártiga v Peña-Irala* (n 41).

[107] Natalie Davidson, 'Shifting the Lenses on Alien Tort Statute Litigation: Narrating US Hegemony in Filártiga and Marcos' (2017) 28 EJIL 147.

[108] This hope has indeed been vindicated, although the absence of a backlash against ATS litigation in more recent times is largely attributable to the Supreme Court reading down the jurisdictional reach of the ATS in the *Kiobel* litigation in light of the presumption against extraterritoriality (a decision which in itself could of course also have been informed by a fear of political backlash). *Kiobel v Royal Dutch Petroleum Co*, 569 US 108 (2013).

[109] Dorothea Anthony, 'Resolving UN Torts in US Courts: Georges v United Nations' (2018) 19(2) MJIL 462. While the United States is perhaps uniquely open to foreign litigation, also in respect of violations of such global values as human rights, the reality is that, according to the Anthony, 'its legitimacy to act [is] constrained by the greater ideological implications of its contribution'. ibid.

in international relations matters. On the grounds that it is incumbent on the executive to conduct foreign relations, they may either defer to the wisdom of the executive (*eg* when the latter brings, or intervenes in the case)[110] or give a restrictive interpretation to the scope of the law for fear of upsetting the executive.[111]

This realist perspective of what domestic courts *actually* do is also borne out by Tonya Putnam's seminal empirical, political-science-based work on judicial extraterritoriality in the United States. In this work, she demonstrates that US courts, in private enforcement cases, have only given extraterritorial application to US laws in two situations: (i) when 'extraterritorial conduct poses a threat to the functioning of US law inside US territory' (domestic rule integrity logic); (ii) when 'US citizens and others with close US ties are accused of violating a short list of rights at the core of American political identity' (rights-based logic).[112] She could not empirically validate alternative hypotheses that the character of a dispute (commercial or non-commercial), the nationality of the defendant (Organisation for Economic Co-operation and Development (OECD) or not), or the place of the conduct (OECD or not) had a bearing on the probability that a US court would exercise extraterritorial jurisdiction.[113] The domestic rule integrity logic corresponds with the above-mentioned economic incentives to exercise extraterritorial jurisdiction, in particular states' desire to prevent rule evasion and to level the playing field for transnational actors, regardless of nationality. The rights-based logic shows overlap, although it does not fully coincide, with the broad interpretation of the national interest that we earlier propounded, as encompassing 'international interests'. Indeed, under the US rights-based logic, US courts are only likely to exercise jurisdiction over international human rights violations insofar as the relevant international rights coincide with *core American political rights*. As the trajectory of ATS litigation shows, this is not always the case.[114] Thus, as Putnam also posits,

110 *Pasquantino* (n 6) 369 (2005) ('The greater danger, in fact, would lie in our judging this prosecution barred based on the foreign policy concerns animating the revenue rule, concerns that we have "neither aptitude, facilities nor responsibility" to evaluate.') (citations omitted). See also *Chicago & S. Air Lines, Inc. v Waterman S.S. Corp.*, 333 U.S. 103, 111 (1948). See for a normative argument in favour of deference to the Executive in extraterritoriality cases in the criminal law: Farbiarz (n 31) 526–27 (arguing that 'there is no reason to think that courts are better positioned than the federal executive branch, acting through its prosecutors, to make decisions about structural concerns, about what might upset the fine balances of give and take that mark the international system or what might constitute an overreach in the context of it.'), and stating at p 528 that this certainly applies when 'the actual federal foreign policy apparatus (including the President's staff) is involved'). Christopher D Totten, 'The Adjudication of Foreign Official Immunity Determinations in the United States Post-*Samantar*: a Circuit Split and Its Implications' (2016) 26 Duke J Comp & Int'l L 517.

111 *Contra* Austen L Parrish, 'Fading Extraterritoriality and Isolationism? Developments in the United States' (2017) 24 IJGLS 207, 215.

112 Putnam (n 80) 4–5.

113 ibid, Table 2.1, 57.

114 See notably *Sosa v Alvarez-Machain*, 542 US 692 (2004) (holding that federal courts should not recognize claims under federal common law for violations of any international law norm with less definite content and acceptance among civilized nationals than the eighteenth-century paradigms familiar when the ATS was enacted, *ie* offences against ambassadors, violations of safe conducts, and piracy). The latter offences posed a distinct threat to US, rather than international, interests.

the rights-based logic is not synonymous with a cosmopolitan logic,[115] and obviously even less so after *Kiobel*.

Apart from Putnam's important work on US judicial extraterritoriality, there is little empirical research testing various theoretical propositions, such as cosmopolitanism, nationalism, or realism, with respect to the extent to which domestic courts apply international law and act extraterritorially in a cosmopolitan manner,[116] or the variables explaining court attitudes.[117] It may happen that courts act in an international law-friendly or cosmopolitan manner because they have *internalized* international law and cosmopolitan values, or because they *assimilate* themselves to certain actors (*ie* the socialization or acculturation hypothesis).[118] As liberal theorists have pointed out, such 'enlightened' action is also more likely to emanate from courts with a liberal-democratic tradition that share a commitment to the rule of law, and boast effective institutions and an active civil society.[119] These theories and parameters may surely generate expectations of empirical outcomes in keeping with cosmopolitan premises. Whether these expectations are also borne out in practice is in need of further social scientific research, however.[120]

Putnam may have concluded, on the basis of thorough empirical research, that courts do not, or only rarely, behave as true cosmopolitans, and only exercise

[115] Putnam (n 80) 253 ('While U.S. courts are internationalist in the sense that they are willing to consider extraterritorial claims, they have been far from cosmopolitan in how they go about it.').

[116] A court's openness to international law does not *perforce* mean that the court will pursue cosmopolitan ends, however, as international law, based on the principle of state consent, may be anti-cosmopolitan. In any event, in the law of jurisdiction, the main function of international law has been to *limit* a state's jurisdictional assertions so as to protect other states' sovereignty. Somewhat counter-intuitively, then, states whose laws do not allow defendants to invoke international law in domestic courts, may have more leeway to realize a cosmopolitan agenda that goes beyond positive international law. See for an example of such a (US) law: Maritime Drug Law Enforcement Act, 46 USCA § 70505. From a defendant's perspective, such laws, especially criminal laws, may however violate the principle of legality, as individuals outside the United States may not be able to predict their subjection to US law. See Kenneth S Gallant, 'The Indeterminate International Law of Jurisdiction, the Presumption against Extraterritorial Effect of Statutes, and Certainty in U.S. Criminal Law' (2014) 27 Pac McGeorge Global Bus & Dev LJ 219, 223.

[117] Conant (n 45) 413.

[118] ibid, 402–03, citing Harold H Koh's transnational legal process approach (which posits that domestic courts' regular interactions with international law may lead to voluntary obedience to international law) and Goodman and Jinks's acculturation hypothesis (pursuant to which domestic courts tend to emulate reference groups that subscribe to an international norm or practice). See Harold H Koh, '1998 Frankel Lecture: Bringing International Law Home' (1998) 35 Hous L Rev 623; Ryan Goodman and Derek Jinks, *Socializing States: Promoting Human Rights Through International Law* (OUP 2013).

[119] Conant (n 45) 404–06, citing, *inter alia* Anne-Marie Slaughter, 'International Law in a World of Liberal States' (1995) 6 EJIL 503.

[120] Compare Steven S Nam, 'Restoring Liberalism to Transnational Corporate Accountability: From Universal Jurisdiction's Ashes to an Afterlife of Multilateral Avenues' (2017) 31 EILR 365, 367 (citing the 'dearth of empirical evidence behind the realist approach', and pointing out that '[s]cholarship empirically assessing the extent to which ATS legislation against foreign corporations caused interstate friction has shown that actual U.S. foreign policy implications were limited and short-lived').

extraterritorial jurisdiction when the state has an economic or identity-based interest in doing so. Still, the scope of her research is relatively narrow, as she only concerns herself with US private enforcement cases where a private plaintiff sues a private defendant in US courts for violations of US regulatory laws. She does not address the large number of US public (criminal/administrative) enforcement cases, such as with respect to anti-corruption and sanctions legislation.[121] In fact, she admits that different dynamics may be at work there,[122] even though historically it was private enforcement that resulted in jurisdictional overreach and sparked foreign complaints.[123] Nor does Putnam address non-US cases and laws, although she notes that with the waning of US political power, the number of (judicial) extraterritoriality cases arising in other jurisdictions, notably in Europe, may increase.[124] It may just be that non-US jurisdictions behave less as pragmatic legal realists (a distinctly US legal tradition),[125] and exercise, inspired by more lofty ideals, extraterritorial jurisdiction 'in the common interest' even where net payoffs for the national interest are relatively low. Any hypothesis obviously needs to be thoroughly tested. The relatively recent vintage of many non-US assertions of extraterritorial jurisdiction—the United States historically being the leader in this field—limits such testing opportunities for now, however.[126]

We can conclude that domestic courts may not always, or most of the time, engage in cosmopolitan extraterritorial action. Taking guidance from more narrow-minded political branches, and applying various prudential doctrines or canons of statutory construction, domestic courts may sometimes be nationalistic, or at least attempt to synchronize cosmopolitan action with the furthering (or not hampering) of the forum state's interests. Still, there is evidence of domestic courts assuming (what looks like) cosmopolitan responsibilities, for example as regards individual criminal accountability for international crimes under the universality principle, or multinational corporations' tort liability for human rights and

[121] Also Austen Parrish, 'The Interplay between Extraterritoriality, Sovereignty, and the Foundations of International Law' (2017), Chapter 12 in Standards and Sovereigns: Legal Histories of Extraterritoriality, SSRN working paper (24 March 2017) 10 (arguing that the US 'retreat from unilateral extraterritorial regulation has been modest and has occurred mostly in the context of private rights of action', whereas '[e]xtraterritorial unilateral regulation from other branches of government ... remains commonplace').

[122] Putnam (n 80) 272 ('Even as U.S. federal courts have made it harder for private entities to bring several types of extraterritorial claims, during this same period, use of extraterritorial regulatory tools on the part of the U.S. executive branch has increased.').

[123] Gallant (n 166) 226 (citing notably securities regulation, the extraterritorial reach of which has been severely curtailed, however, since the 2010 Supreme Court's decision in *Morrison*).

[124] Putnam (n 80) 275 ('European states, in particular, appear increasingly ready to test the relationship between power, domestic institutions, and extraterritorial assertiveness.').

[125] cf Harlan Grant Cohen, 'Are We (Americans) All International Legal Realists Now?' in Chiara Giorgetti and Guglielmo Verdirame (eds), *Concepts on International Law in Europe and the United States* (CUP 2017).

[126] Compare Nam (n 120) 367 (reflecting on the 'recent litigation history of the ATS and pointed out that the 'relatively brief historical record does not give credence to the most dire realist projections of economic downturns and exacerbated national security threats').

environmental abuses under the domicile principle.[127] Adjudicatory jurisdiction over business and human rights torts will be further fleshed out in Chapter 5.4.

3.4 Concluding Observations

Cosmopolitan, unilateral prescriptive jurisdiction is jurisdiction exercised for purely altruistic reasons, in the common interest. Every state could be considered to have a nexus with conduct affecting the common interest, which may ground an entitlement, or a moral imperative to exercise jurisdiction, typically over international crimes, gross human rights violations, or environmental abuses.[128] In practice, however, such pure cosmopolitan jurisdiction is rarely exercised. Scarce resources, fear of retaliation or reciprocity, and lack of local interest in global issues may cause states (legislators, regulators, and courts) to forego assertions of cosmopolitan jurisdiction, unless a 'national interest' can be identified. This is a relatively well-documented empirical phenomenon.

This chapter has shed light on some actual practices of universal and economic jurisdiction. It has been demonstrated that 'abstract' cosmopolitanism may not serve as an incentive to establish jurisdiction.[129] Rather, this incentive is constituted by a more concrete nexus with the state, an 'encounter' of the state with victims of objects of injustice, or an interest of the state.[130] This idea need not be

[127] *Eg* in the Netherlands: *A.F. Akpan v Royal Dutch Shell, plc; E. Dooh v Royal Dutch Shell, plc; F.A. Oguru v Royal Dutch Shell plc.* Court of Appeal of the Hague (18 December 2015); in the United Kingdom: Ekaterina Aristova, 'Tort Litigation against Transnational Corporations in the English Courts: The Challenge of Jurisdiction' (2018) 14 ULR 6; in the United States: Michael Koebele, *Corporate Responsibility under the Alien Tort Statute. Enforcement of International Law through US Torts Law* (Brill 2009). Note that courts may assume cosmopolitan responsibilities while nevertheless downplaying their role as a central cosmopolitan actor, in all likelihood to prevent political censure. See *eg* the *Filartiga* judge's op-ed in The New York Times: Judge Kaufman, 'A Legal Remedy for International Torture?' The New York Times (9 November 1980) 44. 'The courts will not be transformed into some kind of roaming human-rights commission … Nor is the United States, by empowering our courts to hear international claims of torture, engaging in messianic moral imperialism.' It remains nevertheless that *Filartiga* was a cosmopolitan decision in that it held a foreign person responsible for abuses committed abroad against another foreign person.

[128] See on the link between the *erga omnes* obligation to provide reparations for gross human rights violations and the right, or even duty, for states to exercise universal civil (tort) jurisdiction: Andreas Bucher, 'La compétence universelle civile en matière de reparation pour crimes internationaux' (2014) 372 Recueil des Cours 9–127.

[129] Mégret (n 13) 115 (arguing that the forum state 'would tend to typically ignore more virtual assertions of *in absentia* jurisdiction that seem to be based largely on some quixotic concept of abstract justice not based on any meaningful encounter').

[130] See on hybrid motivations for states to exercise extraterritorial jurisdiction: Ireland-Piper (n 30) 10 ('Nation states exercise extraterritorial jurisdiction for three main reasons: first, because they are *legally* obliged to do so; second, because they are *morally* obliged to do so; and, third, because it suits their own *political* or economic agendas. These motivations are not exclusive of one another, and it is likely that all three are present in most exercises of extraterritorial jurisdiction.'). See also Pierik and Werner (n 1) 286–87 (notions of cosmopolitan justice may foster the pursuit of what states perceive to be in their interest, drawing particular attention to the mixture of national security with imperial agendas).

sobering. Instead, it points to the empowering, real-life possibilities of a state exercising jurisdiction in the common interest in ways that at the same time strengthen or reconstitute the territorially bounded political community which the state is supposed to serve, and to whose members (both nationals and non-nationals) it owes fiduciary obligations given the relational character of state sovereignty.[131] Ultimately, the idea is a reflection of the very nature of international law, which oscillates between cosmopolitanism and parochialism,[132] between the celestial and the physically immediate.[133]

Various (territorial) connections and interests may trigger states' extraterritorial legal interventions and justify them internally and externally. However, this does not necessarily make such jurisdiction appropriate in the wider sense of the term. As far as universal criminal jurisdiction is concerned, some examples of inappropriate intervention have already been given. In the next chapter, it is examined at greater length under what circumstances cosmopolitan jurisdictional intervention, or at least intervention with global effects, is appropriate, and in particular, what jurisdictional limitations are required.

[131] Evan Fox-Decent and Evan J Criddle, *Fiduciaries of Humanity: How International Law Constitutes Authority* (OUP 2016) 13.

[132] Mortimer Sellers (ed), *Parochialism, Cosmopolitanism and the Foundations of International Law* (CUP 2012). See Ireland-Piper (n 30) 27 ('the exercise of extraterritorial jurisdiction provides a means by which states can reconcile parochialism with cosmopolitanism. It is a form of transnationalism: a hybrid creature born of both international and domestic law').

[133] Geoff Gordon and Wouter Werner, 'Between the Dog and the Divine: Resistance and Conventionalism in Cosmopolitanism' (2017) 13 ULR 28.

4
Limitations to the Exercise of Prescriptive Jurisdiction in the Common Interest

Non-consent-based unilateralism has undeniable substantive and distributive consequences. It may shift resources, possibly to the asserting state proper, or at least a group or good which the asserting state believes is in need of protection. Such shifts may be justified on scientific or 'uncontested' natural law grounds but they may obscure the *political* character of decision-making by actors bent on entrenching power, selectively pursuing an imperialist agenda, discrediting alternative approaches, and marginalizing particular players.[1] *Who* decides in the end matters a great deal.[2] Cosmopolitan unilateralism then starts resembling Carl Schmitt's theory of decisionism, pursuant to which what really matters in political life is who has the authority to decide on the exception.[3] In this light, the multilateral avenue appears to be far more preferable than unilateral action. Multilateralism can bring about a globally efficient and equitable solution by allowing all affected to have a voice in decision-making while factoring in parameters such as a state's historical contribution to a global public bad, or a state's ability to pay.[4] Relying on consent-based multilateralism also leaves intact the principle of non-intervention, at least in its classic incarnation, pursuant to which,

[1] cf Martti Koskenniemi, 'What Use for Sovereignty Today?' (2011) 1 ASJIL 61, 67 (decrying a managerial decision-making logic that is 'oblivious to the conditions under which it takes place', and highlighting that the resolution of global problems 'is part of everyday political debate and action'); Matthew Craven and Rose Parfitt, 'Statehood Self-determination, and Recognition' in Malcolm Evans (ed) *International Law* (5th edn, OUP 2018) 2015, 235, (observing the 'opacity of the conditions warranting intervention, the selective character of practice that underpins it and, if nothing else, its evidently imperial . . . overtones').

[2] Craven and Parfitt (n 1) 242 (decrying the supposed 'authenticity of the ethical', noting that 'justice always lies in the hands of those who have the capacity to speak its name, although in reality: justice is situational). ibid, 243 (wondering 'how does [the state] claim authenticity for the values it proclaims, and what kind of political action does it entail?', also referring to Martti Koskenniemi, 'The Wonderful Artificiality of States' (1994) ASIL Proceedings 22, 27.

[3] Carl Schmitt, *Nomos der Erde* (Telos Press 2006) 42. Note that Schmitt himself considered the exercise of political authority to be territorially bounded. See also Jens Bartelson, *Sovereignty as Symbolic Form* (Routledge 2014), 34–45.

[4] See also *contra* Jürgen Meyer, 'Dual Illegality and Geoambiguous Law: A New Rule for Extraterritorial Application of U.S. Law' (2010) 95 MLR 110, 158(submitting, with respect to US territoriality, that 'without the input of all parties affected there is little reason to suppose that whatever rule US officials choose will be the most globally efficient and optimal solution'). Compare also Martti Koskenniemi, 'Constitutionalism, Managerialism and the Ethos of Legal Education' (2007) 1 EJIL 1, 14 (advocating a 'nuanced attitude to the jurisdictional conflicts and the attendant choices about distributionary effects').

Selfless Intervention. Cedric Ryngaert, Oxford University Press (2020). © Cedric Ryngaert.
DOI: 10.1093/oso/9780198851783.001.0001

in the Wolffian tradition, it has to be left to each nation to pursue human perfectibility, and each nation's choices in this regard should be respected.[5] Especially unilateralism exercised by states which have a history of avoiding or circumventing international supervision and international procedures, but instead use their domestic laws and courts to realize professed 'global values', may come in for criticism.[6] Still, we live in a non-ideal world where such multilateral solutions are not necessarily forthcoming, and when they are, they may rather be of the lowest common denominator variety.[7] Moreover, states with the strongest nexus to a subject matter may fail to assume their responsibility. Faced with this reality, states have exercised, and may in principle be allowed to exercise, unilateral jurisdiction in the common interest.[8]

If one accepts unilateralism in principle, one should make sure, however, that one takes seriously concerns over self-serving behaviour,[9] undue interference in other nations' internal affairs, normative competency conflicts,[10] and 'false universalism'. States, acting as self-appointed 'trustees of humanity', should not be trusted at face value. Instead, as Benvenisti has pointed out, they 'carry the burden of proving that they serve our interest',[11] the interest of humanity at large. Allowing states to get away with a mere claim that they represent common interests would open the door to domination, which is considered to be the essence of injustice ('subjection to the arbitrary wielding of power').[12] From the perspective of political theory, states should instead ensure that their actions comply with the Kantian

[5] Christian Wolff, *The Law of Nations Treated According to a Scientific Method* 17 (Joseph H Drake trans, 1934), cited in Lorenzo Zucca, 'A Genealogy of State Sovereignty' (2015) 16 Theoretical Inq L 399.

[6] Dorothea Anthony, 'Resolving UN Torts in US Courts: Georges v United Nations' (2018) 19(2) MJIL 462 ('some observers are also likely to be sceptical of a nation [the US] that thinks it can circumvent international procedures, as lacking as they may be, and decide the issues using its own courts').

[7] Gareth Davies, 'International Trade, Extraterritorial Power, and Global Constitutionalism: A Perspective from Constitutional Pluralism' (2012) 13 Ger LJ 1212, 1214.

[8] Maggie Gardner, 'Channeling Unilateralism' (2015) 56 HILJ 297, 302 (arguing that ('channeled unilateralism may be a second-best solution in a world of unequal states', although focusing on unilateral jurisdiction authorized by treaties). Compare Austen L Parrish, 'Fading Extraterritoriality and Isolationism? Developments in the United States' (2017) 24 IJGLS 207, 221 ('A similar persistent reductionist tendency is the notion that in a globalized world, unilateral extraterritorial regulation is inevitable and necessary … The position is only that transnational regulation more meaningfully occurs through cooperative, rather than unilateral, means.'). However, Parrish appears to support extraterritorial regulation in case 'last resort—used when multilateral international cooperation was beyond reasonable grasp and when pressing problems demanded a response'. ibid, 222.

[9] cf Andrew Linklater and Hidemi Suganami, *The English School of International Relations: A Contemporary Reassessment* (CUP 2006) 271.

[10] Indeed, in a cosmopolitan conception of jurisdiction, *every state* may be entitled to exercise jurisdiction in the common interest. The normative competency conflicts to which this may give rise have already been documented with respect to the exercise of universal jurisdiction over international crimes. See *eg* Rain Liivoja, 'The Criminal Jurisdiction of States: A Theoretical Primer' (2010) 7 NoFo 25, 51.

[11] Eyal Benvenisti, 'The Paradoxes of Sovereigns as Trustees of Humanity: Concluding Remarks' (2015) 16 Theoretical Inq L 535, 545.

[12] *Ie*, 'justice as impartiality'. Erik O Eriksen, 'Three Conceptions of Global Political Justice' (2016) Globus Research Papers 1/2016, 4, 9 .

principle of freedom, pursuant to which any state action ought to enhance rather than restrict the autonomy of individual persons.[13]

Thus, states or regional organizations taking unilateral action in the common interest should be cognisant of its potential for abuse and imperial imposition. This awareness need not translate into a wholesale rejection of unilateralism. Instead, in the interest of legitimacy, it calls for a proper explanation of the common interest grounds on which the unilateral action in question is based, and specifically its international aspirations.[14] Also, to avert false universalism, some jurisdictional and substantive limitation may be required.[15] This is especially so as states may perhaps generally agree on objectives but not on the approach to be followed to attain these objectives.[16]

There is no reason to believe that such an endeavour is impossible.[17] In fact, as Bartelson recalled, any exercise of political authority is *intrinsically limited* by the republican principle of liberty; in the absence of a world government, in order to forestall arbitrary domination, this implies in particular that the interests of those subjected to the exercise of power should be taken into consideration.[18]

The pertinent question thus becomes what limitations should be imposed to render such jurisdiction 'reasonable'. After introducing the concept of reasonableness (section 4.1), various jurisdictional mitigating mechanisms are discussed: international recognition of the pertinent common interest (section 4.2), democratic participation of those affected (section 4.3), recognizing foreign

[13] Eriksen is rather pessimistic as to the possibility of state auto-limitation in this regard, arguing that 'any agents sufficiently powerful to carry out these duties are likely to be biased if not corrupt' (n 12) 17, and citing the need for a 'higher-ranking third party that can interpret and make the abstract idea of equal freedom effective' (Eriksen (n 12) 15. See also, although perhaps somewhat less pessimistically, Davies (n 7) 2012 ('the foreign legislator makes an appeal to an abstract and other-determined version of "your own best interests" and uses this to justify its interventions'). In the absence of an international dispute-settlement system of compulsory jurisdiction that extends beyond particular functional domains (*eg* trade, human rights, or the law of the sea), state auto-limitation will, however, remain the next best option.

[14] See, in respect of the Aviation Directive, an instance of the EU unilaterally extending its climate change legislation: Ester Herlin-Karnell, 'The EU as a Promoter of Values and the European Global Project' (2012) 13 Ger LJ 1225, 1244–46. In essence, Herlin-Karnell asks the European Commission to better explain its statement in a Commission Communication of 26 May 2010 that the EU will 'lead the world in demonstrating how this [reducing emissions from aviation] could be done'.

[15] Daniel Bodansky, 'What's in a Concept? Global Public Goods, International Law, and Legitimacy' (2012) 23 EJIL 651. See also Gregory Shaffer, 'International Law and Global Public Goods in a Legal Pluralist World' (2012) 23 EJIL 669 highlighting at 677 the role for international institutions in coordinating decisions, and at 692 advocating the need for international constraints on unilateral action).

[16] Larry C Backer, 'Conceptual, Structural, and Operationalization Constraints on the Right to Remedy Under the Guiding Principles' (Parallel events session of the 3rd UN Forum on Business and Human Rights, Geneva Switzerland, 1 December 2014) http://www.backerinlaw.com/Site/podcasts/speeches-and-remarks/conceptual-structural-and-operationalization-constraints-on-the-right-to-remedy-under-the-guiding-principles-remarks-delivered-at-the-parallel-events-session-of-the-3rd-u-n-forum-on-business-and-h/ (accessed 5 December 2019).

[17] Compare Robert Howse and Ruti Teitel, 'Does Humanity-Law Require (or Imply) a Progressive Theory of History? (and Other Questions for Martti Koskenniemi)' (2013) 27 TICLJ 377, 387.

[18] Bartelson (n 3). See on republicanism also Philip Pettit, *Republicanism: a Theory of Freedom and Government* (OUP 1997).

mechanisms providing equivalent protection (section 4.4), and transfers to, or compensation of those affected (section 4.5). These mechanisms further the normative legitimacy of unilateral jurisdiction in the global interest, as they take the human-centredness of cosmopolitanism truly seriously. They are designed to take account of the interests of all actors affected by state coercion,[19] and thus to limit jurisdictional overreach in violation of cosmopolitan tenets.[20] They may appear to be ideal-typical constructions, drawn in part from moral theories. But at the same time, they have a grounding in existing state and institutional practice, which makes further implementation altogether feasible. More specific implementation of these principles will follow in Chapter 5, which studies the exercise of jurisdiction in the common interest in discrete fields of the law from a more technical and doctrinal perspective.

In line with what was argued earlier, this chapter starts from the assumption that there are such things as 'global values' and 'the common interest', and that states or regional organizations may, and at times do, exercise unilateral prescriptive jurisdiction to serve these values and interests. However, the chapter maintains its relevance even for those who doubt or deny the existence of global values. Irrespective of how one reconstructs or makes sense of what states actually do, there is no denying that they engage in value-based judicial or regulatory unilateralism. For instance, some states have imposed trade measures based on the compatibility with environmental standards of imported products' process and production methods, thereby extending their own laws to foreign production processes short of a global consensus. Such measures can be explained by the asserting actors' desire to protect (what they perceive as) common environmental concerns or supply global environmental goods, for example a stable climate or animal welfare. At the same time, such measures can also be explained by a desire to project abroad local value preferences regarding the (morally) acceptable level of environmental protection, even in respect of foreign activities and in case of foreign effects of such measures. Thus, Gareth Davies considers the adoption of trade measures for environmental and social preferences, as 'an attempt at propagating a specific set of values and choices elsewhere' rather than as a mode of 'enforcing a pre-agreed universal value set', thus locating such practices firmly in the pluralist tradition ('regulatory pluralism').[21]

Regardless of how they are theorized, the regulatory practices themselves remain the same, however. They are unilateral, and raise concerns of imperialism,

[19] Compare Maximo Langer, 'Universal Jurisdiction is Not Disappearing: The Shift from "Global Enforcer" to "No Safe Haven" Universal Jurisdiction' (2013) 13 JICJ 739, fn 11.

[20] Compare Howse and Teitle (n 17) 387 (citing the 'awareness of humanity-law's inner normative logic and its intrinsically self-limiting character').

[21] Davies (n 7) 1215. See also at 1211 ('it is also quite plausible to claim that as human beings, inhabitants of a planet, we have an interest in preserving species, habitats, and the environment as a whole, even outside of the borders of our own state ... the interests of a population are necessarily in those things which they subjectively care about').

jurisdictional overreach, and democratic illegitimacy, as just mentioned. If anything, these concerns may be brought into even starker relief if jurisdictional assertions are interpreted through the lens of regulatory pluralism. If normatively (and not just sociologically) construed, regulatory pluralism may allow states to assert jurisdiction to promote *any* value or *any* interest that is locally perceived, regardless of whether it is internationally shared (*ie* evidenced by its recognition in international legal or political instruments). Pursuant to the cosmopolitan lens donned in this study, such 'parochial' assertions are *prima facie* more suspect than assertions which serve, or at least pretend to serve, the common interest.[22] Absent any grounding in an overlapping consensus, international protest may be more likely to arise, and mitigation mechanisms—the focus of this chapter—may be even more appropriate.[23] Davies urges in this respect to imbue 'states' freedom to exercise regulatory power in the name of out-of-state interests' with constitutional values,[24] which he defines as a set of principles aimed at preventing domination.[25] This is not very different from how 'mitigating principles' are conceived in this chapter. In the pluralist tradition, these mitigating principles, which typically have a procedural and coordinating character, are the only principles that may transcend the particularized value choices made by individually acting states and organizations.[26] Such principles may be conceived of as 'interface norms' as defined by Nico Krisch, as meta-norms that resolve conflict of discourses between suborders of international law,[27] in this case of the geographic rather than functional variety (between states or regional organizations, rather than between specialized fields of international law).[28]

[22] *Eg* Cedric Ryngaert and Marieke Koekkoek, 'Extraterritorial Regulation of Natural Resources: A Functional Approach' in Jan Wouters and others (eds), *Global Governance Through Trade: EU Policies and Approaches* (Edward Elgar Publishing 2016) (doubting the jurisdictional justification of the EU regulation at issue in the *EC Seals* litigation before the World Trade Organization (WTO), as seals are not an internationally protected species; instead, the wish to protect seals, also extraterritoriality, stems from a local, European set of value preferences).

[23] Davies (n 7) 1213, the relevant states—in the trade context, the regulating and producing state—do not contest that it falls within the regulating state sovereignty to impose unilateral measures. Instead, the disagreement is 'about whether they are listening to each other enough, and thus about '[d]ialogue and mutual concern'. This renders the current chapter all the more relevant.

[24] Davies (n 7) 1216.

[25] ibid, 1221.

[26] Compare Dirk Pulkowski, *The Law and Politics of International Regime Conflict* (OUP 2014) 192 (noting that in the pluralist approach, international law is not unified and that there is no regime-transcendent language).

[27] Note that Krisch conceives of interface norms as existing only within the suborders—*ie* in our case within state or EU law—without having a common dimension. This has been criticized by Pulkowski (n 26) 202. At the end of the day, however, such norms will in any event have to be implemented by states, whatever their origin, *eg states* will have to set up mechanisms allowing for participation of foreign affected persons.

[28] Nico Krisch, *Beyond Constitutionalism: The Pluralist Structure of Postnational Law* (OUP 2010). Note, however, that the geographical clash may reveal a functional clash: it may transpire that one state, in projecting its laws abroad, embraces one particular function of international law (*eg* environmental protection) whereas another state, denouncing this 'extraterritorial' projection, emphasizes another function (*eg* free trade, or non-intervention).

4.1 Reasonableness

In jurisdictional theory, the question of reasonableness normally only comes up with respect to jurisdictional assertions that are considered as lawful in the first place: that jurisdiction is *prima facie* lawfully exercised does not mean that exercising it to the fullest extent allowed under international law is necessarily appropriate as a matter of policy. At this point, the study proceeds on the basis of a rather agnostic view as to the (il-)legality of the exercise of unilateral jurisdiction in the common interest. Such assertions may be in tension with the received principles of jurisdiction but as will be demonstrated, notably in Chapter 5, asserting states and organizations, as well as domestic and international courts, tend to legitimize their unilateral action by invoking the classic principles of jurisdiction, in particular territoriality. Because of global interdependence, for a state to find *some* territorial nexus—however tenuous—with a subject matter may not be that difficult. Eventually, perhaps it may be a fruitless exercise to analyse the exercise of prescriptive jurisdiction in the common interest by using the crude binary code through which the law operates (lawful/unlawful). Selfless intervention finds itself in a grey legal zone. It does not easily lend itself to legal coding.

That said, it is uncontested that unilateralism, whether it is legally, politically, morally, or economically justified, creates *externalities* for foreign states, individuals, and operators, which the asserting state may want to internalize. This is where restraining criteria of reasonableness come in. The principle of reasonableness may possibly not *require*, under international law, that states exercise their jurisdiction reasonably, but at least it asks them to take into account the interests of affected foreign actors, of a public or private nature, as a matter of good neighbourliness, so as to prevent chaos resulting from the exercise of overlapping jurisdiction, as well as to prevent the imposition of undue regulatory burdens on third countries and third country actors.

In earlier work, I have expounded at length on the principle of jurisdictional reasonableness,[29] concluding that public international law does not contain hard-and-fast rules of reasonableness and restraint, unlike private international law.[30]

[29] Cedric Ryngaert, *Jurisdiction in International Law* (2nd edn, OUP 2015), ch 5. In this chapter, I refuted the claim that reasonableness is required as a matter of international law, *inter alia* made by the American Law Institute (ALI) in its commentary to section 403 of the Restatement (Third) of US Foreign Relations Law (1987), which codifies the jurisdictional rule of reason. On the basis of an extensive analysis of state practice and *opinio juris*, I came to the conclusion that such a requirement does not currently exist as a matter of positive law. This finding does not mean, however, that reasonableness is not normatively desirable. In this work I went on to praise subsidiarity as a proper criterion of reasonableness. Note that in the Restatement (Fourth) of US Foreign Relations Law (2017), the ALI, while acknowledging reasonableness as a rule of statutory construction, conspicuously refrained from characterized it as a rule of international law. Under the heading 'reasonableness in interpretation', it stated that '[a]s a matter of prescriptive comity, U.S. courts may interpret federal statutory provisions to include other limitations on their applicability'.

[30] See also Alex Mills, 'Rethinking Jurisdiction in International Law' (2014) 84 BYBIL 187, 208–09 (submitting that in the private law context 'states have engaged with the principles and problems of

From a theoretical perspective, as Koskenniemi pointed out, this role of 'reasonableness' is a typical late modern praxis of resorting to 'equity' or 'justice' in order to solve sovereignty problems,[31] a praxis that may be explained by a more general mistrust of the capacity of hard and fast rules to yield legitimate solutions.[32] With respect to the law of jurisdiction, it could be submitted that this equity-based approach was in fact necessitated by the seminal *Lotus* judgment, which affirmed the positive jurisdictional freedom of states as well as states' right not to be subject to regulation without their consent.[33] These 'liberal' affirmations are in tension with each other, as upholding the former, including in its extraterritorial dimension, necessarily undermines the latter. Eventually, circumscribing states' rights to assert jurisdiction and to be free from outside interference, through rather loosely defined interest-balancing tests, could offer a way out.[34] This is not dissimilar to the liberal state balancing the freedoms of its citizens, imposing restrictions on some freedoms so as to protect the freedoms of others as, for example, reflected in the restrictions which states are allowed to impose on the freedom of speech.[35]

Jurisdictional reasonableness, as it was in the past pioneered in US antitrust law,[36] has—not surprisingly—come under severe criticism for failing to provide legal certainty.[37] Reasonableness would at best be subjective,[38] and at worst arbitrary.[39] Where the reasonableness test is carried out by domestic actors delimiting their own jurisdiction, the risk of parochial applications may be high. The challenge then is to develop more specific criteria that could inform a jurisdictional interest-balancing test. This challenge has earlier been taken up by US courts[40] and

(potentially overlapping) international jurisdiction in a more sophisticated and nuanced way than is generally seen in the context of public international law', citing *res judicata*, the application of foreign substantive law as a result of choice of law rules, and the harmonization of choice of law rules).

[31] Martti Koskenniemi, 'The Politics of International Law' (1990) 1 EJIL 4, 16.

[32] ibid, 20.

[33] *Case of the SS Lotus* (France v Turkey) (1927) PCIJ Rep Series A No 10.

[34] Koskenniemi 'The Politics of International Law' (n 31) 1.

[35] See for instance art 10(2) ECHR which provides that the right to freedom of expression 'may be subject to such formalities, conditions, restrictions or penalties as are prescribed by law and are necessary in a democratic society, in the interests of national security, territorial integrity or public safety, for the prevention of disorder or crime, for the protection of health or morals, for the protection of the reputation or rights of others, for preventing the disclosure of information received in confidence, or for maintaining the authority and impartiality of the judiciary'.

[36] See for a strong defence: Larry Kramer 'Extraterritorial Application of American Law After the *Insurance Antitrust Case:* A Reply to Professors Lowenfeld and Trimble' (1995) 89 AJIL 750, 752.

[37] *Eg* Paul B Stephan, 'The Political Economy of Extraterritoriality' (2011) APSA 2011 Annual Meeting Paper, 16 <https://papers.ssrn.com/sol3/papers.cfm?abstract_id=1900156> ('Extraterritorial extension achieved through case-by-case decisionmaking entails considerable uncertainty.').

[38] See also Aravind Ganesh, 'Unilateral Jurisdiction to Provide Global Public Goods: A Republican Account' (2016) 42 Brooklyn JIL 572 (observing that '[p]eople have radically differing visions of what counts as reasonable, extending even to fundamental questions about the survival of the planet', and that 'rather than a pragmatic solution to problems of global coordination, a 'reasonableness' approach to unilateral measures might actually be the perfect recipe for international discord').

[39] Koskenniemi, 'The Politics of International Law' (n 31) 16.

[40] *Timberlane Lumber Co v Bank of America* 749 F.2d 1378 (9th Cir. 1984); *Mannington Mills Inc v Congoleum Corp* 595 F.2d 1287 (3d Cir. 1979).

by the Restatement (Third) of US Foreign Relations Law.[41] This selection of more specific criteria is not a neutral one, however, and it cannot escape natural law-based subjectivism. As Koskenniemi pointed out, 'in justifying its conception of what is equitable, the court will have to assume a theory of justice—a theory, however, which it cannot justify by further reference to the legal concepts themselves'.[42] When exercising unilateral jurisdiction in the perceived common interest, it appears indeed inevitable that states will apply *their* notions of global justice to foreign territories and persons.[43] Absent a globally shared justice conception, a state's quest for an objective test of justice, which will in turn also be *applied* objectively, may ultimately prove futile.

This is simply a limitation that we will have to accept, however. Indeed, to reject reasonableness means to accept either that jurisdictional problems can be solved via hard and fast rules of territoriality or personality, or that such problems cannot be solved at all. The first position is increasingly difficult to maintain in light of the accelerating interdependence of the world, notably following the spread of the Internet. The second position is outright undesirable as it negates the ordering role of international law, and simply stands for lawlessness in international relations, that is, the hardcore realist position. Ultimately, giving in to some form of legal subjectivism, as reflected in an interest-balancing test, however defined, is the only realistic option: after all, the law, and international law in particular, is never applied in a politically neutral fashion.[44] The task at hand is to mitigate the subjective character of this state of affairs by applying principles revolving around *intersubjectivity* (*eg* requiring a substantive or formal international consensus on a common interest; seeking input from affected parties), *openness* to alternative conceptions of the common interest (*eg* devising mechanisms of mutual recognition), and *understanding* of impacts on others (*eg* setting up compensation mechanisms).

How these principles *limit* the exercise of prescriptive jurisdiction in the common interest remains to be seen, however. Bearing in mind that the law of jurisdiction ought to be more responsive to reality and society,[45] the reality of a perceived global urgency (*eg* a global public good risks going undersupplied or global justice risks not being delivered in the absence of unilateral action) may well trump 'traditional' concerns over interference in other states' affairs.[46] A jurisdictional

[41] Section 403 of the Restatement (Third). At the time of writing, a fourth Restatement was in preparation.

[42] Koskenniemi, 'The Politics of International Law' (n 31) 30.

[43] Compare Koskenniemi, 'What Use for Sovereignty Today?' (n 1) 66; John D Haskell, 'Ways of Doing Extraterritoriality in Scholarship' in Daniel Margolies and others (eds), *The Extraterritoriality of Law: History, Theory, Politics* (Routledge 2019) 16.

[44] Compare Koskenniemi, 'The Politics of International Law' (n 31) 31–32.

[45] Compare Mills, 'Rethinking Jurisdiction in International Law' (n 30) 212 (arguing that the artificial disconnection of the law of jurisdiction from reality is 'indeed the condition which has generally afflicted accounts of the law of international jurisdiction').

[46] *Contra Daimler AG v Bauman*, 134 S Ct 746 (2014) (emphasizing the 'risks to international comity' ensuing from the 'expansive view of general jurisdiction posed', and pointing out that '[o]ther nations

assertion could even be considered reasonable on the mere ground that it protects a common interest or is universally condemned.[47] For instance, the US Court of Appeals for the Ninth Circuit held in *United States v Vasquez-Velasco*, a case of extraterritorial drug smuggling, that the principle of jurisdictional reasonableness posed no obstacle to the prosecution '[b]ecause drug smuggling is a serious and universally condemned offense', and thus 'no conflict is likely to be created by extraterritorial regulation of drug traffickers'.[48] Also, to the extent that this interest is recognized in international law, allowing *states*—rather than aloof multilateral institutions that may be seen as undemocratic—to enforce this law will strengthen their sense of ownership and foster implementation.[49] Another reason for not placing the bar of reasonableness too high, is, as legal pluralists have pointed out, that regulatory innovation and error correction, also in respect of common interests, benefits from unilateral action taken by a variety of actors.[50] Moreover, allowing multiple states to exercise jurisdiction, with the attendant international friction this may engender, could, or could even be intended to encourage states to co-operate and reach a negotiated, multilateral solution.[51] This thinking actually harks back to older tropes of Roman greatness stemming from its refusal to embrace one set of moral or religious values, and to Machiavelli's idea of political vitality flowing from social conflict.[52] While at first sight, a 'disorder of orders' may thus ensue,[53] as Shaffer has pointed out, 'the one' may be 'constituted by the interactions of the

do not share the uninhibited approach to personal jurisdiction'). The case concerning a transnational corporation's complicity in kidnapping, torture, and murder, *ie* crimes that are global justice-sensitive.

[47] Compare Haskell (n 43) 15 ('How can it be that there is a strong presumption against extraterritoriality in many spheres of law, and also, at the same time, that it might often be reasonable or necessary to apply extraterritorial jurisdiction?').

[48] *United States v Vasquez-Velasco*, 15 F3 d 833, 841 (9th Cir. 1994). See also *United States v MacAllister*, 160 F.3d 1304, 1308 (11th Cir 1998).

[49] Shaffer (n 15) 687 (supporting unilateral state application of international law via legal pluralism, holding that 'international law is more likely to be implemented if it engages and takes account of state perceptions and concerns through pluralist interaction', also highlighting 'the potential pathologies of centralized institutions').

[50] Paul S Berman 'A Pluralist Approach to International Law' (2007) 32 YJIL 301 (citing as benefits that accrue from having multiple overlapping jurisdictional assertions: greater possibility for error correction, a more robust field for norm articulation, and a larger space for creative innovation, drawing on Robert M Cover, 'The Uses of Jurisdictional Redundancy: Interest, Ideology, and Innovation' (1981) 22 Wm & Mary L Rev 639. See also Joel R Reidenberg, 'Technology and Internet Jurisdiction' (2005) 153 UPLR 1951, 1974 ('the multiplicity of states with jurisdiction over Internet activities is likely to stimulate creativity and new Internet services, such as more accurate and selective filtering technologies, stronger security zones and more robust, customized compliance capabilities').

[51] An Hertogen, 'Letting *Lotus* Bloom' (2015) 26 EJIL 901, 924–25 (noting that the Permanent Court of International Justice's decision in *Lotus* 'prompted negotiations on an alternative allocation of jurisdiction over collisions on the high seas, and this may have been exactly what the Court intended'). Note that Hertogen does not reason from a cosmopolitan perspective, but on the basis of a particular activity's effects occurring in multiple states, which allows the latter to exercise their jurisdiction on the basis of the 'principle of locality'. ibid, 922.

[52] Zucca (n 5) 406.

[53] Neil Walker 'Beyond Boundary Disputes and Basic Grids: Mapping the Global Disorder of Normative Orders' (2008) IJCL 373, 376.

many'.[54] This 'one' does not mean that one legal system prevails over another, however.[55] Instead, the existence of multiple orders may be a check on the arbitrary use of power by one order.[56] Tolerating potentially multiple manifestations of unilateralism could result in a dynamic and innovative regulatory environment that allows for localization.[57] Eventually, although not necessarily, through peer-to-peer learning and normative socialization, this may give rise to globally more uniform standard.

It remains the fact, however, that powerful states and regional organizations which exercise prescriptive jurisdiction in the common interest risk doing so in a heavy-handed manner, with little regard for the foreign addressees of their 'extraterritorial' regulations. The narrative of 'pursuing the common interest' cannot be an excuse for imperial imposition. Therefore, techniques of restraint, which implement jurisdictional reasonableness, may have to be developed. In the following sections, the main techniques of restraint are discussed.[58] We start with the most obvious one in respect of common interests, namely the requirement that those 'common interests' are indeed internationally recognized as common.

4.2 International Recognition of Common Interests

To forestall accusations of 'false cosmopolitanism', states may want to ensure that the activities which their laws jurisdictionally ensnare are proscribed by international or foreign law, or at least have been internationally recognized as threats to the common interest. Such a stance partly pre-empts problems concerning foreign states' lack of consent to another state's regulation. It may also ensure that the foreign persons who are subject to regulation are adequately put on notice that their activities may be caught by unilaterally extended foreign domestic law.[59] After all,

[54] Shaffer (n 15).

[55] Hans Lindahl 'A-Legality: Postnationalism and the Question of Legal Boundaries' (2010) 73 TMLR 30, 56 ('none of these principles succeeds in gaining ascendancy over the others, even though they can display a measure of mutual accommodation').

[56] Zucca (n 52).

[57] Gardner (n 8) 244 ('Interpretive flexibility at the margins of multilateral treaties can empower peripheral states by leaving more space for "localization," or the building of "congruence" by domestic actors between international norms and local beliefs and practices.').

[58] The discussion is non-exhaustive. Nor is it excluded that law-making and applying agencies apply notions of reasonableness to mitigate the foreign impact of a unilateral measures *without* being explicit regarding the doctrinal basis of the applied technique of mitigation. See for an example of *implicit* application of reasonableness: Case C-592/14 *European Federation for Cosmetic Ingredients v Secretary of State for Business, Innovation and Skills and Attorney General*. See the analysis of Ioanna Hadjiyianni, 'The Role of Domestic Courts in Global Environmental Governance: Judicial Review of Extraterritoriality by the Court of Justice of the European Union' (2018) working paper (on file with the author) at fn 102 (herafter Hadjiyianni, 'The Role of Domestic Courts in Global Environmental Governance').

[59] In the United States, this is a requirement that may follow from the Due Process Clause in the US Constitution. See for concerns over whether *international law* sources can, in the criminal law context, ensure that defendants have notice of the content and applicability of extraterritorially applied

as Liivoja has pointed out, 'jurisdiction must be exercised so as to allow individuals to take the law into account when planning their actions'.[60]

This approach is well-known in criminal law where, pursuant to the principle of double criminality, states should only exercise their jurisdiction when the impugned behaviour is criminal under the law of both the asserting state and the foreign territorial state.[61] Arguably, when thus exercising its jurisdiction extraterritorially, the state is just enforcing foreign regulations and, hence, exercising some sort of 'vicarious' jurisdiction. The rule of dual illegality could dispel legitimacy and democracy concerns, preclude tricky determinations as regards the perceived inability or unwillingness to prosecute, or offer remedies on the part of the foreign state, and prevent foreign protest.[62] From a due process and fair warning perspective, it safeguards the legitimate rights of the defendant.[63]

However, what we are mainly concerned with here, given our focus on common interests, is international rather than purely bilateral proscription of particular activities, that is, proscription on the basis of treaties or customary international law. Such proscription may be accompanied by the explicit conferral of unilateral 'cosmopolitan' jurisdiction on individual states. Thus, prosecutions for offences amenable to universal or at least extraterritorial jurisdiction, such as piracy or certain terrorist offences, have been considered as valid, even absent a nexus with the regulating state, in light of the universal proscription of the offence accompanied by the international authorization of the exercise of unilateral state jurisdiction.[64] An explicit conferral of jurisdiction may not be strictly required, however. Even if international law may not have expressly given unilateral prescriptive jurisdiction to individual states to enforce the law's substantive proscriptions, at least the substantive law being enforced is shared and covered by foreign state consent.[65] Given its international character, it is or should be cognisable by the persons subjected

(US) law: Julie R O'Sullivan, 'The Extraterritorial Application of Federal Criminal Statutes: Analytical Roadmap, Normative Conclusions, and a Plea to Congress for Direction' (2018) 106 GELJ 1021, 1093 (considering that it is not 'appropriate to task individual defendants with effective notice of the international law governing prescriptive principles or the content of treaties that require State parties to criminalize defined conduct', and instead favouring embodiment in domestically binding law).

[60] Liivoja (n 10) 28.

[61] Dual criminality is also a mainstay of extradition law. Pursuant to bilateral extradition treaties, states normally only extradite a person when the offence of which he is suspected is a crime in both the requesting and requested state. See Lech Gardocki, 'Double Criminality in Extradition Law' (1993) 27 Is LR 288.

[62] cf Meyer (n 4) 119–20.

[63] See for relevant US case law: *State v Holden*, 217 A 2d 132, 134 (NJ 1966); *Al Kassar*, 606 F3d at 119; *Bin Laden*, 92 F. Supp 2d at 218–19.

[64] See Anthony J Colangelo, 'What is Extraterritorial Jurisdiction?' (2014) 99 CLR 1303, 1326 et seq. Some criminal codes even explicitly limit the exercise of universal jurisdiction to offences amenable to *obligatory* universal jurisdiction, *eg* art 12*bis* of the Preliminary Title of the Belgian Code of Criminal Procedure.

[65] See however Gardner (n 8) 351 (regretting that in many cases of transboundary harms, 'treaty provisions that make appropriate unilateral efforts cheaper and more feasible' are missing).

to enforcement. They cannot advance the argument that they have not adequately been put on notice of the wrongfulness of their conduct.[66] From a sovereignty perspective, because international law proscribes the conduct, states arguably have no reason to complain about jurisdictional overreaching.[67] This legitimacy advantage may in turn encourage motivated states to more actively exercise their jurisdiction.[68] What matters and may suffice is that international law has *proscribed* certain conduct. On the basis of constitutional or statutory authorization to address violations of international law, states could then proceed to exercise jurisdiction. Thus, the US Constitution delegates the power to Congress to 'define and punish ... [o]ffenses against the Law of Nations',[69] which enables the US Congress to create a domestic jurisdictional basis for the prosecution of such offences even absent an explicit international authorization. Similarly, the Alien Tort Statute (ATS) confers on US district courts 'original jurisdiction of any civil action by an alien for a tort only, committed in violation of the law of nations or a treaty of the United States',[70] regardless of whether the international law substantively proscribing the conduct also provides for jurisdiction. Such clauses nevertheless have a limiting effect in that they bar jurisdictional assertions that fail to address violations of international law. Thus, a US court has refused to establish its jurisdiction over drug trafficking, as this offence did not qualify as a violation of customary international law in the context of the Define and Punish Clause.[71] Also, under the ATS, US courts have dismissed jurisdiction where the impugned conduct did not rise to the level of a violation of international law. Notably, in *Sosa*, the US Supreme Court limited the violations falling within the ambit of the United States to those violations accepted by the civilized world, and defined with specificity comparable to the features of the eighteenth-century paradigms.[72]

[66] From that perspective, dual criminality can also broaden rather narrow the exercise of jurisdiction, especially in case dual criminality suffices for the exercise of jurisdiction, *without a nexus being required*. cf Michael Farbiarz, 'Extraterritorial Criminal Jurisdiction' (2016) 114 Mich L Rev 507, 550 (criticizing US court decisions which have required a US nexus for the extraterritorial due process doctrine to be satisfied, and noting the multilateral criminalization of a substantial number of offences).

[67] Uta Kohl, 'Corporate Human Rights Accountability: The Objections of Western Governments to the Alien Tort Statute' (2014) 63 ICLQ 665, 679, discussing the reach of the US Alien Tort Statute (ATS), which on its face provides for universal tort jurisdiction ('human rights are internationally recognized and thus ATS human rights litigation cannot create clashes with foreign law ... Here the US does not force its domestic law on other States [*eg* US antitrust law], but simply enforces law which everyone has agreed upon. Western States can hardly object to this aspect of the litigation, and they have not.').

[68] Gardner (n 8) 315.

[69] Art I sec 8 Cl 10.

[70] 28 USC para 1350.

[71] *United States v Bellaizac-Hurtado*, 700 F 3d 1245, 1248–49 (11th Cir. 2012) (defendants successfully challenging their convictions under the US Maritime Drug Law Enforcement Act for trafficking drugs in Panamanian waters).

[72] *Sosa v Alvarez-Machain*, 542 US 692 (2004). In *Sosa*, this meant that there was no jurisdiction as there was no customary international law prohibition of arbitrary arrests. Also environmental claims have little chance of success, as environmental violations are unlikely to qualify as violations of the law of nations under the *Sosa* standard. Kathleen Jaeger, 'Environmental Claims under the Alien Tort Statute' (2010) 28 Berkeley J Int'l L 519 (arguing that environmental harm may only be addressed in an ATS case where human rights abuses and environmental wrongs overlap)

Requiring international proscription may prevent international tension from coming to a head, although this only applies in theory.[73] In reality, states *have* protested, as states do not normally like another state to pass judgment on territorial conduct or conduct in which its own nationals are implicated.[74] Also, where jurisdictional assertions may, in the abstract, be cosmopolitan in nature, on closer inspection they may well be infused with domestic legal particularities, for example regarding the exact determination of liability, the sanctions imposed, the applicable procedural law, and the focus of enforcement.[75] This may cast doubt on the universal grounding of the assertions, trigger foreign protest, or have unwelcome consequences.[76] Furthermore, individuals targeted by international proscription-based jurisdictional assertions may protest, submitting that the sanctions imposed on them by the state acting 'extraterritorially' are harsher than those normally imposed by the territorial state.[77] Some of these concerns could be met by requiring procedural rather than mere substantive proscription. For others, additional principles of reasonableness, to be expounded shortly, may provide succor. It remains, nevertheless, that, some domestic boundary pushing may be welcome to realize global justice, even if it exceeds internationally agreed minimum standards.[78]

[73] See also Liivoja (n 10) 33–34 (referring, *inter alia*, to differences in the definition of criminal offences, and the general principles of criminal law); Gardner (n 8) 324 (noting the potential impact of power disparity, 'with the motivated state conducting investigations and pushing bilateral cooperation that may be contrary to the interests of affected states').

[74] See *eg* Nigeria's protest against the exercise of US jurisdiction under the Alien Tort Statute, Supplemental Brief for Respondents, *Kiobel v Royal Dutch Petroleum*, No 10-1491 (1 August 2012), at 5; and Dutch and UK protest relating to the same case, Supplemental Brief of the Governments of the Kingdom of the Netherlands and the United Kingdom of Great Britain and Northern Ireland as Amici Curiae in Support of Neither Party, *Kiobel v Royal Dutch Petroleum Co* 133 S Ct 1659 (2013) (No 10-1491) 6.

[75] Gardner (n 8) 343 ('To the extent that multilateral agreements trade generality for consensus, they will leave room for variation in implementation around the margins. In a system of channeled unilateralism, motivated states like the United States can exploit these margins to promote their preferences from within the multilateral framework.'). See for a damning indictment of US extraterritoriality regarding foreign corrupt practices: Ellen Gutterman, 'Extraterritoriality as an Analytic Lens. Examining the Global Governance of Transnational Bribery and Corruption' in Daniel Margolies and others (eds), *The Extraterritoriality of Law: History, Theory, Politics* (Routledge 2019) 192–93 (arguing that 'US extraterritoriality acts as a brake on global anti-corruption efforts, citing the focus of [Foreign Corrupt Practices Act] enforcement on 'specific actors and instances of corrupt transactions rather than tackling the embedded networks and practices in which opportunities for corruption are cultivated in the global economy').

[76] Steven S Nam, 'Restoring Liberalism to Transnational Corporate Accountability: From Universal Jurisdiction's Ashes to an Afterlife of Multilateral Avenues' (2017) 31 EILR 361, 372 ('Contrary to its cosmopolitan intent, [universal tort jurisdiction based on the Alien Tort Statute] could produce new strains of international law informed by U.S. domestic legal understandings yet dressed in universality.'), (citing US Supreme Court Justice Stephen Breyer's 'fear of American international law 'hegemony', Stephen Breyer, *The Court and the World: American Law and the New Global Realties* (Knopf 2015) 148.

[77] Such due process concerns may be soothed if sanctions or sentences are limited to what is common in the territorial state, *eg* on the basis of extradition pledges. Farbiarz (n 66) 544 (submitting that 'it would seem readily possible for U.S. prosecutors to wholly eliminate sentencing conflicts and the due process-triggering unfairness that comes with them-simply by making binding representations that they will not seek certain penalties').

[78] Gardner (n 8) 344 (2015) (arguing that, in the field of transnational criminal law, US-defined standards may not necessarily displace international standards but may instead be 'just another input

What is certain is that international proscription goes a long way to limit jurisdictional overreach. The question arises, however, whether it does not go too long a way. For one thing, international proscription remains strongly tied to the principle of state consent, which allows states to block socially desirable international proscriptions. But more importantly perhaps is that thinking in terms of proscription, which is very much a criminal law notion, does not account for the range of international instruments which oblige states to take action to protect a common interest (*eg* by limiting emissions to combat climate change), rather than proscribing particular conduct. Therefore, a modified international proscription principle may have to be accepted, pursuant to which a third state's exercise of prescriptive jurisdiction aimed at protecting a common interest may derive its legitimacy and reasonableness from its embeddedness in an international instruments recognizing that a particular interest as indeed common to the international community. This embeddedness may offset the asserting state's possibly tenuous territorial or personal links with the subject matter. Again, such an instrument may or may not explicitly provide for unilateral action. It may be legally binding, or perhaps only politically authoritative.[79] What is key, however, is that requiring third states' exercise of prescriptive jurisdiction to be internationally embedded ensures that such jurisdiction accords with the cosmopolitan goal it pretends to serve. This may in turn prevent international conflict.

Along similar lines, in her review of unilateral trade-restrictive measures serving global or extraterritorial environmental objectives, Barbara Cooreman has suggested the use of a 'decision tree', pursuant to which the 'outward concern' of such measures, and their attendant limited jurisdictional link to the regulating state, could be compensated by their embeddedness in international hard or soft regulation.[80] Also, other critiques in the literature on the trade/environment nexus have based the legitimacy of unilateral measures with extraterritorial effect on their relationship with existing international regulation, to which the 'international community', and in particular third countries and third country operators affected by

in a continuing discursive process', citing the 'positive role that U.S. policy has played in the progressive normative development of victim-oriented standards', regarding US unilateralism in the context of human trafficking regulation) (citation omitted).

[79] See *eg* the EU Commission's reference to the (non-binding) Extractive Industry Transparency Initiative (EITI) and the Kimberley Process regarding conflict diamonds in the context of its wish to 'step up efforts to improve transparency in the extractive industries (oil, gas and mining) and the forest sector by allowing effective use of information generated by the EITI and disclosed by companies on their payments to governments from the exploitation of natural resources as part of the new EU legislative requirements on country-by-country reporting'. Communication from the Commission to the European Parliament, the Council, the European Economic and Social Committee, and the Committee of the Regions, A Stronger Role of the Private Sector in Achieving Inclusive and Sustainable Growth in Developing Countries, COM(2014) 263 final, p 12.

[80] Barbara Cooreman, *Global Environmental Protection through Trade: A Systematic Approach to Extraterritoriality* (Edward Elgar 2017). Measures addressing 'inward concerns', *eg* a territorial environmental issue, such as local pollution, need not have a substantive basis in international regulation.

such measures, have arguably consented.[81] In addition, in the field of human rights and security, the extent to which unilateral measures relate, or give effect to international regulation has been cited as a relevant factor with respect to the legitimacy of unilateral jurisdiction. For instance, EU import requirements regarding minerals sourced from conflict-affected and high-risk areas have been considered as justified because they find their basis in a Guidance of the Organisation for Economic Co-operation and Development (OECD) and a UN Security Council resolution.[82]

Embeddedness of a unilateral measure in international norms is no guarantee that such a measure will *necessarily* command international acceptance. One may recall in this respect developing countries' fierce resistance against trade-restrictive measures taken on the ground of non-compliance with international labour standards,[83] or US blocking legislation in relation to the EU Aviation Directive.[84] Nonetheless, it constitutes a major jurisdictional limitation that weeds out entirely self-serving, idiosyncratic, jurisdictional assertions. At the same time, considering such embeddedness as a necessary but also *sufficient* condition for the legitimacy of a jurisdictional assertions strengthens the effectiveness of international regulation. Unilateral measures which build on international regulatory initiatives are not just more legitimate but they also serve as enforcement multipliers. After all, international instruments may well protect particular global values and common interests, but they do not often provide for a strong enforcement machinery, instead putting implementation and enforcement in the hands of states. Vigorous 'extraterritorial' enforcement by bystander states could then compensate for other states' more lacklustre performance, and further the effectiveness of the international regime.[85] Weaker states may even welcome motivated states' enforcement

[81] cf Ryngaert and Koekkoek (n 22) 57 (submitting that 'it is hardly surprising that the EU often seeks to ward opposition by basing its environmental measures giving rise to territorial extension upon an "objective standard" which is embodied in either third country or international law'). Hadjiyianni, for her part, has criticized the CJEU, when it interprets, or rules on the validity of EU environmental legislation with extraterritorial effect, for failing to pay sufficient attention to the extent to which such legislation ties in with international efforts and standards. Hadjiyianni, 'The Role of Domestic Courts in Global Environmental Governance' (n 58) 12, in relation to Case C-424/13 *Zuchtvieh-Export GmbH v Stadt Kempten* [2015] ECLI:EU:C:2015:259; Council Regulation (EC) 1/2005 on the protection of animals during transport and related operations [2005] OJ L3/1.

[82] Enrico Partiti and Steffen Van der Velde, 'Curbing Supply-Chain Human Rights Violations Through Trade and Due Diligence. Possible WTO Concerns Raised by the EU Conflict Minerals Regulation' (2017) 51 JWT 1043, 1061.

[83] *Eg* Onyeka Osuji, 'Transnational Corporations and the Protection of Human Rights: Non-Financial Reporting as an Option' in Derrick M Nault and Shwan L England (eds), *Globalization and Human Rights in the Developing World* (Palgrave Macmillan 2011) 88.

[84] US European Union Emissions Trading Prohibition Act of 2011 (prohibiting compliance of US airlines with 'extraterritorially applied' EU law on aviation emissions). See also Joanne Scott, 'The Global Reach of EU Law' in Marise Cremona and Joanne Scott, *EU Law Beyond EU Borders: The Extraterritorial Reach of EU Law* (OUP 2019) 30–31 (discussing foreign opposition to territorially extended EU law in the environmental field).

[85] Also Gardner (n 8) 300 ('When treaties channel unilateralism, they invite unilateral actions that in turn support the treaty regime, creating a positive feedback loop that improves both compliance and effectiveness over time.').

efforts, as such efforts may prevent that harmful activity is displaced to the former states.[86] This analytical focus on the enforcement dimension may even allow us to locate such action in the realm of enforcement rather than prescriptive jurisdiction. After all, states enforcing a norm laid down in an international instrument are not materially prescribing their own laws, even if their enforcement action will obviously have a domestic legal basis.[87]

Similarly, it may happen that third states, while perhaps not enforcing a norm laid down in an international instrument, may enforce a norm laid down in another state's law, thus exercising vicarious jurisdiction. Also in that case, third states do no more than enforcing an already existing norm, and should thus not be considered as acting fully unilaterally. Some EU unilateral measures with extraterritorial effect are of this type. For instance, the EU Timber Regulation, which aims to fight illegal logging and related trade in timber, defines the term 'illegally harvested' timber as timber 'harvested in contravention of the applicable legislation in the country of harvest'.[88] Accordingly, this Regulation is no more than an enforcement tool which imposes due diligence obligations on operators who place on the EU internal market timber harvested in a manner that violates the law of the country of origin.[89] That there is no *multilateral* agreement on trade in forest products, which addresses illegal logging, is of no moment in this respect.[90] From a legitimacy perspective, it suffices that that the logging

[86] ibid, 315 (focusing on transnational criminal activity).

[87] Compare with how choice of law interacts with jurisdiction in private international law: Alex Mills, 'Private Interests and Private Law Regulation in Public International Law Jurisdiction' (2018) 14, https://papers.ssrn.com/sol3/papers.cfm?abstract_id=3147718 (accessed 5 December 2019) ('In private law disputes, issues of "jurisdiction" (in the international law sense) must therefore involve a careful distinction between the exercise of judicial process (generally referred to, somewhat unhelpfully, as the question of "jurisdiction") and the applicable law which is actualised through that process (generally referred to as the question of "choice of law").'); Paul D Mora, 'Universal Civil Jurisdiction and Forum Necessitatis: The Confusion of Public and Private International Law in Naït-Liman v. Switzerland' (2018) 65 NILR 155 suggesting that choice of law relates to enforcement jurisdiction ('The choice of law enquiry does not form part of the international jurisdiction to prescribe… A decision on the application of the law is on that is concerned with its enforcement.').

[88] Art 2(g) Regulation (EU) No 995/2010 of the European Parliament and of the Council of 20 October 2010 laying down the obligations of operators who place timber and timber products on the market, OJ L 295/23 (2010) ('Timber Regulation').

[89] ibid, art 4.1 EU Timber Regulation (n 88).

[90] cf Commission Staff Working Document, 'Accompanying document to the Proposal for a Regulation of the European Parliament and of the Council determining the obligations of operators who make timber and timber products available on the Market, Impact Assessment, Report on Additional Options to Combat Illegal Logging' (October 2008) 14–15 ('While a number of countries have been fairly open to discuss the control of illegal logging in the international forest policy arena, negotiations on a multilateral framework, which started more than 20 years ago (FAO and following UN forest panels and forest fora), have only known very limited progress. The United Nations Forum on Forests (UNFF) has recently (2007) however made progress towards a non-legally binding instrument on forests, but it is unlikely that in this forum a multilateral agreement on trade in forest products could be established in the foreseeable future. Many governments, including some key forest rich countries like Brazil continue to oppose such an idea. They in particular insist that legislation and law enforcement are issues of national sovereignty.').

activity is illegal under the law of the state of origin.[91] Similarly, the due diligence requirements imposed on the importation of some minerals by the EU Conflict Minerals Regulation tie in with due diligence standards which countries such as the Democratic Republic of the Congo (DRC) and Rwanda had already introduced in their own legislation, under the impetus of the International Conference of the Great Lakes Region.[92] The relevant requirements are moreover based on OECD Guidelines.[93] Thus, also the EU Conflict Minerals Regulation could be conceived of as a legal tool to enforce existing national initiatives which are, on their own, not effective enough to address a particular governance issue that is of global relevance.[94]

In conclusion, international proscription or international embeddedness of a unilateral measure with extraterritorial effect tends to confer legitimacy, preempt international protest, and thus softens the rough edges of unilateralism. However, a mere 'abstract' basis of a unilateral measure in multilateral initiatives may not lay the legitimacy challenge to rest. Especially in case the unilateral measure has distributive consequences which do not *ipso facto* follow from the multilateral initiative, the legitimacy of the measure may remain questionable. This is the case when the measure, while pursuing the multilaterally set goal (*eg* climate change mitigation or tackling pollution), imposes particular burdens on third countries and their operators, on the basis of a tenuous, or artificially constructed territorial nexus. These jurisdictional assertions may have to be subjected to additional mitigation techniques. The next section will explore whether, and how foreign countries and their nationals could have a more direct voice in the design and enforcement of third state extraterritorial regulation in the common interest

[91] That the EU Timber Regulation defers to foreign proscription obviously does not mean, however, that foreign states will automatically accept the legitimacy of the Regulation: 'captured' authorities in those states may well be content with existing levels of non-enforcement and resent strict vicarious enforcement by the importer state. Accordingly, the EU Timber Regulation does not fully shed its unilateral character. Due to the political and technical impossibility of concluding international agreements (voluntary partnership agreements) with every single forest-rich country, the EU may however have had no other option than to apply due diligence requirements across the board unilaterally to any timber imports, while deferring to local interpretations of legality. cf Commission Staff Working Document, 'Accompanying document to the Proposal for a Regulation of the European Parliament and of the Council determining the obligations of operators who make timber and timber products available on the Market, Impact Assessment, Report on additional options to combat illegal logging (October 2008)', 30.

[92] European Commission, Directorate-General for Trade, 'Report on the Public Consultation on a Possible EU Initiative on Responsible Sourcing of Minerals Originating from Conflict-Affects and High-Risk Areas, Contributions from stakeholders' (July 2013) 25–26.

[93] OECD Due Diligence Guidance for Responsible Supply Chains of Minerals from Conflict-Affected and High-Risk Areas (3rd edn 2016).

[94] Directorate-General for Trade, 'Report on the Public Consultation on a Possible EU Initiative on Responsible Sourcing of Minerals' (n 92) 25–26. ibid, p 27 ('Respondents report that while the Rwandan scheme states that all minerals traded in Rwanda must be tagged and certified, the trade in "conflict minerals" is still possible because of corruption and smuggling.').

4.3 Democratic Participation

Extraterritorial laws may be considered to be inherently undemocratic,[95] as they interfere with individuals' right to self-government in the territory of another state, where the latter's laws may be supplanted by the former's.[96] These foreign individuals may never have democratically consented to extraterritorial regulation[97] as they are not represented within the political institutions of the extraterritorially acting state,[98] or at least have little influence on that state's political processes.[99] For instance, states taking unilateral trade measures informed by environmental considerations and thus rendering access to their markets more difficult to foreign producers may do so without the latter having been represented in the decision-making process.[100] This issue of non-representation is not a trivial one, as unilateral acts, in a technical field such as trade and the environment, can have major consequences for foreign actors, who may see their welfare decrease dramatically.[101]

The regulatory challenge then becomes how to involve foreign states and their nationals into the design and enforcement of extraterritorial regulation. This section discusses the foundations and principles of participation of foreign interests in extraterritorial regulation, and provides some empirical information regarding how states and the European Union already pay heed to their interests when designing such regulation. Attention is also paid to how foreign nationals adversely affected by extraterritorial regulation can challenge its validity or influence its interpretation before the courts of unilaterally acting states.

4.3.1 Foundations and principles of participation

The extraterritorial regulation with which we are concerned is aimed at furthering the interests of the international community. This does not render the non-representation of non-citizens unproblematic, however. By unilaterally applying

[95] Austen L Parrish, 'The Effects Test: Extraterritoriality's Fifth Business' (2008) 61 Vanderbilt L Rev 1453, 1483; Austen L Parrish, 'Reclaiming International Law from Extraterritoriality' (2009) 93 MLR 815, 820 ('The rise of extraterritorial domestic law ... poses a greater threat to democratic sovereignty than traditional sources of international law.').

[96] Koskenniemi, 'What Use for Sovereignty Today?' (n 1) 68. Parts of this section have earlier been published in Dutch as Cedric Ryngaert, 'Participatie van derdelanders in extraterritoriale regelgeving: naar een transnationaal bestuursrecht' in Anouska Buijze and others (eds), *Goed bestuur in perspectief—Liber Amicorum Henk Addink* 77–88 (Wolters Kluwer 2019).

[97] Guyora Binder 'Authority to Proscribe and Punish International Crimes' (2013) 63 UTLJ 278.

[98] Shaffer (n 15) EJIL 684 ('national institutions ... make decisions which affect outsiders who are not represented before them'); Meyer (n 4) 157 ('The foreign targets of a U.S. extraterritorial law have little potential democratic redress.').

[99] Parrish, 'Reclaiming International Law from Extraterritoriality' (n 95) 860.

[100] Davies (n 7) 1208.

[101] Marise Cremona and Päivi Leino, 'The New Frontiers of EU Administrative Law, Is There an Accountability Gap in EU External Relations?' (2017) 2 EP 699, 705–06.

such regulation, states effectively render membership of this international community compulsory, thereby weakening non-citizens own 'sense of a community'.[102] From a perspective of contemporary political theory, compulsory community membership, which includes being bound by legal norms, can only be legitimate if the norm-addressees (citizens) can adequately participate in relevant decision-making processes.[103] Participation allows for the transnational repoliticization and 'liberalization' of unilateral national decision-making with extraterritorial effects,[104] in keeping with the tenets of global administrative law as well as political sovereignty and self-government ('with power comes accountability'). Participation and representation of affected foreign persons (states, individuals, operators),[105] transparency, accountability, and international regulatory cooperation, possibly via networks,[106] are therefore advisable[107]—provided of course that foreign persons and regulators also wish to participate.[108] Langer has referred in this respect, in the context of universal criminal jurisdiction, to the 'procedural principle of affected interests', according to which 'whenever a decision of an institution affects the interests of an individual or group, fairness requires that this individual or group has procedural rights to participate and to hold accountable

[102] Doreen Lustig and Eyal Benvenisti, 'The Multinational Corporation as "The Good Despot": The Democratic Costs of Privatization in Global Settings' (2013) GlobalTrust Working Paper Series 01/2013, 26, discussing the tension between corporations 'home states' unilateral regulation http://globaltrust.tau.ac.il/wp-content/uploads/2014/01/Good-Despot-TIL-WP-1-13.pdf (accessed on 5 December 2019) (*eg* by establishing 'extraterritorial' jurisdiction over overseas corporate abuses) and host states' economic self-determination.

[103] Rafael Domingo, 'The New Global Human Community' (2012) 12 CJIL 563, 84.

[104] It has been claimed that exercising unilateral jurisdiction 'is inconsistent with a core tenet of liberalism itself—a state and its constituents should not be subject to the external authority of other states'. cf Nam (n 76) 365. Unlike Nam, who, in the context of universal civil jurisdiction over transnational corporations, instead suggests exploring alternative avenues ('inclusive public–private diplomacy open to all stakeholders', *eg* via compensation funds, and the UN Guiding Principles) (ibid, 365–66), and suggests ceding accountability 'in polycentric fashion to governments, civil society, and business enterprises' (ibid, 391), I am not willing to sacrifice unilateral jurisdiction just yet. Instead, I suggest *remedying*, as far as possible, the undemocratic impact of unilateralism, through the development of participatory mechanisms.

[105] Parrish, 'The Effects Test' (n 95) 1486.

[106] Ralf Michaels 'Global Problems in Domestic Courts' in Sam Muller and others (eds), *The Law of the Future and the Future of the Law* (Torkel Opsahl Academic EPublisher 2011). In the antitrust field, such networked cooperation has been rather successful, with Sassen even suggesting that antitrust regulators share more with each other than with colleagues back home (Saskia Sassen, *Territory, Authority, Rights: From Medieval to Global Assemblages* (PUP 2006) 237).

[107] Shaffer (n 15) 688, citing the following accountability mechanisms proposed by global administrative law (GAL) in the (unilateral) production of global public goods: transparency, access to information, engagement with civil society and national parliaments, reporting, notice and comment procedures, reason-giving, and proportionality. Also Koskenniemi, 'What Use for Sovereignty Today?' (n 1) 68 (arguing, although not in the context of extraterritoriality, but rather with respect to the informal management of social problems by global expert regimes, that transparency and accountability could 'contribute to the re-imaging of what international politics could mean today').

[108] Such procedures of foreign actors' participation in unilateralism are obviously only a second-best option compared to mechanisms of participation in multilateral institutions Nico Krisch, 'The Decay of Consent: International Law in an Age of Global Public Goods' (2014) 108 AJIL 1, 33 ('participation in this mode is far less effective than in classical multilateralism').

the institution's decision-making process'.[109] Similarly, Davies, writing in the context of 'extraterritorial' trade measures, cites the 'need for reflexivity and mutual learning', and posits that the aforementioned principles of participation require that 'lawmakers and courts take account of wider interests than those of their own constituents and listen to those in other jurisdictions' when devising trade measures with extraterritorial effects on foreign producers.[110] In a maximalist interpretation of modes of participation and representation, decision-making bodies could in the interest of legitimacy and fairness even be entirely 'hybridized' in the sense that decision-makers from different states sit on domestic bodies addressing issues of extraterritoriality.[111]

Outsider participation in domestic decision-making processes with respect to unilateral action may at least be a legitimate expectation harboured by norm addressees,[112] even if falling short of a (binding) international law norm.[113] It mitigates global values/public goods consequentialism by re-importing the seminal deontological value of selfhood.[114]

The theoretically most notable contribution to the debate about involving foreign affected persons in domestic decision-making has arguably been made by Eyal Benvenisti in the context of his Global Trust project.[115] While that project does as such not mention the term 'jurisdiction', it clearly has jurisdictional overtones because it focuses on the question whether states, when setting national policies and thereby routinely affecting foreigners in faraway countries, may have to provide the latter with adequate opportunities to participate in shaping the former's policies. When states exercise cosmopolitan jurisdiction with extraterritorial

[109] Langer (n 19) 748 (citing the right to be heard, the right for transparency, and the right that the institution be responsive to one's concerns).

[110] Davies (n 7) 1222.

[111] This applies in particular to *courts*. Paul S Berman 'Global Legal Pluralism' (2007) 80 SCLR 1155, 1218 (giving historical examples). Compare the Extraordinary Chambers in the Courts of Senegal, which have been established within the domestic court system of Senegal to judge former Chad dictator Hissène Habré for international crimes under the universality principle, but which are composed of judges from various African countries. 'Statute of the Extraordinary African Chambers within the courts of Senegal created to prosecute international crimes committed in Chad between 7 June 1982 and 1 December 1990' (22 August 2012). Unofficial translation available here http://www.hrw.org/news/2013/09/02/statute-extraordinary-african-chambers (accessed 6 December 2019).

[112] Thus, as Krisch observed, foreign governments and exporters should been allowed to comment on US environmental, 'turtle-protecting' legislation that applied extraterritorially to foreign fishermen harvesting shrimp (Krisch (n 108) 33). This legislation, which was effectively protecting a global environmental interest, was successfully challenged before the WTO, *US—Import Prohibition of Certain Shrimp and Shrimp Products—Appellate Body Report* (12 October 1998) WT/DS58/AB/R. After the WTO Panel and Appellate Body reviewed the US extraterritorial assertions, the United States changed its legal procedures 'better to assure due process review of the situations and concerns of these countries and their traders'. Shaffer (n 15) 688.

[113] Compare Krisch (n 108) 33 (arguing that representation and consultation of affected actors may replace their consent, but that these mechanisms 'have yet to mature into formal requirements that apply generally to global governance institutions').

[114] Koskenniemi, 'What Use for Sovereignty Today?' (n 1) 69 (submitting that 'authority is not simply about outcomes', but 'also about self-hood and relationship to others').

[115] http://globaltrust.tau.ac.il/ (accessed 5 December 2019).

effects, they tend to affect foreign-based persons. In an influential article in the *American Journal of International Law*, Benvenisti made the (granted, not entirely new) claim that sovereignty entails responsibility, and that sovereign states should be considered as trustees of mankind.[116] Pursuant to this (unfortunately historically charged)[117] concept of trustee sovereignty, 'sovereigns are obligated to provide remedies that can correct, or at least minimize, the loss to individuals of the ability to participate meaningfully in shaping their life opportunities'.[118] Arguing from the perspective of democratic theory and the right to self-determination, Benvenisti went on to suggest the imposition of minimal obligations on states to take others' interests into account, for example by offering reasons and paying due respect.[119] This is a convincing argument that partly draws on global administrative law's suggestion to apply the principles of accountability, transparency, and participation that have matured in domestic settings to global governance.[120] Indeed, insofar as states extend laws beyond their borders to affect global outcomes, they are taking part in global governance. Those who are affected by such laws, whether there are based in the territory or outside it, should have a voice in their design.

Allowing foreign affected persons a voice in domestic deliberative processes is not only desirable from a democratic theory perspective but also from an implementation point of view. Participation of the extraterritorial norm addressees may increase the chances of successful implementation of the relevant norms. They are more likely to support norms in the design of which they were able participate and thus, over which they could claim some ownership.[121] In addition, participation may increase the quality of regulation, and ultimately global welfare and justice, as foreign affected persons may suggest regulatory solutions and perspectives which the asserting state had not yet imagined.[122] Where moral and utilitarian considerations do not suffice to convince unilaterally acting states to

[116] Eyal Benvenisti, 'Sovereigns as Trustees of Humanity: On the Accountability of States to Foreign Stakeholders' (2013) 107 AJIL 295.

[117] Benvenisti was criticized for advocating neocolonialism and domination: trusteeship may be traced back to 'the civilizing mission' of the European colonial powers, and to the continuation of the colonial system via the 'trust system', which required that states responsible for their administration take adequate steps to prepare them for self-government or independence. See Chapter XIII of the UN Charter (all Trust Territories have in the meantime obtained self-government or independence). Benvenisti has countered, however, that the critics did not understand him well: 'my version of trusteeship of humanity did not support giving *more* powers over foreign stakeholders, but just the opposite, requiring more *burdens* on trustees' resources and more *constraints* on trustees' autonomy' (original emphasis). See Eyal Benvenisti, 'Who Trusts the Trustees? (Answer: No One Should)' (*Global Trust*, 8 February 2015), <http://globaltrust.tau.ac.il/who-trusts-the-trustees-answer-no-one-should/ > (accessed 5 December 2019).

[118] Benvenisti, 'Sovereigns as Trustees of Humanity' (n 116) 313.

[119] ibid, 318.

[120] Benedict Kingsbury and others, 'The Emergence of Global Administrative Law' (2005) 68 LCP 15.

[121] Krisch (n 108) 9 ('Broad participation may foster implementation.').

[122] Benvenisti, 'Sovereigns as Trustees of Humanity' (n 116) 300. See also regarding the role of courts in this respect Eyal Benvenisti, 'Community Interests in International Adjudication' GlobalTrust Working Paper 04/2016, 15.

establish consultation and representation mechanisms, strategic reciprocity may perhaps serve as a pull mechanism. A failure to establish such mechanisms may invite other states, and possibly illiberal states to turn the tables, to the detriment of the liberal states which normally engage in regulatory unilateralism,[123] or at the very least to take retaliatory action.[124] In reality, reciprocity and retaliation will exert normative pressure if third states have the power and capacity to respond in a unilateral fashion.[125]

Allowing outsiders to have a say in the adoption of extraterritorial regulation need not deprive territoriality of its continued relevance. True, under a radical conception of global democratic theory, borders collapse, and any person affected by a regulatory decision, wherever the world (s)he may be found, may be allowed to have a voice in the design of such a decision. But as argued earlier, this is not the world in which we live. Moreover it is normatively questionable whether this is the world we *should* live in: in spite of spatio-temporal changes, individuals may still rather strongly identify with the territorially delimited community in which they live. Therefore, while citizens of *other* territorial communities may, and should, have a voice in the design of foreign laws to the extent that they are affected by them, their voice should possibly not be accorded the same weight as the voice of the asserting state's own citizens. Deciding otherwise, and for instance giving foreign-based persons the right to vote—insofar as this would be practically possible at all—might unduly interfere in the life choices of local communities.[126] Allowing foreign-based persons to vote down extraterritorial laws inevitably comes down to allowing them to second-guess local regulatory choices, and thus to violate principles of democracy and self-determination.[127] Such regulatory choices should arguably remain with the territorial community.

It remains that democratic considerations call for the development of mechanisms that factor in—although not necessarily slavishly give effect to—the views of foreign affected persons. How exactly this should be done—the extent to which

[123] Compare Parrish, 'The Effects Test' (n 95) 1453–485.

[124] See in this respect as regards jurisdictional overreach in the field of EU competition law: Luca Prete, 'On Implementation and Effects: The Recent Case-law on the Territorial (or Extraterritorial?) Application of EU Competition Rules' (2018) 9 JECLP 487, 493.

[125] Universality laws in Belgium and Spain were for instance scaled back arguably out of fear that more powerful states would impose political and economic sanctions. See for Belgium, *eg* Antonio Cassese 'Is the Bell Tolling for Universality—A Plea for a Sensible Notion of Universal Jurisdiction' (2003) 1 JICJ 589.

[126] Benvenisti, 'Sovereigns as Trustees of Humanity' (n 116) 313 (relying on JS Mill, who draw attention to the need for communities to pursue their own unique preferences). Compare Langer (n 19) 748, fn 37 ('the procedural principle of affected interests that I am articulating *would not give the right to participate in the decision-making body*, but to be heard by the decision-making body and that this body be responsive to one's concerns') (emphasis added).

[127] Obviously, this argument has less strength in case the law in question is *only* applied extraterritorially, and not domestically, in which case the asserting state may be seen to unjustifiably intervene in the life choices of others, without making its own sacrifices in the global interest. When such action is given shape by trade restrictions, it may be considered as protectionism that runs afoul of the law of the WTO.

such views should be taken into account, and whose views should be solicited—is *context-specific*.

The *extent* to which unilaterally regulating states should pay heed to the interests of outsiders may ultimately be a question of (normatively guided) political choices.[128] Parameters to take into account include the scope of the regulation, the intensity of foreign stakeholders being affected, and state capacity.[129] In this respect, one cannot expect states to incur prohibitively high costs to accommodate participation of foreign affected persons,[130] for example by requiring them to translate all relevant documents into a language understandable to them and to explain complicated aspects of the regulation. What is key, however, is that these mechanisms, while perhaps not enabling the formation of a 'collective will', at least facilitate the definition, generation, and implementation of intersubjectively shared values by giving access or providing accountability to foreign affected persons.[131]

The extent of outsider participation varies depending on the relevant policy field.[132] It may perhaps be argued that foreign input need not be sought or heeded in case a domestic regulation with extraterritorial effect protects common interests,[133] but this is not necessarily persuasive in respect of *all* common interests. There may indeed be less concern over unilateral action to suppress piracy, international crimes, and terrorism, as such acts have been clearly outlawed and even criminalized by international treaties, customary international law, and other mechanisms of international cooperation. In economic terms, they represent

[128] Cremona and Leino (n 109), 707–08 (stating that 'the balancing of interests [between parochial, foreign and international interests] at the micro as well as the macro level is inevitably and rightly a matter for political determination. In the absence of that political debate there is only so much that administrative law can do.').

[129] Benvenisti, 'Sovereigns as Trustees of Humanity' (n 116) 320 ('the question of deciding upon particular "minimal" deliberative obligations raises several secondary questions. They include the extent to which states ought to involve foreign-stakeholders in their decision-making processes, taking into account the costs that are involved; how to determine the circle of those regarded as stakeholders entitled to a hearing; and how information should be made available to them during hearings or when presenting the rationale for the policies chosen. The answers to these and other questions must be sensitive to different areas of regulation, the types of interests that are affected, the relative wealth and capacities of the state, among other considerations.').

[130] Langer (n 19) 751 (observing this in respect of requirements imposed on universal jurisdiction states).

[131] With respect to proceedings under the universality principle, for instance, it has been suggested that states—in particular the rich Western states where such proceedings are initiated—could inform an international audience of these proceedings by means of periodical reports, or allow civil society to file *amicus curiae* briefs. Langer (n 19) 761.

[132] Cremona and Leino (n 109) 704 ('[These] issues are much less easy to determine, both legally and normatively: to what extent should the EU be required to consider as "relevant facts" the situation in a third country or the consequences of an EU action on third country nationals? To what extent is the EU required to take into account the interests of third country nationals affected by its action; what is the scope of its duty of care in such cases?').

[133] Compare Krisch (n 108) 6, Krisch, citing flexibility in democratic theory, and arguing in this respect that, when it comes to protecting global public goods through non-consensual action, the effective protection of such goods in the common interest may trump requirements of consent and the principle of sovereign equality.

'weakest link' problems caused by international outliers that have to be coerced for the global public good to be supplied.[134] Such coercion may also be done unilaterally where the territorial state is unable or unwilling to assume its responsibility,[135] and where a competent multilateral institution is lacking (teeth). Where a global public good is rather in the 'aggregate effort' category, in contrast, a range of positive acts by an internally differentiated international community should be taken to protect the good, without any one specific act being per se illegal. Because action is differentiated, any unilateral determination of how such differentiation should take place necessarily has distributional effects, which affected parties should be able to contest through procedural mechanisms made available by the unilaterally acting state. Thus, for unilateral action in respect of aggregate effort goods such as combating climate change, for example, effectiveness may not prevail over consent as strongly as in respect of weakest link goods.

The precise type of outsiders to involve will depend on who is potentially affected by the envisaged regulation. Actors other than just foreign states may have to be involved. Indeed, in the cosmopolitan approach, which ascribes moral value to every individual—the approach which we espouse in this study—also individuals and other private actors (*eg* corporations) have participatory rights.[136] This means that states or the European Union, while having the cosmopolitan right or even duty to exercise their jurisdiction unilaterally, also have the cosmopolitan duty to take into account the interests of all affected actors, whether they are states, individuals, associations, corporations, etc.[137] After all, selfhood and self-determination, and even (democratic) sovereignty as a concept aggregating individual selfhoods, are global values in their own right.

In case states 'unilaterally' tackle an extraterritorial governance challenge that is located in a *specific country or area*, such as a local human rights or environmental problem, it is advisable that they do so in coordination with *local stakeholders*, in particular community representatives and local businesses. These may have more regional knowledge and their involvement may be key to the successful implementation of an extraterritorial regulatory scheme. A fine example is offered by Western regulatory efforts aimed at stemming the flow of 'conflict minerals' exploited in mines in Central Africa in a manner which sustains civil wars and is accompanied by human rights abuses. Both the United States and the European

[134] Bodansky (n 15) 667.
[135] ibid, 662.
[136] On the participation and legal status of non-state actors in international law: Jean d'Aspremont (ed), *Participants in the International Legal System* (Routledge 2011); Math Noortmann and others (eds), *Non-State Actors in International Law* (Hart 2015); Noemi Gal-Or and others (eds) *Responsibilities of the Non-State Actors in Armed Conflict and the Market Place: Theoretical Considerations and Empirical Findings International Law* (Brill 2015).
[137] Langer (n 19) 740 (contrasting, in the context of the exercise of universal criminal jurisdiction, statist conceptions with cosmopolitan/natural law/global administrative law conceptions; pursuant to the latter, 'all states and all human beings have the right to be heard by domestic authorities that enact and enforce universal jurisdiction statutes').

Union have adopted unilateral regulations to prevent these minerals from ending up on their markets, either by requiring companies to disclose whether their products contain conflict minerals,[138] or by subjecting importers of minerals to mandatory due diligence requirements.[139] These measures, while in themselves not an exercise of extraterritorial jurisdiction in the strict sense of the word, are clearly unilateral acts aimed at having a (positive) extraterritorial impact in the state of origin. Without cooperation of the latter state and private persons in that state, such measures will have little impact: due diligence schemes require that at all levels of the supply chain the minerals can be traced and checked. This requires continuous monitoring and supervision, especially at the mining site where the abuses tend to occur. Involvement of, and engagement with local stakeholders, and sensitivity to their concerns, are called for to guarantee the success of bystander states' regulatory endeavours.[140] This holds true even if in the targeted state, local mining officials and local civil society groups are generally supportive of the bystander states' actions.[141] Also, in such situations, the bystander state may want to make sure that it listens to the voice of all who are (locally) affected, including disenfranchised and marginalized actors who may face difficulties in *proprio motu* bringing their concerns to the bystander state's attention.

This potential participation ultimately points to a more fundamental issue, namely whether all affected third country nationals make, and can make, proper use of the consultation opportunities that may be on offer. Political science research shows that states tend to be particularly interested in providing access to the policy-making process to non-state actors which can provide 'access goods', that is, information, that is crucial in the policy-making process.[142] This research also bears out the fact that organizations which 'command sufficient financial resources, can bring in policy information and have economic clout tend to have better access

[138] Section 1502 of the US Dodd–Frank Wall Street Reform and Consumer Protection Act of 2010.

[139] Regulation (EU) 2017/821 of the European Parliament and of the Council of 17 May 2017 laying down supply chain due diligence obligations for Union importers of tin, tantalum, and tungsten, their ores, and gold originating from conflict-affected and high-risk areas [2017] OJ L 130/1.

[140] cf Christiana Ochoa and Patrick J Keenan, 'Regulating Information Flows, Regulating Conflict: An Analysis of United Stated Conflict Minerals Legislation' (2011) 3 GJIL 129, 153.

[141] See on local DRC support in particular Christopher K Schuele, 'Healing the Congo's Colonial Scars: Advocating for a Hybrid Approach to Conflict Minerals Reporting Regulations in the European Union' 33 Wis Int'l LJ 755, 778, 781, also citing a DRC archbishop's support for Western states' actions ('As I and many of my fellow bishops are firsthand witnesses to the powerful dynamics in regions affected by conflict, having engaged in dialogue with all involved, we can assure that nothing less than a mandatory system will be able to the change the behaviour of companies and other actors.'). Note that the Dodd–Frank Act has been criticized for insufficiently involving African voices in its drafting, although it received African support after its adoption. Thomas Voland and Daly Shona, 'The EU Regulation on Conflict Minerals: The Way Out of a Vicious Cycle?' (2018) JWT 52, 43. The EU Conflict Minerals Regulation has more local ownership as it based on relevant OECD Guidelines which were developed in cooperation with the International Conference of the Great Lakes Region, which consists of the states of that region. See the references in the Preamble of the Regulation

[142] Pieter Bouwen, 'Exchanging Access Goods for Access: A Comparative Study of Business Lobbying in the European Union Institutions' (2004) 43 EJPR 337, 361.

than other groups, which gives them a greater chance to have a say in ... policies'.[143] These organizations are typically business organizations. To counter this access bias, for reasons of equity and effective implementation of policies and rules, states may want to reach out proactively to less resourceful or powerful organizations, which may not master the game of information tactics,[144] or may be unable to participate in consultations regarding impact assessments of proposed extraterritorial regulations.[145] The views of these organizations may still be valuable even if they are unlikely to submit information that may increase the scientific and technical quality of policies and laws. Especially foreign disadvantaged groups may face particular barriers in actually exercising their consultation rights, for example in terms of suffering from an information deficit, inadequate access to the Internet, or insufficient knowledge of the language(s) used by the regulating entity. The basic query here is whether consultation mechanisms may perhaps have been designed with particular individuals and entities in mind whose ways of thinking and organization mirrors those of the regulator setting up the mechanism. This ties in with the broader discussion whether international or global law can ever be truly universal in light of the participation limitations suffered by countries in, and individuals from the Global South, an issue which Third World Approaches to International Law (TWAIL) have continuously emphasized, for example as regards the formation of customary international law.[146]

4.3.2 The reality of participation

While under positive international law there may be no general duty to consult foreign countries and citizens in respect of measures that could have an extraterritorial impact, involvement of foreign stakeholders in the design and application of extraterritorial regulation is not fanciful. As we write, various institutional arrangements urge or even require it.[147] In *Shrimp/Turtle*, for instance, a case concerning

[143] Rainer Eising, 'Institutional Context, Organizational Resources and Strategic Choices Explaining Interest Group Access in the European Union' (2007) 8 EUP 329, 357.

[144] Adam William Chalmers, 'Trading Information for Access: Informational Lobbying Strategies and Interest Group Access to the European Union' (2013) 20 JEPP 39 <https://doi.org/10.1080/13501763.2012.693411>.

[145] For instance, when, as part of the impact assessment process, the European Commission launched a public consultation open to all interested parties to submit views on an EU initiative for responsible sourcing of minerals, most replies came from the business sector: 205 out of the 280). Of 280 replies, only 3 were from government authorities. Non-citizens were not mentioned. European Commission, Directorate-General for Trade, 'Report on the Public Consultation on a Possible EU Initiative on Responsible Sourcing of Minerals Originating from Conflict-Affects and High-Risk Areas, Contributions from Stakeholders' (July 2013). Undeniably, however, the initiative had an impact on stakeholders other than (large) businesses and three foreign governments.

[146] Sara L Seck, 'Transnational Corporations and Extractive Industries' in Shawkat Alam and others (eds), *International Environmental Law and the Global South* (CUP 2015).

[147] See for an overview: Ayelet Berman, 'Taking Foreign Preferences into Account: The Rulemaking Process in the United States and the European Union' (2015) GlobalTrust Working Paper Series

the compatibility with World Trade Organization (WTO) law of a US import ban of shrimp harvested in a turtle-unfriendly manner, a measure arguably aimed at providing a global environmental good, the WTO Appellate Body held that the United States violated WTO law by failing to consult foreign operators affected by its import ban[148]—a failure which the US subsequently addressed.[149] Another example is article 19 of the (as such non-binding) UN Declaration on the Rights of Indigenous Peoples which provides that 'States shall consult and cooperate in good faith with the indigenous peoples concerned through their own representative institutions in order to obtain their free, prior and informed consent before adopting and implementing legislative or administrative measures that may affect them'. This provision could be given extraterritorial application, meaning that states or the European Union, when contemplating the taking of unilateral trade measures which could adversely affect indigenous peoples outside their territory, should consult and cooperate with them.[150]

Consultation with foreign party interests is particularly well-advanced in the European Union. While under general EU law, the EU legislature may not be under an obligation to consult foreign-affected actors in the absence of a specific provision of EU law requiring it to do so,[151] it has been advanced that 'the general objectives as expressed in articles 3(5) and 21 of the Treaty on European Union (TEU) suggest that wider global and [foreign] interests should be a motivating force in Union external action'.[152] Also, an obligation to consult foreign countries and nationals has been derived from the EU institutions' duty to carry out consultations with 'parties concerned' pursuant to article 11 TEU, a duty which is

03/2015, 5 <http://globaltrust.tau.ac.il/wps-2015-03-taking-foreign-preferences-into-account-the-rulemaking-process-in-the-united-states-and-the-european-union/> (accessed on 5 December 2019) citing *inter alia* the Aarhus Convention, the ILC Articles on the Prevention of Trans-boundary Harm From Hazardous Activities, the 2012 OECD Recommendation on Regulatory Policy and Governance, and various US and EU regulations).

[148] *Shrimp/Turtle Case* (n 112) para 172.

[149] Appellate Body Report, *United States—Import Prohibitions of Certain Shrimp and Shrimp Products*, Recourse to Article 21.5 of the DSU by Malaysia WT/DS58/AB/RW (22 October 2011).

[150] This issue came up in *Inuit II* before the EU General Court, in relation to the effects of the EU Seals Regulation on the indigenous Inuit people, but the Court held that the Declaration was not binding. See Case T-526/10, para 112. The Advocate General had observed that art 19 of the Declaration was not a rule of customary international law, without denying its political importance however. Case C-398/13 *Inuit Tapiriit Kanatami and Others v European Commission* (*Inuit II*) [2015] ECLI:EU:C:2015:190, Opinion of AG Kokott, para 94. The CJEU did not touch upon the issue. Case C-398/13 *Inuit Tapiriit Kanatami and Others v European Commission (Inuit II)* [2015] ECLI:EU:C:2015:535, paras 56–58. For a discussion see Simone Vezzani, 'The Inuit Tapiriit Kanatami II Case and the Protection of Indigenous Peoples' Rights: A Missed Opportunity?' (2016) 1 EP 307. See however Scott, 'The Global Reach of EU Law' (n 84) 41 (arguing, in respect of the Inuit exception in the Seals Regulation, 'that the presence of territorial extension serves to soften the stringency of the measure in recognition of the rights and needs of indigenous communities').

[151] Case T-526/10 *Inuit Tapiriit Kanatami v Parliament and Council* (*Inuit II*) [2013] ECLI:EU:T:2013:215, para 113.

[152] Cremona and Leino (n 101) 707–08.

not territorially limited.[153] In any event, the EU Commission has committed itself to 'improve the dialogue with governmental and non-governmental actors of non-member countries when developing policy proposals with an international dimension'.[154] Also, the EU Better Regulation Guidelines, adopted in 2015, urge the institutions to carry out impact assessments which should include the identification of potentially affected non-EU countries, and should list in the final report 'positive and negative impacts, direct and indirect, intended and unintended, including those outside the EU'.[155] Korkea-Aho has carried out an in-depth study of the opportunities for foreign nationals to have their voice heard and has highlighted that these nationals are not formally discriminated against: 'Processes at the policy—and law-making stages are premised on the idea of openness, which is territorially blind.'[156] She has mapped how foreign actors intensively lobby both the EU Commission and EU agencies,[157] highlighted the fact that almost 10,000 non-EU entities had registered in the EU Transparency Register,[158] and stressed that the electronic submission system provides a low threshold for third country actors to give their input.[159] The extent of practices of foreign participation in EU law-making and implementation has led her to conclude that '[non-EU] country consultation is more a norm than an exception in practice', and that non-EU countries are no longer just objects or addressees of EU law but are (fuller) legal subjects,[160] while nevertheless noting that '[t]here is very little said of the rationales for extending participation beyond the EU'.[161]

Some examples of input from, and consultation with foreign actors potentially affected by proposed EU law with extraterritorial effect—or the absence of such input and consultation—are given here. They are based on a close, original analysis

[153] Emilia Korkea-Aho, '"Mr Smith Goes to Brussels": Third Country Lobbying and the Making of EU Law and Policy' (2016) 18 CYELS 45, 57.

[154] Commission of the European Communities, 'European Governance: A White Paper' COM (2001) 428 final, 5.

[155] Better Regulation Toolbox, available at http://www.emcdda.europa.eu/document-library/better-regulation-toolbox-european-commission_en..

[156] Korkea-Aho, 'Mr Smith Goes to Brussels' (n 153) 60 ('the principles that apply to pre-legislative consultations and cost/benefit and impact analyses are open to third country actors. By making it possible to make submissions electronically, barriers to participation are low. This helps third country lobbyists to use the opportunities to participate that are provided to them.').

[157] ibid, 59 (pointing out that a large number of foreign entities participated in the 2003 consultation procedure regarding the REACH Regulation on chemicals).

[158] ibid, 46, 61–62.

[159] ibid, 57, 63. See also Berman, 'Taking Foreign Preferences into Account' (n 147) 18, 21 ('[T]he European Commission has adopted "Minimum Standards" of consultation that set out guidelines which the Commission must follow in its consultations ... consultations are open to all interested parties, including third countries and stakeholders within such countries... A search through comments that are publicly available on the website reveals that while most comments are submitted by EU stakeholders, foreigners and international bodies submit comments too.').

[160] Emilia Korkea-Aho, 'Evolution of the Role of Third Countries in EU Law—Towards Full Legal Subjectivity?' in Samo Bardurtzky and Elaine Fahey (ed), *Framing the Subjects and Objects of Contemporary EU Law* (Edward Elgar 2017) 224.

[161] ibid, 225.

of relevant EU Commission impact assessments of proposed regulatory initiatives serving the common interest, and with potentially extraterritorial effect.

In 2008, after the Commission had taken the initiative to ban the placing on the EU market of seal products, which eventually resulted in the adoption of the EU Seals Regulation, it carried out a wide-ranging consultation pertaining to the initiative's potential impact. This consultation yielded 73,153 answers from citizens in 160 different countries worldwide, the majority of whom resided in the United Kingdom, the United States, and Canada.[162] What was surprising was that a large number of respondents from United States and Canada sided with the proposed EU ban, unlike the Canadian Government itself which opposed the ban.[163] Apart from receiving input from foreigners, the European Union actively participated in meetings with stakeholders 'to explain to the sealing countries the on-going Commission assessment process on the animal welfare aspects of seal hunting and on the other hand, to note their concerns'.[164]

Also in the context of two impact assessments published in 2008 regarding the proposed EU Timber Regulation (a regulation imposed requirements on importers regarding the placement on the EU market of timber products), one by the Commission and one by an independent consultant,[165] serious consultations were held with third countries. Analysis of the Commission's impact assessment demonstrates that the European Union held high-level meetings with other major timber importers, such as China, Japan, and the United States, and meetings were organized with countries with whom the European Union had concluded a voluntary partnership agreement (VPA) (Malaysia, Indonesia, Ghana, and Cameroon), with certain other timber exporting countries (Russia, Brazil) and countries that had shown interest in discussing VPAs with the European Union.[166] The independent consultant, for its part, conducted stakeholder consultation through the arrangement of stakeholder workshops in three non-EU countries (Brazil, Indonesia, Russia), and on the basis of bilateral consultations with selected stakeholders *inter alia* in Gabon and Vietnam.[167] It identified the actors in non-EU countries who would win and those would lose.[168]

[162] Commission Staff Working Document, 'Accompanying document to the Proposal for a Regulation of the European Parliament and of the Council concerning trade in seal products Impact Assessment on the Potential Impact of a Ban of Products Derived From Seal Species' COM (2008) 469 final, 11. Canada had, however, already requested formal WTO consultation with the European Community pursuant to the WTO's Dispute Settlement Understanding in response to Belgian and Dutch trade-restrictive measures (the precursors of the EU Regulation). ibid, 25–26.

[163] ibid, 11 ('Around 50% of the pro-banners come from two non-EU countries: the US and Canada. When looking at the results from respondents in other countries, the results are somewhat less stark.'). The Canadian government itself did not react during the consultation procedure.

[164] ibid, 13.

[165] COM 469 (n 162); European Commission DG Environment, Assessment of the Impact of Potential Further Measures to Prevent the Importation or Placing on the Market of Illegally Harvested Timber or Products Derived from Such Timber, Final Report Indufor Finland (21 January 2008).

[166] COM 469 (n 162) 9.

[167] Indufor Impact Assessment (n 165) 7.

[168] ibid, 35.

EU legal instruments with extraterritorial impacts are, however, not always preceded by extensive consultations with, or input from foreign stakeholders, or at least this could not be gathered from the impact assessments. The impact assessments of notably the EU Financial Reporting on Payments to Governments Directive[169] and the EU Disclosure of Non-Financial and Diversity Information Directive[170] do *not* include explicit references to the views of foreign countries or stakeholders, although these Directives have a direct impact outside the European Union. The former Directive requires large multinational corporations to disclose payment to governments, including payments to foreign governments in relation to business they conduct outside the European Union. The latter Directive requires EU companies to report information on human rights, the environment, and corruption with respect to their business activities, regardless of geographic scope.[171] This Directive in fact has particular relevance for companies operating in third countries 'where legal requirements regulating social impacts are weak or weakly enforced', in the Commission's wording.[172] In its impact assessment, the Commission limited itself to noting that '[n]one of the stakeholders consulted signalled any potential conflict between the law applicable in third countries, and the proposed policy', and '[n]o significant effects on trade flows with third countries were identified nor signalled in any of the consultations carried out'.[173] Possibly because corruption and human rights abuses may be considered as *mala in se*, no elaborate consultation of foreign affected persons and entities was undertaken.

However, some, and perhaps most, activities are not inherently 'evil'. There may be defensible moral reasons why a particular state or community engages in practices that may be considered as globally harmful. Such reasons may often be linked with economic survival strategies. Unilateral 'extraterritorial' regulation addressing the relevant practices may then have major distributive consequences, which the regulating state may have to account for in its regulatory design.[174] Unfortunately, this does not always occur. Two examples can be given.

169 Chapter 10 in Directive 2013/34/EU of the European Parliament and of the Council of 26 June 2013 on the annual financial statements, consolidated financial statements and related reports of certain types of undertakings, amending Directive 2006/43/EC of the European Parliament and of the Council and repealing Council Directives 78/660/EEC and 83/349/EEC [2013] OJ L182/19. There is a proposal for a Directive amending Directive 2013/34.

170 Commission Staff Working Paper Part I Impact Assessment, 'Accompanying the Document Proposal for a Directive of the European Parliament and the Council on the Annual Financial Statements, Consolidated Financial Statements and Related Reports of Certain Types of Undertakings' COM (2011) 684 final.

171 See for the link between reporting and access to remedy for human rights violations, the third pillar of the UN Guiding Principles: Rachel Chambers and Anil Yilmaz-Vastardis, 'The New Rules on Non-Financial Reporting: Potential Impacts on Access to Remedy' (2016) 10 HRILD 18.

172 COM 684 (n 170) 40.

173 COM 684 (n 170) 42.

174 See *contra* Dan E Stigall, 'International Law and Limitations on the Exercise of Extraterritorial Jurisdiction in U.S. Domestic Law' (2012) 35 HICLR 323, 379 (arguing that '*mala in se* crimes can logically be afforded greater extraterritorial reach than *mala prohibita* crimes as the state's need to pursue the former category is naturally greater').

First, in the example of conflict minerals regulation, it is not certain whether the United States and the European Union have accounted for potential distributive consequences of its 'extraterritorial' regulation, even if they profess to have held consultations with foreign stakeholders.[175] Notably, by only recognizing *legal* mining operations, they may have disqualified artisanal mining operations (so-called *débrouillardise*), which may technically be illegal but on which the local population depends for its survival.[176] Also, it is uncertain whether the United States and the European Union have carried out an adequate assessment of the impact which their regulation might have on corporations' sourcing decisions. Faced with a compliance burden, corporations may tend to shun high-risk and conflict areas because satisfying supply chain due diligence requirements in those areas is extremely challenging and sometimes impossible.[177] Such divestment, triggered by well-intentioned extraterritorial regulation, may ultimately make local communities poorer.

Second, Joanne Scott has highlighted how the European Union, when designing and implementing its sustainable fisheries regulation,[178] has failed to evaluate the impact of EU legal measures on particular groups within third countries. Notably, in Scott's view, the European Union appears to have turned a blind eye to small-scale fisheries and associated downstream industries within the Faroe Islands, which were adversely affected by a Commission implementing regulation[179] to ensure the conservation of the Atlanto-Scandian herring stock.[180] That EU impact assessments largely focused on the European Union itself rather than third countries

[175] With respect to US SEC Dodd–Frank implementing rules, SEC officials held meetings with representatives from international organizations and third countries <https://www.sec.gov/comments/df-title-xv/specialized-disclosures/specialized-disclosures.shtml#meetings> (accessed 5 December 2019).

[176] Marie Müller-Koné, 'Débrouillardise: Certifying "Conflict-Free" Minerals in a Context of Regulatory Pluralism in South Kivu, DR Congo' (2015) 53 JMAS 145, 160.

[177] See *eg* a comment submitted by the Minister for Energy and Minerals of the United Republic of Tanzania, to the SEC in the context of the Dodd–Frank Act, stating that 'the mining industry in Tanzania is well regulated and has not been tainted with illegal minerals produced from the DRC', voicing concern that the relevant rules would result in 'disproportionate share[s] of the compliance burden', and end (responsible) sourcing in the region. Cited in McKay S Harline, 'Can We Make Them Obey—U.S. Reporting Companies, Their Foreign Suppliers, and the Conflict Minerals Disclosure Requirements of Dodd–Frank' (2015) 35 Nw J Int'l L & Bus 439, 452. Regarding the EU Conflict Minerals Regulation, it bears notice that the European Union has been informed of the risk of a *de facto* embargo, but nevertheless lent credence to corporate argument relating to better company reputation and higher consumer interest. Directorate-General for Trade, 'Report on the Public Consultation on a Possible EU Initiative on Responsible Sourcing of Minerals Originating from Conflict-Affects and High-Risk Areas, Contributions from Stakeholders' (n 92) 38.

[178] Regulation 1026/2012 of 25 October 2012 on certain measures for the purpose of the conservation of stocks in relation to countries allowing non-sustainable fishing [2012] OJ L16/34.

[179] Commission Implementing Regulation 793/2013 of 20 August 2013 establishing measures in respect of the Faeroe Islands to ensure the conservation of the Atlanto-Scandian herring stock [2013] OJ L223/1.

[180] Scott, 'The Global Reach of EU Law' (n 84) 60. Scott also discusses the near absence of EU attention for negative third country effects of the Commission's proposal for a ship recycling regulation. ibid, 60–61 (highlighting that the Commission did 'not appraise the likely economic impacts on developing countries and on specific groups within these').

may be explained by this EU measure being in large part driven by EU parochial concerns, namely safeguarding the fishing opportunities of EU Member States' fishing fleets.[181] This will be elaborated on in Chapter 5.2.4.

4.3.3 Participation in dispute settlement

Participation does not just require that foreign-affected states and persons can *ex ante* weigh in on the design of unilateral regulations with extraterritorial effects. It may also require that foreign affected persons may have access to the dispute-settlement mechanisms of the regulating state—in the absence of internationally available mechanisms—to contest *ex post* the legality of extraterritorial regulation.[182] Such contestation may pertain to their having been insufficiently consulted, in violation of applicable international, EU, or domestic law. Access to justice is not fanciful. For instance, in 2009, the Air Transport Association of America, which represents the principal US airlines, was allowed to contest the validity of the EU Aviation Directive—which was given extraterritorial effect to combat climate change—under EU and international law, to no avail, however.[183] In 2016, Front Polisario, a national liberation movement fighting for the self-determination of the Saharawi people, and which sought to annul an EU–Morocco Trade Agreement on grounds of incompatibility with—extraterritorially applied—EU fundamental rights, was granted standing by the EU General Court.[184]

In general, however, foreign persons affected by extraterritorially applied domestic law may face major difficulties in accessing justice before the courts of unilaterally regulating states.[185] As far as the European Union is concerned, for instance, strict standing rules under article 263 Treaty on the Functioning of the European Union (TFEU) may prevent affected foreigners from having access to EU courts in the first place. Regarding EU unilateral measures with extraterritorial effects, the Court of Justice of the European Union (CJEU) has interpreted the standing requirements of 'direct' and 'individual' concern rather strictly, and on that basis refused to grant standing to third country applicants challenging the validity of the Seals Regulation, which prohibits the placing of seal products on

[181] ibid, 59–60.

[182] Ioanna Hadjiyianni, 'The Extraterritorial Reach of EU Environmental Law and Access to Justice by Third Country Actors' (2017) 2 European Papers 519, 530.

[183] Case C-366/10 *The Air Transport Association of America, American Airlines, Inc, Continental Airlines, Inc, United Airlines, Inc v The Secretary of State for Energy and Climate Change* [2011] OJ C260/9.

[184] Case T-512/12 *Front Polisario v Council* [2015] ECLI:EU:T:2015:953. The CJEU later refused to grant standing on the ground that the territorial scope of the Agreement did not extend to Western Sahara). Case C-104/16 P *Front Polisario v Council* [2016] ECLI:EU:C:2016:973.

[185] Also Lorand Bartels, 'The EU's Human Rights Obligations in Relation to Policies with Extraterritorial Effect' (2014) 25 EJIL 1071.

the EU market.[186] It has been argued in this context that '[t]he way in which [these measures] are often designed, by imposing direct obligations on EU operators, signifies that [third country] operators will usually be indirectly affected and would not have standing, demonstrating how judicial review before the CJEU currently provides an imperfect transnational accountability avenue.'[187] Oddly, the EU Court of First Instance (General Court) even invoked the international principle of non-intervention and the prohibition of unilateral action to resist remedies regarding EU acts producing extraterritorial effects, although remedies are precisely aimed at *limiting* unilateral, interventionist action affecting outsiders.[188] When the CJEU proves willing to review unilateral measures with extraterritorial effects, it may use a particularly light review standard ('manifestly appropriate'), and tend to defer to the choices made by the political branches.[189]

Resistance to courts offering 'extraterritorial remedies' can also be witnessed in the field of corporate social responsibility, where legal and political obstacles have stood in the way of overseas victims' access to remedies in multinational corporations' home states.[190] This will be elaborated on in Chapter 5.4.

It bears emphasis that access to justice in relation to regulations with extraterritorial effects may not necessarily *limit* the geographic scope of such regulations and thus to mitigate unilateral cosmopolitan action. In fact, sometimes, the availability of remedies may make cosmopolitan action possible in the first place. Remedies may force states and regional organizations to account for the creation of global injustices as a result of self-interested action. In cases where a state or the European Union concludes trade and investment agreements with foreign countries violating human rights, or allows domestically incorporated firms to engage in human rights abuses abroad, it may indeed entrench injustices, which in turns

[186] Case T-18/10 *Inuit Tapiriit Kanatami v Parliament and Council (Inuit I)* [2011] ECLI:EU:T:2011:419; Case C-583/11 *P Inuit Tapiriit Kanatami and others v Parliament and Council (Inuit I)* [2013] ECLI:EU:C:2013:625, challenging the validity of Regulation 1007/2009. Note that *per* art 263 TFEU, an applicant can challenge 'a regulatory act which is of direct concern to them and does not entail implementing measures', without the need to establish individual concern. In this *Inuit* case, the Court however ruled that the Regulation was a legislative rather than regulatory act.

[187] Hadjiyianni, 'The Role of Domestic Courts in Global Environmental Governance' (n 58) 27. See Korkea-Aho, 'Mr Smith Goes to Brussels' (n 153) 64–65 ('the decisions of the EU courts have not allowed much of a role for third country interests').

[188] Case T-212/02 *Commune de Champagne and Others v Commission* [2007] ECLI:EU:T:2007:194, paras 88–89 (ruling that 'the principle of sovereign equality enshrined in Article 2(1) of the United Nations Charter means that it is, as a rule, a matter for each State to legislate in its own territory and, accordingly, that generally a State may unilaterally impose binding rules only in its own territory').

[189] *Inuit II 2013* (n 151); *Inuitt II 2015* (n 150), para 88. Als Hadjiyianni, 'The Extraterritorial Reach' (n 182) 530–31.

[190] Guiding Principles on Business and Human Rights: Implementing the United Nations 'Protect, Respect and Remedy' Framework (A/HRC/17/31) 26 requires that 'States should take appropriate steps to ensure the effectiveness of domestic judicial mechanisms when addressing business-related human rights abuses, including considering ways to reduce legal, practical and other relevant barriers that could lead to a denial of access to remedy'. The commentary to GP 26 further identifies that one such barrier is lack of jurisdiction the part of the home state 'where claimants face a denial of justice in a host State and cannot access home State courts regardless of the merits of the claim'.

calls for remedial action. States and the European Union may even be legally *required* to provide domestic remedies in relation to extraterritorial abuse.[191]

4.3.4 Concluding observations

In this section, it has been argued that unilateral action, even if serving cosmopolitan purposes, may suffer from a democratic deficit. To narrow this deficit, it has been suggested that foreign affected parties be involved in the design of regulations with extraterritorial effects, or be given access to remedies so as to contest the regulation before the courts of the asserting state.[192] This stops short, however, of requiring their—or their state's—formal consent to the exercise of jurisdiction.[193] Representation and consultation mechanisms may provide a modicum of fairness, but there is no guarantee that the state wishing to legislate extraterritorially will take comments from potentially affected persons and states into account when reaching its final decision, let alone that the state will seek the latter's consent, especially not if the latter persons and states are economically or politically dependent on the former state.[194] The decision ultimately rests with the regulating state.[195]

4.4 Equivalence

A third mechanism of jurisdictional restraint consists of the asserting state's recognition of the equivalence, or at least acceptability of a foreign state's regulation, even if such regulation is not *identical* to the former state's regulation. One state's recognition of another state's laws as adequate may accommodate concerns over

[191] Malcolm Langford and others (eds), *Global Justice, State Duties: The Extraterritorial Scope of Economic, Social, and Cultural Rights in International Law* (CUP 2012). See on the extraterritorial application of human rights in particular Marko Milanovic, *Extraterritorial Application of Human Rights Treaties: Law, Principles, and Policy* (OUP 2011). See also Chapter 2.6 and 5.4. See on remedial requirements under international occupation law and the duty of non-recognition, in relation to trade agreements between EU and foreign countries: Cedric Ryngaert and Rutger Fransen, 'EU Extraterritorial Obligations with Respect to Trade with Occupied Territories—Reflections after the Case of Front Polisario before EU Courts' (2017) 2 EIW: a L Rev 1.

[192] See also Daniel Bodansky 'What's in a Concept? Global Public Goods, International Law, and Legitimacy' (2012) 23 EJIL 651, 667.

[193] It may of course happen that a state requests another state to exercise jurisdiction, or at least *consents* to the exercise of jurisdiction by the latter, *eg* because of issues of capacity and safety in the former state. cf Farbiarz (n 66) 513 (describing the practice of Colombia extraditing drug traffickers to the United States for purposes of extraterritorial prosecution there, and justifying it on the grounds of strengthening the fragile Colombian state).

[194] Theoretically, the global regulatory system may be polycentric, but in practice the regime with the greatest resources prevails. See also Pulkowski (n 26) 193. For instance, if a regime has a very large consumer market, it can more or less impose its standards at will, and globally prevail, provided that such standards are effectively enforced and foreign economic operators have few alternative markets to sell their goods and services.

[195] Cremona and Leino (n 101) 700.

foreign regulatory intervention and limit transaction costs for operators doing business transnationally. Thus, mechanisms of recognition acknowledge state sovereignty concerns as well as private actors' concerns over legal certainty and multiple regulatory burdens. They also have a deliberative dimension which links them to the democratic participation mechanisms previously discussed. Indeed, acts of recognition will typically only occur after a process of states and sub-state actors engaging in a (sometimes quite turbulent) transnational dialogue with a view to understanding and possibly approximating various regulatory positions. From a (moral) justice perspective, such a deliberative process allows 'to right the wrongs of the actual formative agency of justice', that is, ensure that the unjust effects of unilateral acts on others (non-citizens) are mitigated or even eliminated in case these others have put in place regulatory solutions that could achieve the same, or at least similar results.[196] It remains, however, that it is the unilaterally regulating state rather than the 'target state' which decides whether the latter's regulatory practices are considered as offering equivalent protection, and thus reviews them in light of its own legislation.[197] In so doing, the former state limits the policy space of the target state, in particular the weaker ones.[198] Accordingly, soothing talk of mutual recognition cannot hide the fact that the unilaterally regulating states may be setting the *de facto* international norm for a particular practice, while only tolerating marginal variations.[199]

Mechanisms of mutual recognition are, in essence, instantiations of a horizontal subsidiarity principle. In a jurisdictional context, this principle could be defined as a principle requiring that bystander states defer the exercise of their jurisdiction when another state with a stronger nexus to the conduct, or a multilateral institution (if one were available), is able and willing to exercise its jurisdiction adequately.[200]

In international law, the standard of equivalence can be traced to the case law of the European Court of Human Rights on the responsibility of Member States

[196] Eriksen (n 12) 19 (theorizing 'justice as mutual recognition', and highlighting that 'justice is not the origin of social relations but the product of practical interaction and contestation over how to regulate common affairs', as well as that 'we cannot know what is just unless all affected are heard').

[197] Christopher Kuner, 'The Internet and the Global Reach of EU Law' in Marise Cremona and Joanne Scott (eds), *EU Law Beyond EU Borders: The Extraterritorial Reach of EU Law* (OUP 2019) 143 ('The need to review third country standards is logically inherent in an evaluation of whether a Commission decision based on those standards results in protection that is essentially equivalent to that under EU law.').

[198] Michael L Buenger, 'Regulatory Legality: Extraterritorial Rule Across Domestic and International Arenas' in Nikolas M Rajkovic and others (eds), *The Power of Legality: Practices of International Law and their Politics* (CUP 2016) 285 ('Equivalent measures requirements, for example, not only present individuals and private entities with a series of compliance challenges, they also limit the regulatory autonomy of actors possessing less relative capacities by presenting a stark choice to their constituents: adapt to a new order and pressure your governments to accede to this order or lose market access.').

[199] ibid, 281 (arguing that the EU's sustainability criteria in the context of the Renewable Energy Directive set the *de facto* 'international norm' for biofuel production).

[200] See Cedric Ryngaert, 'Horizontal Complementarity' in *Max Planck Encyclopedia of International Procedural Law* (OUP 2019).

for the acts of international organizations.[201] Pursuant to this case law, state action taken in compliance with obligations flowing from the state's membership of an international organization to which it has transferred part of its sovereignty 'is justified as long as the relevant organisation is considered to protect fundamental rights, as regards both the substantive guarantees offered and the mechanisms controlling their observance, in a manner which can be considered at least *equivalent* to that for which the Convention provides'.[202]

In the law of jurisdiction, the standard of equivalent protection can usefully be applied by means of techniques of unilateral or mutual recognition. Pursuant to mutual recognition, asserting states recognize that other states' standards, while not providing for identical protection, could also meet the regulatory goal sought, provided that a number of conditions are met.[203] Joanne Scott has characterized such mutual recognition as a jurisdictional 'safety valve', which causes the European Union to cease to apply its own legislation when the foreign conduct 'has been satisfactorily regulated by another state or by an international body'.[204] Elsewhere, she has considered this technique as a type of 'country-level territorial extension'[205] that is often tied to a *de jure* 'Brussels effect', which occurs when 'a third country legislature decides to incorporate the substance of EU standards into its domestic law'.[206]

This is not the place to give an exhaustive overview of all regulations that employ standards of equivalence resulting in mutual recognition. For an understanding of how equivalence works in practice, it suffices to mention just a few examples, notably from EU law, where the principle is widely used to cushion the extraterritorial impact of EU regulations and directives. For instance, the Renewable Energy Directive,[207] a major piece of EU legislation paving the way for a more sustainable energy future, provides that, '[i]rrespective of whether the raw materials were cultivated inside or outside the territory' of the European Union, energy from biofuels and bioliquids 'shall be taken into account for purposes of measuring compliance

[201] See notably *Bosphorus v Ireland* App no 45036/98, 30 June 2005.

[202] ibid, paras 154–156 (emphasis added) (Court going on to state that '[b]y "equivalent" the Court means "comparable"; any requirement that the organisation's protection be "identical" could run counter to the interest of international cooperation pursued', and that '[i]f such equivalent protection is considered to be provided by the organisation, the presumption will be that a State has not departed from the requirements of the Convention when it does no more than implement legal obligations flowing from its membership of the organisation').

[203] Schiff Berman has characterized mutual recognition as a means of managing 'hybridity that the movement across territorial borders inevitably creates' (Berman, 'Global Legal Pluralism' (n 111) 1224 fn 323 for a literature overview).

[204] Joanne Scott 'The New EU "Extraterritoriality"' (2014) 51 CMLR 1343.

[205] Scott, 'The Global Reach of EU Law' (n 84) 29. Scott defines country-level territorial extension in general as 'using the existence of a territorial connection with its Member States to gain leverage over the content of third country law'. ibid, 26.

[206] ibid, 31, 33.

[207] Directive 2009/28/EC of the European Parliament and of the Council of 23 April 2009 on the promotion of the use of energy from renewable sources and amending and subsequently repealing Directives 2001/77/EC and 2003/30/ECRED [2009] OJ L140/16.

with the requirements of this Directive' only if they fulfil certain sustainability criteria elaborated on in the Directive.[208] However, the Directive is reluctant simply to impose detailed regulations on producers from other states, and instead opts for a mutual recognition clause by providing, *inter alia*, that the European Union 'shall endeavour to conclude bilateral or multilateral agreements with third countries containing provisions on sustainability criteria that *correspond* to those of this Directive'.[209] Also, the new EU Accounting and revised Transparency Directives, which require that the extractive industry and loggers of primary forests disclose the payments they make to foreign governments, allow relevant companies to publish a report on the basis of the mandatory requirements of a *third* country considered as equivalent, with a view to 'eliminating the administrative burden that could stem from double or multiple reporting obligations, whilst safeguarding the objective of the Directive'.[210]

A variation on mutual recognition comprise the EU Commission's adequacy decisions in the field of transborder data flows. Pursuant to article 45(1) of the EU General Data Protection Regulation, '[a] transfer of personal data to a third country or an international organization may [only] take place where the Commission has decided that the third country, a territory or one or more specified sectors within that third country, or the international organization in question ensures an adequate level of protection'. On this basis, the Commission may not require that the foreign state complies perfectly with EU law when they or operators under their jurisdiction process EU residents' data abroad. Instead, the Commission looks for regulatory commonalities, and on that base recognizes the 'equivalent protection' offered by foreign regulation. Arguably, the European Union does so to prevent that its assertion of unilateral jurisdiction is seen abroad as unreasonable or disproportionate.[211] Kuner has observed that this quest for internationally shared values may also have cross-border enforcement advantages.[212] It is indeed unlikely that a state will allow another state's data protection regulators to carry out inspections on a company's premises or data systems in the former state's territory if the latter's laws are entirely different from the former's.

Mutual recognition arrangements in relation to third country legislation are not only to be found in the text of relevant regulations and directives with extraterritorial effects, but also in judicial decisions. For instance, in *Zuchtvieh*, the CJEU,

[208] ibid, art 17(1).

[209] ibid, art 18(4) (emphasis added). See also ibid, art 18(5) ('The Commission shall adopt decisions under paragraph 4 only if the agreement or scheme in question meets adequate standards of reliability, transparency and independent auditing.').

[210] European Commission, 'New Disclosure Requirements for the Extractive Industry and Loggers of Primary Forests in the Accounting (and Transparency) Directives (Country by Country Reporting)—Frequently Asked Questions' MEMO/13/541.

[211] Christopher Kuner, *Transborder Data Flows and Data Privacy Law* (OUP 2013) 131–32 (also using the term 'safety valve' in this respect).

[212] ibid, 142.

while applying the requirements of an EU regulation on animal transport to journeys outside the European Union, mitigated this partly extraterritorial application by positing a realistic equivalent protection rule that precludes full compliance.[213] Deference to foreign law offering equivalent protection ensures that EU animal welfare legislation applies extraterritoriality in a reasonable fashion.

Recognition arrangements acknowledge that locally adopted norms, possibly inspired by a cosmopolitan outlook, may in fact not be universally shared. Still, they assume that there is at least convergence on regulatory goals, and thus an overlapping consensus on values, without this consensus consisting of states applying exactly the same norms and procedures. These arrangements require that states defer to another state providing adequate protection, especially when that other state has a stronger nexus to the situation. A failure to defer may amount to a disproportionate and unreasonable exercise of jurisdiction. Obviously, the challenge remains for the regulating state regarding how to establish the adequacy or equivalence *in concreto* of a particular foreign regulatory regime. Put differently, the challenge is how to strike the balance between, on the one hand, the need to safeguard the integrity of its own regulation and the protection of a common interest, and on the other hand, the need to pay heed to alternative foreign regulation addressing the same interest. It is to be borne in mind that an overly strict interpretation of the adequacy standard may fatally undermine the principle of mutual recognition and jurisdictional reasonableness, while a lax interpretation may fail to address the common interest properly.

Two final points are in order regarding equivalence. First, when confronted with a relevant foreign standard aspiring to recognition, the regulating state may want to inquire to what extent this standard commands internal legitimacy in the foreign state. If the standard has been imposed by an elite without adequately consulting its own population, doubts may be cast over its democratic legitimacy. For instance, recognizing a developing country's *official* environmental standard as equivalent on the ground of the principle of common but differentiated responsibilities (CBDR) may do injustice to the environmental desires of sub-state actors.[214] Second, a *uniform* interpretation of the adequacy standard across the

[213] Case C-424/13 *Zuchtvieh-Export GmbH v Stadt Kempten* EU:C:2015:259, para 54 ('Should it nevertheless be the case that the law or administrative practice of a third country through which the transport will transit verifiably and definitely precludes full compliance with the technical rules of that regulation, the margin of discretion conferred on the competent authority of the place of departure empowers it to accept realistic planning for transport which, in the light inter alia of the means of transport used and the journey arrangements made, indicates that the planned transport will safeguard the welfare of the animals at a level equivalent to those technical rules.').

[214] cf Seck (n 146) 390. Seck, writing in the context of environmental regulation regarding mining activities, argued that it 'is not evident that this double standard [of CBDR] is one that mining-impacted local communities of the global South want'. She criticized Principle 11 of the Rio Declaration (1992), pursuant to which '[e]nvironmental standards, management objectives and priorities should reflect the environmental and development context to which they apply. Standards applied by some countries may be inappropriate and of unwarranted economic and social cost to other countries, in particular developing countries.'

(extraterritorially) regulating jurisdiction is called for in order to satisfy the legitimate expectations of third countries and their nationals, and to prevent uneven national application and a regulatory race to the bottom, to the detriment of the promoted concern. This is a problem that may in particular arise in the European Union, whose institutions may require deference to foreign equivalent standards but which leave the practical application of equivalence to the member states without giving specific guidance.[215]

4.5 Transfers

A final technique of mitigating and legitimating the exercise of jurisdiction in the common interest discussed here is the transferring of funds or other resources (*eg* technology) to states or individuals/operators 'targeted' by cosmopolitan extraterritoriality. Such mitigation is called for when the exercise of jurisdiction may come at a considerable financial cost to foreign actors, who may want to be compensated, at least in part, for their efforts to meet the regulatory standards set by the asserting state. Compensation is also called for in cases involving criminal or administrative fines or settlement sums imposed by a unilaterally acting state in respect of overseas abuses disappear in the coffers of its own treasury. Such abuses may have harmed the territorial state interests in the first place, thus grounding an obligation for the bystander state to transfer the proceeds of its enforcement action in the common interest back to the former state or its citizens.

The starting point of the analysis is that non-consent-based unilateralism may, on balance, increase global welfare even if one or more states, such as the targets of the exercise of unilateral jurisdiction, are worse off. In law and economics, this is termed a Kaldor–Hicks improvement.[216] Such an improvement contrasts with a Pareto efficiency improvement which requires that no state is made worse off as a result of one or more being made better off.[217] Obviously, achieving a Kaldor–Hicks improvement is more self-evident than achieving a Pareto improvement, but the flipside is that those who are worse off will tend to resist Kaldor–Hicks-based global welfare improvements, as for instance produced by unilateral action. As Guzman observed, however, 'any Kaldor–Hicks improvement can be made into a Pareto improvement with suitable transfers'.[218] This implies that the blow of a

[215] cf Hadjiyianni, 'The Role of Domestic Courts in Global Environmental Governance' (n 58) 2018 (criticizing the aforementioned para 54 the CJEU's judgment in *Zuchtvieh* on the grounds that 'it is unclear how equivalence decisions by national authorities may be reached or reviewed in light of lack of specific guidance').

[216] For the seminal articles: John Hicks, 'The Foundations of Welfare Economics' (1939) 49 TEJ 696; Nicholas Kaldor, 'Welfare Propositions in Economics and Interpersonal Comparisons of Utility' (1939) 49 TEJ 549.

[217] William BT Mock, 'Pareto Optimality' (2011) Encyclopedia of Global Justice 808–09.

[218] Andrew Guzman, 'Against Consent' (2012) 52 VJIL 747, 759.

state's unilateral action can be cushioned if the addressees of that act—typically the economic operators based in other states with lower levels of regulation—receive financial compensation. While theoretically sensible, this is not to say that a system of transfers can easily be put in place.[219]

In law, compensation typically takes the form of a liability rule: when one actor takes the entitlement of another actor, the former is liable to pay compensation to the latter. In the law and economics literature, this is termed 'efficient breach': an entitlement is taken, but as compensation is paid, no one is made worse off. Thus, as Pauwelyn has argued, relying on earlier research in liability law and economics, an efficient breach may be Pareto efficient, and serve the social function of maximizing overall welfare.[220] The efficient breach doctrine has relevance for our research object insofar as some jurisdictional assertions may be considered to violate international law. Applying efficient breach, a violation of accepted principles of jurisdiction can be tolerated if its net cost is lower than the cost of compliance with the law, provided that compensation is offered.[221]

Discussing such a liability rule in a part on 'reasonableness' may at first sight seem to be somewhat off target, as reasonableness normally only comes into play when jurisdiction is lawfully exercised in the first place. However, as argued earlier, some cosmopolitan jurisdictional assertions may be legally dubious from a positive international law perspective. Accordingly, one could hypothesize that at least some jurisdictional assertions grounded in cosmopolitan extraterritoriality violate international law, in particular the principle of non-intervention. The efficient breach doctrine would then posit that such assertions, in spite of breaching the law, could yet be reasonable because, provided that compensation is offered, they may increase global welfare. Moreover, the doctrine could be expanded to include assertions that do not technically breach the law but at least have injurious consequences or harmful outcomes. Recent scholarship pertaining to the law of international responsibility has, for instance, advocated a departure from the excessive focus on international wrongful acts when determining responsibility and

219 ibid, 759 ('In practice, however, the creation of the necessary transfers can be extremely difficult, and at times impossible. Put another way, the transaction costs are often simply too high for the parties to reach agreement.')

220 Joost Pauwelyn, *Optimal Protection of International Law* (CUP 2008) 6; Guido Calabresi and Douglas Melamed, 'Property Rules, Liability Rules, and Inalienability: One View of the Cathedral' (1972) 85 HLR 1089 (arguing that anyone can take 'liability entitlements' provided that compensation is paid).

221 A liability rule may also serve as a democratic safety valve: as domestic action may be imbued with more democratic legitimacy than international action, violations of international law may well be tolerated, at least if compensation is offered (ibid, 72–74). Such views are particularly prevalent in the United States, where state sovereignty and representative democracy are considered to be higher values than international law. For (some) Americans, a cost/benefit analysis could well yield the result that non-compliance with international law is more efficient. Compare with European absolutism, based on the Kantian ideal that universal values and law prevail over politics, and pursuant to which international entitlements should be inalienable (ibid, 13, 20, 23).

emphasized instead the purportedly responsible actor's contribution to a harmful outcome as the relevant inquiry.[222] Regardless of legality, assertions of unilateral jurisdiction are likely to affect actors outside the state and cause harm in some form. An offer of compensation could legitimize such jurisdiction and soothe foreign opposition.

When applying the doctrine of efficient breach (whether in its restricted or expanded form) to the exercise of unilateral jurisdiction,[223] target states which consider their sovereignty to be violated may claim compensation in the form of transfer payments. This may enable target states, and especially the individuals and operators falling within their (primary) jurisdiction, to comply with the obligations imposed by the asserting state.[224] The challenge, of course, is how to calculate the exact amount of compensation to which the target state and its citizens are entitled. Arguably, the principle of common but differentiated responsibilities may be guiding here. Pursuant to this principle, every state has responsibilities to supply global public goods, but developed states may have to do more, as they have better capabilities than developing states.[225] This may imply that the jurisdictionally assertive state may have to compensate poorer nations much more than rich nations such as the United States.[226] Other criteria than capacity to pay could come into play, however, such as historical contribution. In a jurisdictional context, this criterion posits that states that have historically contributed more to a global public bad, but subsequently change gear by addressing this bad via extraterritorial jurisdiction, should compensate foreign states for the costs associated with the regulatory burden imposed on them. For instance, when Western states require that only sustainably logged tropical timber be imported, with a view to protecting the world's rainforests and thus combating climate change (*eg* the EU

[222] André Nollkaemper and Dov Jacobs 'Shared Responsibility in International Law: A Conceptual Framework' (2012) 34 Mich JIL 359.

[223] Note that under current international law, there are a limited number of efficient breach-based liability rules, none of which relates to the exercise of unilateral jurisdiction, however: (i) the law of cross-border environmental damage, which requires that the state causing this damage compensates the injured state, even if the former's act was not unlawful; (ii) the law of the WTO, which allows Member States to refrain from compliance with WTO law, or rulings of the WTO Dispute Settlement Mechanism, if such non-compliance is compensated by the suspension of trade concessions by the injured party; and (iii) the law concerning investor protection, which allows states to expropriate (foreign) investors if compensation is paid. See Pauwelyn (n 220) 126.

[224] Because these payments may have to funnelled to non-state actors, the recipient state should guarantee that they will indeed trickle down to these actor. This is not given, in which case the state-to-state liability framework for efficient breach will not work. See ibid, 99–100.

[225] See *eg* UNGA 1992 Rio Declaration on Environment and Development (adopted on 14 June 1992) UN Doc A/CONF.151/26 (vol I),

[226] See generally about taking into account the interests of developing nations when 'legislating for humanity' Eyal Benvenisti, 'Legislating for Humanity: May States Compel Foreigners to Promote Global Welfare?' (2013) GlobalTrust Working Paper Series 02/2013, 11–12 <https://papers.ssrn.com/sol3/papers.cfm?abstract_id=2646880> (accessed 5 December 2019) ('the adopted policy must accommodate the legitimate interests of others, especially the interests of developing countries whose economies and capacities require them to modify their order of priorities').

Timber Regulation),[227] these states may have to compensate rainforest states for refraining from logging,[228] or at least for only sustainably logging their rainforests, on the ground that historically, Western states have logged their own forests and contributed to global warming.[229] Practically speaking, transfer payments could take place via the UN REDD programme, a UN collaborative initiative on Reducing Emissions from Deforestation and forest Degradation (REDD) in developing countries.[230] Arguments of historical contribution do not mean that (Western) states cannot act unilaterally in the global interest—they can, and possibly they should—to break a multilateral deadlock. But then, they may have to compensate, via cash or technology transfers, other states to ensure that their citizens can comply with the Western regulations. Such transfers could be arranged bilaterally or multilaterally.[231]

It is of note that not only considerations of equity counsel such transfers, but also considerations of more effectively *enforcing* extraterritorial regulations. If, because of capacity problems rather than sheer unwillingness, foreign operators are unable to comply with such regulations, the latter's effectiveness may be seriously undermined. Especially in case the regulating state, its consumers and producers need the foreign-made products to which the regulations apply, there may be a strong incentive to transfer resources abroad so as to enable compliance. In this vein, an initial assessment of section 1502 of the US Dodd–Frank Act, which imposes extraterritorial due diligence-based disclosure requirements on companies sourcing 'conflict minerals' from the DRC, concluded that '[g]iven the [security and governance] challenges associated with extraterritorially regulating complex, multi-tiered supply chains, home states [*ie* extraterritorially regulating states] need to play a larger role in implementation to facilitate corporate compliance', and should even 'offer support for companies in mapping their supply chains'.[232]

[227] Regulation (EU) No 995/2010 of the European Parliament and of the Council of 20 October 2010 laying down the obligations of operators who place timber and timber products on the market [2010] OJ L295 (entered into force on 1 March 2013).

[228] See on this: Cedric Ryngaert, 'Climate Change Mitigation Techniques and International Law: Assessing the Externalities of Reforestation and Geoengineering' (2017) 30 RJ 273; Chris Armstrong, 'Fairnesss, Free-Riding and Rainforest Protection' (2016) 44 PT 106.

[229] In 2019, however, Brazilian president Bolsonaro rebuffed a 20 million USD pledge to try to halt the destruction by fire of the Amazon rainforest, on the grounds of foreign states considering Brazil 'a colony or no-man's land' and attacking its sovereignty. See 'Amazon fires: Bolsonaro rages at "colonial" G7 leaders over £16m aid deal to fight Brazil blazes', The Independent (27 August 2019) <https://www.independent.co.uk/news/world/americas/amazon-fires-bolsonaro-brazil-g7-summit-aid-deal-a9079586.html>(accessed 5 December 2019).

[230] http://www.un-redd.org.

[231] See on transfers in the context of multilateral agreements, in particular on transnational crime: Gardner (n 8) 315 (arguing that '[b]y entering into a treaty regarding a particular crime, these "limited" states may benefit from shifting the primary cost of enforcement to motivated states in the short term and from the transmission of aid and knowledge in the long term, from shifting the primary cost of enforcement to motivated states in the short term and from the transmission of aid and knowledge in the long term').

[232] Galit A Sarfaty, 'Shining Light on Global Supply Chains' (2015) 56 HILJ 419, 423, 456. See also Alex Brackett and others, 'Revisiting the Conflict Minerals Rule' (2015) 10 GTCJ 73, 76 ('A 2013 report

More generally, extraterritorial regulations serving the common interest, such as the Dodd–Frank Act which is aimed at safeguarding human rights and ending wars, should not just impose stringent import or disclosure requirements: they should also be accompanied by resource transfers, for example in the context of the regulating state's development cooperation, to enable relevant actors in the supply-chain to actually comply with those requirements.[233] Eventually, this will render successful implementation more likely.

So far, we have conceived of compensation payments as mostly accommodating foreign (economic) operators caught in the claws of an assertive bystander state. Because of the regulatory burden which the latter imposes on the former, the cost of doing business for foreign operators increases to possibly prohibitive levels. If the bystander state wishes to keep the stringent regulation in place, it may then want to decrease this cost by making transfer payments. However, compensation payments may also be called for in case the bystander state imposes penalties or fines, negotiates settlement sums, or seizes assets, in public law proceedings against persons, whatever their nationality, which have been involved in wrongful activity overseas. In such a situation, there is a disconnect between on the one hand, the proceeds of the enforcement action of a bystander state being integrally funnelled to its treasury, and on the other hand, the reality that the main victims of the wrongful activity, who are in most need of compensation, may be located in another state. From a cosmopolitan perspective, this disconnect is not defensible. Rigorous enforcement practices by bystander state may possibly have a global deterrent effect on future harmful behaviour, but it appears as self-enrichment for a bystander state to collect money from actors whose violations adversely affect citizens of *foreign* states in the first place. Arguably, it is immaterial in this respect that the person against whom sanctions are taken is a national of, or incorporated in the jurisdictionally assertive state (home state regulation). What *is* material is that the *effects* of the wrongful activity are mainly felt outside that state.

Examples of this situation of potential disconnect are mainly found in the context of enforcement of public economic regulation, for example regarding violations of anticorruption law, antitrust law, embargoes, or sanctions legislation, or criminal law relevant to transnational corporate human rights violations. A limited number of proactive national regulators and law-enforcers, who are typically based in the Global North and have substantial investigative resources and expertise at their disposal, exercise their jurisdiction over such violations. On that basis, they

issued by the OECD indicated that local governments in the DRC and adjoining countries currently lack the capacity to fulfill what is expected of them in ensuring responsible sourcing, including how companies are expected to implement due diligence requirements. This is exacerbated by limited funding for the programs, including for the personnel needed to certify, audit and monitor both the actual mineral supply chains, and the responsible sourcing initiatives that support their assurance, and the infrastructure necessary to support traceability and data management.')

[233] Elena Vyboldina, 'Solving the Conflict Minerals Puzzle' (2015) 10 GTCJ 344.

can go on to impose money penalties on businesses, even if the latter's wrongful activities affect, and sometimes affect very substantially, individuals or even the entire society of another state, or multiple other states. The prosecution of corruption is a case in point. Corruption has the strongest impact on the stability and economic development of the local society whose officials engage in corruption with foreign corporations. At the same time, (relative) bystander states, in particular foreign corporations' home states or states with which the corrupt practice has some minor connection, have proved particularly able and willing to exercise their jurisdiction. Sometimes they have taken very vigorous enforcement action, and imposed heavy fines (typically in the form of settlements), as US experience with the Foreign Corrupt Practices Act testifies.[234] So far, however, there has been scant practice of such bystander states making 'reparations' or 'restitution payments' to locally affected societies. This is partly attributable to the absence of unambiguous restitution requirements in the two main anticorruption conventions (the OECD and UN Conventions).[235] Short of treaty amendment, restitution will have to be based on non-binding international recommendations and on evolving state practice. As far as the latter is concerned, it can be signalled that Switzerland's Foreign Illicit Assets Act (2015) provides for restitution 'in pursuit of the following objectives: (a) to improve the living conditions of the inhabitants of the country of origin, or (b) to strengthen the rule of law in the country of origin and thus to contribute to the fight against impunity'.[236] It remains unclear, however, to whom exactly assets or funds have to be restituted. Restitution directly to foreign state authorities may be frowned upon as this may simply further entrench corruption. Insofar as direct victims of foreign corrupt practices cannot easily be identified,[237] restitution to local non-governmental organizations may appear to be the next best option, provided that they are representative and accountable.[238]

Finally, a danger should be flagged with respect to duties of compensation in the context of cosmopolitan unilateralism, namely the danger that the amount of compensation is set too high, thereby discouraging states from acting in the common

[234] The Foreign Corrupt Practices Act of 1977, as amended, 15 USC §§ 78dd-1 et seq. (See for an overview of the US SEC's enforcement actions under the Foreign Corrupt Practices Act (FCPA): https://www.sec.gov/spotlight/fcpa/fcpa-cases.shtml.

[235] The clause that comes closest to requiring restitution is UN Convention against Corruption (adopted 31 October 2003, entered into force 14 December 2005) 2349 UNTS 41, art 53 which requires States Parties to ensure that their courts can order perpetrators of acts of corruption to pay damages or compensation to another State Party harmed by an act of corruption. This provision is too abstract however to ground restitution obligations between law-enforcers in one state towards particular (undefined) right-holders in another state. The earlier OECD Convention does not contain any relevant clause.

[236] Art 17 Swiss Foreign Illicit Assets Act.

[237] Cecily Rose, 'Restitution in Foreign Bribery Cases under the OECD Anti-Bribery Convention' (paper on file with the author).

[238] Such restitution can also be laid down in a Memorandum of Understanding between states, of which the NGO is a beneficiary. cf *Mercator/Giffin* case, Memorandum of Understanding Among the Governments of the United States of America, the Swiss Confederation, and the Republic of Kazakhstan (2 May 2007), cited in Rose (n 237).

interest, and thus entrenching under-enforcement. Even without having to provide compensation, when intervening in the interest of the international community, states acting in a cosmopolitan manner already spend regulatory and enforcement resources that should in fact be borne by international institutions. Having to transfer funds in excess of these expenses may discourage states from acting in the common interest altogether, thereby making everybody worse off. Accordingly, foreign states and sub-state actors should arguably not be compensated for the entire losses they have suffered as a result of the exercise of unilateral jurisdiction, or for all proceeds which the unilateral enforcer has pocketed as a result of its enforcement action.

4.6 Concluding Observations

This chapter has given an overview of mechanisms that can be used, and are used to ensure that selfless intervention does not descend into outright domination. Its approach was immanent rather than transcendent as it sought to locate limiting principles in actual practice rather than to review practice in light of transcendent moral principles.[239] After all, the law itself has an inner morality.[240] The challenge then is to see through principles of fairness in the law. For our purposes, this means ensuring consistent application of techniques of restraint so as to render the exercise of jurisdiction in the common interest 'reasonable'.

What transpires from the discussion is that applying techniques of reasonableness is inevitably a messy process. Reasonableness is an inherently vague notion that may fail to confer legal certainty on international relations and transactions. But then, even jurisdiction is not a stable category with a fixed meaning, but rather, to recall Berman's words, 'the locus for debates about the appropriate definition of community and the articulation of norms'.[241] The implementation of 'reasonableness' ultimately depends, as Scott has observed, on a 'continuing dialogue' and a dynamic 'discursive process', that may lead to 'ongoing adjustment as new factual scenarios emerge'.[242] What is reasonable cannot be defined in the abstract, but certain techniques, such as international proscription, democratic participation, and equivalent protection, may prove helpful. That being said, mechanisms of restraint should not have a chilling effect on the willingness of states to effectively exercise jurisdiction, as such could lead to under-enforcement and a decrease in global

[239] See for a similar approach to extraterritoriality: Aravind Ganesh, 'Rightful Relations with Distant Strangers: A Kantian Critique of the Law of the European Union in the Wider World' (PhD thesis, VU Amsterdam 2019).

[240] See Lon Fuller, *The Morality of Law* (YUP 1964).

[241] Paul S Berman, 'Conflict of Laws, Globalization, and Cosmopolitan Pluralism' (2005) 51 Wayne L Rev 1105, 1126.

[242] Scott, 'The New EU "Extraterritoriality"' (n 204) 1365.

welfare. Therefore, a flexible application of such mechanisms, which does not set the bar prohibitively high, is required.

The next chapter inquires whether and how the existing jurisdictional framework provides doctrinal entry points for the exercise of prescriptive jurisdiction in relation to discrete common interests in the fields of human rights and the environment. Attention will also be devoted to how mechanisms of jurisdictional restraint can be applied in these fields.

5
The Selfless Exercise of Jurisdiction to Protect Human Rights and the Environment

5.1 Introduction

Unilateral prescriptive jurisdiction in pursuit of the common interest is located between the celestial and the immediate. Intent on realizing global values and protecting common concerns, it may reach for the sky but it needs an anchor in actual law to be effectively exercised. The most pressing challenge for a lawyer is how to fit cosmopolitan extraterritoriality pursued in discrete policy fields, within the long-standing legal systems, forms, and doctrines that govern those fields. The inherent conservativism of the law, its rules-based character, and its path dependency make it rather unlikely that the extant law will somehow magically absorb and give effect to theoretical arguments pertaining to selfless intervention and reasonable, cosmopolitan extraterritoriality. What is called for instead is an epistemic inquiry into the overtures offered by the technical *lex lata* in various fields of law. This inquiry should concentrate on how the various legal regimes may accommodate cosmopolitan extraterritoriality, and on how they offer fine-grained techniques of jurisdictional restraint.

Such an endeavour requires a keen understanding of, and respect for the legal norms and modes of legal reasoning that are socially accepted in selected legal fields. At the same time, it requires the researcher to make full use of the interpretative leeway offered by the relevant law. After all, legal interpretations tend to be critically unstable and to evolve over time, tracking broader social, political, and economic developments.[1] This approach does not exclude the possibility that legal reform could be suggested, that is, a change in legal practices or even the adoption

[1] The critical instability and 'politicization' of the law has obviously been famously theorized by David Kennedy. See for the seminal publication: David W Kennedy, 'A New Stream of International Law Scholarship' (1988) Wis Int'l LJ 1. A fine example of how the law of jurisdiction adjusted to its broader political and economic environment can be found in antitrust law. In the course of the twentieth century, antitrust law moved from strict territoriality to reliance on the effects doctrine, which allowed states to exercise jurisdiction in case foreign-based antitrust conspiracies caused adverse effects in their territory. In the United States, this jurisdictional shift has been attributed to the economy becoming a new object of professional knowledge and political practice. Freya Irani, 'Beyond De Jure and De Facto Boundaries: Tracing the Imperial Geographies of US Law' (2019) 25 EJIR 1, 5 DOI:10.1177/1354066119869801 (accessed 6 December 2019).

Selfless Intervention. Cedric Ryngaert, Oxford University Press (2020). © Cedric Ryngaert.
DOI: 10.1093/oso/9780198851783.001.0001

formal amendments of the *lex lata*. However, such reformist proposals should be in keeping with the overall jurisdictional logic of the legal system under scrutiny. In essence, this calls for a cultural appreciation of the technicalities of the law[2] as well as a retrieving of the space for the political (in this case a political theory of cosmopolitan extraterritoriality) in technical rules of jurisdiction.[3] Or, as John Haskell observed in respect of extraterritoriality: 'Technique, in many respects, is more political than any historical or theoretical analysis, involved to a greater degree in settling the outcomes of actual struggles in the real world.'[4]

5.1.1 The jurisdictional capabilities of territoriality

As argued in Chapter 2, in the face of glaring global governance failures, such as climate change and persistent human rights abuses, the exercise of jurisdiction in the common interest may increasingly be required. However, the foundational principles of territoriality and state sovereignty on which the law of jurisdiction is based (in fact, the principles on which the positivist, modern conception of international law itself is based)[5] appear to be anathema to the development of a more progressive, cosmopolitan agenda furthering the interests of the international community. On closer inspection, however, the capaciousness of the principles of jurisdiction may go quite some way to accommodate the champions of cosmopolitanism. For one thing, the existence of universal criminal jurisdiction over core crimes against international law has been hailed as evidence of rising cosmopolitan solidarity among states and communities,[6] jurisdictional solidarity which in future may possibly also extend to other offenses.[7] For another, the principle of

[2] I borrow here from Annelise Riles, 'A New Agenda for the Cultural Study of Law: Taking on the Technicalities' (2005) 53 Buff L Rev 973.

[3] I borrow here from Asha Kaushal, 'The Politics of Jurisdiction' (2015) 78 TMLR 759, 760. See also Shaunnagh and Shaun McVeigh, *Jurisdiction (Critical Approaches to Law)* (Routledge 2012).

[4] John D Haskell, 'Ways of Doing Extraterritoriality in Scholarship' in Daniel Margolies and others (eds), *The Extraterritoriality of Law: History, Theory, Politics* (Routledge 2019) 18.

[5] See for a problematization: Cedric Ryngaert, 'Territory in the Law of Jurisdiction: Imagining Alternatives' in Martin Kuijer and Wouter Werner (eds), *Netherlands Yearbook of International Law 2016: The Changing Nature of Territoriality in International Law* (TMC Asser Press 2017).

[6] Carly Nyst, 'Solidarity in a Disaggregated World: Universal Jurisdiction and the Evolution of Sovereignty' (2012) 8 JILIR 36, 58 (arguing that 'a study of universal jurisdiction complaints and prosecutions provides countless examples of the abridgement of traditional restrictions of territorial jurisdiction in the name of a community of humankind').

[7] The catalogue of offences amenable to such universal (connection-less) jurisdiction is open-ended and expandable. *Eg* genocide and war crimes committed in non-international armed conflicts were initially not considered to be amenable to universal criminal jurisdiction, as the Geneva Conventions did not provide for it. However, later state practice has confirmed universal jurisdiction over these offences. See for genocide, *eg* ECtHR *Jorgic v Germany*, Appl No 74613/01, 12 July 2007. See for war crimes committed in non-international armed conflicts: International Committee of the Red Cross, *Customary International Humanitarian* Law (CUP 2005) Rule 157. Also, the UN Convention on the Law of the Sea (adopted 10 December 1982, entry into force 16 November 1994) inserted a provision (article 218) allowing for the exercise of apparently universal port state jurisdiction over discharges.

territoriality—although originally devised to keep territorial sovereigns apart—has been, and can be moulded to further the common interest, as states have considered even tenuous territorial connections as sufficient to justify jurisdictional assertions and extend their own laws to foreign situations.[8] Through its objective (effects-based) and subjective (conduct-based) incarnations, territoriality has been given particularly wide interpretations in the criminal law,[9] antitrust law,[10] and cyber law.[11] In fact, the principle allows for the *territorialization* of the *extra-territorial*, depending on how conduct and offences are precisely framed, up to the point that territoriality even becomes an illusory or metaphysical concept.[12] This applies in particular to abstract concepts and intangible phenomena as opposed to physical persons and objects the location of which may be more straightforward.[13] As will be expounded in this chapter, territoriality, being a creature of the law rather than an empirically verifiable phenomenon,[14] may be a potent mechanism to further cosmopolitan extraterritoriality in the fields of human rights and the environment.

This *instrumental* approach to territory, as a 'capability' to address the extraterritorial and the global, can also be found in the social sciences. Thus, Saskia Sassen has observed that state capabilities are multivalent, can actually jump tracks, and get 'relodged in novel assemblages'.[15] For her, this meant that the capabilities of territorially sovereign states enabled the formation of particular global systems,[16] for example the financial system, which is deeply imbricated with 'global' but nevertheless *territorially* based cities such as London. By the same token, geographers

[8] Cedric Ryngaert, 'Whither Territoriality? The European Union's Use of Territoriality to Set Norms with Universal Effects' in Cedric Ryngaert and others (eds), *What's Wrong with International Law, Liber Amicorum Prof. A.H.A. Soons* (Brill 2015). See on how the European Union uses sometimes weak territorial connections to extend the reach of EU law: Joanne Scott, 'Extraterritoriality and Territorial Extension in EU Law' (2014) 62 Am J Comp L 87. See on the uselessness of territoriality, especially in a cyber context, given the ubiquitous territorial connections of conduct in cyberspace: Dan JB Svantesson, 'A New Jurisprudential Framework for Jurisdiction: Beyond the Harvard Draft' (2015) 109 AJILU 69. Actual legal practice is rife with examples of a (territorial) nexus triggering jurisdiction in what could be considered as the common interest. Such practice will obviously be discussed in greater detail later in this chapter.

[9] See on the constituent elements approach underlying application of the territoriality principle in domestic criminal law: Cedric Ryngaert, 'Territorial Jurisdiction Over Cross-frontier Offences: Revisiting a Classic Problem of International Criminal Law' (2009) 9 ICLR 187.

[10] *Eg* Cedric Ryngaert, *Jurisdiction over Antitrust Violations in International Law* (Intersentia 2008).

[11] Dan JB Svantesson, *Solving the Internet Jurisdiction Puzzle* (OUP 2017).

[12] Peter D Szigeti, 'The Illusion of Territorial Jurisdiction' (2017) 52 TILR 359, 398 ('The reasoning used in both "strict territorial" decisions and "extraterritorial effects" decisions are identical. It involves making essentially metaphysical decisions, without geographic substance, about whether an event, a mental state, or a quality "takes place" within or beyond an international boundary.').

[13] Peter D Szigeti, 'In the Middle of Nowhere. The Futile Quest to Distinguish Territoriality from Extraterritoriality' in Daniel Margolies and others (eds), *The Extraterritoriality of Law: History, Theory, Politics* (Routledge 2019) 31 (referring *inter alia* to corporations, conspiracies, responsibilities, and digital data).

[14] ibid, 32, 43.

[15] Saskia Sassen, *Territory, Authority, Rights: From Medieval to Global Assemblages* (PUP 2006) 11.

[16] ibid, 21.

Paul Foley and Elizabeth Havice have argued that territoriality has maintained its importance even in the face of the new politics of transnational sustainability governance; in particular, they have showed that eco-certification initiatives embed international norms in *territorial* specificity.[17] This has led them to conceive of territoriality as 'a set of mediated relationships rooted in ties to the material environment, other groups and mediated by techniques and representations'.[18]

Thus, somewhat counterintuitively, reconstructed territoriality may offer a promising hook to advance a cosmopolitan agenda.[19] Still, this is not too surprising: as we argued in Chapter 2, territoriality's conjoined twin, *sovereignty*, has undergone semantic transformations that have shifted its ambitions from protecting narrow state interests to safeguarding the values and interests of the international community. Territorial sovereignty has become contingent on its serving international interests, and in fact has become an instrument in realizing international community values. In *Sovereignty as Symbolic Form*, political philosopher Jens Bartelson observes in this respect that 'the exercise of political authority is not legitimized with reference to the consent it commands, but with reference to its capacity to maintain the international system in good working order by preventing domestic conflicts, promoting democracy and human rights, and protecting populations from gross violations of the latter'.[20] Sovereignty changes ontologically and is at the mercy of an international political morality that is enforced by 'a thousand petty emperors acting on behalf of an imagined international community'.[21]

If territorial sovereignty is thus reinterpreted, this may obviously invite the question whether *territoriality*, if used to give legal cover to what is in reality the *extraterritorial*, is not forfeiting its traditional role of delimiting spheres of competence between states and preventing international tension. This question can be answered in two ways. First, territoriality may be abandoned altogether on the grounds that it is no longer in keeping with extraterritorial and transnational

[17] Paul Foley and Elizabeth Havice, 'The Rise of Territorial Eco-certifications: New Politics of Transnational Sustainability Governance in the Fishery Sector' (2016) 69 Geoforum 24, 31 (adding that '[t]he territorial re-making of transnational sustainability governance works through integrated networks among territorially embedded seafood production interests, state regulatory and marketing institutions, and international market dynamics and governance norms. It serves to shore up the territorial, often national, industry identities and features of place-specific production and state-based regulatory regimes, and pushes these features beyond the spatial boundaries of the state by promoting them for recognition in global markets.').

[18] ibid.

[19] Szigeti, 'In the Middle of Nowhere' (n 13) 398 ('Exercising jurisdictional power in the global interest (whether determined through economic analyses of efficiency or other means) should be encouraged—as well as critical thinking about power politics disguised in jurisdictional altruism, of course.')

[20] Jens Bartelson, *Sovereignty as Symbolic Form* (Routledge 2014) 88.

[21] ibid, 87. While the empirical basis of Bartelson's claim regarding the changed ontological status of sovereignty pertains rather to the international community's efforts at nation-building in failed states, his theoretical insights can apply with equal, if not more force to states exercising unilateral jurisdiction in the interest of protecting and stabilizing world public order, as if they were the emperors of yesteryear.

realities on the ground.[22] Shedding territoriality may spawn the development of other jurisdictional grounds that are more attuned to these realities, possibly along functional lines. Alternatively, one can simply accept that territoriality will probably only weed out the most outrageous claims, and look instead for principles of jurisdictional reasonableness and restraint along the lines set out in Chapter 4.

5.1.2 Scope and focus of the specific part

A study like this one does not and cannot have the ambition to give an exhaustive overview of the jurisdictional options and limitations of cosmopolitan extraterritoriality in all fields of the law, and in all states or legal systems. Instead, the thematic focus is placed on two 'global values' or 'common interests' which occupy a central place in the contemporary global justice discourse: *human rights* and threats to the *environment*.[23] These fields remain relatively broad, however. Therefore, further delimitation is required. For this specific part, the choice has been made to zoom in on instances of unilateral jurisdiction aimed at a *regulating business activities*. This choice is informed by the nefarious and pervasive human rights and environmental externalities which have accompanied rapid, private business-driven economic globalization over the last few decades, and the subsequent calls for corporate regulation and accountability to counter these externalities.[24]

Private operators affect human rights and the environment in various ways. The impacts of transnational corporations' activities in host states in the Global South,

[22] See for an argument in favour of shedding territoriality: Svantesson, 'A New Jurisprudential Framework' (n 8). See also Paul S Berman, 'Global Legal Pluralism' (2007) 80 SCLR 1155, 1182 (arguing that for state regulation of transactions in cyberspace, this may mean abandoning the pretence that such transactions have specific territorial contacts, and instead admitting that their effects are diffused over many centres).

[23] Chris Armstrong discusses in *Global Distributive Justice* (CUP 2012) as 'issues' of global justice respectively human rights, natural resources, international trade, climate change, and migration. Matthias Risse addresses in *Global Justice* (PUP 2012) immigration, obligations to future generations, obligations arising from climate change, fairness in trade, responsibilities of the WTO, intellectual property rights, labour rights, global inequality, while developing a new foundational theory of human rights. Simon Caney discusses in *Justice Beyond Borders: a Global Political Theory* (OUP 2005), as the first issue 'Civil and Political Justice', which he understands as 'those principles that specify what rights people have to what freedoms, and argues for universal human rights to certain civil and political liberties' (Chapter 2). Caney has however also written extensively on the application of global justice principles to climate change. See *eg* Simon Caney, 'Cosmopolitan Justice, Responsibility, and Global Climate Change' (2005) 18 LJIL 747. See on global environmental justice also Dale Jamieson, 'Global Environmental Justice' (1994) 36 RIPS 199. The legal volume titled *Global Justice, State Duties* (M Langford and others (eds), CUP 2014), for its part, only relates to extraterritorial *human rights* obligations. What these titles have in common is that they give a central place to human rights in global justice. Most of them also address environmental issues, in particular climate change. This justifies this study's focus on human rights and the environment.

[24] *Eg* Liesbeth Enneking and others (eds), *Accountability, International Business Operations and the Law: Providing Justice for Corporate Human Rights Violations in Global Value Chains* (Routledge 2019).

as epitomized by the Rana Plaza disaster, are probably best known.[25] Insofar as host states are unable or unwilling to regulate these activities, calls may be made for third states to provide 'extraterritorial' accountability, for example home states opening up their courts for tort claims brought against domestically incorporated parent corporations. Private operators affect human rights and the environment in other ways too, however. Think of the impacts of emissions from industrial activities on global warming, which have spurred calls to take 'extraterritorial' trade measures, that is to impose regulations or tariffs on imported products that have been produced abroad in an unsustainable manner. Think of private operators' illegal, unreported, and unsustainable fishing practices and pollution of oceans, which in the face of flag state regulatory failures have informed calls for port states to intervene. Or think of operators of Internet intermediaries' practices of gathering Internet users' data worldwide, which have led to calls to regulate such operators (Google, Facebook, etc), possibly extraterritorially, in order to protect privacy rights.

Choosing is losing, and this means that such a mainstay of cosmopolitan extraterritoriality as universal criminal jurisdiction over core crimes against international law falls by the wayside,[26] although we have addressed it in the general part of this study, especially in Chapter 3. In all fairness, universal criminal jurisdiction is a field that is overanalysed by legal scholars. The international legal grounds for exercising universal jurisdiction over core crimes are relatively clear. Modes of universal criminal jurisdiction have been laid down in treaties, and may be authorized by customary international law.[27] Pursuant to treaty-based *aut dedere aut judicare* clauses, the exercise of universal jurisdiction may even be mandatory rather than discretionary.[28] This is not to say that universal criminal jurisdiction is not of academic interest. It is only to say that its doctrinal legal basis is no longer in need of exhaustive scholarly treatment. The focus of academic inquiry regarding international law crimes should rather shift to the empirical variables determining the *actual* exercise of jurisdiction, or to the normative legitimacy of jurisdictional assertions in concrete instances.[29] This was in fact the focus of Chapter 3.3. It remains

[25] Juliane Reinecke and Jimmy Donaghey, 'The "Accord for Fire and Building Safety in Bangladesh", in Response to the Rana Plaza Disaster' in Juliane Reinecke and Jimmy Donaghey (eds), *Global Governance of Labour Rights Assessing the Effectiveness of Transnational Public and Private Policy Initiatives* (Edward Elgar 2015).

[26] See for recent scholarship on universal jurisdiction, *eg* Aisling O'Sullivan, *Universal Jurisdiction in International Criminal Law: The Debate and the Battle for Hegemony* (Routledge 2017); Devika Hovell, 'The Authority of International Law' (2018) 29 EJIL 427; Anthony Reeves, 'Liability to International Prosecution' (2017) 28 EJIL 1047.

[27] See for an overview notably Luc Reydams, *Universal Jurisdiction: International and Municipal Perspectives* (OUP 2003).

[28] *Eg* UN Torture Convention article 5(2).

[29] See in this respect *eg* Maximo Langer and Mackenzie Eason, 'The Quiet Expansion of Universal Jurisdiction' (2019) 30 EJIL 1, 3 and section 2 (forthcoming) <https://www.researchgate.net/publication/332687485_The_Quiet_Expansion_of_Universal_Jurisdiction> (accessed on 6 December 2019) (noting a numerical expansion of universal jurisdiction and listing the following factors as having contributing to this trend: 'the passage of domestic legislation implementing the International Criminal Court framework containing universal jurisdiction provisions; the creation of special units within

the fact, nevertheless, that this study considers universal jurisdiction as a source of inspiration for the cosmopolitan jurisdictional practices which it *does* examine. Universal jurisdiction is inspirational in that its exercise does not depend on the presence of a connecting factor, such as territoriality or nationality, but is instead based on the gravity of the crime, that is on the harm the act caused to a value or interest held dear by the international community. An argument could be made that similar jurisdictional dynamics should be at play in other fields of the law, with respect to (business) activities that are globally harmful while not rising to the level of an international crime. Alternatively, it could be argued, and is in fact argued in this monograph, that the globally harmful character of particular conduct, while not in itself authorizing the exercise of extraterritorial jurisdiction, should guide the application of existing principles of jurisdiction. This may mean that if the objective of a jurisdictional assertion is to protect global values or the common interest, a tenuous territorial link can suffice, and even that states may be under an *obligation* to exercise jurisdiction on the basis of existing permissive principles.[30]

5.1.3 Structure

In section 5.1.2, some examples have been given of how activities of private economic operators can cause externalities for common concerns, and of how states may want to respond by exercising unilateral jurisdiction in the common interest. These examples form the basis of this part's structure. The remainder of this part consists of four sections. Sections 5.2 and 5.3 pertain to environmental concerns, whereas sections 5.4 and 5.5 pertain to human rights. Section 5.2 addresses the exercise of port state jurisdiction over foreign-flagged vessels engaged in illegal, unreported, or unsustainable (IUU) fishing, or which endanger the marine environment on the high seas, an area normally beyond national jurisdiction. Section 5.3 examines the imposition of trade measures (considered here as an exercise of regulatory jurisdiction) in pursuit of global environmental objectives, such as tackling climate change. Section 5.4 studies under what conditions bystander states, such as home states, can exercise adjudicatory jurisdiction in tort matters

domestic law enforcement institutions dedicated to investigating and prosecuting international crimes; the growing number of NGOs dedicated primarily to documenting and advocating for the prosecution of international crimes; officials and advocates incrementally improving their investigation and litigation strategies by learning from past universal jurisdiction cases; the effects of technological change on the cost of gathering and organizing the evidence needed to prosecute crimes committed thousands of miles away from the investigating institution; and the extraordinary number of refugees and other migrants coming to Western states having participated in or bringing reports of international crimes committed in Iraq, Syria and elsewhere').

30 See on the shift in the law of jurisdiction from authorization to obligation: Alex Mills, 'Rethinking Jurisdiction in International Law' (2014) 84 BYBIL 187.

with respect to overseas human rights abuses committed or facilitated by transnational corporations. Section 5.5, finally, analyses how states and in particular the European Union have 'territorially extended' their data protection legislation to protect their citizens' data privacy from abuses committed and facilitated by Internet intermediaries.

It is observed that some states have transferred competencies to a regional organization which may exercise jurisdiction, also externally, on behalf of the member states. The European Union is a case in point. It has turned out to be a major external jurisdictional actor, in particular in the fields of competition law, data protection, and environmental protection. Therefore, this study also incorporates relevant EU practice. From an international jurisdictional perspective, the nature of the regulating actor as a state or a regional organization such as the European Union is immaterial. It is recalled in this respect that in the *ATAA* judgment, the Court of Justice of the EU (CJEU) held, in the context of unilateral environmental regulation with extraterritorial effects, that the European Union is bound by the customary international law rules of prescriptive state jurisdiction.[31]

5.2 Port State Jurisdiction regarding IUU Fishing and Vessel-Source Pollution

Some major global governance problems occur at sea, in maritime areas beyond national jurisdiction (the high seas). IUU fishing[32] and marine pollution stand out in this respect. The remoteness of the high seas, in conjunction with flag states' failure to assume their responsibility in full may render enforcement at sea regarding globally harmful activities problematic. However, at one point, vessels have to dock in *ports*, to unload their cargo, to refuel, to have the vessel repaired, to have the crew disembark, etc. If foreign-flagged vessels which previously engaged or are likely to engage in globally harmful activities visit ports, this may provide an opportunity for the latter to intervene 'selflessly' to further common interests, in particular to support sustainable fishing practices on the high seas and prevent globally harmful vessel-source pollution.[33] Such jurisdiction may have globally beneficial outcomes as it forces vessels and their flag states to comply with higher standards.

[31] Case C-366/10 *Air Transport Association of America and Others v Secretary of State for Energy and Climate (ATAA)* [2011] ECLI:EU:C:2011:864, para 101.

[32] See, for an extensive definition of IUU fishing: Food and Agriculture Organization of the United Nations (Committee on Fisheries), 'International Plan of Action to Prevent, Deter, and Eliminate Illegal, Unreported, and Unregulated Fishing' (23 June 2001) para 3. The eradication of IUU fishing by 2020 is one of UN's sustainable development goals. See UNGA 'The Future We Want' Res 66/288 (27 July 2012) A/RES/66/288 Social Development Goals 14.4.

[33] cf Erik J Molenaar, 'Port State Jurisdiction: Toward Comprehensive, Mandatory and Global Coverage' (2007) 38 ODIL 225, 225–26 ('Port state jurisdiction clearly does not just serve the national interests, but can also further the interests of the international community by, among other things,

The exercise of *port state jurisdiction* (PSJ) can take various forms, such as denial of entry in port, inspections, confiscation of catch, ship detention, or even fines and prosecutions.[34] Port states do not only exercise jurisdiction over visiting vessels on an individual basis, they have also acted jointly by entering into port state control arrangements. Such arrangements, typically concluded in the form of memoranda of understanding, level the international playing field for shipping and eliminate substandard 'ports of convenience'.[35] They enable port states to check, by means of inspections, visiting vessels' compliance with global standards as laid down in treaties relevant to international shipping, notably treaties on marine pollution and maritime labour.[36]

Ports form part of a state's sovereign territory.[37] Accordingly, one may be tempted to posit that port states can rely on the *territoriality principle* to justify any jurisdictional assertion over a visiting vessel in port. However, taking such a position is to conflate prescriptive with enforcement jurisdiction.[38] The territorial presence of a presumed offender, in this case a vessel, may admittedly allow a state, in this case the port state, to exercise territorial *enforcement* jurisdiction, but that state still needs to rely on a principle of *prescriptive* jurisdiction to justify its jurisdictional assertion.[39] One of the complications is that such jurisdiction may well pertain to events which occurred *outside* the port state's territory. The port state might then be viewed as exercising *extraterritorial jurisdiction*,[40] for which it may

ensuring safety at sea (maritime safety), marine environmental protection,and sustainable utilization of marine living resources; safeguarding marine biodiversity; and combating international terrorism.').

[34] See *eg* for an overview of possible US port state measures linked to a failure to comply with MARPOL standards (marine pollution): 33 USC § 1908.

[35] *Eg* Paris Memorandum of Understanding on Port State Control (adopted 26 January 1982, entered into force 1 July 1982) (1982) 21 ILM 1. See for implementation in the EU: Directive 2009/16/EC of the European Parliament and of The Council Of 23 April 2009 On Port State Control (Recast) [2009] OJ L131/59. PSC MoUs do not cover fishing activities, which may however be addressed by PSJ, including through regional fisheries management organizations.

[36] *Eg* Maritime Labour Convention (adopted 23 February 2006, entered into force 20 August 2013) (2006) 45 ILM 792; International Convention for the Prevention of Pollution, as modified Protocol of 1978 Relating to the International Convention for the Prevention of Pollution from Ships (adopted 2 November 1973, entered into force 2 October 1983) (1978) 1340 UNTS 184.

[37] United Nations Convention on the Law of the Sea (adopted 10 December 1982, entered into force 16 November 1994) 1833 UNTS 397, art 11 ('the outermost permanent harbour works which form an integral part of the harbour system are regarded as forming part of the coast').

[38] See for an example of such conflation: Case C-286/90 *Anklagemyndigheden v Peter Michael Poulsen and Diva Navigation Corp* [1992] ECR I-06019, para 28 ('once within port vessels are subject to the unlimited jurisdiction of the port state').

[39] Compare with the exercise of universal criminal jurisdiction, which is typically triggered by the territorial presence of the presumed offender, jurisdiction *in absentia* hardly being exercised. However, the exercise of prescriptive jurisdiction over this person is not justified by his mere territorial presence but rather by norms of treaty or customary international law which allow states to exercise jurisdiction over a limited number of particularly serious offences, the commission of which the presumed offender stands accused.

[40] Compare Robin Churchill, 'Port State Jurisdiction Relating to the Safety of Shipping and Pollution from Ships—What Degree of Extra-territoriality?' (2016) 31 IJMCL 442, 454 (considering

need special authorization under international law. The UN Convention for the Law of the Sea (UNCLOS) provides for such (optional) PSJ in the service of collective interests only with respect to discharges on the high seas.[41] It remains silent on the exercise of PSJ regarding other globally harmful conduct such as other forms of vessel-source pollution or IUU fishing. The absence of specific UNCLOS authorization to exercise PSJ need not render it unlawful, however. This section examines the overtures offered by international law allowing port states to exercise jurisdiction in the common interest. The thematic focus of the analysis is on IUU fishing and vessel-source pollution.

The structure of this part is as follows.[42] Section 5.2.1 argues that port states in principle have discretion to deny entry to visiting vessels. If they want to go further and take enforcement action in port against visiting vessels, they normally (will have to) rely on an accepted principle of jurisdiction. Citing relevant practice, section 5.2.2 goes on to show that states normally rely on territorial offenses in this respect. However, port states' territorialization of underlying activities which in fact take place in areas beyond national jurisdiction raises questions regarding the viability of territoriality as a persuasive jurisdictional ground. Therefore, section 5.2.3 examines whether a novel jurisdictional ground for port state measures in the common interest could possibly be found, with full respect for the particularities of (functional) jurisdiction in the law of the sea. Section 5.2.4 demonstrates that regardless of the precise doctrinal justification of 'cosmopolitan' port state jurisdiction, the more immediate trigger for such jurisdiction is the national interest rather than global common concerns. In section 5.2.5, it is submitted that the exercise of PSJ may have *beneficial extraterritorial consequences*, in that it may pave the way for more protective multilateral solutions. Section 5.2.6 argues that port state should take into account the legitimate interests of foreign countries

a measure to be extraterritorial when its 'primary purpose' is the regulation of extraterritorial circumstances).

[41] UNCLOS (n 37) art 218(1), titled 'enforcement by port states' ('When a vessel is voluntarily within a port or at an off-shore terminal of a State, that State may undertake investigations and, where the evidence so warrants, institute proceedings in respect of any discharge from that vessel outside the internal waters, territorial sea or exclusive economic zone of that State in violation of applicable international rules and standards established through the competent international organization or general diplomatic conference.'). See on the collective interest rationale of UNCLOS (n 37) art 218: Jutta Brunnée, 'Common Areas, Common Heritage, and Common Concern' in Daniel Bodansky and others (eds), *Oxford Handbook of International Environmental Law* (OUP 2007) 550; Henrik Ringbom, *The EU Maritime Safety Policy and International Law* (Brill 2008) 216.

[42] I am partly indebted for this part to Dr Arron Honniball and Dr Nelson Coelho, who successfully defended their PhDs on the port state jurisdiction at Utrecht University in 2019, in the framework of the UNIJURIS project of which I was the Principal Investigator. Arron N Honniball, 'Extraterritorial Port State Measures. The Basis and Limits of Unilateral Port State Jurisdiction to Combat IUU Fishing' (PhD, Utrecht University 2019); Nelson F Coelho, 'Unilateral Port State Jurisdiction. The Quest for Universality in the Prevention, Reducation and Control of Ship-Source Pollution' (PhD, Utrecht University 2019).

and operators when exercising PSJ, and suggests some legal tools and techniques in this respect.

5.2.1 Residual port state powers and denial of entry

It is widely accepted that it is within a port state's residual powers to deny entry to foreign-flagged vessels,[43] or to impose entry conditions or restrictions (such as denial of services), as long as port states refrain from regulating the internal affairs of a vessel.[44] In principle, port states can deny entry or impose conditions as they please, that is they have discretionary powers in this respect.[45] After all, vessels, like natural persons, have no right of entry to port, unless specific treaties have been concluded to this effect. Thus, port states can deny entry to foreign-flagged vessels which they suspect of IUU fishing or of supporting IUU fishing (*eg* via bunkering) or of posing a danger to the local environment. If port states act in concert, such entry denials will have a major deterrent effect on IUU fishing as fish have to be landed somewhere in order to reach consumer markets.

From a doctrinal perspective, entry denials or entry conditions find their legal basis in the sovereignty of the state.[46] As Honniball has argued, such denials and conditions may even belong to the state's *domaine réservé*, which would mean that states need not rely on international rules of jurisdiction to justify their exercise of authority.[47] Port states can deny and have denied entry not only to suspected individual vessels (or subject them to more stringent inspections) but also to all vessels flying the flag of suspected states. States may be suspect where they are non-cooperating, non-contracting parties to regional fisheries management organizations and arrangements, or non-parties to multilateral agreements such as the Port

[43] Louisse de La Fayette, 'Access to Ports in International Law' (1996) 11 IJMCL 1, 22. *Contra*, but clearly dated: *Saudi Arabi v Arabian American Oil Co. (ARAMCO)* (1963) 27 ILR 117, 212. ('According to a great principle of public international law, the ports of every State must be open to foreign merchant vessels and can only be closed when the vital interest of the State so require.').

[44] *Spector v Norwegian Cruise Lines Ltd* 545 US 119 (2004) (holding that except insofar as Title III of the US Americans with Disabilities Act regulates a vessel's internal affairs, the statute is applicable to foreign-flag cruise ships in US waters). In the United States, the internal affairs rule is derived from the presumption against extraterritoriality, pursuant to which a statute may only regulate the internal affairs in case of a clear indication of congressional intent. See also *Wildenhus's Case* 120 US 1, 11 (1887); *Benz v Compania Naviera Hidalgo, S.A.* 353 US 138 (1957); *McCulloch v Sociedad Nacional de Marineros de Honduras* 372 US 10 (1963). In *Lauritzen v Larsen* 345 US 571 (1953), the Court derived this rule also from international law (at 576–79) (holding the US Jones Act inapplicable in a suit by a foreign seaman against a foreign shipowner for an injury sustained in a foreign port).

[45] See on possible limitations to port state discretion, however: Australia House of Representatives Committee, 10 May 2013 *Imposition of conditions on port access for cruise ships: requirements regarding crimes at sea* (advisory opinion stating that 'there is little guidance, either in treaties or in the academic literature, about the sorts of conditions of access which would be permitted').

[46] *Eg* Case concerning Military and Paramilitary Activities in and against Nicaragua (*Nicaragua v USA)* (Merits) [1986] ICJ Rep 3, para 213.

[47] Honniball, 'Extraterritorial Port State Measures' (n 42) section 2.5.

State Measures Agreement,[48] and are thus presumed not to do enough to address IUU fishing.[49]

In some situations, there is not just a right to deny entry in the context of the exercise of PSJ, but even a *duty*. This duty may also extend to the taking of other port state measures, for example a duty to carry out minimum level of inspections in port. Notably regarding IUU fishing, the exercise of PSJ has shifted from a discretionary right to an international duty.[50] Such treaties as the UN Fishing Stocks Agreement[51] and in particular the Port State Measures Agreement[52] and constitutive instruments of regional fisheries management organizations and arrangements,[53] as well as soft law initiatives such as the International Plan of Action to Prevent, Deter and Eliminate, Illegal, Unreported and Unregulated Fishing (IPOA IUU)[54] set out minimum measures which port states must take in order to address IUU fishing.[55] These relate primarily to denial of entry,[56] and required minimum levels of inspection.[57] In due course, such a duty may possibly crystallize under customary international law too, provided that evidence of sufficient state practice and *opinio juris* can be advanced. The existence of mandatory PSJ in any event demonstrates that international duties to exercise jurisdiction are also found outside the narrow confines of the international law governing the prosecution of core crimes.

[48] Agreement on Port State Measures to Prevent, Deter and Eliminate Illegal, Unreported and Unregulated Fishing (adopted 22 November 2009, entered into force 5 June 2016) art 23(2) ('[All] Parties shall take fair, non-discriminatory and transparent measures consistent with this Agreement and other applicable international law to deter the activities of non-Parties which undermine the effective implementation of this Agreement.').

[49] See for an application by US authorities: NOAA, 'Notification to Mexican Fishing Vessels Subject to Port Denial under the High Seas Driftnet Fishing Moratorium Protection Act' (2017).

[50] See at length Honniball, 'Extraterritorial Port State Measures' (n 42) ch 3.

[51] See *eg* United Nations Agreement for the Implementation of the Provisions of the United Nations Convention on the Law of the Sea of 10 December 1982 relating to the Conservation and Management of Straddling Fish Stocks and Highly Migratory Fish Stocks (adopted 4 August 1995, entered into force 11 December 2001) 2167 UNTS 3, art 23(1) ('A port State has the right and the duty to take measures.'). However, the remainder of art 23(1) is couched in optional terms: art 23(2) ('A port State *may*, inter alia, inspect documents, fishing gear and catch on board fishing vessels, when such vessels are voluntarily in its ports or at its offshore terminals.'); art 23(3) 'States may adopt regulations empowering the relevant national authorities to prohibit landings and transshipments where it has been established that the catch has been taken in a manner which undermines the effectiveness of subregional, regional or global conservation and management measures on the high seas.').

[52] PSMA (n 48) art 9. See for mandatory port state measures in the PSMA: mandatory designation of port, minimum advance notification requirements, mandatory denial of entry or use of port. PSMA (n 48) arts 7–9.

[53] *Eg* South East Atlantic Fisheries Organization, System of Observation, Inspection, Compliance and Enforcement (2016) (adopted 3 December 2016, entered into force 15 February 2016), art 22(4).

[54] IPOA IUU (n 32). On the basis of this non-binding instrument, port states should use measures to prevent, deter, and eliminate IUU fishing, should require advance notice for entry, with sufficient information to ascertain IUU fishing involvement, and should deny landing or transhipment where clear evidence of IUU fishing activity exists. ibid, paras 52, 55–56. See also FAO, *Model Scheme PSM*, paras 2–3.10, Appendices A–D (describing inspection regimes that should be implemented).

[55] See on the evolution towards mandatory coverage: Molenaar (n 33); Judith Swan, 'Port State Measures—from Residual Port State Jurisdiction to Global Standards' (2016) 31 IJMCL 395.

[56] PSMA (n 48) art 9.

[57] PSMA (n 48) art 12(1) ('Each Party shall inspect the number of vessels in its ports required to reach an annual level of inspections sufficient to achieve the objective of this Agreement.').

5.2.2 Port state jurisdiction over territorial offences

States may want to take more onerous measures that go beyond denying entry to vessels calling at port, and beyond merely conducting inspections to check compliance with international standards. In particular, they may consider taking enforcement measures against vessels *in port*, with respect to globally harmful conduct that took place in areas beyond their national jurisdiction. Enforcement measures can range from the imposition of civil penalties to criminal prosecution, confiscation, ship detention, or forfeiture.[58]

Typically, in order to justify the taking of such measures, port states will *territorialize* extraterritorial conduct by prescribing territorial offences.[59] When using territorial offences, port states exercise prescriptive jurisdiction on the basis of the territoriality principle. Reliance on territoriality pre-empts jurisdictional problems connected to extraterritoriality. However, as discussed earlier, in principle, the mere *presence* of a vessel in port does *not* suffice for the exercise of prescriptive jurisdiction over the extraterritorial activities in which the vessel has engaged, even if enforcement is undeniably territorial (in port). Instead, a valid ground of *prescriptive* jurisdiction, in particular territoriality, should be advanced.

Territorial offences do not punish the extraterritorial conduct itself but rather its territorial manifestation. Examples are rife: a territorial failure to present an accurate logbook or accurate documentation after entering the port,[60] refusing inspection in port,[61] the establishment of vessel deficiencies during control in port, a vessel's failure to meet static construction, design, equipment, or manning (CDEM) standards in port (*eg* having a double hull[62] or possessing prohibited driftnets in port),[63] landing or transhipment of fish in spite of port state

[58] See *eg* for confiscation of fish imported without a valid catch certificate: Council Regulation (EC) No 1005/2008 establishing a Community system to prevent, deter and eliminate illegal, unreported and unregulated fishing, amending Regulations (EEC) No 2847/93, (EC) No 1936/2001, and (EC) No 601/2004, and repealing Regulations (EC) No 1093/94 and (EC) No 1447/1999 [2008] OJ L 286/1, art 18(3). See generally for enforcement of that Regulation: arts 43–44.

[59] International agreements may contain jurisdictional savings clauses to this effect. See *eg* Paris Memorandum of Understanding on Port State Control, Including 38th Amendment (adopted 22 May 2015, efffective date 1 July 2015), 1.7 ('Nothing in the Memorandum will be construed as restricting the powers of the Authorities to take measures within its jurisdiction in respect of any matter to which the relevant instruments relate.'); Straddling Fish Stock Agreement (n 51) art 23(4) ('Nothing in this article affects the exercise by States of their sovereignty over ports in their territory in accordance with international law.').

[60] British Branch Committee on the Law of the Sea, 'Report of the 56th Session of the ILA' (New Delhi 1974), pp 407–08. For relevant US court cases based on oil record book violations: *US v Royal Caribbean Cruises, Ltd* (1998) 11 F Supp 2d 1358 (SD Fla 1998) 1364; *US v Jho* (2008) 534 F 3d 398 (5th Cir 2008); *United States v Ionia Management S.A.*, 498 F Supp 2d 477 (D. Conn. 2007) 487.

[61] See on the territoriality of inspections in port, *eg*, International Convention for the Prevention of Pollution of the Sea by Oil (adopted 12 May 1954, entered into force 26 July 1958) 327 UNTS 3, Article IX(2) (hereafer OIPOL); MARPOL (n 36) Annex I, Regulation 20; ibid, Annex II, Regulation 9(7). ibid, Annex VI, Regulation 18(5)(a).

[62] Ringbom (n 41) 214.

[63] Such offences could be seen as continuous in the sense that, while originating extraterritorially, they continue in port. See on the territoriality of static standards, regardless of their extraterritorial

denial,[64] being a stateless vessel (regardless of the nature of its extraterritorial activities),[65] or the danger which the vessel or its activities pose to the port state (as coastal state), such as the emission of pollutants through dirty fuel combustion.[66] To combat IUU fishing, some states, notably the United States on the basis of the Lacey Act, even consider the mere landing, importation, or possession of fish caught on the basis of IUU fishing[67] to be an offence committed in port which grounds territorial PSJ.[68] It is observed that port state measures enforcing territorial offences are in principle discretionary, that is, not mandatory, as they are based on a permissive principle of jurisdiction. Sometimes, states decide against prosecution on grounds of international comity.[69]

Reliance on territorial offences is a clear example of the extent to which one can territorialize extraterritorial activities. This territorialization, in spite of its undeniable extraterritorial impact, has not given risen to strong protest by foreign states such as flag states,[70] and may thus be acceptable under customary international law. Nevertheless, concerns have at times been raised as to their compatibility with the freedom of the high seas, in light of their extraterritorial effects.[71] Most notably,

effects: Churchill (n 40); Veronica Frank, *The European Community and Marine Environmental Protection in the International Law of the Sea* (Brill 2007), 203–04.

64 IUU Regulation EU (n 58) art 11(2).

65 IUU Regulation EU (n 58) art 3(1)(l). However, stateless vessels will normally be denied entry rather than be subject to enforcement action via territorial offences. cf Honniball, 'Extraterritorial Port State Measures' (n 42) section 5.5.3.6.

66 This may ground *territorial* fuel content regulation, even though in fact a continuous activity is regulated and such regulation does produce *extraterritorial* effects. cf Sophia Kopela, 'Making Ships Cleaner: Reducing Air Pollution from International Shipping' (2017) 26 RECIEL 231, 40 ('a port State could adopt and enforce measures requiring the carrying of certain types of fuel on board, as the breach in this instance will arise in the port'). See regarding vessel fuel rules justified by the territoriality principle also *Pacific Merchant Shipping Association v Goldstene* 639 F.3d 1154 (9th Cir 2011) 17.

67 US Lacey Act, 16 USC § 3372(2)(a); 16 USC § 1857(1)(q); 50 CFR § 600.1203(a)(5)(6).

68 Admittedly, some states or the European Union may require a transfer of jurisdiction from other states with respect to serious infringements detected in port but relating to extraterritorial activities. cf art 11(4), 41(3) IUU Regulation EU (n 58). However, broad constructions of what counts as a territorial infringement, on the basis of the territorialisation techniques cited above, may drastically reduce the need for a transfer of jurisdiction.

69 cf *US v Jho* (n 60) (noting that although 'a state's exercise of jurisdiction over foreign-flagged ships in its ports is permissive ... a port state may, based on comity concerns, decide not to exercise its jurisdiction').

70 Coelho (n 42) section 3.3.2.

71 See the position of the European Union in the *Swordfish* dispute with Chile, regarding Chile's violation of the freedom of the high seas as a result of its port state measures pertaining to fishing practices conducted by EU-flagged vessels on the high seas: *WTO Chile—Measures affecting the Transit and Importing of Swordfish* [2000] WTO DSB DS193; *Conservation and Sustainable Exploitation of Swordfish Stocks (Chile/European Community)* (Order of 20 December 2000) ITLOS Reports 2000, 148. Compare, however, with the current EU position regarding PSJ and IUU, *eg*, per the IUU Regulation EU (n 58), which clearly does not consider port state measures to violate the freedom of the high seas. See also *Sellers v Maritime Safety Inspector* (1998) 120 ILR 586 (New Zealand, Court of Appeal) [48, 57] (stating that 'effect, if not the purpose, of the provision is to place requirements on the exercise of the freedom to navigate on the high seas', and that port states have 'no general power to unilaterally impose its own requirements ... if the requirements are to have effect on the high seas').

in *M/V Norstar* (2019), the International Tribunal for the Law of the Sea (ITLOS) ruled that 'any act which subjects activities of a foreign ship on the high seas to the jurisdiction of States other than the flag State constitutes a breach of the freedom of navigation, save in exceptional cases expressly provided for in the Convention or in other international treaties', and that 'the principle of exclusive flag State jurisdiction ... prohibits not only the exercise of enforcement jurisdiction on the high seas by States other than the flag State but also the extension of their prescriptive jurisdiction to lawful activities'.[72] This judgment was accompanied, however, by a strongly worded dissenting opinion signed by seven judges, who submitted that

> nothing in the text of the Convention, in its *travaux préparatoires*, in other international treaties, in customary international law, or in the practice of States suggests that article 87 and its corollary article 92 [UNCLOS] altogether excludes the right of non-flag States to exercise their prescriptive criminal jurisdiction with respect to activities on the high seas.[73]

As the majority's approach appears to be contrary to actual state practice, it remains to be seen whether it will be followed in future cases, possibly heard by other international tribunals.[74]

It is submitted here that UNCLOS has not supplanted the customary principles of jurisdiction.[75] Thus, reliance on territoriality and residual jurisdiction to justify PSJ is compatible with international law. However, this does not mean that all port state measures are internationally lawful. In fact, some of these measures do *not* appear to be based on a territorial link (apart from the vessel calling at, or being present in port). A notable example is the use of prior notification requirements which require vessels to give notification and information while they are still sailing.[76]

[72] International Tribunal for the Law of the Sea, The M/V 'Norstar' Case (*Panama v Italy*) (Judgment of 10 April 2019) paras 224–225.

[73] M/V 'Norstar' (*Panama v Italy)* (Joint dissenting opinion of Judges Cot, Pawlak, Yanai, Hoffmann, Kolodkin, Lijnzaad, Judge Ad Hoc Treves) para 19.

[74] Richard Collins, 'Delineating the Exclusivity of Flag State Jurisdiction on the High Seas: ITLOS issues its ruling in the M/V 'Norstar' (EJIL:Talk!, 4 June 2019) https://www.ejiltalk.org/delineating-the-exclusivity-of-flag-state-jurisdiction-on-the-high-seas-itlos-issues-its-ruling-in-the-m-v-norstar-case/ (accessed 6 December 2019); Arron N Honniball, 'Freedom of Navigation Following the M/V "Norstar" Case' (JCLOS Blog, 4 June 2019) https://site.uit.no/jclos/2019/06/04/freedom-of-navigation-following-the-m-v-norstar-case/ (accessed 6 December 2019).

[75] See also M/V 'Norstar' (n 73) Joint dissenting opinion Judge Ad Hoc Treves, paras 31–36.

[76] In this respect, Article 8 of the PSMA (n 48) provides that '[e]ach Party shall require, as a minimum standard, the information requested in Annex A [to the Agreement] to be provided before granting entry to a vessel to its port', and 'shall require [this] information ... to be provided sufficiently in advance to allow adequate time for the port State to examine such information'. The exercise of such jurisdiction cannot be grounded on an existing territorial nexus as the vessel is not yet in port. Still, one could use an extended version of territoriality as including anticipatory presence to justify the jurisdictional assertion. See for PSJ over vessel information: Bevan Marten, 'Port State Jurisdiction over Vessel Information: Territoriality, Extra-Territoriality and the Future of Shipping Regulation' (2016) 31 IJMCL 470.

Another example is Australia's requirement that vessels passing through the Torres Strait (*ie* an area beyond Australian jurisdiction) use compulsory pilotage, a requirement that would be enforced in Australian ports by making it an offence to enter port after a voyage through the strait without a pilot.[77] The prohibition and the attendant Australian port state measures were severely criticized by other International Maritime Organization (IMO) members,[78] after which Australia no longer considered it an offence to transit without a pilot outside the internal waters or territorial sea of Australia.[79] Foreign protest against the Australian port state measure may in fact have been justified on the ground that port state prescription in the case appeared to be wholly *extraterritorial.* No relevant conduct *in port* was proscribed, and as already mentioned, mere presence of a vessel in port does not suffice for the exercise of prescriptive jurisdiction.[80]

5.2.3 A novel jurisdictional ground for port state measures in the common interest?

If port states redeploy territory for cosmopolitan purposes, the question may arise whether territoriality still serves its original purpose of preventing one state's intrusion into another state's affairs. Given the cosmopolitan purpose of PSJ (or at least the global, non-territorial effects of a port state's regulatory intervention, in combination with the artificiality of the port state's territorial link), one is left to wonder whether such jurisdiction is ultimately not based on a more cosmopolitan principle of jurisdiction. Universal jurisdiction may perhaps lend itself to this, but for various reasons reliance on it may not be entirely apt to explain the workings of port state jurisdiction: (i) universal jurisdiction is normally associated with international crimes, whereas PSJ is typically exercised over offences or wrongful activities not rising to the level of international crimes (*eg* IUU fishing is not an international crime, possibly because there is no international consensus on what activities precisely constitute IUU fishing); (ii) in its pure form, the exercise of universal jurisdiction does not depend on a territorial link, whereas PSJ is triggered precisely by the territorial presence of the vessel; (iii) the concept of universal jurisdiction is relatively alien to the allocation of jurisdiction in the law of the sea.

[77] Australian Maritime Safety Authority, 'Marine Notice 8/2006' (16 May 2006) ('the owner, master and/or operator of the ship may be prosecuted on the next/entry into an Australian port, for both ships on voyages to Australian ports and ships transiting the Torres Strait en route to other destinations'). See for a discussion: Coelho (n 42) ch 3.4.6.

[78] International Maritime Organization, 'Report of the Marine Environment Protection Committee on its Fifty-Fifth Session' (16 October 200) MEPC.55/23, paras 8.10–14.

[79] Australian Navigation Act 2012, 167.

[80] See also Robert C Beckman, 'PSSAs and Transit Passage—Australia's Pilotage System in the Torres Strait Challenges the IMO and UNCLOS' (2007) 38 ODIL 325, 345 (considering such PSJ to be a violation of UNCLOS, and arguing that at most Australia could have denied entry).

Developing that last issue, the international law of the sea system, as codified in UNCLOS, is largely a system of *functional jurisdiction*, meaning that states can exercise elements of sovereign jurisdiction not necessarily over territory but rather over particular, functionally delineated activities, matters, and objects in designated maritime areas, such as the territorial sea, the contiguous zone, or the exclusive economic zone.[81] Nelson Coelho has argued that this system of functional jurisdiction, ingrained in the law of the sea, may also explain—and encourage—the exercise of PSJ regarding globally harmful activities occurring on the high seas.[82] PSJ could thus be considered as a form of functional jurisdiction in the common interest. Arguably it is a *function* of port states to provide protection to the global environment, a function already recognized in UNCLOS itself, also in respect of port states. Indeed, article 211(3) UNCLOS, in the context of marine pollution, refers to states establishing 'particular requirements for the prevention, reduction and control of pollution of the marine environment as a condition for the entry of foreign vessels into their ports'. The requirements mentioned in this provision are not geographically limited, which implies that they can as well pertain to activities in areas beyond national jurisdiction that threaten common concerns. To protect the global environment, port states could take measures to enforce existing multilateral rules and standards, for example, relating to discharges and dumping,[83] or by unilaterally prescribing novel standards (and subsequently enforcing them too), for example, relating to the protection of the marine environment, the preservation of biological diversity, the mitigation of climate change, or the conservation of natural heritage.[84] Reliance on states' functions to protect the global environment may eventually remove doubts as the international legality of a state's exercise of PSJ, especially if such jurisdiction does not have a strong territorial connection.[85]

Obviously, to prevent subjective interpretations of what measures may serve the global environment pursuant to a theory of functionalism, port state unilateralism needs to be imbued with a measure of *objectivity*. As Coelho has argued, such objectivity could be found in scientific knowledge which signals the urgency of tackling environmental problems, for example as caused by vessel-source pollution.[86] Based on scientific studies, states and the European Union could set emission standards that go beyond those provided in MARPOL,[87] or introduce

[81] Maria Gavouneli, *Functional Jurisdiction in the Law of the Sea* (Brill 2007). UNCLOS provisions give a detail overview of a (coastal) state's functional jurisdiction regarding various maritime zones.

[82] Coelho (n 42) ch 6.3 ('[P]ort state jurisdiction over common concerns is best explained by the principle of functionality. [P]ort states have certain functions and ... those functions are the normative ground that allows the exercise of regulatory functions over ship-source pollution.').

[83] UNCLOS (n 37) arts 216, 218. See Coelho (n 42) ch 6.2.2.1.

[84] Coelho (n 42) ch 6.2.3.2.

[85] *Eg* Kopela (n 66) 240.

[86] Coelho (n 42) ch 6.2.4.

[87] Directive 2005/33/EC of the European Parliament and of the Council of 6 July 2005 amending Directive 1999/32/EC [2005] OJ L191/59.

a monitoring, reporting, and verification system with which all visiting vessels should comply, even absent consensus at the IMO.[88] Also, when denying entry to vessels from states considered as not sufficiently addressing IUU fishing, states or the European Union may review these states' laws and practices in light of considerations of scientific desirability, for example fisheries conservation and management measures of regional fisheries management organizations of which they are supposed to be a member but are not in fact, soft law standards, or even best practices such as due diligence-based catch traceability schemes.[89]

5.2.4 Port state jurisdiction as parochial cosmopolitanism

While territoriality could be reconceptualized to serve the common interest, such as the fight against overfishing and marine pollution, as argued in Chapter 3, the immediate trigger for the exercise of jurisdiction is typically a desire to protect an aspect of the national interest. PSJ is no exception. Port states may tackle vessel-source air pollution in the first place because it affects coastal and port communities (a national public health interest), or they may clamp down on IUU fishing because it adversely affects the competitive opportunities of their own law-abiding fishing fleet (a national economic interest).[90]

National or EU legislation may sometimes even be explicit about protecting parochial concerns. For instance, EU Regulation No 1026/2012 on certain measures for the purpose of the conservation of fish stocks in relation to countries allowing non-sustainable fishing[91] (also) applies to extraterritorial fish stocks in with the European Union has a common interest on the ground that its fishing fleets are active in the relevant areas.[92] On the basis of this Regulation, the European Union applied restrictive measures, including port state measures, against the Faeroe Islands in relation to common interest stocks of Atlanto-Scandian herring, in

[88] Regulation (EU) 2015/757 of the European Parliament and of the Council of 29 April 2015 on the monitoring, reporting and verification of carbon dioxide emissions from maritime transport, and amending Directive 2009/16/EC [2015] OJ L123/55. See for a discussion: Natalie Dobson and Cedric Ryngaert, 'Provocative Climate Protection: EU "Extraterritorial" Regulation of Maritime Emissions' (2017) 66 ICLQ 333.

[89] See for a review of EU practice on the basis of the EU listing mechanism based on the IUU Fishing Regulation: Honniball, 'Extraterritorial Port State Measures' (n 42) s 6.5.2.11, unilateral non-cooperating third country list and emergency measures.

[90] Insofar as port states brazenly protect national interests by singling out particular foreign vessels and leaving their own vessels unharmed, these states may well violate the non-discrimination principle laid down in international trade law, as well as various principles of UNCLOS. See on such general UNCLOS safeguards and limitation as non-discrimination of foreign, abuse of right, and good faith fulfilment of obligations: Honniball, 'Extraterritorial Port State Measures' (n 42) ss 4.4.2, 4.4.3.

[91] Regulation (EU) No 1026/2012 of the European Parliament and of the Council of 25 October 2012 on certain measures for the purpose of the conservation of fish stocks in relation to countries allowing non-sustainable fishing [2012] OJ L316/34.

[92] ibid, art 2(a) ('stock of common interest' being defined as a 'fish stock the geographic distribution which makes it available to both the Union and third countries').

which EU fishermen had an interest.[93] In particular, the European Union argued that the Faeroe, by setting a unilateral catch limit, had scuttled a joint management plan, failed in its duties of cooperation based on UNCLOS and the UN Fish Stocks Agreement, and thus engaged in unsustainable fishing.[94] The EU's measures, such as the prohibition of introduction into EU territory and denial of services in EU ports, were apparently effective, as the Faeroe subsequently reduced its catch limits, thereby causing the European Union to repeal its restrictive measures against the Faeroe.[95] This contributed to stock conservation and increased economic opportunities for EU-flagged vessels in the relevant area. This example goes to show that the existence of a national interest will incentivize states and regional organizations to exercise PSJ in what ultimately is also in the common interest.

Contrariwise, in the *absence* of a strong immediate national interest to address IUU fishing or marine pollution, states may well sit still and allow 'ports of convenience' or 'ports of non-compliance' (*ie* non-compliance with international and regional standards) to operate on their territory, for example to attract port fees. Such practices could, however, be countered by stronger states and regional organizations, which may impose sanctions on states that fail to implement more stringent port state measures. This will be illustrated below by the EU's practice of using a unilateral listing mechanism in relation to states which fail to adequately address IUU fishing, including states operating ports of convenience. Again, however, such listings may be informed by the 'parochial' desire to level the international playing field and safeguard competitive opportunities for one's own fishing fleet.

5.2.5 Port state jurisdiction between unilateralism and multilateralism

When exercising PSJ, port states may or may not rely on global standards. As argued in Chapter 4.2, jurisdictional assertions that give effect to global standards may be imbued with higher international legitimacy. Examples are entry denials and instances of territorial port state enforcement to address IUU fishing which follow internationally accepted definitions of IUU fishing, inspections on the basis of memoranda of understanding on port state control which check compliance with international conventions, or port state measures addressing vessel-source

[93] Commission Implementing Regulation (EU) No 793/2013 of 20 August 2013 establishing measures in respect of the Faeroe Islands to ensure the conservation of the Atlanto-Scandian herring stock [2013] OJ L223/1. See for the PSMs taken: arts 5–6 of the Regulation.

[94] ibid.

[95] Commission Implementing Regulation (EU) No 896/2014 of 18 August 2014 repealing Implementing Regulation (EU) No 793/2013 establishing measures in respect of the Faroe Islands to ensure the conservation of the Atlanto-Scandian herring stock 2014 [2014] OJ L244/10, preamble 3–4, art 1.

pollution which give effect to 'generally accepted international rules and/or standards' (GAIRAS).[96]

When port states merely enforce multilaterally agreed standards, they may not be considered as acting unilaterally. Nonetheless, even when, at first sight, port states do no more than implement international law, room for unilateralism remains. For instance, while port state control does not create special jurisdictional rights and does not impose novel standards, states exercising such control do not normally distinguish between vessels of flag states that are parties to relevant treaties, and states that are not.[97] Accordingly, to the extent that states exercising port state control apply treaties to vessels of non-contracting parties, there may be an element of unilateral, non-consensual jurisdiction. For that matter, some of these treaties call on contracting parties to apply the treaty's rules and standards to the vessels of non-contracting parties 'as may be necessary to ensure that no more favourable treatment is given to such ships'.[98] As regards GAIRAS then, which are often developed by the IMO, precisely to prevent unilateral action,[99] such rules and standards need not necessarily find their basis in universally binding international law: they could also be based on international agreements that are far from universally ratified, or on 'soft' international agreements and recommendations. Again, this may allow port states to impose standards on flag states which have not formally consented to be bound. Accordingly, the application of GAIRAS by port states may also have a unilateral dimension, even if mitigated by the existence of a relevant international legal or political instrument featuring such standards.[100]

Jurisdictional assertions may obviously be more clearly unilateral—and hence suspect—when they are not based on international standards at all. Nevertheless, as set out in section 4.2.2, port state jurisdiction is, formally speaking at least, ordinarily grounded on territoriality, and thus *prima facie* internationally lawful. However, while, in principle, reliance on territoriality allows states to apply their own laws, from a broader legitimacy perspective, some embeddedness of a domestic regulation in international law may be advisable (see also Chapter 4.2).[101]

[96] cf UNCLOS (n 37) arts 211(2), 211(5), 211(6), 226(1)(a) (which pertain to coastal state rather than port state jurisdiction); Part XII UNCLOS.

[97] Paris Memorandum (n 59) paras 2.3 and 2.4 ('Each Authority will apply those relevant instruments which are in force and to which its State is a Party... In applying a relevant instrument, the Authorities will ensure that no more favourable treatment is given to ships of non-Parties.').

[98] MARPOL (n 36) art 5(4).

[99] cf International Maritime Organization (Assembly Resolution) 'Strategic Plan for the Organization (for the six-year period 2014–2019)' (29 November 2013) A.1060(28), para 2.2. 'provide an effective and efficient response to shipping trends, developments and incidents and, in so doing, stave off regional or unilateral tendencies that conflict with the Organization's regulatory framework'.

[100] *Eg* EU Directive 2005/35 on ship-source pollution and on the introduction of penalties for infringements [2005] OJ L255/11, which implements MARPOL (a binding treaty), but also refers to non-binding (although authoritative) IMO Guidelines. See also Coelho (n 42) ch 2.5.

[101] However, insofar as global standards lack ambition and fail to tackle the global governance problem at hand, non-consensual, unilateral action need to be considered illegitimate *per se*. See also B Marten, 'Port State Jurisdiction, International Conventions, and Extraterritoriality: An Expansive

As it happens, relevant multilateral agreements rarely explicitly *exclude* the exercise of unilateral jurisdiction, and instead tend to preserve the residual jurisdiction of the state as long as it complies with international law.[102]

Even if PSJ is unilateral in nature, it can in due course have an impact on multilateral regulatory initiatives, as it puts pressure on international organizations to adopt more ambitious norms, in line with the preferences of the unilaterally acting state or regional organization. An example of unilateral action influencing global regulation is the adoption of the US Oil Pollution Act (1990).[103] Pursuant to this Act, all tankers constructed under contracts awarded after 1990 must be fitted with double hulls and all existing single hull tankers, and all other tankers should be phased out. US authorities controlled, *in port*, whether visiting vessels complied with these requirements. At the time, there were no international standards on double hulls[104] but the Act rather quickly paved the way for an amendment of MARPOL (1992) in respect of double-hull tankers.[105] In turn, dissatisfied with the implementation calendar of this amendment, the European Union unilaterally decided to put pressure on the IMO to accelerate implementation by proposing its own phasing-out implementation mechanism (2000),[106] backed up by EU port state jurisdiction. The EU's threat immediately bore fruit as the IMO did indeed accelerate the calendar.[107] The European Union then proceeded to implement the new IMO regulation (2002),[108] and relied explicitly on PSJ as an enforcement tool.[109] In 2003, the European Union decided to accelerate the IMO calendar even more,[110] which again led to IMO amendments. It is of note that a number of IMO members did not particularly appreciate the EU's unilateral action as a means to

Interpretation' in H Ringbom (ed), *Jurisdiction over Ships* (Brill 2015) 110 (arguing that 'unless the convention in question prohibits such a rule, a port state can legitimately enact rules of this kind from an international law perspective'). ibid, 118 (arguing that port state jurisdiction does not rely on international conventions for its existence).

[102] Possibly the only counter-example is Regulation 15(1) of Annex VI of MARPOL (n 36). 'If the emissions of [Volatile Organic Compounds] from a tanker are to be regulated in a port or ports or a terminal or terminal sunder the jurisdiction of a Party, they shall be regulated in accordance with the provisions of this regulation.'

[103] Oil Pollution Act of 1990, 101 HR1465, PL 101–380.

[104] 46 USC § 3703. 'The Secretary may prescribe regulations that exceed standards set internationally.').

[105] International Maritime Organization (Assembly Resolution) 'Application of tonnage measurement of segregated ballast tanks in oil tankers' (4 November 1993) A.747(18).

[106] European Council Meeting, Doc. 11711/00 (Presse 347); Council Doc 14004/00 (Presse 470).

[107] MEPC 45 draft agreement to Regulation 13G of Annex 1, approved in MEPC 46.

[108] Regulation (EC) No 417/2002 of the European Parliament and of the Council of 18 February 2002 on the accelerated phasing in of double-hull or equivalent design requirements for single-hull oil tankers and repealing Council Regulation (EC) No 2978/94 [2012] OJ L64/1.

[109] ibid, art 4: 'No oil tanker shall be allowed to operate under the flag of a Member State, nor shall any oil tanker, irrespective of its flag, be allowed to enter into ports or offshore terminals under the jurisdiction of a Member State after the anniversary of the date of delivery of the ship in the year specified hereafter, unless such tanker is a double hull oil tanker.'

[110] Regulation (EC) No 1726/2003 of the European Parliament and of the Council of 22 July 2003 amending Regulation (EC) No 417/2002 on the accelerated phasing-in of double-hull or equivalent design requirements for single-hull oil tankers [2003] OJ L249/1.

put pressure on multilateral mechanisms,[111] even if assertions of port state jurisdiction over double-hull tankers are formally grounded on territoriality (a static CDEM standard is violated while in port, regardless of the inevitable extraterritorial impact of such jurisdiction). Similar international norm-setting EU unilateralism occurred with respect to the sulphur content of marine fuels (an EU Directive went beyond the standards contained in MARPOL Annex V, and led to MARPOL amendments),[112] and to a monitoring, reporting, and verification (MRV) mechanism regarding carbon emissions from maritime transport (an EU Regulation informed the proposal of amendments to MARPOL).[113] In all these instances, compliance with relevant standards is controlled by *port state* authorities,[114] as only a vessel's presence in port allows for inspection and enforcement.

Unilateral jurisdiction may not only lead to upward migration of norms, from the national/regional to the global level, but also to horizontal dissemination, from one state or regional organization to another. In particular, to avoid losing access to lucrative markets of port states, foreign operators and states may well fall in line with the latter's regulatory wishes. For instance, the prospect of requirements regarding catch certificates for imported and landed fish[115] may incentivize importers to change their extraterritorial fishing practices so as to satisfy the port state's requirements, especially if they have few alternative lucrative markets to sell their wares. Strict port state requirements may, however, not only lead to foreign operators changing their ways but they could also inform legislative change abroad. This will especially be the case if port state measures do not just apply to individual vessels but to all vessels flying the flag of a non-compliant state. The beneficial effect on foreign regulation of the EU's identification and penalization of non-cooperating port states in the context of IUU fishing can be cited in this respect.[116] *Per* the EU's IUU Fishing

[111] See for a discussion of the interplay between EU unilateralism and IMO action: Ringbom (n 41) 271.

[112] Directive 2005/33/EC (n 87); Directive 2012/33/EU of the European Parliament and of the Council of 21 November 2012 amending Council Directive 1999/32/EC as regards the sulphur content of marine fuels [2012] OJ l327/1; Directive (EU) 2016/802 of the European Parliament and of the Council of 11 May 2016 relating to a reduction in the sulphur content of certain liquid fuels [2016] OJ L132/58. From 2020 onwards, IMO/MARPOL maritime fuel content requirements mirror unilateral EU standards that were adopted earlier. See International Maritime Organization, 'Report of the Marine Environment Protection Committee on its 57th Session' (7 April 2008) MEPC 57/21.

[113] Regulation (EU) 2015/757 (n 88); Draft amendments to Chapter 4 of MARPOL Annex VI regarding a data collection system for fuel consumption. It is arguable that the MARPOL amendments remain lacking in ambition if compared to the EU Regulation. See for a discussion of the international legality of the EU Regulation: Dobson and Ryngaert (n 88).

[114] Article 1 of Regulation (EU) 2015/757 (n 88) (referring to 'ships arriving at, within or departing from ports under the jurisdiction of a Member State').

[115] See for the unilateral EU catch certification/documentation scheme: arts 6–16 IUU Regulation EU (n 58). Also, art 37(9) of this Regulation ('the importation of fishery products caught by IUU fishing vessels shall be prohibited, and according catch certificates accompanying such products shall not be accepted or validated'). See for US traceability requirements: 50 CFR § 300.324 Seafood Traceability Program; facilitating enforcement of 16 USC § 1857(1)(q).

[116] Honniball, 'Extraterritorial Port State Measures' (n 42) ch 6.3.

Regulation,[117] the EU's unilateral listing mechanism, pursuant to which 'yellow' and 'red' cards are given to foreign states which fail to take action to prevent, deter, and eliminate IUU fishing, has more or less *forced* these states to improve their legislative framework and enforcement practices,[118] lest they lose access to the vast EU market for fish products, or lest their products be confiscated in EU ports.[119]

5.2.6 Reasonableness

Even if PSJ promotes common environmental interests, it may have to be mitigated to accommodate foreign operators and states. Stringent unilateral port state measures may create compliance burdens for private operators, who may be under an obligation to comply with multiple national, regional and international regulations at the same time.[120] Moreover, insofar as such unilateral measures (as well as measures laid down in international instruments that have been adopted *as the result* of unilateral jurisdiction) force third countries to change their legislation and enforcement practices, they could be viewed as intruding on foreign state sovereignty. Thus, in the fisheries context, some developing states have raised concerns over a possibly 'unnecessary and disproportionate burden of conservation' that is imposed on developing state ports, tasked with implementing ambitious international and regional conservation and management measures.[121] The imposition of such a burden may perhaps not be considered as internationally unlawful but clearly as inappropriate and unfeasible. Therefore, it is a common occurrence that, for capacity reasons, formal ambitions laid down in global or regional arrangements, to which states have signed up, are not borne out in practice, for example, minimum levels of inspections

[117] IUU Regulation EU (n 58), ch VI.

[118] ibid, art 31.

[119] ibid, art 18. See for the impact of the EU IUU Fishing Regulation's listing mechanism on the implementation of treaty-based minimum port states standards, and the expansion of port state offences in third countries: Arron N Honniball, 'What's in a Duty? EU Identification of Non-Cooperating Port States and Their Prescriptive Responses' (2020) 35 IJMCL 1, who also demonstrates that the EU's global leadership regarding IUU fishing has led to expansions of port state offences and more onerous enforcement measures to denial of entry or use, as compared to EU port state measures.

[120] Compare the IMO's obligatory data collection scheme for maritime emissions (2016) with the EU's unilateral maritime MRV. Marine Environment Protection Committee (Resolution MEPC.278(70)) 'Amendments to the Annex of the Protocol of 1997 to amend the International Convention for the Prevention of Pollution from Ships, 1973, as modified by the Protocol of 1978 relating thereto—Data Collection System for Fuel Oil Consumption of Ships' (28 October 2016) MEPC 70/18/Add.1, Annex 3.

[121] *Eg* 'FFA fires off grim warning on impacts of inaction at Western and Central Pacific Fisheries Commission' (Pacific Islands Forum Fisheries Agency, 5 December 2014) https://www.ffa.int/node/1421 (accessed 6 December 2019).

required by treaty may not be met.[122] Failures of the latter kind are not attributable to bad faith, but to inability.

To mitigate the regulatory burden imposed by PSJ, mutual recognition may be an appropriate mechanism. Thus, states and regional organizations have sometimes recognized foreign regulatory schemes as essentially equivalent to their own schemes. For instance, the EU recognizes fish catch documentation/certification schemes of regional fisheries management organizations to the extent that they meet EU standards.[123] Implementation problems caused by lack of capacity could in turn be remedied by building capacity in developing countries. Unilaterally acting states and regional organizations may want to enable foreign states and their operators to comply with strict standards by providing them with financial and technical assistance. Also, duties of assistance (typically North–South) could be incorporated into international or regional instruments, which have often been adopted at the behest of the same states acting or threatening to act unilaterally. Thus, the Port State Measures Agreement, which provides for mandatory PSJ, has suggested, in its Part 6, the setting up of an Assistance Fund to help developing states struggling with the implementation of the agreement. The Food and Agriculture Organization (FAO), which is to administer this fund, may assist non-contracting parties as well.[124] The IMO for its part has indicated that it takes into account the special needs of developing countries in light of the principle of common but differentiated responsibilities when addressing the contribution of shipping to climate change.[125] Also, regional initiatives may invest in building capacity of port states,[126] including port states in non-cooperative, non-contracting parties, with a view to enhancing the effectiveness of the conservation and management measures laid down in the relevant instrument.[127]

[122] There is little information regarding enforcement levels. Gathering such information is very challenging, for that matter, as port state may not be willing to disclose data and may not record cases where they failed to take necessary port state measures. See Honniball, 'Extraterritorial Port State Measures' (n 42) s 7.5.4.

[123] IUU Regulation EU (n 58) art 13(1).

[124] PSMA (n 48) Article 21(6). See the Food and Agriculture Organization, 'Draft Terms of Reference: Funding Mechanisms under Part 6 of the FAO Agreement on Port State Measures to prevent, deter and eliminate illegal, unreported and unregulated fishing' in 'Report of the First Meeting of the Ad Hoc Working Group Established by the Parties to the Agreement on Port State Measures to Prevent, Deter and Eliminate Illegal, Unreported and Unregulated Fishing' (June 2017) FAO Fisheries and Aquaculture Report 1212 Appendix 3.

[125] Submission by the International Maritime Organization 'Control of Greenhouse Gas Emissions from Ships Engaged in International Trade' United Nations Climate Change Conference—Eighth Session of the Ad Hoc Working Group on Long-Term Cooperative Action, Fifteenth Conference of the Parties (Denmark, Copenhagen, 7–18 December 2009).

[126] *Eg* International Commission for the Conservation of Atlantic Tunas, 'Recommendation 14–108 To Support Effective Implementation of Recommendation 12–107 by ICCAT for an ICCAT Scheme for Minimum Standards for Inspection in Port' (2014) para 2.

[127] *Eg* Southern Indian Oceans Fisheries Agreement (adopted 7 July 2006, entered into force 21 June 2012) 2835 UNTS 412, preamble (recalling the 'need for non-Contracting Parties ... to apply the conservation and management measures adopted').

5.2.7 Concluding observations

By denying access to foreign-flagged vessels engaging in harmful extraterritorial activity, and by exercising jurisdiction in port over such vessels, port states can effectively address threats to common concerns, such as IUU fishing and marine pollution. Doctrinally, PSJ can be grounded on the state's *domaine réservé* and on the territoriality of in-port offences. Often, PSJ may be based on multilateral instruments. This decreases concerns over unilateralism. However, port states have also acted more unilaterally by prescribing and enforcing their own laws. While the legitimacy of such unilateral action may derive from its contribution to the protection of common interests, port states may want to make sure that they can scientifically justify their assertions, as well as taking the interests of foreign states and their operators into account. In any event, prescient unilateralism by regulatory first movers has at times had a beneficial effect on the global protection of common interests. The exercise of unilateral PSJ has forced foreign-flagged vessels to change the ways they operate worldwide, and has accelerated the adoption of international standards on marine environmental protection.

5.3 Unilateral Trade Measures regarding Global Environmental Challenges

There is no denying that some of the most pressing global challenges pertain to the protection of the environment. The very development of global public goods theory has even been triggered by the international cooperative challenges posed by environmental problems, such as climate change, threats to the ozone layer, and the loss of biodiversity.[128] As multilateral efforts to address these problems may lag behind in ambition, states and regional organizations, such as the European Union, may wish to 'go it alone', and exercise unilateral prescriptive jurisdiction in the common interest.

'Selfless' extraterritoriality in the environmental field typically takes the form of trade measures. Where environmentally harmful practices take place in the context of industrial production, supply chains have become global, and goods are traded internationally, bystander states may have a practical opportunity to unilaterally address global environmental challenges by conditioning the access of a product to its market on that product satisfying particular environmental process and production requirements in the country of origin.[129] When a market

[128] Inge Kaul and others, *Global Public Goods: International Cooperation in the 21st Century* (OUP 1999).

[129] Alternatively, a state or the European Union may allow the product on its market, but nevertheless price it out of the market by not considering it as counting towards mandatory environmental targets. See *eg* EU Renewable Energy Directive, pursuant to which only sustainably sourced renewable energy

state sets unilateral standards, it exercises a form of prescriptive jurisdiction with an extraterritorial dimension because it influences production processes *outside* the market state.[130] Relevant standards may or may not correspond to foreign or international law.

The extraterritorial overtones of unilateral trade measures raise concerns over their legality and legitimacy. Admittedly, such measures are only enforced *at the border* of the regulating state,[131] and do not directly 'sanction' foreign states and producers, as these are not barred from maintaining their environmentally unfriendly production processes and from exporting their goods to more lenient markets.[132] However, where foreign producers have few alternatives to export their products than to a strictly regulating state or trade bloc with a large consumer population such as the European Union, unilateral trade measures may seem to limit the sovereign economic policy space of foreign states.[133]

This part studies, through a jurisdictional lens, how the law of the World Trade Organization (WTO) can accommodate the unilateral pursuit of global environmental concerns by means of trade measures. WTO law is taken as the focal point of the analysis, for the following reasons: (i) prescriptive environmental extraterritoriality typically takes the form of trade measures;[134] (ii) the

counted towards EU Member States' mandatory national targets. Directive 2009/28/EC on the promotion of the use of energy from renewable sources and amending and subsequently repealing Directives 2001/77/EC and 2003/30/EC [2009] OJ L140/16, arts 3 and 4.

[130] Because of the impact of PPM measures outside the territory of the regulating state, such measures could well be characterized as *extraterritorial.* See Lorand Bartels, 'Article XX of GATT and the Problem of Extraterritorial Jurisdiction—The Case of Trade Measures for the Protection of Human Rights' (2002) 36 JWT 353, 381 (arguing that extraterritoriality is a function of the legal connection between the legislation and the extraterritorial subject-matter, as well as the 'denial of opportunities normally open to the person against whom enforcement is directed'.)

[131] The fact that the exercise of enforcement jurisdiction over the relevant imported products is exercised at the border, and hence is territorial, does not normally suffice as a justification. After all, enforcement jurisdiction, even if territorial, cannot be lawful if there is no underlying justification of the assertion under the rules of prescriptive jurisdiction. cf Bartels (n 130) 378.

[132] Robert Howse and Donald Regan, 'The Product/Process Distinction—an Illusory Basis for Disciplining "Unilateralism" in Trade Policy' (2000) 11 EJIL 249, 274; Laurens Ankersmit and others, 'Diverging EU and WTO Perspectives on Extraterritorial Process Regulation' (2012) 21 Min JIL 12, 24.

[133] These concerns can notably be found in the 1992 Rio Declaration on Environment and Development, and in a decision of a GATT panel in the *Tuna/Dolphin* case (1994). UNGA 'The Rio Declaration on Environment and Development' (United Nations Conference on Environment and Development) Rio de Janeiro, Brazil 1992, A/CONF.151/26 (Vol I) principle 12 ('unilateral actions to deal with environmental challenges outside the jurisdiction of the importing country should be avoided' and environmental measures addressing transboundary or global environmental problems 'should, as far as possible, be based on an international consensus'); *Tuna/Dolphin.* WTO, *United States—Restrictions on Imports of Tuna—Report of the Panel* (16 June 1994) DS29/R, para 5.26 (stating that allowing such unilateral environmental measures under art XX GATT would 'permit contracting parties to take trade measures so as force other contracting parties to change their policies within their jurisdiction').

[134] There is also an *adjudicatory* dimension to environmental extraterritoriality: bystander states could open their courts (establish adjudicatory jurisdiction) for tort claims in respect of environmental abuses committed abroad. This dimension is addressed below in Chapter 5.4 on business and human rights tort litigation, which also covers environmental abuses with human rights overtones.

fragmentation of global governance appears to be addressed by international trade law in particular,[135] which interacts, albeit on its own terms, with other norms of international law;[136] (iii) as a related matter, international trade law, as one of the few fields of international law, boasts a compulsory dispute-settlement mechanism (DSM) with jurisdiction over the WTO compatibility of unilateral trade measures, for example taken in pursuit of global environmental objectives.

After briefly explaining the WTO's dispute-settlement mechanism's approach to the trade/environment interface so far (**section 5.3.1**), this part examines the role which the general international law notion of jurisdiction might play in determining the lawfulness of unilateral trade measures in pursuit of extraterritorial or global environmental objectives (**section 5.3.2**). Particular attention is paid to mitigating mechanisms which ensure that unilateral measures remain within the bounds of jurisdictional reasonableness (**section 5.3.3**).

In the analysis, the system of WTO law is considered as given, although at the same time as hermeneutically unstable. Proceeding from an immanent WTO-systemic perspective, the aim is to find, from within the existing system of WTO law, overtures to the general law of jurisdiction.[137]

5.3.1 Trade and the environment: the WTO approach

The WTO agreements do not contain a jurisdictional clause setting out under what circumstances states can take unilateral trade measures to pursue global or extra-territorial environmental objectives.[138] Instead, trade-restrictive environmental unilateralism has piggybacked on the more general debate regarding the tension between trade and environmental norms. This debate has informed fundamental epistemic inquiries into issues of unity, cohesiveness, and fragmentation of international law, in which the quest for mechanisms to solve norm conflicts and pursue normative integration has occupied a central place.[139]

[135] *Eg* Frank Biermann and others, 'The Fragmentation of Global Governance Architectures: A Framework for Analysis' (2009) 9 GEP 14, 19.

[136] Study Group of the International Law Commission, 'Fragmentation of International Law: Difficulties Arising from the Diversification and Expansion of International Law' (13 April 2006) UN Doc A/CN.4/L.682, 29.

[137] I am partly indebted for this part to Dr Natalie Dobson, who successfully defended her PhD on the topic at Utrecht University in July 2018, in the framework of the UNIJURIS project of which I was the Principal Investigator. Natalie Dobson, 'Extraterritorial Climate Protection under International Law: A Jurisdictional Analysis of EU Unilateralism' (PhD thesis, Utrecht University 2019).

[138] In the *Shrimp/Turtle* case, the WTO Appellate Body famously declined to pronounce on the existence of an implicit jurisdictional clause in the 'exceptions' of art XX GATT. WTO AB, *United States—Import Prohibition of Certain Shrimp and Shrimp Products—Report of the Appellate Body* (12 October 1998) WT/DS58/AB/R, para 133.

[139] *Eg* Dirk Pulkowski, *The Law and Politics of International Regime Conflict* (OUP 2014); Joost Pauwelyn, *Conflict of Norms in Public International Law. How WTO Law Relates to Other Rules of International Law* (OUP 2003).

Trade measures pursuing environmental objectives typically make regulatory distinctions on the basis of non-incorporated process and production methods (PPMs). These are PPMs that do not leave a specific physical trace in the relevant product, as a result of which the physical properties of the product do not differ from other products. Viewed from a WTO law perspective, it appears that such measures, including 'non-territorial' PPMs (*ie* those relating to process and production methods abroad), are in principle incompatible with WTO law as they discriminate between like products. They affect the competitive opportunities for (producers from) some WTO Member States and may thus run foul of the principles of national treatment and most-favoured nation (articles I.1 and III.4 General Agreement on Tariffs and Trade (GATT)).[140] Nevertheless, WTO panels and the Appellate Body (AB) have proved willing to accept such restrictions to the extent that they can, at least *prima facie*, be justified under one of the exceptions of article XX GATT, or as a legitimate public policy objective under article 2.2 of the Agreement on Technical Barriers to Trade (TBT),[141] also where the restriction pertains to a harvesting or production method that takes place *outside* that state's territory.[142] This is an emanation of the basic principle that 'it is within the authority of a WTO Member to set the public health or environmental objectives it seeks to achieve, as well as the level of protection that it wants to obtain, through the measure or the policy it chooses to adopt'.[143] Trade liberalization (opening up market access) has not removed unilaterally acting states' sovereign policy space to take trade restrictive measures in pursuit of particular public policy objectives.

Relevant public policy objectives pertaining to global environmental law and policy can be accommodated in particular by the exception of article XX(g) GATT,

[140] WTO, *European Communities—Measures Affecting Asbestos and Asbestos-Containing Products—Report of the Appellate Body* (5 April 2001) WT/DS135/AB/R, para 101 (emphasizing a product's physical characteristics in determining the 'likeness' of a product); WTO, *European Communities—Measures Prohibiting the Importation and Marketing of Seal Products—Report of the Appellate Body* (22 May 2014) WT/DS400/AB/R and WT/DS401/AB/R para 5.125 (rejecting the relevance of a state's (legitimate) regulatory objectives in the context of determining 'less favourable treatment'); WTO, *Canada—Certain Measures Affecting the Automotive Industry—Appellate Body Report (Canada—Autos)* (31 May 2000) WT/DS139/AB/R para 10.29 (considering origin-based distinctions in principle to in violation of art I.1 GATT).

[141] The exceptions enshrined in these provisions countenance trade restrictions that are promulgated with a view to protecting environmental interests. See notably the clauses citing the protection of human, plant, and animal life and health (art XX(b) GATT), the preservation of exhaustible natural resources (art XX(g) GATT), and the protection of public morality (art XX(a) GATT, or implicitly in art 2.2 TBT).

[142] WTO, *European Communities—Measures Prohibiting the Importation and Marketing of Seal Products—Report of the Panel* (25 November 2013) WT/DS400/R and WT/DS401/R, para 8.2.c ('The EU Seal Regime is not inconsistent with Article 2.2 [TBT] because it fulfils the objective of addressing the EU public moral concerns on seal welfare to a certain extent, and no alternative measure has been demonstrated to make an equivalent or greater contribution to the fulfilment of the objective as the EU Seal Regime.').

[143] WTO, *Brazil—Measures Affecting Imports of Retreaded Tyres—Appellate Body Report* (3 December 2007) WT/DS332/AB/R, para 140. See also WTO, *Korea—Measures Affecting Imports of Fresh, Chilled and Frozen Beef—Appellate Body Report* (11 December 2000) WT/DS161/AB/R and WT/DS169/AB/R, para 176; *EC—Asbestos AB Report* (n 140) para 168.

which provides that nothing in GATT 'shall prevent the adoption or enforcement of measures ... relating to the conservation of exhaustible natural resources'. This accommodation was initially hard-fought, however. In *Tuna/Dolphin* (1991), a case concerning a US trade measure aimed at protecting dolphins—considered here as a global environmental interest—accidentally caught by tuna fishers, a GATT panel did not approve of unilateral measures to further a purportedly global environmental interest, instead putting a higher premium on free trade.[144] The United States continued to apply similar measures, however. Eventually, in the *Shrimp/Turtle* case, it managed to convince the WTO AB of the permissibility of the exercise of its jurisdiction aimed at protecting global environment interests; in this case, the interests of sea turtles which happen to find themselves in the nets of shrimp fishers.[145] This US action has been usefully described as an instance of 'unfriendly unilateralism' that helped 'reconcile competing objectives within the law' in the case, by giving global environmental interests more weight within the trade regime.[146]

5.3.2 Trade law and jurisdictional nexus

This monograph beholds unilateralism from a jurisdictional perspective. At first sight, the concept of jurisdiction has not played a prominent role in the debate on reconciling free trade and environmental protection, as WTO law is concerned with the *justification* of trade measures rather than with their *jurisdictional authorization*. Nevertheless, elements of jurisdictional doctrine can be traced in WTO law and in case law relevant to the trade/environment nexus. Notably, in *Shrimp/Turtle*, the AB, called on to interpret the exception of article XX(g) GATT, limited the categories of states which could invoke this provision to those which have a 'sufficient [jurisdictional] nexus' with the subject matter.[147] Thereby, it appeared to exclude states with no connection whatsoever to the regulated matter.

In *Shrimp/Turtle*, this jurisdictional nexus was, in the WTO's view, constituted by the highly migratory nature of a fishing species, which passed in (and out) of waters subject to the jurisdiction of the regulating state.[148] This might appear somewhat artificial, but the idea was clearly to preclude an unrestricted number

[144] Report of the Panel, *United States—Restrictions on Imports of Tuna*, DS21/R (3 September 1991), GATT BISD (39th Supp) at 155 (1991) ILM 1594 (1991); Report of the Panel, *United States—Restrictions on Imports of Tuna*, DS29/R (16 June 1994), 33 ILM 936 (1994).

[145] *US Shrimp Turtle AB report* (n 138) para 133.

[146] Monica Hakimi, 'Unfriendly Unilateralism' (2014) 55 HILJ 105, 129. US leadership thus had an undeniable effect on international law-making or at least interpretation, by the WTO bodies. ibid, 130 ('All of these restrictions ... were part of a broader effort to create more space for the environment within the trade regime. WTO bodies eventually responded by giving states some discretion to use trade restrictions for the global environment.') (footnote omitted).

[147] *US Shrimp Turtle AB Report* (n 138) para 133.

[148] ibid.

of states from exercising 'universal' jurisdiction with a view to protecting non-territorial or global environmental interests via unilateral trade measures. Some have thus read an 'implicit jurisdictional clause' into WTO law on the trade/environment nexus.[149] Pursuant to this clause, a state can only take unilateral trade measures or exercise unilateral jurisdiction if it can show a substantial connection to the regulated matter.

In keeping with classic jurisdictional doctrine, this connection may primarily have to be territorial or geographic. This is also borne out by the AB's decision in *Shrimp/Turtle,* which required that the animals pass through the regulating state's waters. This decision could thus be construed as applying a version of the territoriality principle. A substantial connection need not necessarily be territorial, however.[150] Arguably, states may also claim a substantial connection to an environmental problem that is of a global nature, and which affects every single state,[151] although not in equal measure. A good example is offered by emissions contributing to climate change. Doctrinally, unilateral trade measures addressing high-emission-based products and services could be justified under the territoriality principle, insofar as climate change is likely to affect (the territory of) every single state. However, problems relating to the required quantity of effects and to causality undermine the legitimacy of exclusive reliance on objective territoriality to address global problems producing global effects. It may then be more appropriate to locate the substantial connection in the global nature of an environmental problem which has not been sufficiently addressed by multilateral solutions. In this case, jurisdiction sails close to the universality principle. However, a combination of universal common concern with the requirement of minimum territorial links, for example, the inevitable effects of climate change on any given state, or the existence of territorial consumption patterns fuelling the production of environmentally unfriendly imported goods and services, could serve as the doctrinal justification of such jurisdiction.[152]

[149] Peter van den Bossche and others, *Unilateral Measures Addressing Non-Trade Concerns: A Study on WTO Consistency, Relevance of other International Agreements, Economic Effectiveness and Impact on Developing Countries of Measures concerning Non-Product-Related Processes and Production Methods* (The Hague: the Ministry of Foreign Affairs of the Netherlands 2007) 94–6, 150 (referring to 'implicit jurisdictional limitation').

[150] cf International Law Commission, 'Report of the International Law Commission on its fifty-eighth session' (1 May–9 June and 3 July–11 August 2006) UN Doc A/61/10.

[151] Dobson (n 137) ch 5.2. See also Francesco Francioni, 'Extraterritorial Application of Environmental Law' in Karl Meessen and others (eds), 'Extraterritorial Jurisdiction in Theory and Practice' (Kluwer Law International 1996) 122 (arguing that 'the extraterritorial application of environmental law can be justified on the basis of the policy argument that national regulation must also protect the elements of the global environment, such as the ozone layer and the climate, or contribute to the conservation of common resources, such as those of the high seas, of outer space, and of Antarctica, and to the preservation of biodiversity').

[152] Dobson (n 137) ch 5.3; Geert De Baere and Cedric Ryngaert, 'The ECJ's Judgement in Air Transport Association of America and the International Legal Context of the EU's Climate Change Policy' (2013) 18 EFAR 389.

Regardless of broad constructions that may be given to the jurisdictional nexus requirement, this requirement may possibly only apply in the context of article XX(g) GATT, the exception pertaining to the exhaustion of natural resources. Instead, global environmental problems could also be addressed under other *litterae* of article XX, in particular to article XX(a), which allows for the (unilateral) adoption or enforcement of measures 'necessary to protect public morals'. In an animal welfare context, the WTO Panel and AB in *EC—Seals* (2013–14) have foregrounded the potential of the public morals exception to tackle extraterritorial phenomena which upset the moral standards of the importing state's consumers, in this case concerns over the methods of killing seals in areas outside the importing state.[153] In essence, the WTO Panel and AB deferred to the importing state's certification that its consumers' public morals had been offended,[154] with the *locality* of the moral concern being decisive rather than the universal proscription of the phenomenon. *EC—Seals* may pave the way for a host of unilateral trade measures that are justified on the mere ground that a particular extraterritorial phenomenon offends local public morality,[155] regardless of the existence of a jurisdictional nexus, and irrespective of the formal or informal international legal recognition of the undesirability of such a phenomenon.

5.3.3 Jurisdictional reasonableness and the GATT

As shown above, the system of WTO law can and does accommodate trade measures pursuing global environmental objectives. While such trade measures may *prima facie* be in breach of WTO law, they could be justified under the exceptions of article XX GATT (in particular *litterae* (a) and especially (g)). The WTO DSB appears to employ a relatively low jurisdictional threshold when applying the relevant exceptions. This may render a large number of 'extraterritorial' trade measures pursuing global environmental objectives *prima facie* justifiable.

[153] See for a discussion Barbara Cooreman, 'Extraterritorial Environmental Concerns and Public Morals: Testing the Limits of Article XX(a) GATT after *Seals*' (2016) 5 JITAL 519.

[154] At least insofar as the European Union and its Member States had taken action in respect of these morals (in the case animal welfare). cf *EC—Seals Panel Report* (n 142) para 7.34.

[155] Note that such measures could even be under-inclusive insofar as there is an attitude–behaviour gap, *ie* a gap between citizens' attitudes and their actions as consumers. Due to informational deficits, citizens may continue to purchase products that are produced in circumstances which they may find morally objectionable. This may limit the regulatory pressure to bring to bear on their governments, or if the government enacts regulation render this regulation difficult to justify under art XX(a) GATT, pursuant to which only actual consumer attitude may count. cf Aleydis Nissen, 'Can WTO Member States Rely on Citizen Concerns to Prevent Corporations from Importing Goods Made from Child Labour' (2018) 14 ULR 70. See for a broader understanding Cooreman (n 153) 158–59 ('[S]hould trade measures based on public morals reflect consumer preferences, voters' opinions, or a compromise of both? It is submitted that both must be taken into account when examining the evidence of a genuine public moral, especially in light of information asymmetries and information manipulation.').

In order to prevent unjustifiable domination by one state over another, application of second-order jurisdictional principles of reasonableness may then be required, and in fact, take on particular relevance in the analysis.[156] In WTO law, these principles are partly laid down in the text of the various *litterae* of article XX GATT, and partly in the *chapeau* of article XX. Article XX(g) requires that the measure relates to the objective of conserving exhaustible natural resources, whereas article XX(a) requires that the measure be *necessary* to protect public morals.[157] In addition, and perhaps most importantly, the *chapeau* of article XX GATT requires non-discrimination, even-handedness, and seeking the least trade-restrictive measure possible. The aim of the *chapeau* is to weed out protectionist and/or discriminatory trade restrictions, thereby balancing the exporting states' freedom to trade (arguably a global public good in its own right),[158] with the importing states' sovereign right to set public policy, including in respect of non-territorial environmental problems.

The *chapeau* prohibits trade measures that are 'applied in a manner which would constitute a means of arbitrary or unjustifiable discrimination between countries where the same conditions prevail, or a disguised restriction on international trade'. In practice, this means *inter alia* that the regulating state should make serious efforts to negotiate before restricting trade,[159] that is, to 'provide effective

[156] See also Barbara Cooreman, 'Addressing Environmental Concerns through Trade? A Case for Extraterritoriality' (2015) 65 ICLQ 229, 235.

[157] See also art XX(b) GATT concerning measures necessary 'to protect human, animal or plant life or health'. See on necessity *Brazil—Measures Affecting Imports of Retreaded Tyres AB Report* (n 143) para 210 ('To be characterized as necessary, a measure does not have to be indispensable. However, its contribution to the achievement of the objective must be material, not merely marginal or insignificant, especially if the measure at issue is as trade restrictive as an import ban. Thus, the contribution of the measure has to be weighed against its trade restrictiveness, taking into account the importance of the interests or the values underlying the objective pursued by it.'); *EC—Seals AB Report* (n 140) para 5.169 ('In the context of Article XX(a), this means that a Member wishing to justify its measure must demonstrate that it has adopted or enforced a measure "to protect public morals", and that the measure is "necessary" to protect such public morals. As the Appellate Body has explained, a necessity analysis involves a process of "weighing and balancing" a series of factors, including the importance of the objective, the contribution of the measure to that objective, and the trade-restrictiveness of the measure.').

[158] Eyal Benvenisti and Sivan S Agon, 'The Law of Strangers: The Form and Substance of Other-Regarding International Adjudication' (2016) GlobalTrust Working Paper Series 08/2017, 15 https://papers.ssrn.com/sol3/papers.cfm?abstract_id=3013014 (accessed on 6 December 2019) (referring, in a WTO context, to a 'duty of exporting members to consider the interests of global others who in an interconnected economy are dependent on their exports').

[159] *US Shrimp Turtle AB Report* (n 138), para 166 (emphasizing the need to engage with other Members 'in serious, across-the-board negotiations with the objective of concluding bilateral or multilateral agreements for the protection and conservation of sea turtles, before enforcing the import prohibition against the shrimp exports of those other Members'). WTO, *United States—Import Prohibition of Certain Shrimp and Shrimp Products, Recourse to Article 21.5 of the DSU by Malaysia—Report of the Appellate Body* (22 October 2001) WT/DS58/AB/RW, paras 115–34. It is of note, however, that the WTO Panel in *EC—Seals* did *not* address Canada and Norway's arguments, based on *Shrimp/Turtle*, that the regulating state should have made efforts to engage in negotiations to regulate conduct that takes place outside its territory. See *EC—Seals Panel Report* (n 142) fn 518 and para 7.643. Canada further argued that where a measure is premised on an objection to conduct that takes place outside the territory of the regulating Member, there should be additional efforts to engage in

opportunities to foreign individuals who might have been adversely affected by such policies to voice their concerns',[160] should explore less trade-restrictive, reasonably available alternative measures that could realize its policy objective,[161] and should not apply its own laws in a rigid and inflexible manner but instead recognize foreign or international measures that provide protection comparable in effectiveness.[162]

To the extent that a trade-restrictive measure finds its normative basis in multilateral agreements, the *chapeau* requirements could relatively easily be fulfilled.[163] Where the international community (or some part of it) addresses a 'global value' via soft law only,[164] or does not address it at all, this is more difficult, but certainly not impossible.[165] As such, however, the *chapeau* does *not* require an

negotiations to regulate the conduct in question. (See Canada's response to Panel question No 135(a), paras 118 and 119).

[160] Eyal Benvenisti, 'Legislating for Humanity: May States Compel Foreigners to Promote Global Welfare?' (2013) GlobalTrust Working Paper Series 02/2013, 12–13 https://papers.ssrn.com/sol3/papers.cfm?abstract_id=2646880 (accessed on 6 December 2019).

[161] *US Shrimp Turtle AB Report* (n 138) para 171.

[162] ibid, paras 164–65, 177 (holding 'that discrimination results not only when countries in which the same conditions prevail are differently treated, but also when the application of the measure at issue does not allow for any inquiry into the appropriateness of the regulatory program for the conditions prevailing in those exporting countries' and that 'rigidity and inflexibility also constitute 'arbitrary discrimination' within the meaning of the chapeau'). See also *US—Shrimp Turtle Recourse to Article 12* (n 159) para 144: 'conditioning market access on the adoption of a programme *comparable in effectiveness*, allows for sufficient flexibility in the application of the measure so as to avoid "arbitrary or unjustifiable discrimination'".

[163] Enrico Partiti and Steffen van der Velde, 'Curbing Supply-Chain Human Rights Violations Through Trade and Due Diligence. Possible WTO Concerns Raised by the EU Conflict Minerals Regulation' (2017) 51 JWT 1043, 1063 ('the conformity of a measure with a multilaterally negotiated agreement on the issue in question would bring such a measure in line with the requirements of the Chapeau for the purpose of the dispute at hand'), relying on the interpretative rule contained in Article 31(1)(c) VCLT. See also WTO, *China—Measures Affecting Trading Rights and Distribution Services for Certain Publications and Audiovisual Entertainment Products—Report of the Appellate Body* (12 August 2009) WTO Doc WT/DS363/AB/R ('a measure is "necessary" involves a process of weighing and balancing a series of factors that prominently include the contribution made by the measure to secure compliance with the law or regulation at issue, *the importance of the common interests or values protected by that law or regulation*, and the accompanying impact of the law or regulation on imports or exports') (emphasis added); *EC—Asbestos AB Report* (n 140), para 172 ('The more vital or important [the] common interests or "values" pursued, the easier it would be to accept as "necessary" measures designed to achieve those ends. In this case, the objective pursued by the measure is the preservation of human life and health through the elimination, or reduction, of the well-known, and life-threatening, health risks posed by asbestos fibres. The value pursued is both vital and important in the highest degree.').

[164] Partiti and van der Velde (n 163) 1067 (referring to the non-binding OECD Due Diligence Guidance for Responsible Supply Chain of Minerals in the context of the justification of the 2017 EU Conflict Minerals Regulation).

[165] Katie Sykes, 'Sealing Animal Welfare into the GATT Exceptions: The International Dimension of Animal Welfare in WTO Disputes' (2014) 13 WTR 471, 496 (arguing that '[t]he extent to which a moral value is internationally shared is one factor (albeit not the only one) that can help to distinguish justifiable morality-based regulation from impermissible protectionism', although technically doing so in the context of a determination whether a measure is *necessary*, rather than in the context of the *chapeau* of art XX GATT).

international consensus on the value that is pursued by a trade-restrictive measure to be non-discriminatory.[166] This means that states may be allowed to condition market access on a good's foreign production process satisfying home-grown requirements that are not shared universally. Seen through a legal pluralist lens, this allows communities to give expression to their own opinions of what constitutes a good life,[167] but it remains the fact that idiosyncratic trade measures enacted by major powers possessing large consumer markets may well be perceived as unduly unilateral and imperialistic by exporting states. Some embeddedness of the trade measure's objective in international values may therefore be advisable as a jurisdictional constraint.[168] At the very least, it appears to be good practice, and possibly even an obligation, for states to take into account the interests of foreign country nationals and communities affected by unilateral environmental measures,[169] including by actively soliciting their views when designing the measures.[170]

[166] Deciding otherwise would empty art XX(a) GATT—which allows states to take trade measures to protect public morality—of much of its potential as an exceptional regime; only *international public morality* (as *eg* enunciated in international human rights treaties), would qualify.

[167] *Eg* Robert Howse and Joanne Langille, 'Permitting Pluralism: The Seal Products Dispute and Why the WTO Should Permit Trade Restrictions Justified by Non-Instrumental Moral Values' (2012) 37 YJIL 367, 418. Note that WTO Panels had earlier already implied that states could themselves (subjectively) determine public morals in the sense of art XX(a) GATT. cf WTO, *United States—Measures Affecting the Cross-Border Supply of Gambling and Betting Services—Report of the Panel* (10 November 2004) WT/DS285/R, para 6.461; WTO, *China—Measures Affecting Trading Rights and Distribution Services for Certain Publications and Audiovisual Entertainment Products—Report of the Panel* (12 August 2009) WT/DS363/R, para 7.759. Note that the WTO DSM may sometimes misinterpret importing states' citizens' public morality attitudes. *Eg* Elizabeth Whitsitt, 'A Comment on the Public Morals Exception in International Trade and the EC—Seal Products Case: Moral Imperialism and Other Concerns' (2014) 3 CJICL 1376, 1379–80 (criticizing the DSM for failing to take into account the moral preferences of EU citizens regarding the protection of the traditional practices of indigenous seal-hunting communities, moral preferences which could coexist and compete with the general moral condemnation of seal-killing practices).

[168] Steve Charnovitz, 'The Moral Exception in Trade Policy' (1998) 38 VJIL 689, 742–43; Sykes (n 165) 492 ('It seems reasonable to think that there is at least some outer limit to the proposition that public morals are defined by the community in question . . . The justifiability of a trade measure based on moral judgments that are completely at odds with those of the international community might be difficult to defend.'). 'Public morality' in art XX(a) GATT would then be construed as *international* public morality. In fairness, in *EC—Seals*, the WTO Appellate Body appears to have been cognizant of this concern, where it referred to 'international doctrines and measures of a similar nature in other WTO Members' as evidence of animal welfare being 'a matter of ethical responsibility for human beings in general'. cf *EC—Seals AB Report* (n 140) para 7.409. But eventually this was not the *ratio decidendi* of its decision.

[169] See on the involvement of (substate) local communities in the transnational regulation of the extractive sector: Sara L Seck, 'Transnational Corporations and Extractive Industries' in Shawkat Alam and others (eds), International Environmental Law and the Global South (CUP 2015) 380–98.

[170] Ayelet Berman, 'Taking Foreign Preferences into Account: The Rulemaking Process in the United States and the European Union' (2015) GlobalTrust Working Paper Series 03/2015, 5 http://globaltrust.tau.ac.il/wp-content/uploads/2015/03/Ayelet-Berman-US-EU-Rule-Making-Process-WPS-03-15.pdf (accessed 6 December 2019). See on the extent to which WTO law gives effect to the principle of other-regardingness: Eyal Benvenisti and Sivan Agon, 'The Law of Strangers: The Form and Substance of Other-Regarding International Adjudication' (2017) GlobalTrust Working Paper Series 08/2017, 8 https://papers.ssrn.com/sol3/papers.cfm?abstract_id=3013014 (accessed 6 December 2019).

An important aspect of jurisdictional restraint in a WTO context is also the requirement that unilaterally regulating states defer to foreign or international measures that provide protection that is comparable in effectiveness. In practice, however, it may not be obvious to determine when exactly other measures offer equivalent protection.[171]

In respect of developing countries, particular regulatory flexibility may be required, in accordance which the principle of common but differentiated responsibilities (CBDR) to reach a globally set environmental goal, such as the reduction of greenhouse gas emissions. Pursuant to CBDR, equity demands that states which contributed more to a global environmental problem, and which have more capacity to address it (in practice developed states), do more than others (in practice developing states).[172] Also *per* the *chapeau* of article XX GATT, which refers to 'countries where the same conditions prevail', trade measures pursuing global or extraterritorial environmental objectives should incorporate this differentiation.[173] Unfortunately, sensitivity to states' different stages of development is not always present in the regulatory design of 'extraterritorial' environmental measures.[174] If no distinction is made between states in different stages of development, the unilaterally acting state may at least have to put affected foreign operators in a position to comply with stringent 'Western' environmental regulation, through technology transfer and financing opportunities, a long-standing demand of Third World Approaches to International Law scholars.[175] Such flanking measures may soothe concerns in the Global South over Western regulatory overreach that limits the former's development opportunities.

[171] At the time of writing, for instance, it was unclear whether the European Union would, or should abandon its unilateral approach towards aviation emissions regulation in the face of an international agreement reached at the International Civil Aviation Organization, which may well be (far) less stringent than the EU's Aviation Directive. Amendments adopted by the European Parliament on 13 September 2017 on the proposal for a regulation of the European Parliament and of the Council amending Directive 2003/87/EC to continue current limitations of scope for aviation activities and to prepare to implement a global market-based measure from 2021 [2017] (COM(2017)0054—C8-0028/2017—2017/0017(COD)). Insofar as the European Union has made good faith efforts to increase international regulation, arguably it remains its sovereign right to maintain its unilateral action if, and as long as such regulation differs considerably from relevant EU regulation.

[172] *Eg* art 4(4) of the Paris Agreement (2015) (calling on country Parties to 'continue taking the lead by undertaking economy-wide absolute emission reduction targets', while developing country parties should 'continue enhancing their mitigation efforts').

[173] See on this last issue, Joanne Scott and Lavanya Rajamani, 'EU Climate Change Unilateralism' (2012) 23 EJIL 469.

[174] See on the 'considerate design' approach: Dobson (n 137) ch 6.

[175] Shawkat Alam, 'Trade and the Environment: Perspectives from the Global South' in Shawkat Alam and others (eds), *International Environmental Law and the Global South* (CUP 2015) 316. Note that the diffusion of EU norms to the EU's neighbourhood has largely not been based on market accession conditions, but rather on capacity-building and socialization to induce domestic reforms. See Tanja A Börzel and Thomas Risse, 'When Europeanisation Meets Diffusion: Exploring New Territory' (2012) 35 WEP 192, 195.

5.3.4 Concluding observations

WTO law may well give ample leeway for unilateral, trade-restrictive action in the global environmental interest, in particular given the public policy exceptions codified in article XX GATT. While in *Shrimp/Turtle,* the AB appeared to require some territorial nexus for unilateral measures to pass muster with article XX GATT, it is not clear whether the permissive principles of jurisdiction govern the interpretation of GATT provisions. However, even if they do, they may not serve a limiting purpose: requirements of 'territoriality' or 'substantial connection' are so capacious that they may presumptively justify almost all unilateral trade measures. Therefore, to prevent unilateral action from running amok and resulting in abusive domination rather than selfless intervention, some additional limiting principles may be called for. This applies even if the objective of such intervention is internationally shared, such as combating climate change.[176] If these requirements are interpreted strictly, the number of instances where states could successfully invoke unilaterally defined public policy exceptions with extraterritorial effect may be rather limited in fact. It is recalled that the EU's measures in *EC—Seals* stranded in the WTO Panel and AB precisely on these grounds.[177]

5.4 The Right to a Remedy in Tort in Transnational Business and Human Rights Litigation

Our world is characterized by powerful, internationally active corporations that are not always a force for good. Especially the impact of transnational corporations on individuals' and groups' enjoyment of human rights, notably in the Global South, where production tends to be concentrated for reasons of costs, has been a particular concern. The reality of corporate power, which sometimes dwarfs the power of the state, has informed calls to extend human rights obligations to corporations,[178] and to increase corporate accountability and liability, whether under international or domestic law.[179]

[176] Compare Dobson (n 137) ch 7 ('tensions do not so much arise out of disagreements as to the objective, but rather from the fact that one state seeks to impose the design of its "solution" on foreign actors who also have an interest in the situation').

[177] *EC—Seals Panel Report* (n 142) paras 7.344, 7.340, 7.398, 7.410, 7.460. See also Partiti and van der Velde (n 163) 1067, regarding EU trade measures in respect of conflict minerals (calling for 'thorough justification of the requirements generating detrimental impact under the Chapeau of Article XX GATT, which would result in a higher burden of proof and a potentially open outcome of the dispute', especially in the context of the application of the EU Conflict Minerals Regulation to conflict-affected and high-risk areas, the geographic scope of which is wider than under the OECD Due Diligence Guidance regarding conflict minerals).

[178] See for the most extensive resource centre for advocates of corporate human rights accountability: https://www.business-humanrights.org/ (accessed 23 January 2020).

[179] See at length Liesbeth Enneking and others (eds), *Accountability, International Business Operations and the Law: Providing Justice for Corporate Human Rights Violations in Global Value Chains* (Routledge 2019).

Providing (legal) accountability in respect of harmful transnational corporate activities has a strong jurisdictional dimension. As there are no international dispute-settlement mechanisms yet with special jurisdiction over corporate abuses,[180] it falls to states to regulate global corporate activities and supply chains, and to offer a forum, that is, establish their jurisdiction, with a view to providing remedies if harm occurs. If such courts offer a remedy to foreign victims of corporate abuse in situations where victims are unable to pursue remedies in the host state of investment,[181] they may be deemed to promote the international community's interest in human rights compliance. At the same time, however, these jurisdictional assertions have a possibly suspect 'extraterritorial' dimension, as they pertain to events that largely take place outside the territory of the forum state.

Notably the adoption of the UN Guiding Principles on Business and Human Rights (UNGP 2011)[182] has thrust the exercise of jurisdiction over transnational corporations into the limelight. The foundational principle of UNGP Pillar III provides that

> [a]s part of their duty to protect against business-related human rights abuse, States must take appropriate steps to ensure, through judicial, administrative, legislative or other appropriate means, that when such abuses occur within their territory and/or jurisdiction those affected have access to effective remedy.[183]

Access to a remedy logically requires that states first establish their jurisdiction before they can grant a substantive remedy (*ie* hold a corporation liable and order compensation to be granted).[184] These states also include third states.[185] The UNGP remain silent on the jurisdictional basis for third state intervention, and only urge states to consider 'ways to reduce legal, practical and other relevant barriers that could lead to a denial of access to remedy'.[186] In the face of this silence, it is the aim of this section to uncover the (potential) legal basis for third

[180] But see Katerina Yiannibas, 'The Adaptability of International Arbitration: Reforming the Arbitration Mechanism to Provide Effective Remedy for Business-related Human Rights Abuses' (2018) 6 NQHR 214–31.

[181] See also Michael Kidd, 'Minerals' in Elisa Morgera and Kati Kulovesi (eds), *Research Handbook on International Law and Natural Resources* (Edward Elgar 2016) 348.

[182] UN, 'Guiding Principles on Business and Human Rights: Implementing the United Nations "Protect, Respect and Remedy" Framework' (2011) UN Doc HR/PUB/11/04.

[183] UNGP (n 182) principle 25.

[184] See Commentary to Principle 25 UNGP (n 182) ('Access to effective remedy has both procedural and substantive aspects.').

[185] See *eg* Commentary to Principle 26 UNGP (n 182) (mentioning the situation 'where claimants face a denial of justice in a host State and cannot access home State courts regardless of the merits of the claim').

[186] UNGP (n 182) principle 26.

states' exercise of jurisdiction over corporate human rights abuses, as well as its legal limitations.[187]

The analysis in these pages only extends to the question of *jurisdiction*. Whether states can also hold a corporation *liable* after having established jurisdiction over it is a different question which is governed by rules of applicable law under private international law, corporate law (*eg* regarding the possible piercing of the corporate veil in parent–subsidiary relationships), and obviously domestic liability law (*eg* regarding negligence and duties of care). Nevertheless, even if only the more narrow question of jurisdiction—which logically precedes the question of liability—is addressed, it will transpire that, in practice, jurisdictional issues are intertwined with substantive law issues.[188] Hence, liability questions cannot entirely be left out of the analysis.

Another limitation is that the analysis only extends to jurisdiction in *civil or tort* matters. This is not to deny the relevance of the exercise of domestic *criminal* jurisdiction over corporate human rights abuses. In fact, the author has highlighted this relevance in earlier publications.[189] In reality, however, criminal jurisdiction in extraterritorial business and human rights cases has so far hardly been exercised, whereas by now there are a sizeable number of relevant court decisions in civil matters that are ripe for analysis.[190]

The focus on civil litigation also implies a focus on the *adjudicatory* rather than *prescriptive* dimension of jurisdiction, as we are concerned with the availability of a forum rather than with the prescription and application of particular substantive norms. However, adjudication and prescription are not entirely separate categories, as a court adjudicating a case may go on to apply (prescribe) its own laws to the case, for example in case the *lex loci delicti* that is normally applied on the basis of private international law rules of applicable law is considered to be incompatible

[187] I am partly indebted for this part to Dr Lucas Roorda, who successfully defended his PhD on the topic at Utrecht University in December 2019, in the framework of the UNIJURIS project of which I was the Principal Investigator. Lucas Roorda, 'Jurisdiction over Foreign Direct Liability Claims against Transnational corporations in EU Member States. Increasing Access to Remedy for Victims of Corporate Human Rights Violations' (PhD thesis, Utrecht University 2019). See on legal remedies more generally also Axel Marx and others, 'Access to legal remedies for victims of corporate human rights abuses in third countries', February 2019, Brussels: European Parliament Policy Department for External Relations, available at http://www.europarl.europa.eu/RegData/etudes/STUD/2019/603475/EXPO_STU(2019)603475_EN.pdf. This report recommends strengthening jurisdictional bases.

[188] See also Roorda (n 187) 3.7.4.1.

[189] Cedric Ryngaert, 'Accountability for Corporate Human Rights Abuses: Lessons from the Possible Exercise of Dutch National Criminal Jurisdiction over Multinational Corporations' (2018) 29 CLF 1; Emma van Gelder and Cedric Ryngaert, 'Dutch Report on Prosecuting Corporations for Violations of International Criminal Law' [2017] IRPL 113.

[190] A detailed overview of relevant European cases is given in Roorda (n 187) ch III. Most cases were brought in English courts. See also Marx and others, (n 187). See Liesbeth Enneking and others, 'Zorgplichten van Nederlandse Ondernemingen Inzake Internationaal Maatschappelijk Verantwoord Ondernemen, Een rechtsvergelijkend en empirisch onderzoek naar de stand van het Nederlandse recht in het licht van de *UN Guiding Principles*' (2015) Utrecht Centre for Accountability and Liability Law, https://english.wodc.nl/onderzoeksdatabase/2531-maatschappelijk-verantwoord-ondernemen-in-het-buitenland.aspx?cp=45&cs=6796 (last accessed 6 December 2019).

with the *ordre public* of the forum state. Moreover, and more importantly perhaps, as Parrish has observed, the exercise of adjudicatory jurisdiction in civil litigation is one of the ways for states to engage in the international arena, permitting 'unilateral private initiative to advance global justice',[191] while raising concerns over jurisdictional overreach, just like the exercise of prescriptive jurisdiction.

The structure of this section is as follows. Section 5.4.1 argues that the basic principle of adjudicatory jurisdiction is the principle of domicile, which allows a corporation to be sued in its home state. In a number of states, a parent corporation's foreign subsidiary or another related foreign person could also be sued in the parent's home state, typically on the ground that such a claim is connected to the claim against the parent. The other sections explore jurisdictional bases that allow for autonomous suits against a foreign corporation.[192] Two bases will be discussed in more detail: forum of necessity, that is, a jurisdictional principle which is aimed at averting a denial of justice, and which is laid down in some states' law of civil procedure (section 5.4.2), and universal civil jurisdiction, which is triggered by the gravity of a particular violation but is not laid down in existing law, at least not in its pure form (section 5.4.3). Other, more out-of-the box jurisdictional grounds could also be contemplated, however (section 5.4.4).

Technically speaking, the jurisdictional aspects of civil litigation are governed by rules of *private international law*, as such litigation involves private parties: victims of human rights abuses sue a private corporation. However, *public international law* is not wholly alien to such litigation. For one thing, the public international law rules of jurisdiction may mark the outer limits of the permissible exercise of jurisdiction under private international law.[193] For another, the substantive values underlying business and human rights litigation feature in public international law instruments, notably human rights treaties. This also means that the value-neutrality which characterizes private international law may have to give way to a conceptualization of private international law as a legal instrument aimed at realizing the common interest. Applied to the law of jurisdiction, this means that the nature of the abuse, namely the abuse of *human rights*—a violation of international law—coupled with the victim's human right to a remedy as highlighted by the UNGP, should inform a wider, more cosmopolitan construction of jurisdictional techniques in private international law. Safety valves

[191] Austen L Parrish, 'Fading Extraterritoriality and Isolationism? Developments in the United States' (2017) 24 IJGLS 207, 208.

[192] See also FRA, 'Improving Access to Remedy in the Area of Business and Human Rights at the EU level—Opinion of the European Union Agency for Fundamental Rights—1/2017 [B&HR]' (10 April 2017), available at http://fra.europa.eu/en/opinion/2017/business-human-rights (accessed 6 December 2019). Council of Europe Committee of Ministers, 'Recommendation CM/Rec(2016)3 of the Committee of Ministers to Member States on Human rights and Business' (2 March 2016), 1249 Meeting, CM(2016)18-addfinal.

[193] L Roorda and C Ryngaert, 'Public International Law Constraints on the Exercise of Adjudicatory Jurisdiction in Civil Matters' in S Forlati and P Franzina (eds), *Universal Civil Jurisdiction* (forthcoming Brill 2020).

should be foreseen in order to prevent jurisdictional overreach, but overly strict interpretations of doctrines of jurisdictional restraint could render victims' right to a remedy illusory (section 5.4.5).

5.4.1 Domicile and connected claims

In civil cases, jurisdiction could non-controversially be established over a corporation on the basis of the domicile principle, regardless of the location of the abuse. The domicile principle has been considered as a form of 'fictitious territoriality',[194] or 'ascriptive jurisdiction', a separate ground of jurisdiction linked to the hypermobility of corporations, whose registration in states may be based on an 'act with minimal geographical content'.[195] Because of the lack of territorial 'fixity' of a corporation's domicile (place of incorporation), the domicile principle may be an uncertain accountability principle. Scott has observed in this respect: 'Faced with demanding regulation, it is more likely that an elastic target, such as a corporation, will change its nationality or alter its corporate form to avoid a harsh regulatory burden, creating a high likelihood of regulatory arbitrage.'[196] Nevertheless, a corporation's choice to incorporate in a particular state tends to depend on a variety of criteria, with the level of regulation and the possibility of local adjudication being only one of them. In any event, pursuant to the domicile principle, a corporation's home state, the state on whose territory the corporation is incorporated or registered, can, and possibly even should exercise jurisdiction over that corporation, also in respect of human rights abuses committed abroad in the context of the corporation's transnational activities. In the European Union, domicile jurisdiction is mandatory,[197] but in Anglo-Saxon states, doctrines have been developed to restrict its application. Among these are the doctrine of *forum non conveniens*, which allows a defendant to move to dismiss on the basis that a court in a foreign country is a more appropriate forum in which to proceed, even if the forum court has jurisdiction,[198] and the doctrine that claimants need to have a 'good arguable case' on the merits.[199]

[194] Szigeti, 'The Illusion of Territorial Jurisdiction' (n 12) 389.
[195] Szigeti, 'In the Middle of Nowhere' (n 13) 42–44 (noting how easy it is to change a place of registration).
[196] Joanne Scott, 'The Global Reach of EU Law' in Marise Cremona and Joanne Scott (eds), *'EU Law Beyond Borders: The Extraterritorial Reach of EU Law* (OUP 2019) 58.
[197] *Eg* in the European Union: Council Regulation (EU) No 1215/2012 of 12 December 2012 on jurisdiction and the recognition and enforcement of judgments in civil and commercial matters (Brussels-I Recast) [2012] OJ L/351, art 4 ('persons domiciled in a Member State *shall*, whatever their nationality, be sued in the courts of that Member State') (emphasis added).
[198] See for a discussion of US legal practice (from the perspective of the plaintiff): Brett J Workman, 'Deference to the Plaintiff in Forum Non Conveniens Cases' (2017) 86 Ford LJ 871.
[199] *Eg Young v Anglo American South Africa Ltd and others* [2014] EWCA Civ 1130; [2014] WLR(D) 370 (refusing to hear a case filed by South African miners who worked in mines owned by

It s not certain whether domicile-based jurisdiction can provide a remedy for all abuses that are committed in the corporation's supply chain, notably by subsidiaries and suppliers. While a home state court may have jurisdiction over the corporation on the basis of the domicile principle, in light of the principle of limited liability it may be difficult, if not impossible, to hold it liable for abuses committed by separate legal entities. Admittedly, parent corporations can be held liable for violating their duty of care vis-à-vis the activities of their subsidiaries and suppliers, but restrictive judicial interpretations of such duties (*eg* interpretations which require effective rather than just overall control of the parent over the subsidiary), may render establishing a breach of the duty of care a tall order.

This elicits the question whether third states could possibly also exercise direct jurisdiction over *foreign corporations* in respect of *foreign harm*. Such jurisdiction would not normally be covered by the domicile principle nor by the territoriality principle. However, some states allow the establishment of jurisdiction over a (foreign) defendant in case the claim is *closely connected* to a claim against another defendant over which it duly has jurisdiction.[200] The International Law Association's Committee on International Civil Litigation (ILA 2012) has indicated in its Sofia Guidelines on Best Practices for International Civil Litigation for Human Rights Violations that claims are closely connected if 'it is efficient to hear and determine them together; and the defendants are related'.[201] In a human rights context, the connected claims doctrine, which is informed by the principle of procedural economy, may enable a forum court to exercise jurisdiction over a subsidiary or other related entity of a corporation amenable to domicile jurisdiction. In *Akpan v Shell*, for instance, a Nigerian farmer brought a case before a Dutch court in respect of environmental harm (oil spills, which could be conceptualized as violating environmental rights) that occurred in Nigeria, both against a Dutch parent corporation (Shell, amenable to domicile jurisdiction) and against the latter's Nigerian subsidiary. Dutch courts established jurisdiction over the Nigerian subsidiary on the basis of the connected claims doctrine as codified in Dutch law, holding that the claim against the parent was not manifestly unfounded, that the factual

an English parent corporation, and who alleged that the corporation had not sufficiently protected them against dust).

[200] cf Brussels-I Recast regulation 2012 (n 197) art 8(1). However, that this provision only applies to EU-domiciled defendants. In business and human rights cases, at least one of the defendants will ordinarily be domiciled outside the European Union. That being said, domestic codes may give the principle a general scope of application (*eg* art 7(1) Rv, Dutch Code of Civil Procedure).

[201] International Law Association 'Resolution No 2/2012, Sofia Guidelines on Best Practices for International Civil Litigation for Human Rights Violations' (August 2012) para 2.2(2). The Guidelines indicate that '[d]efendants are related ... in particular if at the time the cause of action arose: (a) they formed part of the same corporate group; (b) one defendant controlled another defendant; (c) one defendant directed the litigious acts of another defendant; or (d) they took part in a concerted manner in the activity giving rise to the cause of action'.

connection between both the defendants and the object of the claims justified them being joined together before the same court, and that separate treatment would risk irreconcilable decisions on issues that are both factually and legally connected.[202] As Roorda suggested, the Dutch approach to the connected claims doctrine is commendable from a cosmopolitan perspective, as Dutch courts use a particularly light test to assess the connectedness of claims.[203] Dutch courts limit themselves to ascertaining whether the claims arise from the same set of facts, subject to an abuse of process limitation, as would be proper indeed in the jurisdictional stage.[204] This is unlike, for instance, English courts, which also inquire into the substantive strength of the claim on the merits when inquiring whether the person outside the jurisdiction is a 'necessary and proper party' to the claim.[205] Even if English courts conclude that the claim is 'arguable', they still have to find that England is the 'proper place' to bring the claim.[206] To ascertain this, they have regard to the risk of not obtaining justice in a foreign forum, that is, an analysis which resembles the analysis carried out under forum of necessity (as discussed in section 5.4.2). However, as *Vedanta v Lungowe*, a case decided by the UK Supreme Court in 2019, shows, English courts may well determine that such a risk exists, and allow the case to proceed.[207]

[202] Gerechtshof (Court of Appeal) Den Haag, 18 December 2015, ECLI:NL:GHDA:2015:3586, 3587 and 3588, paras 2.2–2.5. See also District Court Den Haag, 1 May 2019, ECLI:NL:RBDHA:2019:4233, paras 4.23–4.25 in the Dutch case of *Kiobel v Shell* (upholding jurisdiction over Dutch-incorporated Shell's Nigerian subsidiary on the basis of connected claims).

[203] Roorda (n 187) ch 7.2.1.

[204] A restrictive interpretation of abuse of process would obviously be desirable from a cosmopolitan point of view. In Dutch legal practice, in any event, if the claimant has a perspective, if only a remote one, of winning the claim, he can be accused of an abuse of process. cf *Akpan v Shell* (n 202) para 2.2.

[205] CPR (1998) SI 1998/3132, RSC Order 11, Rule 1(1)(c). See for an application in a case concerning leakages of Shell oil pipelines in Nigeria: *His Royal Highness Emere Godwin Bebe Okpabi v Royal Dutch Shell* [2018] EWCA Civ 191 (holding that there was no arguable case to be made against the parent company, based on its lack of proximity to its subsidiary, and hence that the connected claims doctrine could not apply in the case). See for an application in a case concerning Unilever's alleged failure to take precautions to protect employees of its Kenyan subsidiary against ethnic violence: *AAA and others v Unilever PLC and Unilever Tea Kenya Limited* [2017] EWHC 371(QB) (holding that there was no arguable claim against the parent, as a result of which the claim against the subsidiary was also bound to fail). While the English test may appear more stringent, it need not always result in dismissal. See *eg Dominic Liswaniso Lungowe & Others v Vedanta Resources Plc & Konkola Copper Mines Plc*, 2017] EWCA Civ 1528 (holding, in a case concerning pollution in Zambia, that the Zambian subsidiary of an English corporation whose discharges allegedly contributed to the pollution, was a necessary and proper party to the claim, and that there was no prospect of substantial justice in Zambia). See for criticism of English practice: Roorda (n 187) s 3.7.4.2 (arguing that 'making the standard of 'arguable case' that a duty of care exists as the lynchpin for the feasibility of [foreign direct liability] cases creates a strong incentive for parent companies not to intervene in the activities of their subsidiaries', as active intervention may result in its subsidiary becoming a party to the claim as a 'necessary and proper party').

[206] See *Vedanta Resources PLC v Lungowe* [2019] UKSC 20, para 66 et seq.

[207] ibid, para 88 et seq. (Holding that because of lack of proper funding and lack of legal representation of the claimants in Zambia, they risked not obtaining substantial justice there). This case was brought by a group of 1,800 Zambians against UK-incorporated Vedanta and its Zambian subsidiary. The claimants alleged that they suffered personal injury, property damage, and loss of livelihood as a result of mining operations in Zambia.

5.4.2 Forum of necessity

The requirements of the connected claims doctrine are relatively strict in the sense that a relationship between multiple defendants needs to be established so that it is foreseeable for the foreign defendant to be hauled before the forum court alongside the other (domiciled) defendant. If a claim proves unsuccessful under the connected claims doctrine, other jurisdictional doctrines may have to be envisaged. An obvious candidate is forum of necessity (*forum necessitatis*), which does not require a relationship with a claim against another defendant. In the aforementioned Guidelines, the ILA Committee defines forum of necessity as the exercise of jurisdiction by the 'courts of any State with a sufficient connection to the dispute ... in order to avert a denial of justice'.[208] A denial of justice occurs, according to the ILA, if 'no other court is available; or the claimant cannot reasonably be expected to seize another court'.[209] The Committee lists a variety of—alternative rather than cumulative—connections as satisfying the requirement that the connection be sufficient, such as the presence of the claimant, the nationality of the claimant or the defendant, the presence of assets of the defendant, or some activity of the defendant.[210]

In essence, forum of necessity creates an exceptional forum to ensure that justice is served for claimants who cannot rely on another jurisdictional ground. The rationale of forum of necessity may be cosmopolitan in the sense that it allows for 'distant strangers' to have their day in a court which is not normally be accessible to them. Still, the extent to which such jurisdiction is truly cosmopolitan is a function of the interpretation of the connection requirement. A strict interpretation of this requirement may drastically dampen the doctrine's potential to further human rights through unilateral jurisdiction. Arguably, because of the nature of the abuses—human rights abuses—a liberal interpretation of the connection requirement is required.

As it happens, most states espouse a relatively conservative interpretation of forum of necessity, requiring, in particular, strong connections to the forum. In the case of *Naït-Liman*, for instance, Swiss courts ruled that a claim regarding foreign torture filed by a foreigner who was later granted political asylum in Switzerland did not have a strong enough connection to the forum for forum of necessity-based jurisdiction to be exercised.[211] The European Court of Human Rights (ECtHR) did

[208] 'Sofia Guidelines' (n 201) para 2.3.1.

[209] ibid, para 2.3.2.

[210] ibid, para 2.3.3 (which also refers to 'a civil claim based on an act giving rise to criminal proceedings, in the court seized of those proceedings, to the extent that court has jurisdiction under its own law to entertain civil proceedings').

[211] Swiss Federal Supreme Court, Judgment of 22 May 2007, *Naït-Liman*. See for the relevant legal provision: art 3, Loi Fédérale sur le Droit International Privé du 18 Décembre 1987 (LDIP; RS 291) ('Lorsque la présente loi ne prévoit aucun for en Suisse et qu'une procédure à l'étranger se révèle impossible ou qu'on ne peut raisonnablement exiger qu'elle y soit introduite, les autorités judiciaires ou administratives suisses du lieu avec lequel la cause présente un lien suffisant sont compétentes.').

not consider this dismissal of jurisdiction to be a violation of the right of access to a court under article 6 ECHR.[212] The ECtHR's decision is understandable insofar as only a relatively limited number of states have incorporated forum of necessity-based jurisdiction into their codes in the first place. In this situation, states which happen to be Contracting Parties to the European Convention of Human Rights (ECHR) cannot be faulted for espousing a narrow interpretation of forum of necessity. Nevertheless, precisely because of the global values which the application of forum of necessity may serve, it is advisable for courts to give an expansive interpretation to relevant statutory clauses.

Forum of necessity-based jurisdiction has been successfully relied on by claimants in a limited number of human rights cases (relating to torture).[213] As far as the exercise of jurisdiction in the context of business and human rights is concerned, however, no successful cases have been reported, although at least in in one case claimants relied on forum of necessity.[214] Arguably, in business and human rights cases, courts may want to consider the parent corporation's presence in the forum to be sufficient for the establishment of jurisdiction over the defendant subsidiary, even if the claim is not directed at the parent itself.[215] Also, they may want to take into account relevant facts that occurred after the harm, unlike what the Swiss courts in *Naït-Liman* did. This would mean, for instance, that a court also has jurisdiction over a corporation which acquired another corporation responsible for the human rights harm, after such harm occurred and before the claim was filed, if such a corporation has a strong connection to the forum.[216]

A low threshold for a finding of connection may be advisable in business and human rights cases, as long as the corporation can somehow foresee being hauled before a (foreign) court. It is less certain, however, whether an equally low threshold for the 'denial of justice' prong of forum of necessity is called for. In particular, the risk of imperialism looms large when courts from the Global North pass judgment on the quality of court proceedings in the Global South.

[212] *Naït-Liman v Switzerland*, Application no 51357/07, 15 March 2018.

[213] See Ontario Supreme Court (Canada), *Bouzari v Bahremani* [2013] ONSC 6337; District Court The Hague, Judgment of 21 March 2012, *El-Hojouj v Unnamed Libyan Officials*, ECLI:NL:RBSGR:2012:BV9748.

[214] Canadian Superior Court, *Canadian Association Against Impunity (CAAI) v Anvil Mining Ltd* [2011] 500-06-000530-101. However, in the related context of labour law, in a case of alleged wrongful termination of employment contracts by French companies in Congo, a French Court of Appeal applied forum of necessity and establish its jurisdiction on the basis that the claimants risked a denial of justice in Congo. As reported in Jean-Baptiste Jacquin, 'Comilog-Eramet: Justice, Libre Entreprise et Compétitivité' *Le Monde* (11 September 2015) http://www.lemonde.fr/economie/article/2015/09/11/comilog-eramet-justice-libre-entreprise-et-competitivite_4753022_3234.html. Note that jurisdiction in this case could in any event be based on the domicile principle. See, in the same case, Arrêt n° 145 du 28 janvier 2015 (13-22.994 à 13-23.006)—Cour de Cassation—Chambre Sociale—ECLI:FR:CCASS:2015:SO00145 (ruling that the co-defendants were French companies and could thus be sued under the domicile principle).

[215] Roorda (n 187) 7.2.2.4.

[216] ibid.

The former may want to carry out a culture-sensitive analysis of whether the foreign forum is indeed not reasonably available. As Roorda suggested, a high evidentiary burden should rest on plaintiffs to establish that the legal system of the foreign forum (in practice the host state of the corporation) does not meet basic fair trial standards and thus cannot be an acceptable forum.[217] In addition, forum courts may want to inquire to what extent foreign states may take issue, on sovereignty grounds, with the forum state's jurisdictional assertion, bearing in mind that public international law constraints remain applicable in disputes governed by private international law. Obviously, evidentiary requirements should not become overly strict, and forum courts should not readily defer to foreign courts in case of foreign protest. Otherwise, the victim's access to a remedy—a global value—risks becoming illusory.

5.4.3 Universal civil jurisdiction

A pure form of cosmopolitan jurisdiction in civil matters is the exercise of 'universal civil jurisdiction', that is, the exercise of jurisdiction based on the gravity of a violation, regardless of any connections of the violation or the dispute to the forum state. Reference has already been made to the US Alien Tort Statute (ATS), which on its face provides for universal civil jurisdiction where it reads: 'The district courts shall have original jurisdiction of any civil action by an alien for a tort only, committed in violation of the law of nations or a treaty of the United States.'[218] After the US Supreme Court's *Kiobel* judgment (2013), however, it has become clear that the ATS does not authorize universal jurisdiction.[219] The Court, relying on the presumption against extraterritoriality, required that a dispute 'touch and concern' the United States.[220] Even before *Kiobel*, however, assertions of jurisdiction arising under the ATS were never truly universal, as separate requirements for the establishment of personal jurisdiction precluded that defendants were hauled before US courts if they had no minimum contacts with the United States.[221] Outside the United States, universal civil jurisdiction can possibly be read into existing statutory provisions on forum of necessity that do not require a connection,[222] but most

[217] Roorda (n 187) 7.2.2.3. See also *Vendata v Lungowe* 2019 (n 206) 96.

[218] 28 USC s 1350.

[219] See also *Jesner v Arab Bank*, 138 S Ct 1386 (2018) (ruling that foreign corporations cannot be sued under the ATS).

[220] *Kiobel v Royal Dutch Petroleum Co.*, 569 US 108, 124–25 (2013).

[221] cf *International Shoe Co. v Washington*, 326 US 310 (1945). Lately, such requirements have become even stricter, since the US Supreme Court required that the defendant be essentially at home in the United States. *Goodyear Dunlop Tires Operations, S.A. v Brown*, 564 US 915 (2011); *Daimler AG v Bauman*, 571 US (2014).

[222] *Eg* art 9(b) of the Dutch Code of Civil Procedure, which allows for the exceptional exercise of jurisdiction when a judicial procedure outside the Netherlands turns out to be impossible.

such provisions do require a connection. As a result, for universal civil jurisdiction to apply, statutory amendment would be required.

State support for universal civil jurisdiction is however lukewarm, to put it mildly, even if some scholars have endorsed the concept.[223] Foreign states' *amicus curiae* briefs in the *Kiobel* litigation have been largely negative toward it,[224] with the exception of Argentina.[225] The European Union supported it, insofar as it would be limited to the international crimes to which universal criminal jurisdiction applies.[226] Given the absence of actual state practice in support of universal civil jurisdiction (both verbal and physical), the international legality of universal civil jurisdiction may be in doubt.[227] Also, the ECtHR in *Naït-Liman* was sceptical towards it,[228] even though the case itself concerned forum of necessity. In light of hostility towards the concept in conjunction with the scarcity, or even total absence, of relevant practice, it is unlikely that states will amend their codes of civil procedure to include universal civil jurisdiction.

From a cosmopolitan point of view, this may be regrettable as universal civil jurisdiction has the potential to provide a remedy to those victims who cannot access any other court for practical or legal reasons. At the same time, however, it bears notice that in some legal systems victims can file reparation claims with criminal courts in the context of the latter exercising universal criminal jurisdiction; when the court hears such claims, it effectively exercises universal civil jurisdiction.[229] Also, liberal interpretations of forum of necessity, which notably use a low threshold regarding the connection requirement, may shift that concept toward universal civil jurisdiction. Finally, especially in the context of business and human rights claims, corporate groups typically have connections all over the world, as a result of which connection-less universal jurisdiction may not be needed to bring them, or members of their group, to account.

[223] See for scholarly support notably Commission Bucher, 'Universal Civil Jurisdiction with Regard to Reparation for International Crimes, Resolution' (2015) 75 Yearbook of the Institute of International Law 265–66 (supporting 'subsidiary' universal civil jurisdiction, *ie* in case other states do not have a closer connection, or do not make a substantive remedy available).

[224] See notably Brief of the Governments of the United Kingdom of Great Britain and Northern Ireland and the Kingdom of the Netherlands as *amici curiae* in support of the respondents, *Kiobel et al v Royal Dutch Petrol et al*, no 10-1491 (2012). See for a survey of all *amicus* briefs filed by states in ATS cases (not just limited to *Kiobel*): OHCHR, 'Business and Human Rights: Enhancing Accountability and Access to Remedy: *State positions on the use of extraterritorial jurisdiction in cases of allegations of business involvement in severe human rights abuses: a survey of amicus curiae briefs filed by States and State agencies in ATS cases (2000–2015)*' (April 2015) Working paper 2 http://www.ohchr.org/Documents/Issues/Business/DomesticLawRemedies/StateamicusATS-cases.pdf (accessed 6 December 2019).

[225] Brief of the Republic of Argentina (June 2012), *Kiobel v Royal Dutch Petroleum* (n 224).

[226] Brief of the European Commission on behalf of the European Union (June 2012) *Kiobel v Royal Dutch Petroleum* (n 224).

[227] Abhimanyu Jain, 'Universal Civil Jurisdiction in International Law' (2015) 55 IJIL 209.

[228] *Naït-Liman v Switzerland* (n 212) paras 187–88.

[229] ibid, 185.

5.4.4 Other jurisdictional grounds

Apart from domicile, connected claims, forum of necessity, and universality, also other jurisdictional grounds could be envisaged to ensure a remedy for foreign victims of overseas corporate abuses. In his study, Roorda has examined three possible grounds that build on existing jurisdictional grounds as well as legal evolutions in liability or regulatory law: jurisdiction based on the presence of assets, jurisdiction disregarding separate personality, jurisdiction based on the presence of goods, and jurisdiction based on profiting.

Asset-based jurisdiction has the advantage of already existing in a number of codes of civil procedure such as in continental Europe.[230] Under this jurisdictional head, the forum would have jurisdiction over a corporation as soon as the latter has assets of some value in the territory. However, some states consider asset-based jurisdiction as exorbitant. Moreover, corporations can move assets out of the territory, thereby nullifying its effect. Therefore, the legitimacy and effectiveness of asset-based jurisdiction are questionable.[231]

Jurisdiction that disregards the separate legal personalities of entities of a transnational corporate group could take a variety of forms. The most far-reaching one is probably 'enterprise jurisdiction', which would allow the group—which legally consists of a number of separate legal entities—to be sued in any forum where it is present in relation to torts committed by any entity of the group. Such a jurisdictional ground obviously facilitates victims' obtaining of a remedy, but it may open the floodgates of litigation, thereby overburdening domestic courts and possibly leading to inter-state conflict.[232] Moreover, it overlooks the fact that, within corporate groups, entities may operate relatively autonomously. Instead, jurisdiction could possibly be tied to ownership and control, which would enable a subsidiary to be sued in its parent home state (without the possibly stringent requirements of 'connected claims' applying). This jurisdictional ground has some pedigree in corporate liability law: in some jurisdictions, parents may be held liable for the debts of their subsidiaries, and *vice versa*.[233] However, it is not self-evident for a claimant to demonstrate that a subsidiary is really controlled by a parent.[234] Moreover, control-based jurisdiction may lead parents to relinquish control over their subsidiaries, thereby possibly making matters worse in terms of human rights compliance.

Alternatively, one could allow victims of corporate abuses committed during production processed abroad to sue corporations in the forum where the goods

[230] German Code of Civil Procedure (*Zivilprozessordnung*) of 5 December 2005, BGBl I 3202, § 23; Austrian Court Jurisdiction Act (*Jurisdiktionsnorm*) of 1 August 1895, Reichsgesetzblatt no 111/1895, § 99; Swedish Code of Judicial Procedure (*Rättegångsbalken*) of 1 January 1948, Ds 1998:000, ch 10 s 3. See also Brussels-I Recast regulation 2012 (n 187) Commission Draft (2010) draft art 25.

[231] Roorda (n 187) ch 7.2.3.

[232] ibid, ch 7.3.2.1.

[233] ibid, ch 7.3.2.2.1.

[234] See on reversing the burden of proof: ibid, 7.3.2.2.3.

are subsequently present, that is, where they have been imported. Under administrative regulations, goods produced abroad in substandard conditions can already be kept off the market through import prohibitions and conditions, as expounded in **section 5.3** of this chapter in the context of 'extraterritorial' environmental regulation. Extrapolated to adjudicatory jurisdiction over corporations, this means that if such goods happen to enter the forum's market, the forum has jurisdiction over corporations involved in the supply chain of such goods, even if they are not domestically incorporated. However, the personal scope of jurisdiction based on presence of goods remains unclear. Bearing in mind that sometimes a large number of corporations are involved in transnational supply chains, some limitation appears appropriate.[235]

Finally, jurisdiction could be based on benefiting. There is some precedent for this in liability law: under the criminal law of some states, a person could be held liable for benefiting or profiting from the proceeds of a crime.[236] Extrapolated to adjudicatory jurisdiction, this means that the forum could exercise jurisdiction over any corporation which benefits in the forum's territory from overseas corporate abuses, even if it is incorporated elsewhere. Such jurisdiction may hold some promise to exercise jurisdiction over holding companies to whom profits of the corporate group accrue, but often it may be complicated to determine who exactly profited from extraterritorial corporate abuse.[237]

5.4.5 Sovereignty concerns and reasonableness

Transnational human rights tort cases operate at a distance from the place where the wrongful acts took place, or at least had their effects. Typically, they involve Western courts (home states) sitting in judgment of acts occurring in the Global South (host states), with victims being represented by Western lawyers and Western non-governmental organizations (NGOs).[238] In this respect, concerns have been raised that 'foreign, private judicial proceedings will not be able to internalize and give proper space to the preferences and values of the domestic community'.[239] From a classic public international law perspective, those concerns are normally channelled through the concept of (foreign state) sovereignty. Arguably,

[235] Roorda (n 187) ch s 7.4.1 (suggesting focusing on the top tiers of the value chain, although not excluding lower tiers).
[236] *Eg* art 273f Dutch Penal Code (providing for criminal liability for benefiting from human trafficking).
[237] Roorda (n 187) ch 7.4.2.
[238] *Eg* the plaintiff in the Dutch case of *Akpan v Shell* (n 202) was supported by Milieudefensie, a Dutch environmental NGO.
[239] Doreen Lustig and Eyal Benvenisti, 'The Multinational Corporation as "The Good Despot": The Democratic Costs of Privatization in Global Settings' (2013) GlobalTrust Working Paper Series 01/2013, 16 http://globaltrust.tau.ac.il/wp-content/uploads/2014/01/Good-Despot-TIL-WP-1-13.pdf (accessed 6 December 2019).

this sovereignty would be trampled upon by the 'extraterritorial application' given to the home state's law. Thus, some early home states' initiatives to regulate the overseas business activities of 'their' corporations have been aborted on the basis that, in the view of the home state, that is, the regulating state, they caused 'conflict with the sovereignty of foreign states',[240] or would be considered by foreign states as 'arrogant, patronising, paternalistic and racist'.[241] In respect of more recent initiatives on transnational business regulation, for example the French act on a corporate duty of vigilance,[242] and the Swiss Responsible Business initiative,[243] both of which could be enforced via tort law, such sovereignty concerns were no longer prominent, however, or at least the home state did not voice them.

Concerns over home states intervening in the domestic affairs of host states, and supplanting host state policies, should be taken seriously. This applies in particular to economic and social rights, as the relevant conventions give Contracting Parties some room to develop their own policies to realize these rights, in light of their developmental status.[244] Host state governments may want to exploit their state's competitive advantages as states of inward investment, by setting lower labour and environmental standards. That being said, the attitudes of governments do not necessarily coincide with the attitudes of their citizens who may well prefer *higher* regulatory protection as potentially enforced by home states and their courts. Venal governmental elites may act hand in glove with foreign corporations, and fail to properly represent their citizens. Corporate payments for industrial and extraction activities may disappear into private pockets rather than into accounts of the treasury, a state of affairs which Leif Wenar has denounced in *Blood Oil*.[245] Also, judges may side with governmental elite interests or be prone to take bribes in return for outcomes favourable to corporations. As a result, victims of corporate misconduct may be left without a remedy. In another scenario, host states may perhaps

240 cf Government response to proposed Canadian 'extraterritorial' business regulation, cited in Sara L Seck, 'Home State Responsibility and Local Communities: The Case of Global Mining' (2008) 11 YHRDJ 177, 181.

241 Australian Parliamentary Joint Statutory Committee on Corporations and Securities, hearings to determine whether to enact a proposed Corporate Code of Conduct Bill 2000 ('Bill 2000'), cited in ibid.

242 See Loi no 2017-399 du 27 Mars 2017 Relative au Devoir de Vigilance des Sociétés Mères et des Entreprises Donneuses d'ordre, https://www.legifrance.gouv.fr/affichTexte.do?cidTexte=JORFTEXT000034290626&categorieLien=id (accessed 6 December 2019).

243 Swiss Coalition for Corporate Justice 'The Responsible Business Initiative' (April 2015) http://konzern-initiative.ch (accessed 6 December 2019).

244 See *eg* International Covenant on Economic, Social and Cultural Rights (adopted 19 December 1966, entered into force 3 January 1976) 993 UNTS 3, art 2(1) ('Each State Party to the present Covenant undertakes to take steps, individually and through international assistance and co-operation, especially economic and technical, to the maximum of its available resources, with a view to achieving progressively the full realization of the rights recognized in the present Covenant by all appropriate means, including particularly the adoption of legislative measures.') See also Seck, 'Home State Responsibility and Local Communities' (n 240) 194 ('These concerns touch upon economic, social, and cultural rights; environmental rights; indigenous rights; and the right to development. Accordingly, home state regulation of these matters is more likely to be perceived as infringing host state sovereignty than is home state legislation that addresses an international criminal law norm.').

245 Leif Wenar, *Blood Oil: Tyrants, Violence, and the Rules that Run the World* (OUP 2016).

be willing to provide remedies for foreign corporate misconduct, but simply lack the capacity to do so because the civil service (especially inspection services and courts) is not functioning properly, or because they have no control over parts of their territory. These transparency, regulatory, and accountability gaps between citizens and rulers, especially of those countries plagued by a resource curse, could possibly only be remedied by third states rising to the occasion. In fact, when third states exercise jurisdiction in respect of overseas corporate abuses, they may strengthen rather than weaken the host state's sovereignty insofar as the home state offers the enforcement machinery which the host state is lacking,[246] or the home state satisfies popular accountability demands better than the host state.

It is striking that, by and large, host states have not protested the exercise of transnational tort jurisdiction by third states. On the contrary, at times they appear to have actually supported it.[247] Arguably, host states do not consider tort litigation regarding corporate activities taking place on their territory as sufficiently threatening their sovereign interests to warrant protest. Effects of such litigation on sovereignty are also less direct than the effects of universal criminal jurisdiction. In the latter case, the state is often directly implicated where one of its officials is indicted by a prosecutor from another state, whereas in the former case, the home state merely provides a forum for litigation against its 'own' corporations (albeit in respect of extraterritorial business activities). If host states do indeed not protest unilateral home state regulation, it appears disingenuous for home states to cite potential violations of host state sovereignty as a justification for the non-exercise of jurisdiction. Sara Seck put it as follows: '[H]ome state concern to avoid infringement of host state sovereignty is revealed as an excuse—or worse, a denial of responsibility.'[248]

It remains that home state or third state jurisdictional authority should be exercised judiciously and reasonably. As it happens, jurisdictional restraint is part of

[246] Compare also the international regulation of conflict diamonds: Virginia Haufler, 'Orchestrating Peace? The United Nations and the Kimberley Process' in Kenneth W Abbott and others (eds), *International Organizations as Orchestrators* (CUP 2015), 226 (arguing that the definition of conflict diamonds as 'those originating from areas controlled by rebel forces, a definition later adopted by the Kimberley Process', 'reinforced state sovereignty and established rebel forces as the ultimate target of the campaign against conflict diamonds'). The fact that the Kimberley Process is aimed at rebels rather than government forces is also problematic, however, as it shields governmental misconduct from accountability. See Global Witness, 'An Inside Job. Zimbabwe: The State, the Security Forces, and a Decade of Disappearing Diamonds' (Global Witness, 11 September 2017) https://www.globalwitness.org/en/campaigns/conflict-diamonds/inside-job/ (uncovering new evidence linking Zimbabwe's state and partisan security forces to a decade of disappearing diamond wealth).

[247] UNCHR, Open-ended intergovernmental working group on transnational corporations and other business enterprises with respect to human rights, Draft Legally Binding Instrument to Regulate, in International Human Rights law, the Activities of Transnational Corporations and Other Business Enterprises (3rd Session, 16 July 2018) https://www.ohchr.org/Documents/HRBodies/HRCouncil/WGTransCorp/Session3/DraftLBI.pdf. This instrument was drafted by Ecuador and supported by a number of developing countries. In art 5, it provides for mandatory jurisdiction for *home state courts*.

[248] Sarah L Seck, 'Unilateral Home State Regulation; Imperialism or Tool for Subaltern Resistance' (2008) 46 Osgoode Hall LJ 565, 585.

the very structure of private international law. On the basis of rules of private international law regarding applicable law, third state courts, after having established their jurisdiction, will normally determine the corporation's liability on the basis of host state law as the *lex loci delicti* (the place of the wrongful act).[249] This implies that home states only exercise *adjudicatory* jurisdiction by offering a forum, whereas the exercise of *prescriptive jurisdiction* remains in the hands of the host state. Put differently, the third state is not prescribing or setting its own laws, but *enforcing the host state's laws*, thereby deferring to the host state. In addition, for third states other than home states, stringent—and sometimes overly stringent—requirements may apply already in the jurisdictional stage, for example in respect of connected claims or forum of necessity, as discussed above. Moreover, in some common law states, pursuant to the doctrine of *forum non conveniens*, courts may refuse to exercise their jurisdiction if, all things considered, a more appropriate (foreign) forum is available.[250]

It is undesirable, however, for a court to exercise too much restraint. After all, it is precisely the current restrictive interpretation of various jurisdictional doctrines that has prompted our inquiry into more expansive interpretations that give adequate consideration to substantive and procedural human rights.[251] Accordingly, opportunities for jurisdictional expansion rather than restraint may have to be explored. In this context, states may possibly even be under an *obligation* under international (human rights) law to exercise particular forms of jurisdiction over extraterritorial corporate abuses. Such an obligation could form part of extraterritorial state obligations in the context of business activities. For instance, in 2017, the UN Committee on Economic, Social and Cultural Rights, which monitors compliance with the eponymous UN Covenant, issued a General Comment on State Obligations in the Context of Business Activities, in which it stated that

[249] Regulation (EC) No 864/2007 of the European Parliament and of the Council of 11 July 2007 on the law applicable to non-contractual obligations (Rome II) [2007] OJ L199/40, art 32.

[250] See for the United Kingdom: *Spiliada Maritime Corporation v Cansulex Ltd.* [1987] AC 460. This is obviously not to say that human rights tort claims are particularly likely to be dismissed on *forum non conveniens* grounds. In *Connelly v RTZ Corporation plc* [1997] UKHL 30, a lawsuit filed in English courts by an employee of a English parent corporation's subsidiary in Namibia, who claimed that the parent breached its duty of care to ensure proper health and safety in the workplace, the House of Lords ruled that England was the appropriate forum as the case could not be heard in Namibian courts. Likewise, in *Lubbe & others v Cape plc.*, [2000] UKHL 41, the House of Lords allowed a case, brought against an English parent company by South African miners affected by asbestos, to proceed on the grounds that they risk a denial of substantive justice in South African courts. EU Member States (in practice the United Kingdom) can no longer rely on *forum non conveniens* in matters falling within the scope of the Brussels Convention. See Case C-281/02 *Andrew Owusu v N.B. Jackson, trading as 'Villa Holidays Bal-Inn Villas' and Others* [2005] ECR I-01383 (holding that the 'Brussels Convention precludes a court of a Contracting State from declining the jurisdiction conferred on it by Article 2 of that convention on the ground that a court of a non-Contracting State would be a more appropriate forum for the trial of the action even if the jurisdiction of no other Contracting State is in issue or the proceedings have no connecting factors to any other Contracting State'). After Brexit, *forum non conveniens* could possibly again be relied on.

[251] See also Roorda (n 187) 3.7.5 (regretting that in recent cases, '[c]onsiderations of access to justice and access to remedy abroad have . . . been pushed to the background').

> [t]he extraterritorial obligation to protect requires States parties to take steps to prevent and redress infringements of Covenant rights that occur outside their territories due to the activities of business entities over which they can exercise control, especially in cases where the remedies available to victims before the domestic courts of the State where the harm occurs are unavailable or ineffective.[252]

This debate is not yet settled[253] and need not be entered into here. Short of hard law extraterritorial obligations, it is in any event advisable policy for bystander states to open up their courts to victims of human rights abuses who cannot reasonably access host state courts. For the assumption of responsibility by a bystander state may be victims' only hope for remedies for corporate human rights abuses.

5.4.6 Concluding observations

This section has demonstrated that existing jurisdictional grounds in domestic codes of civil procedure hold particular promise for 'selfless intervention'. Third states can, and sometimes are even required, on the basis of principles of private international law, to provide a forum for tort claims alleging overseas corporate human rights abuses. Third state courts exercising such jurisdiction could be considered as 'cosmopolitan actors' who vindicate victims' right to a remedy, a global value laid down in international human rights instruments.

Such selfless intervention is not self-evident, however. Third states, in particular home states, have sometimes construed their jurisdiction narrowly, possibly out of a 'parochial' fear that doing otherwise would undermine the competitive position of locally-incorporated firms, would open the floodgates of litigation, would amount to interference in host state's affairs, or stunt foreign investment in developing countries.[254] Moreover, in more practical terms, victims may face particular

252 CESCR 'General comment No. 24 (2017) on State Obligations under the International Covenant on Economic, Social and Cultural Rights in the Context of Business Activities' (2017) UN Doc E/C.12/GC/24, para 30. See also para 44 on preventing denial of justice. See on such obligations also ETOs, 'Maastricht Principles on Extraterritorial Obligations in the Area of Economic, Social and Cultural Rights' (2011) https://www.etoconsortium.org/nc/en/main-navigation/library/maastricht-principles/?tx_drblob_pi1%5BdownloadUid%5D=23, in particular Principle 9, suggesting obligations for states 'in a position to exercise decisive influence or to take measures to realize economic, social and cultural rights extraterritorially, in accordance with international law'.

253 A later study by O'Brien has concluded that, as a matter of positive law, such obligations do not yet exist: engaging with the progressive literature, she argues, rather convincingly, that the authorities cited by the relevant scholars do not support the rule that states have extraterritorial obligations in the context of business activities. Claire O'Brien, 'The Home State Duty to Regulate the Human Rights Impacts of TNCs Abroad: A Rebuttal' (2018) 3 BHRJ 47. Legal authority regarding extraterritorial obligations indeed pertains primarily to instances of state military control abroad. Such control is ordinarily absent in the context of business activities, even if states may influence the overseas activities of their corporate nationals by concluding bilateral investment agreements, granting export credits, tax breaks, etc.

254 *Eg Jesner v Arab Bank, PLC*, No. 16-499, 584 US (2018) 24, citing Brief for United States as *Amicus Curiae* in *American Isuzu Motors, Inc. v Ntsebeza* (2007), No 07–919, 20 (ruling that holding foreign

obstacles accessing third state courts. Victims may not have the resources, connections, or knowledge to file lawsuits in third states, and may not able to gather sufficient evidence to convince a judge to rule in their favour. All this explains why there have been relatively few relevant court cases so far, let alone cases that have reached the merits stage.[255]

From a normative perspective, however, third states, alongside host states, may have to do more to ensure the right to a remedy for victims of human rights abuses. This right should inform broad interpretations of existing jurisdictional grounds and possibly give rise to the adoption of new grounds that have less of a territorial flavour. Ultimately, underlying all deliberations of courts hearing transnational business and human rights claims should be the double imperative of preventing a denial of justice, and preventing transnational corporations, because of their global structure, from evading accountability for their activities. Third states may have an enhanced responsibility in this respect to the extent that 'their' corporations have been able to reap the benefits of economic globalization.[256] States which have close connections with, and can exert a strong influence over the activities of transnational corporations are expected to assume leadership.[257] These states may even be considered as (morally) complicit in overseas corporate abuses to the extent that they fail to regulate their own corporations.[258] Such regulation includes offering remedies for victims of extraterritorial abuses, a crucial element of which is facilitating access to third state courts.

5.5 Extraterritoriality in the Internet Era—The Case of Data Protection

The spread of the Internet and communications technology has triggered debate as to who can regulate online activities.[259] As there is no international agreement on how to regulate these activities, let alone a global regulator, states prescribe their laws unilaterally to cross-border online activity that affects them, even if

corporations liable under the ATS may hinder 'global investment in developing economies, where it is most needed').

255 As the likelihood of success for transnational tort claims remains small, Parrish has observed that 'the illusion [is given] that serious steps are being taken, when in actuality little progress has been made'. *Contra* Parrish, 'Fading Extraterritoriality and Isolationism?' (n 191) 220.

256 Roorda (n 187) s 8.5.

257 See Maastricht Principles' (n 252) principle 9.

258 See in respect of corporate environmental abuses: Scott, 'The Global Reach' (n 196) 58 (stating that 'it seems highly probable that there are circumstances in which the EU's failure to take available steps to constrain environmental wrongdoing by EU corporations in third countries would constitute a complicit act').

259 Uta Kohl (ed), *The Net and the Multidisciplinary Perspectives on Internet Governance* (CUP 2017); D Svantesson, *Solving the Internet Jurisdiction Puzzle* (OUP 2017).

geographically locating such activity may prove challenging. As online activities tend to have links with multiple states, the exercise of jurisdiction tends to overlap and may even lead to international conflict.[260]

Questions of unilateral Internet jurisdiction rose to prominence in the late 1990s, especially after the seminal case involving US Internet service provider Yahoo. The *Yahoo* case concerned a US Internet service provider allowing the sale of Nazi memorabilia by online auction in violation of French law which prohibits wearing or exhibiting in public uniforms, insignia, and emblems recalling those used by the Nazis.[261] As the auction was also open to bidders based in France, and Yahoo specifically targeted French residents through advertisements, a French court established its jurisdiction over the case, and went on to order Yahoo to use geolocation technology to prevent French residents from accessing the auctions.[262] In so deciding, the French court did not consider the location of Yahoo's servers in the United States, or a clash with the freedom of speech as guaranteed by the US Constitution, to be relevant considerations.[263] The French decision epitomized how the exercise of unilateral jurisdiction over the deterritorialized Internet could be used to advance a state's particular value conceptions,[264] if perhaps not global value conceptions.

As the use of the Internet has increased dramatically since *Yahoo*, jurisdictional questions have become ever more important. It is not the aim of this part to give an overview of the various forms of unilateral jurisdiction over Internet-related matters. Others have already done so at great length.[265] As this monograph pertains to the 'selfless' exercise of unilateral jurisdiction with cosmopolitan overtones, that is, the exercise of jurisdiction to further extant or nascent global values or common interests, this monograph has opted to focus on online privacy, in particular data protection. The UN General Assembly has recognized the international right to

[260] Christopher Kuner, 'The Internet and the Global Reach of EU Law' in Marise Cremona and Joanne Scott (eds), *EU Law Beyond EU Borders. The Extraterritorial Reach of EU Law* (OUP 2019) 115.

[261] Article R645-1 French Penal Code ('Est puni de l'amende prévue pour les contraventions de la 5e classe le fait, sauf pour les besoins d'un film, d'un spectacle ou d'une exposition comportant une évocation historique, de porter ou d'exhiber en public un uniforme, un insigne ou un emblème rappelant les uniformes, les insignes ou les emblèmes qui ont été portés ou exhibés soit par les membres d'une organisation déclarée criminelle en application de l'article 9 du statut du tribunal militaire international annexé à l'accord de Londres du 8 août 1945, soit par une personne reconnue coupable par une juridiction française ou internationale d'un ou plusieurs crimes contre l'humanité.').

[262] Case No. RG: 00/05308, Association 'l'Union des Etudiant Juifs de France', la 'Ligue contre le Racisme et l'Antisemitisme' c. Yahoo! et Yahoo France [2000], 22 May 2000; Case No RG: 00/05308, Association 'l'Union des Etudiant Juifs de France', la 'Ligue contre le Racisme et l'Antisemitisme' c. Yahoo! et Yahoo France [2000], 20 November 2000.

[263] A US court later establish personal jurisdiction in a declaratory judgment action against the French NGOs which had sued Yahoo! in France, ruling that these NGOs caused harm to Yahoo! as the latter's servers were based in the US. *Yahoo! Inc. v La Ligue Contre Le Racisme et l'Antisemitisme*, 433 F 3d 1199 (9th Cir 2006).

[264] See Horatia Muir Watt, '*Yahoo*! Cyber-Collision Of Cultures: Who Regulates?' (2003) 24 Mich JIL 673.

[265] U Kohl, *Jurisdiction and the Internet* (CUP 2007); Svantesson, *Solving the Internet Jurisdiction Puzzle* (n 11).

privacy in the digital age as an international human right,[266] and has even appointed a special rapporteur on the right to privacy who specifically studies challenges arising from new technologies.[267] Derived from the right to privacy is the right to personal data protection. As early as 1988, in its General Comment on the Right to Privacy, the UN Human Rights Committee considered that '[t]he gathering and holding of personal information on computers, data banks and other devices, whether by public authorities or private individuals or bodies, must be regulated by law'.[268] Europe in particular, given its experiences with totalitarianism, has taken data protection issues very seriously.[269] In the European Union, it has been codified as a separate fundamental right in Article 8 of the EU Charter on Fundamental Rights. The European Union and its courts have not shrunk from giving its data protection legislation 'extraterritorial' application, or at least it has extended the territorial reach of its legislation to foreign service providers.[270]

This section focuses on the European Union as it is the international actor which has most aggressively pushed the geographic boundaries of data protection legislation.[271] It is argued that, while the EU's unilateralism in the field may not yet be firmly backed up by a global consensus on the specifics of personal data protection, data protection may be considered at least as an emerging global value (section 5.5.1). When exercising its jurisdiction, for example over foreign operators collecting data of EU subjects, the European Union has mainly relied on the territoriality principle (section 5.5.2). Spurred by its own courts, it has gone on to give relatively wide interpretations to the territorial reach of its data protection law, arguably on the grounds that data protection rises to the level of a fundamental right in the Union (section 5.5.2). This assertiveness has set the European Union on a collision course with foreign states and foreign-based operators (section 5.5.3). International tensions could be eased, however, by a reasonable 'extraterritorial' application of EU data protection law (section 5.5.4).[272]

[266] UNGA Res 68/167 (18 December 2013) UN Doc A/RES/68/167.

[267] See 'Special Rapporteur on the Right to Privacy' (UNCHR) https://www.ohchr.org/EN/Issues/Privacy/SR/Pages/SRPrivacyIndex.aspx.

[268] UNHRC 'General Comment No. 16: Article 17 (Right to Privacy): The Right to Respect of Privacy, Family, Home and Correspondence, and Protection of Honour and Reputation' (1988) UN Doc HRI/GEN/1/Rev.9. The NGO *Privacy International* later went on to derive a number of principles of data protection from regional and international frameworks. See '*A Guide for Policy Engagement on Data Protection. Part 3: Data Protection Principles*' (2018–19) Privacy International https://privacyinternational.org/sites/default/files/2018-09/Part%203%20-%20Data%20Protection%20Principles.pdf.

[269] The threat of totalitarianism is typically brandished in relation to (state) surveillance. See *eg* Bart Jacobs, 'Keeping our Surveillance Society Non-Totalitarian' (2009) 1 ALF 19.

[270] Case C-131/12 *Google Spain SL v Agencia Española de Protección de Datos (AEPD) and Mario Costeja González* [2014] ECLI:EU:C:2014:317.

[271] See for an overview Kuner, 'The Internet and the Global Reach' (n 260).

[272] I am partly indebted for this part to Dr Mistale Taylor, who successfully defended her PhD on the extraterritoriality of EU data protection law at Utrecht University in June 2018, in the framework of the UNIJURIS project of which I was the Principal Investigator. Mistale Taylor, 'Transatlantic Jurisdictional Conflicts in Data Protection Law: How the Fundamental Right to Data Protection Conditions the

This monograph's focus on data protection does not imply that global values do not or may not inform (the legitimacy of) other assertions of unilateral jurisdiction in the field of cyber regulation. One example taken from the criminal law is the exercise of unilateral enforcement jurisdiction by law-enforcement agencies (police, prosecutors) over evidence (data) located abroad, that is, jurisdiction that bypasses traditional cooperation through mutual legal assistance treaties, considered as too cumbersome. Such jurisdiction can take two forms: either the law-enforcement agency requires that a foreign service provider (*eg* Google or Yahoo) disclose data (*eg* relating to an email account),[273] or it carries out direct extraterritorial network searches, possibly using hacking-like techniques against foreign-based computers.[274] All this may happen without the explicit consent of the state on whose territory the data are located—if that state can be identified at all, given the reality of loss of data location in the Internet era. States increasingly exercise such jurisdiction, even if it remains controversial in light of the international law prohibition of extraterritorial enforcement jurisdiction.[275] Concerns over jurisdictional overreach may, however, be soothed insofar as the underlying crime is particularly grave and rises to the level of an international crime or treaty-based transnational offence. In such cases, the infringement on the sovereignty of the state on whose territory the data is located, may be considered to be less severe, and the exercise of enforcement jurisdiction (more) legitimate. Obviously,

European Union's Exercise of Extraterritorial Jurisdiction' (PhD thesis, Utrecht University 2018, forthcoming with CUP). Sections of this part have earlier been published as C Ryngaert and M Taylor, 'The *Global* Data Protection Regulation?', forthcoming AJIL Unbound 2020.

[273] See for the United States: the 2018 US Cloud Act—Clarifying Lawful Overseas Use of Data Act or CLOUD Act (HR 4943), amending the Stored Communications Act and the Electronic Communication Privacy Act. The adoption of the US CLOUD Act rendered moot a case on the issue which was pending before the Supreme Court. *United States v Microsoft Corp* 138 S Ct 1186, 1188 (2018). See for the appeals decisions disallowing the practice: *United States v Microsoft Corp* No 17-2, 2017 WL 2869958, at *1 (US 16 October 2017). See for the European Union: Proposal for a Regulation of the European Parliament and of the Council on European Production and Preservation Orders for Electronic Evidence in Criminal matters [2018] COM/2018/225 final—2018/0108 (COD). See for national case law, *eg* Belgian case law: Court of Cassation, 1 December 2015, P13.2082.N (upholding a prosecutor's order to Yahoo to disclose subscriber information relating to a Yahoo count, and rejecting a challenge that such an order amounted to an exercise of unlawful extraterritorial enforcement jurisdiction); Court of Cassation, 19 February 2019, P.17.1229.N/4 (upholding an investigative judge's warrant to compel Skype to set up a wiretap for a Skype phone call between suspects).

[274] *Eg* art 39 bis, § 3 and § 4 of the Belgian Criminal Code; art 125i, m, j of the Dutch Code of Criminal Procedure.

[275] The Convention on Cybercrime authorizes unilateral access without prior notification in art 32, but this provision is limited to two rather exceptional cases, namely in case the stored data are publicly available, and after consent by the person with lawful authority to disclose data. See for a potential amendment of the Convention: Cybercrime Convention Committee, 'Terms of Reference for the Preparation of a Draft 2nd Additional Protocol to the Budapest Convention on Cybercrime' (8 June 2017) T-CY (2017)3. See for a discussion on the extent to which unilateral cross-border access to data violates the prohibition of enforcement jurisdiction: Ahmed Ghappour, 'Searching Unknown Place: Law Enforcement Jurisdiction on the Dark Web' (2017) 69 SLR 1075; Ahmed Ghappour, 'Tallinn, Hacking, and Customary International Law' (2017) 111 AJILU 224, 225.

additional techniques of restraint could enhance the legitimacy of such jurisdiction still further.[276]

Whilst not gainsaying the conceptual potential of linking other types of Internet jurisdiction to a cosmopolitan discourse, the focus of this section, however, lies on the unilateral prescription of standards regarding data protection, a *fundamental right* and arguably a subspecies of the internationally recognized *human right* to privacy.

5.5.1 Data protection as an emerging global value

At first sight, it may appear to be a stretch to consider EU jurisdictional assertions regarding data protection as vindicating global values. After all, such assertions are normally aimed at protecting (the data pertaining to) EU citizens and residents rather than foreign persons. Moreover, they yield the application of idiosyncratic EU data protection law which may not give effect to a global normative consensus. While the EU Charter on Fundamental Rights contains a right to data protection, international human rights treaties such as the International Covenant on Civil and Political Rights (ICCPR) do not.[277] Nor is there a global instrument setting out data protection principles and standards. Thus, EU data protection norms and principles appear to be *regionally* rather than universally shared. This has led to normative conflicts with third countries, which may cherish rival values, such as freedom of speech, the free flow of information, or security concerns. Conflicts between the European Union and the United States (as well as US economic operators) have been widely documented and discussed, for example over the transfer of passenger name records,[278] the right to erasure ('right to be forgotten'),[279] and

[276] See *eg* European Parliament, Committee on Civil Liberties, Justice and Home Affairs, Study, 'Legal Frameworks for Hacking by Law Enforcement: Identification, Evaluation, and Comparison of Practices' (2017) PE 583.137.

[277] Art 8 of the EU Charter on Fundamental Rights provides as follows: '1. Everyone has the right to the protection of personal data concerning him or her. 2. Such data must be processed fairly for specified purposes and on the basis of the consent of the person concerned or some other legitimate basis laid down by law. Everyone has the right of access to data which has been collected concerning him or her, and the right to have it rectified. 3. Compliance with these rules shall be subject to control by an independent authority.'

[278] For a discussion, *eg* Maria Tzanou, 'The War Against Terror and Transatlantic Information Sharing: Spillovers of Privacy or Spillovers of Security?' (2015) (80) UJIEL 87; Valentin M Pfisterer, 'PNR in 2011: Recalling Ten Years of Transatlantic Cooperation in PNR Information Management' (2012) 2 NSACLR 111; Rocco Bellanova and Denis Duez, 'A Different View on the "Making" of European Security: The EU Passenger Name Record System as a Socio-Technical Assemblage' (2012) 17 EFAR 109.

[279] Regulation (EU) 2016/679 of the European Parliament and of the Council of 27 April 2016 on the protection of natural persons with regard to the processing of personal data and on the free movement of such data, and repealing Directive 95/46/EC (General Data Protection Regulation) [2016] OJ L/199, art 17. ('The data subject shall have the right to obtain from the controller the erasure of personal data concerning him or her without undue delay and the controller shall have the obligation to erase personal data without undue delay where one of the following grounds applies.'). There are a number of publications on the international conflicts engendered by the 'extraterritorial application' of the right

the EU–US transfer of data by commercial providers.[280] The CJEU, which has repeatedly emphasized the importance of data protection in the face of countervailing considerations, has played no small part in fanning the flames of such conflicts, *eg* when rendering its judgments in *Google Spain* (concerning the right to erasure)[281] and *Schrems* (concerning the protection of data by the EU–US Safe Harbour Agreement),[282] or when it considered parts of the EU–Canada passenger names records agreement to be incompatible with EU fundamental rights.[283]

Nevertheless, the normative environment of EU data protection law is not exactly empty. There is a Council of Europe Convention for the Protection of Individuals with regard to Automatic Processing of Personal Data (Convention 108), which has just been modernized,[284] and counts fifty-three ratifications or accessions. Also, the ECtHR has considered the protection of a person's data to be an aspect of his right to privacy.[285] In addition, according to Graham Greenleaf's study, 120 states have national data protection (or 'data privacy') laws.[286] Even if the substantive protection offered by these laws may not be comparable to that offered by EU law,[287] there seems to be an international tendency to protect individual persons' data. Therefore, data protection could be characterized as an *emerging global value* the crystallization of which may be boosted by its characterization as

to erasure after the CJEU's judgment in *Google Spain* (n 270). See *eg* Brendan Van Alsenoy and Marieke Koekkoek, 'Internet and Jurisdiction after *Google Spain*: The Extraterritorial Reach of the 'Right to be Delisted' (2015) 5 IDPL 105; Dan JB Svantesson, 'The Google Spain case: Part of a harmful trend of jurisdictional overreach' (2015) European University Institute Robert Schuman Centre for Advanced Studies Research Paper No RSCAS 2015/45.

280 Christopher Kuner, *Transborder Data Flows and Data Privacy Law* (OUP 2013).

281 *Google Spain* (n 270).

282 Case C-362/14, *Maximilian Schrems v Data Protection Commissioner* [2015] ECLI:EU:C:2015:650, para 106 (declaring the Commission's 2000 adequacy decision invalid as US security and law enforcement considerations could override data protection principles laid down in the Safe Harbour agreement); para 94 (US 'legislation permitting the public authorities to have access on a generalised basis to the content of electronic communications must be regarded as compromising the essence of the fundamental right to respect for private life'). See for Safe Harbour: US Department of Commerce, 'U.S.–EU Safe Harbor Framework Guide to Self-Certification', 10–14 http://trade.gov/media/publications/pdf/safeharbor-selfcert2009.pdf.

283 Opinion 1/15, *Draft agreement between Canada and the European Union—Transfer of Passenger Name Record data from the European Union to Canada* [2017] ECLI:EU:C:2017:592.

284 On 18 May 2018, the 128th Ministerial Session of the Council of Europe's Committee of Ministers adopted the Protocol (CETS No. 223) amending the Convention for the Protection of Individuals with regard to Automatic Processing of Personal Data (ETS No 108) and endorsed its Explanatory Report. The Protocol has been open for signature since 25 June 2018.

285 *S and Marper v United Kingdom* [2008] Applications nos 30562/04 and 30566/04, 4 December 2008 ('The protection of personal data is of fundamental importance to a person's enjoyment of his or her right to respect for private and family life.').

286 Graham Greenleaf, 'Global Data Privacy Laws 2017: 120 National Data Privacy Laws, Including Indonesia and Turkey' (2017) 145 PL & B International Report, 10–13 https://papers.ssrn.com/sol3/papers.cfm?abstract_id=2992986 (accessed on 6 December 2019).

287 See on non-Western countries also Payal Arora, *The Next Billion Users. Digital Life Beyond the West* (HUP 2019) (arguing that new, poorer users in the Global South are willing to trade privacy for cheap online access).

a fundamental right in Europe. This elevated status implies that data protection is not considered as just a public policy goal, but instead, at least in the European view, inheres in the human being as it aims to protect human dignity. Regardless of the largely regional character of the right, this renders data protection a candidate for recognition at the global level.[288] Thus, Christopher Kuner writes that 'data protection law should be oriented towards the protection of universal values, and not just those that are local or national', adding that '[t]his should be seen not as a weakening of local values, but as a strengthening of fundamental rights at a global level'.[289] The EU's data protection 'norm entrepreneurship',[290] backed up by its strong market power vis-à-vis foreign economic operators, may serve as the bridge between the local and the global.[291] In due course, this may lead to

[288] See in a transatlantic context: Working Party on the Protection of Individuals with regard to the Processing of Personal Data, 'Opinion 1/99 concerning the level of data protection in the United States and the ongoing discussions between the European Commission and the United States Government (26 January 1999) 5092/98/EN/final WP 15, 1 http://ec.europa.eu/justice/data-protection/article-29/documentation/opinion-recommendation/files/1999/wp15_en.pdf ('Data protection rules are not only intended to protect users of new technologies [but] express also the adherence to a certain number of fundamental principles and rights based on a common culture of respect for privacy and other values that are inherent in the human being and which is shared equally by the Member States of the European Union and the United States.').

[289] Kuner, Transborder Data Flows (n 280) 183. ibid, 159 (arguing that '[t]here is tension between the nature of transborder data flow regulation as a topic of inherently global significance, and the fact that many States and regional organizations treat it mainly as a vehicle for exporting their own standards and values').

[290] See for seminal literature on norm entrepreneurship: Cass Sunstein, 'Social Norms and Social Roles' (1996) 96 Col LR 903; Martha Finnemore and Kathryn Sikkink, 'International Organization at Fifty: Exploration and Contestation in the Study of World Politics' (1998) 52 Int'l Org 887, 916 (describing 'how people's ideas about what is good and what "should be" in the world become translated into political reality'). Finnemore and Sikkink famously adopted the term 'norm cascade' to describe the diffusion of norms. ibid, at 902 ('After the tipping point ... [m]ore countries begin to adopt new norms more rapidly even without domestic pressure for such change. Empirical studies suggest that, at this point, often an international or regional demonstration effect or "contagion" occurs in which international and transnational norm influences become more important than domestic politics for effecting norm change.').

[291] Kuner, Transborder Data Flows (n 280) 186–87 (submitting that the European Union has become an actor promoting the 'universality of fundamental rights' through 'the application of local values outside national borders'). Notably the art 29 Working Party, *ie*, the EU advisory body on data protection, has actively promoted the data protection legislation outside the European Union. See art 29 Working Party and the Working Party on Police and Justice, 'The Future of Privacy Joint contribution to the Consultation of the European Commission on the legal framework for the fundamental right to protection of personal data' (2009), para 31 http://ec.europa.eu/justice/data-protection/article-29/documentation/opinion-recommendation/files/2009/wp168_en.pdf (calling upon the European Commission, '[i]n the absence of global standards, to promote the development of data protection legislation providing an adequate level of protection ... in countries outside the European Union'); art 29 Working Party, 'Opinion 10/2006 on the processing of personal data by the Society for Worldwide Interbank Financial Telecommunication (SWIFT)' (22 November 2006) 01935/06/EWP128, 28 http://ec.europa.eu/justice/data-protection/article-29/documentation/opinion-recommendation/files/2006/wp128_en.pdf (submitting that it is 'essential' that EU data protection principles be 'fully respected in any framework of global systems of exchange of information'). Also the Commission has donned the cloak of data protection norm entrepreneur. See European Commission, 'Communication from the Commission to the European Parliament and the Council on Exchanging and Protecting Personal Data in a Globalised World' (10 January 2017) COM 2017/7 final, 2 and 16 https://ec.europa.eu/newsroom/document.cfm?doc_id=41157 (acknowledging that world consumers 'increasingly cherish and value

internalization or socialization by the 'receiving' operators and the third countries where they are located. Following a normative rationality or a logic of appropriateness, these operators and countries may redefine their identities and interests,[292] and accept data protection as a norm or fundamental right,[293] following EU data protection legislation as the gold standard.[294] The remarkable spread of data protection over the last few years[295] appears to be testimony to this process. It bears emphasis, however, that internal dynamics in third countries will play a major role in adopting and crafting data protection principles. Third countries' agency may lead to selective diffusion, differential adaptation, cultural translation, and even resistance to some interpretations,[296] especially in cases where the European Union has little direct influence over third countries such as the United States[297] (which they *may* have vis-à-vis countries that are candidates for EU membership or EU association). Regardless of legislative variation, in due course, basic principles of data protection may be identified, allowing for the characterization of data protection as a global value, even in the absence of an international agreement on data protection.[298]

their privacy', and that the European Union should 'strive to seek greater upward convergence of data protection principles internationally [and the Commission will take measures to] develop high personal data protection standards globally', while mentioning the modernization of Council of Europe Convention No 108).

[292] cf Tanja A Börzel and Thomas Risse, 'From Europeanisation to Diffusion: Introduction' (2012) 35 WEP 1, 5.

[293] This may happen via 'harmonization networks'. See Paul M Schwartz and Karl-Nikolaus Peifer, 'Transatlantic Data Privacy' (2017) 106 GELJ 115, 174. See also US FTC Commissioner Julie Brill, 'Keynote Address at the Amsterdam Privacy Conference' (2015) 9 https://www.ftc.gov/system/files/documents/public_statements/836443/151023amsterdamprivacy1.pdf (stating that the CJEU's decision in *Schrems* 'may, in the longer term, help restart efforts in the United States to put in place stronger privacy and data security laws that will benefit all').

[294] See Giovanni Buttarelli, 'The EU GDPR as a Clarion Call for a New Global Digital Gold Standard' (2016) 6 IDPL 77.

[295] See Greenleaf (n 286) 14–26.

[296] Börzel and Risse (n 292) 204.

[297] See *eg* in the context of EU–US data transfers after the *Schrems* decision: HR 1428 (114th): Judicial Redress Act of 2015 Sec. 2(1)(c) (authorizing a state to be included on the list of those whose citizens may obtain redress in the United States according to the Privacy Act if it permits US companies to transfer personal data from that state's territory to the United States and if the transfer arrangements 'do not materially impede the national security interests of the United States'). Pursuant to this Act, security may still trump data protection regarding the EU residents whose data have been transferred to the United States. See also European Commission press release, 'Article 29 Working Party Statement on the decision of the European Commission on the EU–U.S. Privacy Shield' (2016) http://ec.europa.eu/justice/data-protection/article-29/press-material/press (regretting 'the lack of concrete assurances' that the collection of 'mass amounts of data without discriminants' does not take place).

[298] See for a normative argument: Siva Vaidhyanathan, *Antisocial Media: How Facebook Disconnects Us and Undermines Democracy* (OUP 2018) 216 ('The least we should is embrace European-style data protection laws worldwide ... Other major states such as Brazil, India, Australia, Canada, Mexico, Japan, and the United States should follow and model data protection laws after the European Union's.').

5.5.2 The (extra-)territoriality of EU data protection legislation

While EU data protection legislation does not explicitly feature a jurisdictional clause, its jurisdictional reach can be derived from the provisions governing its scope of application. These provisions, as interpreted by EU courts, bear out that EU data protection jurisdiction is largely based on the *territoriality* principle. Still, such jurisdiction, while not as such extraterritorial, clearly has extraterritorial effects as it affects persons and conduct outside the European Union.[299]

The EU Data Protection Directive (DPD, no longer in force) provided that the DPD applied where 'the processing is carried out in the context of the activities of an establishment of the controller on the territory of [a] Member State', and even if 'the controller is not established on Community territory', but 'for purposes of processing personal data makes use of equipment, automated or otherwise, situated on the territory' of an EU Member State.[300] In its 2014 *Google Spain* judgment, the CJEU famously relied on this provision to subject US-based Internet intermediary Google to the DPD, holding that

> the processing of personal data for the purposes of the service of a search engine such as Google Search, which is operated by an undertaking that has its seat in a third State but has an establishment in a Member State, is carried out 'in the context of the activities' of that establishment if the latter is intended to promote and sell, in that Member State, advertising space offered by the search engine which serves to make the service offered by that engine profitable.[301]

The Court added that

> [i]n such circumstances, the activities of the operator of the search engine and those of its establishment situated in the Member State concerned are inextricably linked since the activities relating to the advertising space constitute the means of rendering the search engine at issue economically profitable and that engine is, at the same time, the means enabling those activities to be performed.[302]

[299] Compare also Kuner, 'The Internet and the Global Reach' (n 260) 124 ('With regard to EU data protection law, it is less important to categorize the exact form of extraterritoriality used, than to recognize that it exerts its influence in different ways on persons and activities in third countries.').

[300] Directive 95/46/EC of the European Parliament and of the Council of 24 October 1995 on the Protection of Individuals with Regard to the Processing of Personal Data and on the Free Movement of Such Data [1995] OJ L/281, art 4(1).

[301] *Google Spain* (n 270) para 55. The Court applied art 4.1(a) DPD (n 300) which provides that '[e]ach Member State shall apply the national provisions it adopts pursuant to this Directive to the processing of personal data where: (a) the processing is carried out in the context of the activities of an establishment of the controller on the territory of the Member State'). See also art 3.1 GDPR ('This Regulation applies to the processing of personal data in the context of the activities of an establishment of a controller or a processor in the Union, regardless of whether the processing takes place in the Union or not.').

[302] ibid para 56.

Pursuant to the very terms of Article 4(1)(c) DPD, as interpreted by the CJEU, data jurisdiction over foreign operators is clearly based on territoriality.

The General Data Protection Regulation (GDPR), which currently constitutes the EU data protection legal framework, applies to

> the processing of personal data of data subjects who are in the Union by a controller or processor not established in the Union, where the processing activities are related to: (a) the offering of goods or services ... to such data subjects in the Union; or (b) the monitoring of their behaviour ... within the Union.

GDPR may appear to be less explicitly based on territoriality because it emphasizes the EU *residence* of persons 'targeted' by foreign operators.[303] Nevertheless, the relevant provision bears the title 'territorial scope'. Moreover, the term 'data subjects in the Union' almost necessarily refers to those who reside on EU territory, even if they do not have an EU nationality. Residence has a clear territorial dimension. Therefore, also after the entry into force of the GDPR, jurisdiction in the field EU data protection law remains largely based on territoriality. In practice, the territorial nexus of the regulated activity with the European Union may be relatively weak, for example, a foreign operator's use of tracking cookies in the European Union, which track a user's browsing habits, typically for marketing purposes, may suffice to apply EU data protection law.[304]

The EU's jurisdictional assertions may not appear to be 'cosmopolitan', as through the territoriality and residence principles, they aim at ensuring the broadest protection possible for *EU residents* (in practice largely EU citizens), in the context of transfers of EU subjects' data to substandard jurisdictions,[305] or of third-country operators targeting EU subjects.[306] As practices of EU territorial extension do not aim at raising the level of data protection for *non-EU residents*, it may be a stretch to posit that the European Union acts 'selflessly' and is intent on normatively shaping the world.[307] Still, higher data protection for non-EU residents may follow from third countries and corporations aligning their laws and

303 GDPR Regulation (n 279) art 3(2).

304 See notably art 4(1)(c) DPD (n 300); art 29 Working Party, 'Opinion 8/2010 on Applicable Law (16 December 2010) 0836-02/10/EN WP 179, 21; Rechtbank van Eerste Aanleg Brussel, *Voorzitter van de Belgische Commissie voor de bescherming van de persoonlijke levenssfeer v Facebook Ireland Limited*, 26 February 2018, AR/2016/153-A (herafter *Voorzitter van de Belgische Commissie voor de bescherming van de persoonlijke levenssfeer v Facebook Ireland Limited)*; Scott, 'The Global Reach' (n 196) 39 (stating in this context that 'the EU is relying upon a novel and flimsy territorial connection').

305 Art 45(1) GDPR (n 279) ('A transfer of personal data to a third country or an international organisation may take place where the Commission has decided that the third country, a territory or one or more specified sectors within that third country, or the international organisation in question ensures an adequate level of protection.'

306 Art 3(2) GDPR (n 279).

307 See also Joanne Scott, 'Extraterritoriality and Territorial Extension in EU Law' (2014) 62 Am J Comp L 87.

practices with EU law, a tendency which may be nurtured by the long arm of EU law,[308] the success of which however depends on normative socialization and EU bargaining power.[309] The territorial extension of the right to erasure post-*Google Spain*,[310] as well as EU Commission adequacy decisions conditioning the transfer of data from the European Union to third countries,[311] may indeed allow for the migration of EU data protection principles abroad. Accordingly, while EU unilateralism is not exactly selfless intervention, as a form of 'consequentialist cosmopolitanism', or 'Brussels effect',[312] it may shape global values and affect data privacy rights elsewhere.

5.5.3 Extraterritorial obligations

That data protection rises to the level of a fundamental right in the European Union may persuade other states to consider the adoption of data protection legislation, but it may also give rise to particular obligations for the European Union itself to protect the right to data protection extraterritorially. Precisely because data protection is a fundamental right, the European Union may have extraterritorial obligations to respect, protect, and fulfil that right, even if primarily to safeguard EU data subjects' interests. Accordingly, giving a wide geographic scope to data protection legislation may not be a discretionary choice for the European Union but instead be *required by law*.

Unlike some international human rights treaties such as the ICCPR or the ECHR, the EU Charter on Fundamental Rights does not have a limiting jurisdictional clause. Instead, the geographic scope of a fundamental right follows

[308] *Eg* Facebook CEO Zuckerberg stated that the GDPR protections would in spirit (although not necessarily in detail) extend worldwide. 'Facebook refuses to promise GDPR-style privacy protection for US users', The Guardian, 4 April 2018. See also Council Decision of 3 December 2011 on the signing, on behalf of the union, of the Agreement on the Use and Transfer of Passenger Name Records (PNR) to the US Department of Homeland Security (DHS) [2012] OJ L215/1, 13, which provides for judicial redress for EU data subjects *in the United States*.

[309] Relatively weak EU bargaining power may result in agreements between the European Union and third countries which insufficiently EU subjects' data transferred abroad. See *eg* CJEU, *Opinion 1-15 on EU-Canada PNR Agreement* [2017] ECLI:EU:C:2017:592, para 232 (ruling that parts of the agreement did not comply with the EU fundamental rights to respect for private life and protection of personal data). It is likely that also the EU–US PNR Agreement (see previous footnote) violates EU fundamental rights. Such agreements would have to be renegotiated to make them compatible with EU fundamental rights law. See on various mechanisms of global reach of EU data protection law: Kuner, 'The Internet and the Global Reach' (n 260) 130–34.

[310] See on this term: Scott, 'Extraterritoriality and Territorial Extension in EU Law' (n 307).

[311] GDPR (n 279) art 45(1) ('A transfer of personal data to a third country or an international organisation may take place where the Commission has decided that the third country, a territory or one or more specified sectors within that third country, or the international organisation in question ensures an adequate level of protection.')

[312] The Brussels effect is defined as the 'unprecedented and deeply underestimated global power that the EU is exercising through its legal institutions and standards' which 'it successfully exports . . . to the rest of the world'. See Anu Bradford, 'The Brussels Effect' (2012) 107 NULR 1.

the scope of the competences of the European Union and the application of the EU law.[313] The absence of a jurisdictional clause may pose fewer doctrinal limitations to the extraterritorial application of the Charter. Thus, it may inform the application of a 'control' standard that is more relaxed as compared to the control standards used by notably the ECHR to delineate the extraterritorial application of that Court. Given the 'virtual' nature of threats to data protection, application of a functional 'virtual' control standard may be apt.[314] This means that, insofar as the EU exercises virtual control over an EU resident's data, it incurs extraterritorial obligations. More specifically, insofar as the European Union has the capacity to influence how an EU resident's data are treated abroad, it should harness this influence to have her data respected and protected. The European Union should refrain from giving assistance to (extraterritorial) third parties' breaches (duty to respect), and should prevent such parties from committing breaches (duty to protect). This implies that the European Union should construe EU data protection legislation in such a way that it safeguards EU residents' fundamental right to data protection against encroachment by third states and third state-based operators. In practice, the European Union may have to make sure that decisions and agreements on the transfer of data from the European Union to third countries contain adequate data protection guarantees, and that foreign-based data controllers and processors targeting EU residents sufficiently protect the latter's data. All this may also explain why the CJEU has, in a string of well-known cases with a transatlantic dimension, such as *Google Spain*,[315] *Schrems*,[316] and *Canada–EU PNR*,[317] so strongly emphasized the right to data protection over countervailing interests, such as security and the free flow of information. Thereby, the CJEU forced the European Union to renegotiate agreements with third countries, or forced foreign-based data controllers targeting the EU market to enhance the protection of EU residents' data.

5.5.4 Data protection extraterritoriality and international conflict

Given its wide geographic scope, the 'extraterritoriality' of EU data protection legislation or, rather, its territorial extension, risks conflict with third states. Third states may claim that they have an equally strong, or even stronger link to a situation than the European Union does. For instance, the United States may claim that it is entitled, on security grounds, to request name records of passengers boarding

313 Violeta Moreno-Lax and Cathryn Costello, 'The Extraterritorial Application of the EU Charter of Fundamental Rights: From Territoriality to Facticity, the Effectiveness Model' in Steve Peers and others (eds), *The EU Charter of Fundamental Rights: A Commentary* (Hart Publishing 2014) 1662.
314 Taylor (n 272) 3.5.3.
315 *Google Spain* (n 270).
316 *Maximilian Schrems v Data Protection* (n 282).
317 *Opinion 1-15* (n 309).

aircraft bound for the United States. It is not self-evident that the European Union, wishing to protect these passengers' data adequately, necessarily has the stronger jurisdictional link. Ultimately, the EU–US stand-off over these records was resolved on the basis of a passenger names records (PNR) agreement. Regardless of whether an agreement with a third country could be envisaged,[318] it is in any event advisable for the European Union to take into account the legitimate interests of third countries. This mitigation exercise may be walking a fine line, as at the same time, the European Union is required to guarantee the protection of EU residents' data, also in an extraterritorial context.

As it happens, data protection is a field in which unilateral assertions of jurisdiction have not often met with foreign sovereign protest. This state of affairs may raise the impression that such assertions are considered lawful and reasonable under customary international law. An explanation for the absence of foreign sovereign protest is that such assertions are often brought to bear on private operators controlling and processing data. Typically, these operators have strong economic clout and may be viewed by foreign governments as being able to fend for themselves, that is, being able to protest unlawful or unreasonable jurisdictional assertions on their own, without foreign sovereign intervention. Doctrinally speaking, however, private actors' protest at a state's or the EU's jurisdictional assertion does not 'count' for the determination of the lawfulness of such assertions under customary international law. After all, for customary law to crystallize then *state* practice is required. Nevertheless, there are some instances of states—notably the United States—voicing concerns over the extraterritoriality of EU data protection legislation, although it is not always clear whether their concerns amount to protest on legal grounds. For instance, while the United States undeniably resisted the EU's attempts to have EU data protection law applied to the PNR transfer from the European Union to the United States, it is doubtful whether this resistance was based on a perception that the application of EU law to PNR amounted to an unlawful exercise of prescriptive jurisdiction. Similarly, with respect to data transfers, while the US may have opposed the inclusion of strong EU-style data protection norms in the US–EU Safe Harbour and its post-*Schrems* Privacy Shield,[319] it may

[318] See on EU–US agreements and procedures in the field of privacy: Paul Schwartz, 'The EU–US Privacy Collision: A Turn to Institutions and Procedures' (2013) 126 HLR 1966.

[319] See *eg* US Mission to the European Union, 'Statement From U.S. Secretary of Commerce Penny Pritzker on EU–U.S. Privacy Shield' (2016) https://www.commerce.gov/news/press-releases/2016/02/statement-us-secretary-commerce-penny-pritzker-eu-us-privacy-shield (arguing that giving EU data protection law a broad scope would significantly impede upon individual rights and the free flow of information). See on the Privacy Shield: Commission Implementing Decision (EU) 2016/1250 of 12 July 2016 pursuant to Directive 95/46/EC of the European Parliament and of the Council on the adequacy of the protection provided by the EU–U.S. Privacy Shield (notified under document C(2016) 4176) [2016] C/2016/4176, OJ L 207, 1.8.2016, 1–112, see 48–67; Commission Implementing Decision of 12 July 2016 pursuant to Directive 95/46/EC of the European Parliament and of the Council on the adequacy of the protection provided by the EU–US Privacy Shield, Brussels [2016] (COM 2016) 4176 final http://ec.europa.eu/justice/data-protection/files/privacy-shield-adequacy-decision_en.pdf.

not necessarily have viewed the extension of EU law to US-bound data transfers as unlawful.[320]

5.5.5 Reasonableness

While the United States may not necessarily have deemed EU assertions unlawful, it may have considered them to be unreasonable because they interfere in its capacity to regulate or condone activities which have strong links with its territory or have been carried out from its territory. Moreover, reasonableness, in line with private international law thinking, may require that not only foreign sovereign protest is taken into account, but in fact a host of factors, including the legitimate expectations and interests of private actors,[321] as they have been vigorously defended by the likes of Google or Facebook.[322]

It is good practice in this respect to take into account solicit input from third countries potentially affected by EU data protection legislation. As Kuner has observed, unfortunately impact assessments in the field of Internet legislation tend to focus on impact in the European Union itself.[323] Relatedly, the European Union may want to assist third countries and third country operators when seeking compliance with EU data protection legislation.[324] This could occur via capacity-building or advisory services offered by the European Union.[325] It should be borne in mind that lack of knowledge of the GDPR, or uncertainty as to its interpretation, may confuse third country operators and cause them not to enter the EU market

320 See also Taylor (n 272). In *Schrems II*, an Irish judge authorized the US government to file an *amicus curiae* brief in support of Facebook. It remains to be seen what position the US will exactly take in this case. The High Court Commercial Ireland, [2016 no. 4809] *Data Protection Commissioner v Facebook Ireland Limited and Maximillian Schrems* [2017] para 19 ('The United States has a significant and *bona fide* interest in the outcome of these proceedings. At issue in the proceedings is the assessment, as a matter of EU law, of the applicant's law governing the treatment of EU citizens' data transfer to the United States. The imposition of restrictions on the transfer of such data would have potentially considerable adverse effects on EU–US commerce and could affect US companies significantly'). In *Schrems II*, Schrems has requested that the Irish Data Protection Commissioner halt data transfers between Facebook Ireland and Facebook Inc. on the basis of Standard Contractual Clauses, on the ground that the relevant data may be subject to US mass surveillance in violation of EU data protection law.

321 Thus, section 403(2) of the Restatement (Third) of US Foreign Relations Law, provides that whether exercise of jurisdiction over a person or activity is unreasonable is determined by, *inter alia*, '(b) the connections, such as nationality, residence, or economic activity, between the regulating state and the person principally responsible for the activity to be regulated, or between that state and those whom the regulation is designed to protect; ... (d) the existence of justified expectations that might be protected or hurt by the regulation'.

322 See eg *Voorzitter van de Belgische Commissie voor de bescherming van de persoonlijke levenssfeer v Facebook Ireland Limited* (n 304); 'Google takes right to be forgotten battle to France's highest court', The Guardian 19 May 2016.

323 Kuner, 'The Internet and the Global Reach' (n 260) 141–42.

324 ibid, 142.

325 Christopher Kuner and others, 'The GDPR as a Chance to Break Down Borders' (2017) 7 IDPL 231, 232.

for fear of incurring high penalties.[326] Not only may foreign operators forfeit legitimate economic opportunities, EU residents may be denied access to useful information.[327] Accordingly, it may also be in the EU's interest to assist third countries and their operators.

In addition, the European Union may want to show lenience or reasonableness in the application of data protection legislation in respect of foreign countries and operators. Applying the principle of reasonableness, the European Union could for instance satisfy itself with third countries and third country operators complying with the basic thrust of EU data protection legislation, rather than with all manner of detailed rules.[328] The Commission's adequacy decisions per article 45 GDPR, in the context of data transfers to third countries, could play a major role in this respect, as they allow for the recognition of equivalent rather than identical data protection legislation. Much depends of course on how the Commission interprets the criteria set forth in article 45(2) GDPR:[329] how high or low does it set the bar? If in the future, global and regional agreements on data protection expand, both qualitatively and quantitatively, and data protection becomes a true *global value*, the work of the Commission may be eased, as states parties to such agreements, provided that these offer high standards of protection, may be presumed to offer adequate protection. It is no surprise that article 45(2)(c) GDPR stipulates that when assessing the adequacy of the level of protection, the Commission shall take into account, 'the international commitments the third country or international organisation concerned has entered into, or other obligations arising from legally binding conventions or instruments as well as from its participation in multilateral or regional systems, in particular in relation to the protection of personal data'. Thus, the rise of the value of data protection to the level of a global value may not

[326] See *eg* GDPR (n 279) Article 83(6) ('Non-compliance with an order by the supervisory authority as referred to in Article 58(2) shall, in accordance with paragraph 2 of this Article, be subject to administrative fines up to 20 000 000 EUR, or in the case of an undertaking, up to 4% of the total worldwide annual turnover of the preceding financial year, whichever is higher.').

[327] *Eg* the Dutch newspaper NRC Handelsblad reported that hundreds of US (news) sites remained inaccessible after the entry into force of the GDPR, over concerns that the use of tracker cookies would violate the GDPR. NRC Handelsblad, 'Honderden Amerikaanse sites nog steeds op zwart in Europa' NRC Handelsblad (7 August 2018). The newspaper quoted a lecturer of American studies at Leiden University who stated that students now can no longer write their thesis on, for example, the Los Angeles Times' coverage during the Second World War. 'Honderden Amerikaanse Sites Weren EU-burgers', *NRC Handelsblad* (8 August 2018).

[328] Compare Article 29 Working Party, Opinion 8/2010 (n 304) (suggesting the application of only basic principles of EU data protection law, such as security and legitimacy, in case an act has only very weak links with the EU). See also Christopher Kuner, 'Extraterritoriality and Regulation of International Data Transfers in EU Data Protection Law' (2015) IDPL 235, 243 (arguing that parts of data protection law 'could be seen to constitute the "essence" of the fundamental right of data protection and should thus be presumed to apply extraterritorially'). Obviously, foreign lobbying efforts could play a major role in this respect. See regarding foreign (US) lobbying of EU institutions with respect to the ePrivacy Directive: 'The Next Privacy Battle in Europe Is Over This New Law' New York Times (27 May 2018) (stating that Cisco, Facebook, Google, IBM, Microsoft, SAP, the American Chamber of Commerce, have all lobbied officials at the European Commission about ePrivacy).

[329] GDPR (n 279) Article 45(2).

only serve to legitimize the EU's data protection expansive unilateralism. It may also serve as a tool of jurisdictional restraint, provided that third countries have committed themselves to this global value. The cynic may obviously observe that the mentioned conventions and instruments will only be accepted insofar as their content mirrors EU preferences regarding the level of data protection.

In another example, it may be *unreasonable* for the European Union or for national data protection agencies supervising compliance with the GDPR, to require *global implementation* of the right to erasure.[330] Global implementation means that the relevant search results are delisted *everywhere*, on all versions of the search engine (*eg* Google), also if accessed outside the European Union.[331] It may be more reasonable to require implementation *in the European Union only*, that is, on all versions of the search engine accessed from EU territory (although perhaps not only on versions of the search engine accessed in the state from which the data subject requested delisting, as was Google's position at one point).[332] This does not exclude that EU-based users can view non-redacted results via virtual private networks, or that non-EU-based users can view them via regular channels, but that may be the price to pay for reasonableness. This solution protects EU residents' right to erasure in the European Union while allowing third states (such as the US) to guarantee the free flow of information for their own residents, unencumbered by delisting of search results.[333] The CJEU has, more or less, followed this reasoning in *Google v CNIL* (2019), in which the Grand Chamber held that an operator like Google 'is not required to carry out that de-referencing on all versions of its search engine, but on the versions of that search engine corresponding to all the Member States'.[334] The Court grounded this jurisdictional restraint *inter alia* on

[330] See for a jurisdictional reasonableness-informed discussion of the right to erasure: van Alsenoy and Koekkoek (n 279).

[331] In favour of global implementation: Article 29 Data Protection Working Party, 'Guidelines on the implementation of the Court of Justice of the European Union judgment on Google Spain inc v Agencia Española de Protección de Datos (AEPD) and Mario Costeja González' (2014) C-131/12, 2 ('[D]e-listing decisions must be implemented in a way that guarantees the effective and complete protection of these rights and that EU law cannot be easily circumvented ... In practice, this means that in any case de-listing should also be effective on all relevant domains, including .com.'); Supreme Court of Canada, *Google Inc v Equustek Solutions Inc* [2017] 1 SCR 824, para 47 (herafter *Google Inc v Equustek Solutions Inc)* ('it hardly seems equitable to deny Equustek the extraterritorial scope it needs to make the remedy effective ... We are dealing with the Internet after all, and the balance of convenience test has to take full account of its inevitable extraterritorial reach when injunctive relief is being sought against an entity like Google.').

[332] Peter Fleischer, 'Adapting our approach to the European right to be forgotten' (blog, 2016) <https://europe.googleblog.com/2016/03/adapting-our-approach-to-european-right.html>. See on Google's position also *Equustek Solutions Inc., v Jack*, 2018 BCSC 610 ('Google has now changed its system so that it now delivers search results based by default on the user's location, regardless of the Google URL the user enters. That means website delisting would continue to be effective for all users identified as being in Canada, unless those users took specific steps to alter the settings on their computers.').

[333] See also Taylor (n 272) 7.6.

[334] Case C-507/17 *Google LLC v Commission Nationale de l'Informatique et des Libertés (CNIL)* [2014] September 2019 (Grand Chamber), ECLI:EU:C:2019:772, para 73 (adding, however: 'using, where necessary, measures which, while meeting the legal requirements, effectively prevent or, at the very least, seriously discourage an internet user conducting a search from one of the Member States on the basis

the fact that 'numerous third States do not recognise the right to de-referencing or have a different approach to that right', and that 'the balance between the right to privacy and the protection of personal data, on the one hand, and the freedom of information of internet users, on the other, is likely to vary significantly around the world'.[335] However, the Court did not exclude global implementation in specific circumstances, when ruling that while 'EU law does not currently require that the de-referencing granted concern all versions of the search engine in question, it also does not prohibit such a practice'.[336] A case-by-case, reasonableness-informed analysis will thus be required.[337]

Also the US/Canadian *Equustek v Google* litigation (2017) shows that, especially when delisting orders made by one state (Canada in the case) may directly conflict with free speech protections in another (the United States in the case), global implementation of the right to erasure may be considered as unreasonable. In that case, the Supreme Court of Canada affirmed a Canadian trial court order requiring Google to delist search results worldwide relating to a company which had engaged in intellectual property theft.[338] However, it left the door open for local implementation only, where it held that '[i]f Google has evidence that complying with such an injunction would require it to violate the laws of another jurisdiction, including interfering with freedom of expression, it is always free to apply to the British Columbia courts to vary the interlocutory order accordingly'.[339] Google subsequently filed a motion for injunctive relief with respect to this order with a US District Court, which was granted on the grounds that '[b]y forcing intermediaries to remove links to third-party material, the Canadian order undermines the

of a data subject's name from gaining access, via the list of results displayed following that search, to the links which are the subject of that request'). The Court held that '[i]t is for the referring court to ascertain whether, also having regard to the recent changes made to its search engine ... the measures adopted or proposed by Google meet those requirements.' ibid, para 71.

335 ibid, paras 59–60.

336 ibid, para 72 ('Accordingly, a supervisory or judicial authority of a Member State remains competent to weigh up, in the light of national standards of protection of fundamental rights, a data subject's right to privacy and the protection of personal data concerning him or her, on the one hand, and the right to freedom of information, on the other, and, after weighing those rights against each other, to order, where appropriate, the operator of that search engine to carry out a de-referencing concerning all versions of that search engine.') (citation omitted).

337 This is more or less in line with van Alsenoy and Koekkoek argued. See van Alsenoy and Koekkoek (n 279).

338 Supreme Court of Canada, *Google Inc v Equustek Solutions Inc* (n 331). Compare also Case C-324/092011, *L'Oréal and Others* [2011] ECLI:EU:C:2011:474, para 63 (ruling that the effectiveness of EU trademark rules 'would be undermined if they were not to apply to the use, in an internet offer for sale or advertisement targeted at consumers within the EU, of a sign identical with or similar to a trade mark registered in the EU merely because the third party behind that offer or advertisement is established in a third State, because the server of the internet site used by the third party is located in such a State or because the product that is the subject of the offer or the advertisement is located in a third State').

339 *Google Inc v Equustek Solutions Inc* (n 331) para 52. ibid, para 44 ('Google's argument that a global injunction violates international comity because it is possible that the order could not have been obtained in a foreign jurisdiction, or that to comply with it would result in Google violating the laws of that jurisdiction is, with respect, theoretical.').

policy goals of Section 230 and threatens free speech on the global internet'.[340] Varying the Canadian interlocutory order, that is, restricting its extraterritorial effect, on grounds of international comity/reasonableness could then seem called for. However, unlike the EU *Google Spain* case, the delisting in *Equustek* pertained to the selling of pirated products rather than the right to erasure. Accordingly, Canadian courts' deference to the United States, based on freedom of speech considerations, might not be fully warranted insofar as intellectual property violations may be considered as reprehensible everywhere,[341] and thus as potentially rising to the level of transgressions of 'global values'.[342] At the very least it may be a value shared between Canada and the United States. As expected, in the wake of the US District Court's decision, Google applied to the Supreme Court of British Columbia (Canada, 2018) to set aside or vary the earlier interlocutory order. The Court went on to dismiss the application,[343] on different although not entirely unrelated grounds. Giving a restrictive interpretation to the change of circumstance mentioned by the Supreme Court of Canada, it held that the 'US decision does not establish that the injunction requires Google to violate American law' or 'core American values', that the US court did not rule on Google's freedom of speech rights under the First Amendment, and that it has the ability 'to protect the integrity of its own process through orders directed to parties over whom it has personal jurisdiction'.[344] On the specific facts of the case, *Equustek* may ultimately not be a major precedent for cases pertaining to right to erasure. In such cases, comity may militate more strongly against global implementation of delisting orders as the

[340] *Google LLC v Equustek Solutions Inc.*, 2017 WL 5000834 (ND Cal 2 Nov 2017).

[341] *Google Inc v Equustek Solutions Inc* (n 331) 44–45 (approving the observations of lower court judges that 'Google acknowledges that most countries will likely recognize intellectual property rights and view the selling of pirated products as a legal wrong', and that 'there is no realistic assertion that the judge's order will offend the sensibilities of any other nation', as '[i]t has not been suggested that the order prohibiting the defendants from advertising wares that violate the intellectual property rights of the plaintiffs offends the core values of any nation'). The US District Court, however, applied Section 230 of the US Communications Decency Act 'which immunizes providers of interactive computer services [such as Google] against liability arising from content created by third parties', and held that 'Google is harmed because the Canadian order restricts activity that Section 230 protects'. The US Court added that '[s]ince Google is likely to prevail on the merits of its Section 230 claim, it is unnecessary to address Google's arguments based on the First Amendment and international comity' (fn 2 of the judgment).

[342] See for relevant international law regarding the industrial designs at issue in *Equustek*: art 25(1) of the WTO Agreement on Trade-Related Aspects of Intellectual Property Rights (TRIPS) ('Members shall provide for the protection of independently created industrial designs that are new or original.'). See also art 3 of the World International Property Organization (WIPO) Convention (listing as the main aim of WIPO 'to promote the protection of intellectual property throughout the world through cooperation among States and, where appropriate, in collaboration with any other international organization'); the WIPO has 191 Member States.

[343] *Equustek Solutions Inc., v Jack* (n 332).

[344] ibid, paras 19–22. See in particular para 20 ('The U.S. decision does not establish that the injunction requires Google to violate American law. That would be the case if, for example, the Datalink Defendants obtained an order from a U.S. court requiring Google to link to their websites. But there is no suggestion that any U.S. law prohibits Google from de-indexing those websites, either in compliance with the injunction or for any other reason.').

right to erasure may clash head-on with the freedom of speech as constitutionally protected in the United States.[345]

5.5.6 Concluding observations

The European Union has lately rather vigorously stretched the long arm of its data protection legislation. The EU's jurisdictional assertions appear to be largely based on the territoriality principle, as they apply to providers targeting the Union, and protect the data of EU residents (mostly EU citizens in fact) transferred outside the European Union. Where such links may in themselves be considered as insufficiently strong to ground jurisdiction,[346] the character of data protection as a fundamental right and an emerging global value may possibly serve as a factor legitimating or even mandating the broad jurisdictional scope of EU data protection law. This scope cannot be unlimited, however. The European Union should make sure that it pays due regard to the interests of economic operators, as well as to foreign states' rival value conceptions. This may mean, for instance, that in transnational settings, the European Union and its Member States refrain from seeking global implementation of the right to erasure, or requiring strict equivalence of foreign data protection legislation.

[345] Muge Fazlioglu 'Forget Me Not: The Clash of the Right to Be Forgotten and Freedom of Expression on the Internet' (2013) 3 IDPL 149 (arguing that the right to be forgotten contrasts with the safeguards for free expression afforded by the First Amendment in the United States). See also Case C-507/17 *Google v CNIL et al* [2019] ECLI:EU:C:2019:15, Opinion of Advocate General Szpunar, points 50–53 (acknowledging that in connection with trade mark law, extraterritorial effects are accepted in EU law, but considering this to be an extreme situation of an exceptional nature, that could not be compared with the right to erasure pursuant to data protection law).

[346] *Eg* Brussels Court of Appeal, *Facebook Ireland Ltd., Facebook Inc. and Facebook Belgium B.V.B.A. v Belgian Data Protection Authority (DPA)*, 2018/AR/410, 8 May 2019 (Court refusing to exercise jurisdiction over Facebook Ireland Ltd. targeting Belgian residents).

6

Concluding Observations

6.1 Cosmopolitanism and the State

The aim of this monograph was to inquire how a cosmopolitan agenda could be implemented in the law of jurisdiction. At first sight, such an inquiry might look like an attempt at marrying fire and ice. Cosmopolitans tend to focus on the individual as the ultimate unit of moral concern, and are interested in bringing about 'global justice' (whether of the human or environmental variant), regardless of geographical location. They are always concerned with the negotiation and overcoming of delineated political borders.[1] In contrast, the law of jurisdiction, given its close connection to the seminal concept of state sovereignty in international relations, has 'borders' written all over it.

Nevertheless, political allegiance to territorially delineated states and allegiance to an international community project based on universal human solidarity need not be mutually exclusive. Kwame Appiah, one of the leading political philosophers of cosmopolitanism, has coined the term 'constitutional patriotism' in this respect:

> We cosmopolitans can be patriots, loving our homelands (not only the states where we were born but the states where we grew up and the states where we live); our loyalty to humankind so vast, so abstract, a unity does not deprive us of the capacity to care for lives nearer by.[2]

Accordingly, the actual existence of borders need not prove fatal to the cosmopolitan project.

Some authors have even suggested that the 'state' could be considered as a cosmopolitan construct in its own right.[3] A somewhat less extreme position, taken by this monograph, is that states may perhaps have primarily been set up or conceived to serve their own citizens, but that this does not bar them from serving a global citizenship and protecting humankind's common concerns. This cosmopolitan, global citizenship-based authority and responsibility of states has gained increased attention from political theorists disenchanted with the disconnect

[1] Marina Calloni, 'Cosmopolitanism and the Negotiation of Borders' (2012) 20 IJS 153.
[2] Kwame A Appiah, 'Cosmopolitan Patriots' (1997) 32 CI 617, 622.
[3] H Patrick Glenn, *The Cosmopolitan State* (OUP 2013) (arguing that all states are cosmopolitan in character and that the cosmopolitan state is the only appropriate conceptualization of the state in a time of globalization).

Selfless Intervention. Cedric Ryngaert, Oxford University Press (2020). © Cedric Ryngaert.
DOI: 10.1093/oso/9780198851783.001.0001

between moral idealism and actual international political practice, which revolves around states very much indeed. Thus, in a praiseworthy and wide-ranging volume on the cosmopolitan responsibilities of the state, Beardsworth and colleagues investigate 'the possibility that states can become bearers of cosmopolitan responsibilities while also remaining vehicles for popular self-determination'.[4] Along the same lines, for an international lawyer interested in jurisdictional questions, the challenge is to investigate how the law of state jurisdiction—the initial aim of which was to prevent state sovereignties from clashing with each other—is, and can be reinterpreted to serve cosmopolitan or 'selfless' ends, alongside parochial, national interest-based ends.

6.2 Selfless Intervention, Jurisdiction, and State Sovereignty

Inevitably, the quest to conceive the notion of jurisdiction as a vehicle for selfless intervention by states is closely bound up with epistemic evolutions regarding jurisdiction's twin concept of state sovereignty. After all, jurisdiction is the legal emanation of the political notion of state sovereignty. The state manifests its sovereign power by exercising jurisdiction, that is prescribing and enforcing its laws, and adjudicating disputes on the basis of these laws. In Chapter 2, it was argued that the concept of sovereignty is malleable and allows for novel, contemporary understandings of sovereignty being in the service of the international community. It is logical, then, that jurisdiction could fulfil the same function.

However, jurisdiction is not simply an emanation of sovereignty, that is originating or issuing from sovereignty.[5] As Irani suggested, jurisdictional assertions

> not only form, border, and construct 'the state': they *are* the state. The state is instantiated in its jurisdictional assertions . . . Changing jurisdictional assertions do not simply change what 'the state' does: they further change what the state is, who and what it includes and excludes, and crucially, *where it is located*.[6]

Thus, the nature of the state and of state sovereignty may change as a result of actual jurisdictional practices. This also means that jurisdictional assertions may yield the formation of new political communities that do not necessarily track the physical borders of the state.[7] For our research object, it means that a state becomes

[4] Richard Beardsworth and others (eds), *The State and Cosmopolitan Responsibilities* (OUP 2019) 4.

[5] cf *Oxford English Dictionary* online, defining 'emanation' as 'something which originates or issues from a source'.

[6] Freya Irani, 'Beyond De Jure and De Facto Boundaries: Tracing the Imperial Geographies of US Law' (2019) 25 EJIR 1, 5 (original emphasis).

[7] Roxana Vatanparast, 'Data and the Elasticity of Sovereignty' (2019), paper on file with the author (suggesting the formation of new political communities in the context of assertions of state

cosmopolitan to the extent that it engages in cosmopolitan jurisdictional practices. Accordingly, to grasp fully the contemporary epistemic transformation of state sovereignty, a fine-grained analysis of actual instances of the exercise of jurisdiction by states is imperative.

6.3 The Capaciousness of Territoriality

This monograph has demonstrated that, regardless of the dynamics of globalization, interconnectedness, deterritorialization, or international solidarity characterizing the current era, when addressing transnational or global challenges, states continue to give pride of place to the core principle of the law of jurisdiction: the principle of territoriality. While use of territoriality to capture the extraterritorial may seem somewhat incongruous, as Rajkovic has pointed out, 'territorial boundaries have been always, to varying degrees, in temporal flux'.[8] Hence, the newly minted concept of 'territorial extension',[9] which has played a prominent role in this monograph, may not be a conceptual revolution in the law of jurisdiction. Still, it does point to an expanding state praxis of states formally relying on territoriality to, in fact, reach beyond state borders.[10]

In addition, to roll out a cosmopolitan agenda, the principle of territoriality has been the primary jurisdictional gateway. Certainly, *universality*—which is triggered by the gravity of an offence rather than a (territorial) connection to the regulating state—is well-known in the law of jurisdiction, but it only has purchase in respect of a limited number of offences, and arguably only in the field of criminal law.[11] This renders universality, as it is currently understood, ill-suited to address the range of global governance challenges confronting humanity such as climate change, unsustainable fishing practices, or corporate human rights abuses. Territoriality then emerges as an unlikely saviour for the cosmopolitan project as its capaciousness allows states to 'territorialize the extraterritorial' and contribute to the realization of global justice.

jurisdiction over data, relying on Richard T Ford, 'Law's Territory (A History of Jurisdiction)' (1999) 97 Mich LR 843, 844).

[8] Nikolas M Rajkovic, 'The Visual Conquest of International Law: Brute Boundaries, the Map, and the Legacy of Cartogenesis' (2018) 31 LJIL 267, 275, adding that 'territory has never been constituted by an absolute and fixed materiality, but more accurately involving an evolving assemblage and materialization of things, actors and ideas'.

[9] Also Joanne Scott, 'Extraterritoriality and Territorial Extension in EU Law' (2014) 62 Am J Comp L 87.

[10] Also Marise Cremona and Joanne Scott (eds), *EU Law Beyond EU Borders. The Extraterritorial Reach of EU Law* (OUP 2019).

[11] See on universal civil jurisdiction: Abhimanyu George Jain, 'Universal Civil Jurisdiction in International Law' (2015) 55 IJIL 209.

There are many instances of states using a territorial hook to address essentially extraterritorial activities, both historic and more recent ones. Some of these jurisdictional assertions have a cosmopolitan dimension in that they have the realization of global justice as their *goal* (deontological cosmopolitanism) or as their *effect* (consequentialist cosmopolitanism). In the field of criminal law, where the origins of the international law of jurisdiction lie, the long-standing ubiquity principle has enabled states to exercise territorial jurisdiction over the whole of an offence as soon as a constituent element could be located on the territory.[12] The seminal idea that it suffices for an element of a particular offence or event to be linked to the territory for territorial jurisdiction to be validly exercised has cast a long shadow. It has paved the way for a host of jurisdictional assertions that rely on tenuous, artificial, or even fictitious territorial connections,[13] assertions which may also serve the common interest. In Chapter 5, it has been set out how territoriality has been creatively used in such diverse areas as the environment, fisheries, business and human rights litigation, and data protection, to further (sometimes only nascent) global values and common interests.

As was indicated, this area analysis is by no means exhaustive. Territoriality has been similarly instrumentalized in other areas such as competition law, foreign corrupt practices, and secondary sanctions legislation. In the field of competition law, US and European courts have exercised jurisdiction over foreign-origin restrictive practices that are implemented or have direct, substantial, and reasonably foreseeable anti-competitive effects on the territory.[14] While this effects jurisdiction has traditionally been relied upon to protect the national economy,[15] wider goals such as boosting global deterrence of anti-competitive conduct and increasing global welfare for both domestic and foreign consumers have been propounded and arguably pursued.[16] Also as regards enforcement of foreign corrupt practices and

[12] Cedric Ryngaert, 'Territorial Jurisdiction Over Cross-frontier Offences: Revisiting a Classic Problem of International Criminal Law' (2009) 9 ICLR 187.

[13] See also Peter Szigeti, 'The Illusion of Territorial Jurisdiction' (2016) 52 TJIL 369.

[14] See for the seminal US judgment: *United States v Alcoa*, 148 F 2d 416 (2d Cir 1945). See for the European Union: Case T-286/09 *Intel v Commission* [2014] ECLI:EU:T:2014:547, para 244 ('[I]n order to justify the Commission's jurisdiction under public international law, it is sufficient to establish either the qualified effects of the practice in the European Union or that it was implemented in the European Union.'), confirmed by Case C-413/14 P *Intel v Commission* [2017] ECLI:EU:C:2017:632. See also, Joined Cases 89/85, 104/85, 114/85, 116/85, 117/85, and 125/85 to 129/85 *Ahlström Osakeyhtiö and Others v Commission* [1988] EU:C:1988:447 (implementation doctrine); Case T-102/96 *Gencor v Commission* [1999] ECR II-753 (effects doctrine).

[15] Irani (n 6) 22.

[16] See on states' tackling of export cartels to increase global welfare: Michael Ristaniemi, 'Export Cartels and the Case for Global Welfare' [2017] GAR 173. See also Brief of *Amici Curiae* Economists JE Stiglitz and PR Orszag in Support of Respondents, *F Hoffmann-LaRoche Ltd v Empagran SA*, 542 US 155 (2004) (No 03-724) (urging the US Supreme Court to take into account global deterrence and the imperative to provide a remedy for antitrust harm suffered in foreign transactions). In legal practice, the effects doctrine has been relied upon to address foreign practices and agreements that were as such not implemented nor had effects on the territory, but only had effects if *taken together* with other practices and agreements. See Case T-447/14 *NKT v Commission* [2018] ECLI:EU:T:2018:443, para 90.

economic sanctions legislation, which could be considered cosmopolitan insofar as this contributes to the stamping out of global corrupt practices blighting the developmental prospects of foreign populations, or to clamping down on commercial transactions with regimes violating human rights or threatening international security,[17] courts, especially in the United States, have given wide interpretations to territoriality.[18] A US court has considered the mere routing of emails through a US server to be sufficient for the exercise of territorial jurisdiction over underlying foreign corrupt practices, even if the defendant lacked personal knowledge that his communications would be so routed.[19] Another US court has considered the mere routing of US dollar payments to or through the United States in apparent violation of US sanctions programs to amount to use of the US financial system, and an 'exportation of services from the United States',[20] even if the underlying economic transaction was essentially foreign. All this speaks to the enduring attractiveness of territoriality to address transnational and global challenges.

6.4 Territoriality and the Common Interest

In themselves, some territorial connections may be too tenuous to support successful reliance on the territoriality principle. After all, the permissive principles of jurisdiction should be interpreted in light of the substantial connection requirement undergirding the law of jurisdiction.[21] However, one of the main arguments

[17] See on the link between US economic sanctions and international standards: Sarah H Cleveland, 'Norm Internalization and U.S. Economic Sanctions' (2001) 26 YJIL 1, 71–72. This is not to say, however, that US economic sanctions are always based on international standards. See Tom Ruys and Cedric Ryngaert, 'Secondary Sanctions: A Weapon Out of Control? International Legality of, and European Responses to, US Secondary Sanctions', forthcoming BYBIL 2020.

[18] See also Anthony J Colangelo, 'What is Extraterritorial Jurisdiction?' (2014) 99 CLR 1303, 1306 (arguing that the United States has proved willing to establish jurisdiction, for example, to tackle international corruption or drugs-trafficking, as soon as some aspect of a transnational activity has a connection with the United States, 'even if that aspect is fleeting and minor relative to the rest of the conduct comprising the claim'). However, on other occasions, the United States has rejected jurisdiction where a nexus was clearly present, *eg* in *Morrison v National Australia Bank*, 561 US 247 (2010).

[19] *Securities and Exchange Commission v Straub*, 921 F Supp 2d 244 (SDNY 2013) ('The emails were "routed through and/or stored on network servers located within the United States". The mere fact that Defendants may not have had personal knowledge that their emails would be routed through or stored in the United States does not mean that they did not, in fact, use an instrument of interstate commerce sufficient for purposes of conferring jurisdiction. Second, the Court rejects Defendants' argument that it was not foreseeable that emails sent over the Internet in a foreign country would touch servers located elsewhere.').

[20] *United States v Reza Zarrab*, 15 Cr 867 (RMB) (SDNY 2016) https://www.courtlistener.com/recap/gov.uscourts.nysd.451245.90.0.pdf, 12 ('the Indictment is not an extraterritorial application of the IEEPA and the ITSR ... [because] Zarrab is charged in connection with his scheme to intentionally export and supply financial services from the United States and to cause U.S. banks to export and supply financial services—in other words, with causing conduct and effects in the United States').

[21] See on the essential role of substantial connection: Dan JB Svantesson, *Solving the Internet Jurisdiction Puzzle* (OUP 2017), ch 3 (even suggesting to abandon territoriality in favour of, *inter alia*, substantial connection).

in this monograph is that the legality of jurisdictional assertions resting on weak territorial links may be boosted by these assertions' very contribution to the common interest, and preferably by their embeddedness in, or relationship with international regulatory instruments. Thus, trade restrictions aimed at tackling climate change may derive their jurisdictional legality from their contribution to the goals of the Paris Climate Agreement, regardless of the diffuse character of the effects which emissions tend to have on the territory of the regulating state.[22] By the same token, the insertion of an unqualified territorial principle in the UN Convention against Corruption and the Organisation for Economic Co-operation and Development (OECD) Convention against Bribery[23] may give international backing for wide interpretations of the principle by Contracting Parties; the nature of corruption as a global scourge[24] may compensate for the weak territorial link which certain foreign practices may have.[25]

It could even be argued that, from a normative perspective, territoriality should more often and more expansively be relied on when it comes to global values and common interests in order to prevent that no state's law applies.[26] As it happens, some conventions *require* that states exercise territorial jurisdiction, not only in the field of core international crimes (*eg* torture)[27] but also as regards transnational offences such as corruption.[28] The Port State Measures Agreement, for its part, *requires* that states deny entry or privileges to visiting foreign-flagged vessels which engaged in illegal, unreported, and unregulated (IUU) fishing.[29] In addition,

[22] See Chapter 5.

[23] UN Convention against Corruption (adopted 13 October 2003, entered into force 14 December 2005) 2349 UNTS 41, art 42; OECD Convention on Combating Bribery of Foreign Public Officials in International Business Transactions (adopted 7 December 1997, entered into force 15 February 1999) 2802 UNTS 228, art 4.

[24] See UNCAC (n 23), preamble (voicing concerns 'about the seriousness of problems and threats posed by corruption to the stability and security of societies, undermining the institutions and values of democracy, ethical values and justice and jeopardizing sustainable development and the rule of law', and being convinced 'that corruption is no longer a local matter but a transnational phenomenon that affects all societies and economies, making international cooperation to prevent and control it essential').

[25] Régis Bismuth, 'Pour une appréhension nuancé de l'extraterritorialité du droit américain—quelques réflexions autour des procédures et sanctions visant Alstom et BNP Paribas' (2015) LXI AFDI 785, 795 ('Indéniablement, sans aller jusqu'à évoquer une quelconque compétence universelle, le caractère international de l'infraction et les critères de compétence retenus par la Convention OCDE autorisent un certain assouplissement des critères de rattachement. Une telle habilitation internationale n'existe toutefois pas pour certaines des mesures de sanctions économiques adoptées par les États-Unis.').

[26] Compare the denunciation of the strict US presumption against extraterritoriality by Julie R O'Sullivan, 'The Extraterritorial Application of Federal Criminal Statutes: Analytical Roadmap, Normative Conclusions, and a Plea to Congress for Direction' (2018) 106 GELJ 1021, 1083 ('Where there is no potential for conflict, application of the strong presumption may result in cases where no State's law will apply to objectionable conduct.').

[27] UN Convention against Torture and Other Cruel, Inhuman or Degrading Treatment or Punishment (adopted 10 December 1984, entered into force 26 June 1987) 1465 UNTS, 85 art 5.1.

[28] Art 42 UNCAC (n 23); OECD Anti-Bribery Convention (n 23).

[29] Art 9.4 Port State Measures Agreement ('when a Party has sufficient proof that a vessel seeking entry into its port has engaged in IUU fishing ... the Party shall deny that vessel entry into its ports').

human rights treaties or fundamental rights instruments may mandate that states exercise their jurisdiction more vigorously. The human right to a remedy may require state courts to give a liberal interpretation to principles of adjudicatory jurisdiction, such as the principles of domicile, connected claims, or forum of necessity (all of which can be considered as variations of territoriality), so that victims of (corporate) human rights abuses have their day in court, even if they sustained harm outside the territory.[30] In the same vein, the nature of data protection as a fundamental right in the European Union[31] exerts pressure on EU regulators and courts to give wide interpretations to territorial jurisdiction with a view to safeguarding the rights of EU residents.[32]

Conversely, expansive jurisdictional assertions which do not further widely recognized common interests may, in the absence of a strong nexus with the regulating state, be more difficult to justify. For instance, the US imposition of 'secondary' sanctions on non-US persons engaging in commercial transactions with non-US sanctioned entities may well violate the law of jurisdiction, as the territorial or personal nexus of sanctions with the United States is typically very tenuous, and such sanctions may not give effect to an international consensus on the harmful activities of the sanctioned entity.[33] Also, expansive assertions of effects-based jurisdiction in the field of competition (antitrust) law may be problematic, insofar as such assertions are based on weak territorial connections,[34] and insofar as an international agreement on the illegality of particular anti-competitive practices remains elusive.[35] Jurisdictional assertions that are not based on a strong nexus to the state and do not build on international instruments recognizing particular values and common interests are likely to unjustifiably intrude on the policy space of other states and violate the principle of non-intervention.[36]

[30] See Chapter 5.3.

[31] Art 8 EU Charter on Fundamental Rights.

[32] See Chapter 5.4.

[33] Ruys and Ryngaert (n 17) (considering that US corporate control, re-exportation of US items, use of the US financial system, and trafficking in US property are insufficient US connections to justify US jurisdictional assertions under the principles of territoriality, nationality, or passive personality).

[34] Case C-413/14 P *Intel v European Commission* [2016] ECLI:EU:C:2016:788, Opinion of Advocate General Wahl, point 300 ('I consider it to be particularly important that jurisdiction is asserted with restraint in relation to behaviour that has not, strictly speaking, taken place within the territory of the European Union. Indeed, to comply with a certain form of comity and, by the same token, to ensure that undertakings can operate in a foreseeable legal environment, it is only with a great deal of caution that the effect of the conduct complained of can be used as the yardstick for asserting jurisdiction. That is all the more important today. There are over 100 national or supranational authorities worldwide that claim jurisdiction over anticompetitive practices.').

[35] Brendan Sweeney, 'International Competition Law and Policy: A Work in Progress' (2009) 10 MJIL 58, 63.

[36] See in the context of competition law *eg* Luca Prete, 'On Implementation and Effects: The Recent Case-law on the Territorial (or Extraterritorial?) Application of EU Competition Rules' (2018) 9 JECLP 487, 495 (considering it, as regards the scope of competition law, 'of the greatest importance that States (or polities) stay away from policing economic behaviour that is essentially extraneous to their markets').

This is not to say, however, that jurisdictional assertions of which the object is internationally recognized pass muster with the law of jurisdiction as soon as some territorial link can be discerned, however tenuous. To prevent territorial jurisdiction from degenerating into connectionless universal jurisdiction,[37] a some (territorial) connection may still be required. This may prevent the eruption of international conflict[38] and the wasting of precious domestic resources.[39] In light of loss of territoriality in an era of economic globalization and of revolutions in communication technology, the quest for this minimum connection under customary international law in still ongoing.[40] For instance, in the context of the vigorous enforcement of US foreign corrupt practices legislation, commentators have argued that territorial connections such as routing emails via a US server or transferring funds electronically via the US financial system are too tenuous to ground jurisdiction, regardless of the international proscription of corruption.[41] These critics will have welcomed a recent US Court of Appeals decision holding that the presumption against extraterritoriality bars the US Government from using conspiracy and complicity statutes to charge a foreign-based defendant who had not set foot in the United States during a bribery scheme and performed all relevant activities outside the United States.[42] This presumption against extraterritoriality more generally serves as a potent tool to limit the geographic reach of US law.[43]

[37] Note that universal jurisdiction typically also operates on the basis of a territorial link, in that, under domestic law, universality tends to be triggered by the presence of the suspect. On universal jurisdiction in the absence of the suspect: Tim Kluwen, 'Universal Jurisdiction in Absentia Before Domestic Courts Prosecuting International Crimes: A Suitable Weapon to Fight Impunity?' (2017) 8 GJIL 7.

[38] *EEOC v Arabian Am. Oil Co.*, 499 US 244, 248 (1991) (holding that the presumption against extraterritoriality aims 'to protect against unintended clashes between our laws and those of other nations which could result in international discord').

[39] *United States v Phillip Morris USA Inc.*, 566 F 3d 1095, 1130 (DC Cir 2009) (deeming a case domestic if there were sufficient territorial conduct and effects present to warrant a belief that 'Congress would have wished the precious resources of United States courts and law enforcement agencies to be devoted to them').

[40] See also Maggie Gardner, 'Channeling Unilateralism' (2015) 56 HILJ 297, 304 (arguing that 'the closer that one state gets to the outer limits of the permissive grounds, the more likely it is that other states will feel threatened', and discussing in particular expansive interpretations of territoriality).

[41] Annalisa Leibold, 'Extraterritorial Application of the FCPA under International Law' (2015) 51 WLR 225, 260, submitting that 'current extraterritorial enforcement of the FCPA has the potential to violate international law'; Sarah Routh, 'Tweet to Defeat Government Bribes: Limiting Extraterritorial Jurisdiction under the Foreign Corrupt Practices Act to Combat Global Corporate Corruption' (2018) 51 Vanderbilt J Transnat'l L 625, 647 ('US agencies' current expansive exercise of extraterritorial jurisdiction under the FCPA violates norms of international sovereignty by impeding a foreign government's ability to maintain control over its citizens and prosecute them for conduct that the foreign government, not the United States, designates a crime.'). See for an overview of tenuous territorial connections: Amy Deen Westbrook, 'Enthusiastic Enforcement, Informal Legislation: The Unruly Expansion of the Foreign Corrupt Practices Act' (2011) 45 GELR 489, 552–53. Note, however, that sovereignty concerns flowing from broad US interpretations of territoriality should not be overstated. As Gardner has observed, FCPA investigations of foreign firms correlate with the existence of memoranda of understanding on transnational cooperation which US law-enforcement agencies have signed with their foreign counterparts. See Gardner (n 40) 329. For 'extraterritorial' investigations to be successful, ultimately foreign states' cooperation will be required.

[42] *United States v Hoskins*, 902 F 3d 69 (2d Cir 2018).

[43] O'Sullivan (n 26) 1056 (submitting that the US Supreme Court's 'most recent cases demonstrate that the Court is committed to a muscular presumption against extraterritoriality'); William

Still, application of the presumption is fraught with difficulty, as a determination whether a particular event with links to multiple states is domestic or extraterritorial appears to be inherently subjective.[44] In Europe, efforts to limit the reach of the territoriality principle continue. In the field of EU data protection, for instance, the geographic scope of the implementation of the right to erasure has proved particularly contentious.[45] After the Court of Justice of the European Union (CJEU) held, in *Google Spain* (2014), that the processing of personal data carried out in the context of the activity of a search engine such as Google Search fell within the territorial scope of application of EU data protection legislation,[46] the question arose whether decisions on de-referencing had to be implemented worldwide or only in the European Union. On this question, in 2019, the CJEU ruled in *Google v CNIL* that 'there is no obligation under EU law, for a search engine operator who grants a request for de-referencing made by a data subject, as the case may be, following an injunction from a supervisory or judicial authority of a Member State, to carry out such a de-referencing on all the versions of its search engine',[47] but that instead 'the de-referencing in question is, in principle, supposed to be carried out in respect of all the Member States'.[48] Nevertheless, the CJEU does not exclude the possibility of global implementation.[49] However, ultimately it leaves it to domestic courts in EU Member States to decide on the geographic scope of implementation of the right to erasure, without giving much guidance as to how to reach such a decision. This means that, in the years to come, EU Member States will continue to grapple with how jurisdictionally to localize borderless Internet activity in a more principled manner.[50] Technological evolutions may bring new challenges in this respect.

All these efforts at restricting the reach of territoriality speak to a desire to safeguard the traditional role of the principle of territoriality as a principle of jurisdictional *order* rather than justice. In its original Westphalian incarnation, territoriality aims at delimiting spheres of competence and preventing undue intervention in other states' affairs. As the limits of territoriality are pushed almost to breaking point in order to address global and transnational challenges, some

Dodge, 'The New Presumption Against Extraterritoriality' (2020) 133 HLR 1582 https://ssrn.com/abstract=3429336.

[44] O'Sullivan (n 26) 1060.
[45] See also Chapter 5.4.
[46] Case C-131/12 *Google Spain SL and Google Inc. v Agencia Española de Protección de Datos (AEPD) and Mario Costeja González* [2014] EU:C:2014:317.
[47] Case C-507/17 *Google LLC v Commission nationale de l'informatique et des libertés (CNIL)* [2019] ECLI:EU:C:2019:772, para 64.
[48] ibid, para 66.
[49] ibid, para 72.
[50] Christopher Kuner, 'The Internet and the Global Reach of EU Law' in Marise Cremona and Joanne Scott (eds), *EU Law Beyond EU Borders. The Extraterritorial Reach of EU Law* (OUP 2019) 140 ('EU law is still searching for a paradigm for its application to Internet-related activities that is based on firm legal principles, secures the rights of EU individuals, and avoids jurisdictional overreach.').

pushback against overly loose interpretations which undermine the principle's function as competence delimiter is expected.

At the same time, precisely because of the poor fit of the concept of territoriality and the reality of global challenges, more revolutionary jurisdictional thinking no longer focuses on territoriality as the main jurisdictional linchpin but instead suggests reliance on other connections to the regulating state, or on the goals of regulatory intervention. As regards connections, scholars of global legal pluralism have urged increased attention to personal or community connections,[51] whereas others have emphasized the substantiality of connections mitigated by the principle of reasonableness.[52] Especially in the context of access to data in the 'extraterritorial cloud', multiple, technology-driven connecting criteria have been proposed.[53] Yet others have advanced a broad construction of the national interest as the jurisdictional trigger,[54] or suggested conceiving of cosmopolitan jurisdiction as a form of functional jurisdiction, the exercise of which is, in given circumstances, justified by its furthering of the common interest.[55] At the far end of the spectrum, the link between jurisdiction and the state has been abandoned altogether, and jurisdictional empowerment of private actors in a transnational legal space has been mooted.[56]

It is appropriate to observe, finally, that no scheme of jurisdictional (al-)location is ever politically neutral. All schemes have important distributive effects in that they may further the interests of one actor (*eg* a multinational corporation) to the detriment of those of another (*eg* victims of human rights abuses).[57]

[51] Paul S Berman, *Global Legal Pluralism: A Jurisprudence of Law Beyond Borders* (OUP 2012). See as regards Internet regulation: Cedric Ryngaert and Mark Zoetekouw, 'The End of Territory?: The Re-Emergence of Community as a Principle of Jurisdictional Order in the Internet Era' in Uta Kohl (ed), *The Net and the Nation State* (CUP 2017).

[52] Svantesson (n 21). See also Kuner (n 50) 140 (noting 'the tendency of [data protection agencies] to prioritize the protection of individuals with a substantial connection to the EU').

[53] Paul M Schwartz, 'Legal Access to the Global Cloud' (2018) 118 Col LR 1681.

[54] See *Kiobel v Royal Dutch Petroleum Co*, 133 S Ct 1659 (2013) (Breyer J, concurring), at II (arguing that the United States should exercise jurisdiction under the Alien Tort Statute if 'the defendant's conduct substantially and adversely affects an important American national interest', such as the interest of the United States not becoming 'a safe harbor for violators of the most fundamental international norms').

[55] Nelson F Coelho, 'Unilateral Port State Jurisdiction. The Quest for Universality in the Prevention, Reducation and Control of Ship-Source Pollution' (PhD, Utrecht University 2019) ch 6.3 (arguing that the system of functional jurisdiction, ingrained in the law of the sea, rationalizes the exercise of port state jurisdiction over globally harmful activities on the high seas such as marine pollution). See also Chapter 5.1 of this monograph.

[56] Peer Zumbansen, 'Defining the Space of Transnational Law: Legal Theory, Global Governance and Legal Pluralism' in Gunther Handl and others (eds), *Beyond Territoriality Transnational Legal Authority in an Age of Globalization* (Brill 2012).

[57] Asha Kaushal, 'The Politics of Jurisdiction' (2015) 78 TMLR 759; Cedric Ryngaert, 'Territory in the Law of Jurisdiction: Imagining Alternatives' in Martin Kuijer and Wouter Werner (eds), *Netherlands Yearbook of International Law 2016: The Changing Nature of Territoriality in International Law* (TMC Asser Press 2017); Philip Liste, 'Geographical Knowledge at Work: Human Rights Litigation and Transnational Territoriality' (2015) 22 EJIR 217; Philip Liste, 'Transnational Human Rights Litigation and Territorialized Knowledge: Kiobel and the "Politics of Space"' (2014) 5 TLT 1.

6.5 Limitations

However the exercise of state jurisdiction in the common interest is doctrinally conceived (as a form of territorial, community, functional, or universal jurisdiction), care should be taken to prevent jurisdictional overreach and imperial imposition. After all, such jurisdiction is enacted *unilaterally* by individual states or regional organizations, even if the common interest which is (supposedly) served is international in nature. Unilateral action carries the risk that the regulating state imposes its own value conceptions and furthers its own interests, thereby impinging on foreign persons' right to self-government. To limit this risk, in Chapter 3 this monograph has suggested a number of techniques of restraint, such as allowing foreign affected states, communities, and persons a voice in the design and enforcement of regulation with extraterritorial effect, recognition of equivalent foreign regulation, and compensation of affected persons and entities. These techniques of jurisdictional reasonableness discipline unilateralism and increase its legitimacy as a tool to further the common interest in the absence of adequate multilateral or host state regulation and enforcement.

Techniques of restraint should however not be interpreted too strictly lest states prove unwilling to exercise their jurisdiction. Bearing in mind that global public goods tend to be underprovided because of free-riding,[58] the risk of normative conflicts among states should not be inflated.[59] Thus, states should be offered sufficient jurisdictional leeway to assume their responsibility in respect of the common interest. To give just one example, international comity-inspired principles of adjudicatory jurisdiction may be in need of an overhaul, or at least a more liberal interpretation, so that they can be more effectively relied on to deliver justice for individuals suffering extraterritorial human rights abuses.[60]

6.6 Selfless Intervention and the National Interest

In spite of the title of this monograph, ultimately, *selfless* intervention remains somewhat of a mirage. As argued in Chapter 4, states are unlikely to exercise jurisdiction in the common interest if it is not *also* somehow in their own interests.

[58] Inge Kaul, 'Global Public Goods: Explaining Their Underprovision' (2012) 15 JIEL 729 (2012).

[59] Gardner (n 40) 348–49 (arguing, in the context of transnational criminal law, that 'the number of cases that will instigate jurisdictional conflicts is likely to be small', and accordingly that '[t]he risk of jurisdictional conflict will therefore be greatest when significant fines or forfeitures are at stake (for example, with foreign bribery) or political valence is high (for example, with terrorism)'). Gardner nevertheless points out that in bilateral cooperation agreements, states could agree on 'the division of cases and any resulting fines'. ibid, 349.

[60] Lucas Roorda, 'Jurisdiction over Foreign Direct Liability Claims against Transnational corporations in EU Member States. Increasing Access to Remedy for Victims of Corporate Human Rights Violations' (PhD thesis, Utrecht University 2019) ch 8.6.

In this respect, states may consider the existence of a jurisdictional *connection* as a proxy for the existence of an *interest*, so that framing extraterritorial as territorial conduct ('territorializing the extraterritorial') may have enforcement advantages. In practice, however, especially in the social, economic, and environmental fields, a domestic rule integrity logic tends to inform common interest-oriented unilateralism. The danger of foreign regulatory leakage as a result of strict domestic regulation serving common interests (*eg* addressing climate change, combating foreign corrupt practices, protecting data) more or less compels first-moving states to extend their regulation extraterritorially. In so doing, states pursue *prima facie* parochial interests (safeguarding the competitive opportunities of their own businesses) alongside common interests.

In the field of human rights and international crimes, a less selfish justice logic may be expected, but also in this fieldextra-legal incentives may be required before states exercise their jurisdiction. For instance, Germany's vigorous prosecution of Syrian war criminals, mainly under the universality principle,[61] may be informed by the presence of a large number of Syrian refugees, whose integration in Germany might be furthered if and when their torturers (some of whom have posed as refugees themselves) are brought to justice.[62] Alternatively, a state's exercise of jurisdiction over gross human rights violations could be informed by a desire to brandish its liberal values and to set itself apart from an amoral world dominated by *Realpolitik*.[63]

6.7 Unilateralism as Global Governance

Faced with governance deficits at international and national levels, third states' exercise of unilateral jurisdiction has its rightful place in the international legal order, as third state legal prescription and adjudication may well be the only means to safeguard common interests. Therefore, states' extensions of national laws into the global sphere can promote world order and justice.[64] However, safety valves should be provided to ensure that such jurisdiction, as a tool of global governance, is

[61] Beine Ye, 'How Germany is Leading the Way for Accountability for Crimes in Syria' (International Justice Monitor, 19 April 2019) https://www.ijmonitor.org/2019/04/how-germany-is-leading-the-way-for-accountability-for-crimes-in-syria/ (accessed 6 December 2019). See for statistical data on asylum application, showing Syrians as by far the largest category of applicants in 2018: AIDA and ECRE, 'Applications and Granting of Protection Status at First Instance' (Asylum in Europe 2018), available at https://www.asylumineurope.org/reports/country/germany/statistics (accessed 6 December 2019).

[62] See Chapter 3.3 on universal criminal jurisdiction and the national interest.

[63] See on US and European 'exceptionalism': Georg Nolte and Helmut P Aust, 'European Exceptionalism?' (2013) 2 GC 407 (2013); Michael Ignatieff (ed), *American Exceptionalism and Human Rights* (PUP 2004).

[64] Ellen Gutterman, 'Extraterritoriality as an Analytic Lens' in Daniel Margolies and others (eds), *Extraterritoriality of Law: History, Theory, Politics* (Routledge 2019) 184–85 (discussing the usefulness of deploying 'extraterritoriality as a central concept for reasoning about global governance').

exercised responsibly and reasonably.[65] Ideally, unilateral jurisdiction with extraterritorial effects is just a *temporary* means of providing protection and justice. It should not displace multilateral and foreign regulation and enforcement but rather emphasize the latter's urgency.[66] Obviously, this regulation and enforcement are likely to mirror the preferences of powerful first-moving states, who may only be willing to forego their unilateralism provided that international and foreign norms and practices approximate their own.[67] Such 'contingent unilateralism' should not be considered as holding the multilateral process hostage but rather as a welcome tool to overcome the tyranny of consent and address its anti-commons streak.

65 Compare the gist of the argument in Eyal Benvenisti, *The Law of Global Governance* (Brill 2014).

66 Joanne Scott and Lavanya Rajamani, 'Contingent Unilateralism—International Aviation in the European Emissions Trading Scheme' in Bart van Vooren and others (eds), *The EU's Role in Global Governance: The Legal Dimension* (OUP 2013) 209–23.

67 See on the influence of US law on international anti-corruption conventions: Elizabeth K Spahn, 'Implementing Global Anti-Bribery Norms: From the Foreign Corrupt Practices Act to the OECD Anti-Bribery Convention to the UN Convention against Corruption' (2013) 23 IICLR 1. See on the global influence of EU law with extraterritorial effect: Anu Bradford, 'The Brussels Effect' (2012) 107 NULR 1; Anu Bradford, *The Brussels Effect* (OUP 2020).

Index

Note: *For the benefit of digital users, indexed terms that span two pages (e.g., 52–53) may, on occasion, appear on only one of those pages.*